Anthropology and Antihumanism
in Imperial Germany

Anthropology and Antihumanism in Imperial Germany

By

Andrew Zimmerman

The University of Chicago Press

Chicago and London

Andrew Zimmerman is assistant professor of history at George Washington University.

The University of Chicago Press, Chicago 60637
The University of Chicago Press, Ltd., London
© 2001 by The University of Chicago
All rights reserved. Published 2001
Printed in the United States of America

10 09 08 07 06 05 04 03 02 01   1 2 3 4 5
ISBN: 0-226-98341-2 (cloth)
ISBN: 0-226-98342-0 (paper)

Library of Congress Cataloging-in-Publication Data

Zimmerman, Andrew,
    Anthropology and antihumanism in Imperial Germany / Andrew Zimmerman.
        p.   cm.
    Includes bibliographical references and index.
    ISBN 0-226-98341-2 (cloth : alk. paper) — ISBN 0-226-98342-0 (paper : alk. paper)
        1. Anthropology—Germany—History—19th century.   2. Humanism—
    Germany—History—19th century.   3. Science—Germany—History—19th
    century.   I. Title.

    GN17.3.G3 Z54   2001
    306'.0943'09034—dc21   2001035163

CONTENTS

ACKNOWLEDGMENTS

While writing this book I have been supported, provoked, and inspired by mentors, colleagues, family, friends, and institutions. I am delighted to have the opportunity to express my gratitude. Judith Hughes, David Luft, Tanya Luhrmann, John Marino, Martin Rudwick, Steven Shapin, and Tracy Strong not only offered counsel on the dissertation that formed the earliest version of this project but also helped me begin the process of turning it into this book. Much of this book was written while I was a member of the Society of Fellows in the Humanities at Columbia University, where my colleagues read drafts and helped me work through conceptual and other issues. Volker Berghahn and John Toews read and commented generously on earlier versions of the entire manuscript. My colleagues in the History Department at the George Washington University have provided a stimulating and supportive environment in which to complete the final stages of this project. I have been fortunate to work with Susan Abrams of the University of Chicago Press, who has offered invaluable encouragement and advice.

I enjoyed helpful discussions with Sierra Bruckner, Rainer Buschmann, Rob Gordon, Pascal Grosse, and Glenn Penny, who all are pursuing research related to the history of German anthropology and who have inspired and informed my work. This book has also benefited from the generosity of four Berlin anthropologists who shared their own research, collections, and recollections: Gustav Mahr, Peter Bolz, Ulrich Creutz, and the late Hans Grimm. The development of this project has also been shaped by conversations at conferences, colloquia, coffee shops, and other venues. I cannot name everyone who has helped me, but I would like to single out Adam Daniel, Nick Hopwood, and Jonathan Zatlin, who have contributed much to this project.

The Fulbright Commission made it possible for me to spend two years in Berlin, conducting research for this book. In Berlin I enjoyed the advice and support of Rüdiger vom Bruch and the intellectual community of his colloquium at the Humboldt University. I am grateful to the archives I used in Germany, which are listed in my bibliography. My research has also been facilitated by a number of libraries, especially the Staatsbibliothek in Berlin, the library of the Berlin Museum of Ethnology, the library of the Museum of Ethnography in Budapest, the libraries of the University of California and Columbia University, the New York Public Library, and the Library of Congress. I have published earlier versions of some of the material presented here in *Central European History,* the *European Studies Journal, Journal of the Pacific Arts Association, Studies in History and Philosophy of Biological and Biomedical Sciences,* the *Zeitschrift für Geschichtswissenschaften,* and *Wissenschaft und Öffentlichkeit in Berlin 1870–1930,* edited by Constantin Goschler (Wiesbaden: Franz Steiner, 2000). I would like to thank the editors and the readers for those publications for their perceptive suggestions.

My parents, Muriel and Everett Zimmerman, and my brother Daniel read drafts of this book and discussed the project with me many times. I am grateful for their insights and advice. In the acknowledgments to my dissertation I thanked Johanna Bockman for her comments on the earliest version of each of my chapters. I thank her here for reading and commenting on the final version of this book and for the discussions of the intervening years, which have fundamentally shaped what follows.

ABBREVIATIONS

AA	*Archiv für Anthropologie*
ABGAEU	Archiv der Berliner Gesellschaft für Anthropologie, Ethnologie und Urgeschichte, Schloß Charlottenberg, Berlin
Andree	Christian Andree, *Rudolf Virchow als Prähistoriker* (Cologne: Bohlau, 1976), vol. 2. Contains transcriptions of letters held in NL Virchow.
BAP	Bundesarchiv Potsdam. Records of the Imperial German Government.
BGAEU	Berliner Gesellschaft für Anthropologie, Ethnologie und Urgeschichte
BLHA	Brandenburgisches Landeshauptarchiv, Potsdam
CBDAG	*Correspondenz-Blatt der Deutschen Anthropologischen Gesellschaft*
GStA PK	Geheimes Staatsarchiv Preußischer Kulturbesitz, Berlin. Records of the Prussian government.
HU	Archiv der Humboldt-Universität, Berlin
LAB	Landesarchiv Berlin (Stadtarchiv)
MfV	Archiv des Museums für Völkerkunde, Berlin
NL Luschan	Nachlaß Felix von Luschans, Handschriftenabteilung, Staatsbibliothek Berlin (Haus II)
NL Virchow	Nachlaß Rudolf Virchows, Akademie der Wissenschaften, Berlin
VBGAEU	*Verhandlungen der Berliner Gesellschaft für Anthropologie, Ethnologie und Urgeschichte*
ZfE	*Zeitschrift für Ethnologie*

INTRODUCTION

T he human sciences have long grappled with profound methodological and ideological crises, crises that began as colonial expansion
drew Europe into global cultural, economic, and political structures, as
popular urban cultures challenged the monopoly of academic elites, and as
natural science demanded to be recognized as a comprehensive worldview.
The humanist project of interpreting the textual monuments of European
history had for centuries served Europeans as a privileged mode of understanding what it meant to be human and as a hegemonic ideology and civic
identity. By the late nineteenth century, critics of humanism pointed to its
narrow focus on Europe, its elitism, and its disregard of the natural sciences. Defenders of humanism emphasized the utopian potential of hermeneutic interpretation, in which the humanity of both interpreter and
subject of interpretation is recognized and elevated. The outlines of the
major positions in contemporary debates about humanism originated in
nineteenth- and twentieth-century Germany.[1] The historical methods of
Leopold von Ranke, the hermeneutics of Wilhelm Dilthey, and the work
of the historian Hans Baron on "civic humanism" in Renaissance Florence
have provided a vocabulary still active in much contemporary discussion of
the humanities.[2]

While the discipline of anthropology emerged all over Europe in the
nineteenth century, it was above all in Germany that it functioned as a new
antihumanist worldview, and it was in Germany that this anthropological
antihumanism had some of its most important and far-reaching effects.[3]
Anthropologists argued that the global culture initiated by imperialism,

the increasing power of natural scientific methods, and the need for broader participation in the creation of knowledge had rendered traditional humanism obsolete. The history of German anthropology in the nineteenth and early twentieth centuries sheds light both on the politics of knowledge in the German *Kaiserreich* and on the political and cultural valences of the crises that continue to mark the human sciences even today.

If German anthropology was peculiar, it was in the peculiar clarity with which it exhibited the global processes that shaped anthropology, humanism, and the human sciences in the late nineteenth and early twentieth centuries. Germany, after all, was the most important center of academic humanism at the time.[4] Humanism had defined German national self-understandings at least since the Prussian reform movement, when Wilhelm von Humboldt's model of the humanist research institution and Johann Gottlieb Fichte's language-centered understanding of German nationality galvanized Prussian opposition to French rule. In 1848, German patriotism was again bolstered by the historical scholarship of Johann Gustav Droysen and other members of the Prussian school of history writing. Memories of this scholarly nationalism survived throughout the *Kaiserreich,* as evinced peculiarly well in the work of Wilhelm Dilthey, who connected German historicism with the German armies that drove Napoleon out of Europe and with later nineteenth-century distinctions between Germany and the positivist, ratiocinating West.[5] The social, political, and economic forces of the later nineteenth century, themselves accelerated by the founding of the German Empire in 1871, however, undermined the humanist self-understandings on which German liberal nationalism rested: Germany may indeed have been a nation of poets and thinkers, but poetry, thought, and the nation had been fundamentally transformed since the early nineteenth century.

Already in the late eighteenth century, the German humanities (or *Geisteswissenschaften*) had been engaged with, and informed by, imperialism. For Hegel, Ranke, and the ensuing tradition of historicism, the subject of humanistic knowledge was identified as European through the self-conscious and explicit exclusion of Africans, Asians, and others. The goal of history, for both Hegel and Ranke, was self-knowledge, and the self was defined in Manichaean ethnic terms. The paradox of non-Europeans for the European human sciences—a paradox that dated back at least to sixteenth-century debates about the inhabitants of the Americas or perhaps even to Aristotle's theorizing about slavery—was that they were human yet could not be acknowledged as possessing full "humanity." Humanist notions of the self were both defined and profoundly threatened by the existence of humans whom Europeans regarded as inferior. A number of scholars have recently shown how this very notion of a European self was worked out in the colonies so that the "self" of humanism and the "other" of imperialism were twin births.[6] For all its provincialism, German humanism was, from the very beginning, a global discourse that made sense of the colonial encounter by defining a European self unaffected by it.

In the last third of the nineteenth century, the global networks of imperialism intensified dramatically, thus threatening to collapse the cool distance that German humanists had previously kept from societies outside Europe. The new imperialism exacerbated humanist anxieties about the European self and allowed for new, posthumanist configurations of the human sciences. Quinine allowed Europeans to survive in tropical regions; developments in gun technology allowed them to impose their will on remote societies; steamships and telegraphy allowed them to communicate with the entire globe.[7] Although Germany did not take colonies until 1884, by then the world had already become a much smaller place, as Germans traveled to all parts of the globe and visitors from all over the world came to Germany, especially to perform in ethnographic spectacles so popular among audiences in growing metropolises. The dismissive exclusion of the non-European, which continues to mark humanism even today, became increasingly precarious as the "colonial fantasies" of the period before 1870, brilliantly elucidated by Susanne Zantop, were realized in actual colonial encounters.[8] The crisis of humanism only increased as Germany began taking colonies in Africa and the Pacific and as colonial enthusiasts persuaded increasingly large sectors of the population and the German state that the nation's "place in the sun" depended on global engagement, or *Weltpolitik*.

This new global situation allowed anthropologists to challenge humanism and the academic humanities. Anthropologists proposed a new basis for working out the European self through human scientific scholarship: rather than excluding the colonized other, anthropology would focus explicitly on societies that, all agreed, were radically separate from narratives of Western civilization. Instead of studying European "cultural peoples" (*Kulturvölker*), societies defined by their history and civilization, anthropologists studied the colonized "natural peoples" (*Naturvölker*), societies supposedly lacking history and culture. Anthropologists proposed that their study of so-called natural peoples would reveal human nature directly, unobscured by the masks of culture and the complications of historical development. For the empathetic interpretation characteristic of humanism, anthropologists substituted what they regarded as objective, natural scientific knowledge of a non-European other. Anthropology focused not on canonical texts of celebrated cultural peoples but on the bodies and the everyday objects of the colonized natural peoples. The European self should no longer, anthropologists suggested, work itself out through a solipsistic repression of the rest of the world. Anthropology offered Europeans a modern identity as a cultural people whose status depended less on humanist *Bildung,* or self-cultivation, than on the development of the natural sciences—including anthropology as the study of natural peoples.[9]

In working out this new relation between the European self and the colonized other, anthropology proposed a new identity for the human scientist, one no less "civic" than the identity of the humanist had been. With the growth of cities and urban culture, new mass spectacles and voluntary associations vied with academic institutions as sites of culture and knowledge. Most relevant for anthropology, and fundamentally related to colonialism and natural science, were the "freak" shows and ethnographic performances, or *Völkerschauen,* which provided entertainment and instruction to audiences including both the curious everyman and amateur and professional anthropologists. Freak shows, which often presented individuals as monstrous intermediaries between humans and animals, relied on a new interest in biological aspects of human nature generally and Darwinism in particular. This democratization of the sources and locations of scientific knowledge was further bolstered by the growth of a middle-class public sphere, separate from the state, which allowed a range of voluntary associations to challenge the hegemony of official academic institutions. Anthropology displaced the elite, academic "mandarin" with a group of enthusiasts organized by professionals but incorporating contributions even by untrained amateurs.[10] The discipline challenged not only the intellectual project of academic humanism but also the social structure of the academic humanities and the distinctions between professional and popular science. Anthropology's roots in popular culture also raised doubts about the scientific legitimacy of the discipline, which to critics and even to some practitioners bordered on what they referred to as the leering "voyeurism" (*Schaulust*) of the carnival.

Berlin was the center of German anthropology well into the twentieth century. The anthropological society in Berlin had the largest, most active membership and the widest international contacts both within and outside

Europe. The Berlin museum was the largest and best funded in Germany, if not in the world. The Berlin branch of the German Society for Anthropology, Ethnology, and Prehistory (Berliner Gesellschaft für Anthropologie, Ethnologie und Urgeschichte) was the most important anthropological society in the country. In 1869, the year the German society and the Berlin branch were founded, local organizations were also set up in Leipzig, Würzburg, Munich, Hamburg, Freiburg, Vienna, Bonn, Frankfurt, Mainz, and Heidelberg.[11] The German society met once a year both to give members of local societies a chance to present their work and to provide a more public forum in which to promote the study of anthropology.[12] After a few years, many of the smaller branches seem to have lost momentum, becoming increasingly inactive.[13] As one anthropologist from Heidelberg acknowledged in 1871, "One would have to be blind not to see that the focus of all anthropological activity in Germany is in the Berlin group."[14] Some of the most interesting questions were worked out in the yearly meetings of the German Anthropological Society, for it was here that scientific standards could be made binding throughout Germany rather than in a single locality. However, among the local groups, only the Berlin society regularly produced significant research.

Berlin anthropology focused on the study of regions outside Europe, an enterprise that not only generated much public enthusiasm but also placed the discipline in dialogue with international anthropological discourse. Most German anthropological societies outside Berlin focused on collecting prehistoric German artifacts and on discussing general anatomical questions. The Munich anthropologist Johannes Ranke, for example, did not appear to consider non-Europeans worthy of scholarly attention and found "'piquant' glances at foreign regions" at odds with "the dignity of science."[15] The founding of the Royal Museum of Ethnography in Berlin in 1886 only further emphasized both the centrality and the uniqueness of Berlin anthropology. While anthropology museums also existed in other German cities, the Berlin museum was the best funded, had privileged access to collections from Germany's overseas colonies, and served as an example to other museums in Germany and in Britain and the United States. The regional anthropological societies and museums outside Berlin were certainly of great importance for German cultural life.[16] However, the national German Anthropological Society and its Berlin chapter constituted the central institutions of German anthropology and provided the discipline's most direct contacts to the global context of imperialism. Not surprisingly, it was above all in Berlin, the so-called Athens on the River Spree (*Spreeathen*) and global capital of the academic humanities, that the

anthropological attack on humanism emerged with its greatest clarity and
force.

The natural scientific study of natural peoples could challenge the humanities in Germany because of the massive increase in the prestige of the natural sciences at the end of the nineteenth century.[17] The very thought of
applying natural scientific methods to the questions of the humanities
rested on a reevaluation of the cultural significance of disciplines that had
earlier seemed of peripheral interest. The Berlin anthropologist and museum director Adolf Bastian, himself aware of the novelty of answering
humanistic questions with natural scientific methods, proclaimed: "The
hand of the clock of history points to the hour when the natural scientific
method . . . is to be applied . . . to the subject matter of the humanities [*Geisteswissenschaften*] and therefore to the humanistic studies."[18] Before the late
nineteenth century, the natural sciences took a clear second place to the humanities in Germany as sources of knowledge and cultural prestige. The
second-rate status of the natural sciences clearly informed, for example,
Hermann von Helmholtz's 1862 lecture defending the natural sciences
against the charge that they had abandoned "the other sciences, which are
bound to each other through common philological and historical studies."
Helmholtz insisted that the natural sciences pursued with "logical induction" the same goal—knowledge, presumably—that the humanities
sought using "artistic induction."[19] Anthropologists, themselves mostly
natural scientists and physicians, were part of a larger movement to give
the natural sciences authority commensurate with what was perceived to
be their importance in the contemporary world.

European expansion made possible the natural scientific transformation of the humanities that anthropologists proposed. As the founders of
the Berlin Anthropological Society explained to the Prussian minister of
culture: "A science called forth by the needs and born by the currents of our
time is that of the human, which in the inductive sense of natural science
was previously unknown. It also could not have been undertaken earlier,
until modern voyages of discovery had brought the necessary comparative
materials from the newly opened regions of the world."[20] Natural science,
these anthropologists explained, could be applied to humanistic topics only
after imperialist exploration had brought enough material to Europe to
conduct inductive, comparative studies. Anthropology thus also, its practitioners claimed, answered the new demands of the modern era, which required natural scientific knowledge of the peoples of the globe, not just of
Europeans and their classical ancestors. Anthropologists considered their
discipline a natural science not only because they considered supposedly

"natural" people but also because they approached humanity empirically and inductively, considering all humans around the globe. A natural science of humanity was, for anthropologists, both required and made possible by the globalization brought about by European imperialism.

Notions of biological evolution were conspicuously absent from most anthropologists' understanding of the natural sciences throughout the nineteenth century. Nature functioned in German anthropology as an unchanging realm of eternal truth, which contrasted with the ephemeral developments of history. This understanding of nature was diametrically opposed to that embodied in the theory of evolution, and those few anthropologists who did accept the Darwinistic "monkey doctrine" (*Affenlehre*) in the nineteenth century fit uneasily into the mainstream of the German Anthropological Society. Applying a static concept of nature to living humans, however, presented insurmountable theoretical and practical difficulties. From the beginning, anthropologists complained that the people they encountered were corrupted by contact with Europeans and thus were poor examples of natural peoples. By the early twentieth century, presenting the customs and artifacts of particular societies as instances of a timeless nature would come to seem arbitrary and artificial to anthropologists. In a single conceptual shift just after the turn of the twentieth century, anthropologists would embrace the idea of a changeable nature, thus abandoning their search for ahistorical natural peoples and accepting theories of biological evolution. However, throughout the last third of the nineteenth century, nature functioned as a timeless opposite to culture and history and provided the conceptual grounding for anthropology's challenge to the Eurocentric humanism of the German academy.

The history of German anthropology is not a story of modernity blithely triumphant over hoary humanism. Anthropologists never fully mastered the modern world with which they allied themselves, for imperialism, natural science, and mass culture were not passive resources but active forces with their own dynamics. Imperialism was the sine qua non of anthropology, for without imperialism anthropologists never would have had access to the ethnographic performers, artifacts, body parts, and—in the early twentieth century—field sites that provided the empirical data that they valued above all else. However, the imperialist world system that made these resources available also threatened anthropology. Performers resisted anthropologists' designs, for they were cosmopolitan cultural hybrids, often with political agendas of their own, rather than the pure natural peoples anthropologists wished to study. Similarly, far from being traces of an ahistorical humanity, artifacts and body parts often bore indelible marks of the modern imperialist world system that made them available to anthropologists in the first place. The field also challenged anthropological practice, for it demanded a level of intersubjectivity at sharp odds with the anthropological project of objective natural science. Because of its connections to imperialism, anthropology was an extraordinarily heteroglossic science, containing voices of both colonized and colonizer, which anthropologists themselves could never fully master. Anthropology's roots in popular spectacles gave the discipline a similarly fraught relation to the voyeuristic culture of the commercial arcades. The classical discourse of the humanist, which strictly policed its own boundaries, gave way to a global cultural sphere that European scientists could only partially dominate. While there is no doubt that the imperialism of the late nineteenth century raised the global power of Europe to an unprecedented level, it also allowed for new challenges to that power from a wide range of European and non-European actors. German anthropology illustrates, to a greater extent than any other human scientific discipline, the tremendous challenge presented by imperialism, mass culture, and natural science to traditional humanism and to the former certainties of the European self.

The existence of a connection between anthropology and imperialism has become a commonplace observation, but studies of this connection have tended to focus on the ideological distortions and uses of anthropological knowledge to the exclusion of a broader range of associations.[21] However, as the essays collected in the pathbreaking 1973 *Anthropology and the Colonial Encounter* emphasize, the ideological support and practical suggestions that anthropologists gave to colonialists are but elements of a larger social, cultural, and political context of an "unequal power encounter between the West and Third World which goes back to the emergence of bourgeois Europe."[22] Although European anthropologists and the people they studied were often connected only via a distant colonial military and economic network, they cohabited what Richard White has called a "middle ground," a space that neither fully dominated.[23] While anthropologists could usually exercise overwhelming power over their subjects, this power, like all power, was never so absolute as to subordinate reality itself.[24] The subjects of German anthropology did not—indeed could not have—become natural peoples simply by force of European colonial fantasies. Rather, these colonial interlocutors played an active role in the construction and also in the deconstruction of anthropological knowledge.[25] To overlook the actions and perspectives of anthropology's colonized subjects, even in the name of an ideological critique of anthropology, would allow a myth of objective distance, originally constructed by anthropologists themselves, to obscure a more historically accurate account of anthropology.[26] German anthropology was not the rarefied product of an isolated German intellectual history but rather an active participant in world history.

The first part of this book considers anthropology as a shift in the theories and practices of the human sciences, a shift that reflects an intensification of imperialist relations between Europe and the rest of the world. The first chapter focuses on the global context of this transformation by following individuals from colonized societies who traveled to Europe to stage ethnographic performances. The second chapter then discusses the intellectual shift corresponding to this transformation in imperialism, in which the rejection of non-European societies by humanist historians gave way to the counterhumanistic study of these supposed natural peoples by anthropologists. In the third chapter, I look at how anthropologists sought to ground an antihumanist conception of the human in static conceptions of nature that were themselves under attack by theories of biological evolution. The fourth chapter presents controversies about the measurement and representation of the human skull to show how this paradigmatic anthropological object allowed the discipline to work out a social and epistemological identity that differed sharply from that of the humanist scholar.

The second part focuses on how anthropologists sought to redefine German national identity to give their discipline a privileged place in modern German political and cultural life. In the fifth chapter, I argue that the inductive scientific practices of the German and Berlin Anthropological Societies displaced an earlier civic humanism rooted in the university and the state with a middle-class sociability that was simultaneously open and authoritarian. In the sixth chapter, I look at how, in a massive survey of the "race" of German schoolchildren, anthropologists propagated a new national identity that rendered Germany itself as a racialized space, subject, like the colonized world, to natural scientific anthropology rather than to historicist humanism.

The third part reconstructs the international culture and political economy of anthropological objects to show how the discipline developed in relation both to the new imperialism and to popular consumer culture. In the seventh chapter, I discuss the collection and circulation of anthropological objects in the German colonies to situate the discipline's challenge to humanism in a larger political and economic project of ruling Germany's overseas colonies. For political and scientific reasons, anthropologists and colonists attempted to strip the historical traces from the possessions and the bodies of their colonial subjects. This colonialist reinterpretation of the objects was to be stabilized in natural scientific displays of the Royal

Museum of Ethnology in Berlin, which is the subject of the eighth chapter. In Berlin the objects entered a fraught relation with mass culture, for a fascination with objects and with the exotic was a characteristic not only of anthropology but also of an emerging consumer culture. While anthropologists hoped that the museum would end the ambiguous relations of their discipline with mass culture and with colonial subjects, in fact it exacerbated these tensions and engendered a crisis in anthropological theory and practice.

The fourth and final part of the book focuses on how anthropology transformed itself by acknowledging, rather than seeking to deny, its fundamental connections to mass culture and imperialism. The public demand for narrative coherence in the museum of ethnology led a new generation of curators, after the turn of the century, to seek a rapprochement between anthropology and history, which is the topic of the ninth chapter. While, on the one hand, curators acknowledged the failure of the discipline to create a discourse radically separate from humanism, their move to history also demonstrated a new confidence by anthropologists, who now attempted to appropriate historical narrative to their own designs. In the tenth chapter, I consider anthropologists' attempt to engage more actively with imperialist politics in the early twentieth century by conducting extended field research. Anthropologists initially had difficulty accepting the results of fieldwork because it relied on a model of the human that they regarded as too subjective and individualistic, too like the individual interpreters and subjects of analysis presupposed by humanism. The early failure of fieldwork—far more than its success later in the twentieth century—thus illustrates the limitations of anthropology as a human science without humanism and the ways in which colonialism not only transformed but also fundamentally challenged the European human sciences.

Humanism and the human sciences have, at least in the last two centuries, been marked by a nearly perpetual crisis—from Leopold von Ranke's anxious exclusion of all non-Europeans from "world history," to anthropologists' science of "natural peoples," to the "culture wars" that have recently preoccupied academics in the United States. These various positions on Eurocentrism and humanism have been, in the last instance, responses to global economic, political, and cultural configurations. German anthropology was one of the most important witnesses to, and participants in, this fraught global history of humanism. Anthropology challenged the elitism of an academic humanism that consisted of professors interpreting an ethnocentric canon in the name of humanity. It also provided a series of prac-

tices, theories, and ideologies for some of the greatest evils of human history: colonialist and Nazi genocide. While anthropology's expansion of the
scope of humanistic study represents a democratization of the human sciences, its displacement of hermeneutic notions of understanding and interpretive empathy with models of objective observation borrowed from the
natural sciences devalued the human both as an inquirer and as a subject of
inquiry.[27] The shift in the human sciences represented by anthropology
thus had, from the beginning, multivalent and contradictory potentials.
The purpose of my account is not to denounce or defend anthropology
specifically or studies of formerly excluded others generally. The present-
day U.S. academic descendants of both anthropology and the Eurocentric
humanism that it attacked—for example, world history and Western civilization—are as fundamentally related to global political, economic, and
cultural configurations as were their nineteenth-century forebears. In this
book, I take a global rather than a Eurocentric perspective, not because I
am a committed partisan in contemporary methodological controversies,
but rather because it is the only perspective empirically adequate to the history of the human sciences. I do not want to celebrate the "low"—or to defend the "high"—but rather to historicize this imaginary system of
coordinates that continues to structure debates about the humanities in a
world even more marked by global politics, economics, and culture than
the one in which anthropology first emerged.

PART I

CHAPTER   I

🕊🕊

Exotic Spectacles and the Global Context
of German Anthropology

T he history of anthropology has been written inside out. At least in Germany, it depended not so much on European scientists venturing out into the colonies as on colonial subjects venturing into a Europe that was dangerous, exciting, and potentially profitable for them, much as the colonies were for Europeans. In the years before the First World War, the majority of encounters between German anthropologists and the people they studied occurred in Germany, in circuses, panopticons, and zoos.[1] To dismiss science of this sort as "armchair anthropology," as groundless speculation based on unreliable sources, would be to ignore the foundations of anthropology in a global culture of imperialism and in the popular culture of exotic spectacles. Although anthropologists themselves rarely conducted research abroad, they did study individuals from around the world who traveled to Europe to perform in popular ethnographic shows, or *Völkerschauen*. Performers, however, were not merely shaped according to anthropological expectations; they often came to Europe with personal and political agendas that sometimes led to conflicts with anthropologists. They often disrupted—and thereby illuminated—the conceptual and political structures presupposed by anthropology.

Even before the late nineteenth century, a considerable number of individuals from every part of the globe visited or lived in Germany.[2] Some came to learn a trade or to go to school.[3] Non-European sailors took shore leave when their ships were docked in German ports.[4] A large number of Africans who fought in the French army against Germany in 1870–71 came as prisoners of war.[5] Most importantly for the development of anthropology, individuals were enlisted to perform in German zoos and variety shows. Such shows of non-Europeans had taken place in Germany since the eighteenth century and became much more frequent in the second half of the nineteenth century.[6] In one case, two enslaved individuals from the Aka society were brought by the German colonial hero Franz Stuhlmann; they were then used by the German Colonial Society for promotional demonstrations. They were also presented in the Royal Museum of Ethnology in Berlin, where the anthropologist Rudolf Virchow was invited to study them.[7]

Non-Europeans in Berlin could perform in the so-called panopticons (*Panoptiken*), institutions of popular entertainment where visitors could, as the name implies, see everything. There were two such panopticons in Berlin's commercial arcades, Castan's Panopticon, which opened in 1873, and the Passage-Panopticon, which opened in 1888 (see fig. 1.1).[8] Both were centered around wax museums presenting figures from history and popular culture. Castan's Panopticon presented displays of ethnographic objects and wax "racial busts" depicting various ethnic groups (see fig. 1.2). Several times a day, both panopticons staged humorous song-and-dance

FIGURE 1.1
Castan's Panopticon, date unknown. This was one of the most important institutions presenting "exotic" performers, who were one of the major sources of contact between anthropologists and the people they studied.
Source: Landesarchiv Berlin.

FIGURE 1.2

"Racial busts" from Castan's Panopticon. These wax figures were originally displayed in Castan's Panopticon in the nineteenth century and until quite recently were still displayed in Berlin. They were considered contributions to anthropological knowledge. The brothers Louis and Gustav Castan, the owners of this panopticon, both belonged to the Berlin Anthropological Society.

Source: Berliner Panoptikum (brochure purchased at the Panoptikum in 1995).

routines as well as appearances by remarkable individuals such as the Captain of Köpenick or the "hunger artists," accurately described in Kafka's story.[9] The Passage-Panopticon had a thousand-seat theater in which "natural wonders such as giants, dwarves, two-headed children, etc." performed every day.[10] Castan's Panopticon similarly presented numerous freak shows. The Passage-Panopticon offered an "Anatomical Museum and Hall of Abnormalities," and Castan's Panopticon boasted a display of wax medical statues, many of which represented both diseased and healthy sexual organs.[11] Attendance at certain unusually risqué shows, such as an 1898 display of a hermaphrodite, was limited to medical doctors and university faculty and students.[12] Apart from these occasional restricted shows, the panopticons were enormously popular, and Castan's reported that, on Sundays and holidays, more than five thousand people visited. Tourist guidebooks presented the panopticons as important sights, and one suggested a visit even during a stay in Berlin of only three days.[13]

The panopticons, as well as zoological gardens and other arenas of popular amusement, were ready markets for non-European performers, who could draw large crowds to ethnographic displays, or *Völkerschauen*, in which they presented what were supposed to be their native customs, dances, and other entertaining practices. The most important promoter of these so-called *Völkerschauen* was the animal importer and zookeeper Carl Hagenbeck, whose first show consisted of a group of Laplanders whom he included in an 1874 reindeer exhibition (see fig. 1.3). The show turned out to be so popular and profitable that Hagenbeck began regularly to organize displays of humans.[14] Louis and Gustav Castan, the brothers who owned Castan's Panopticon, were also very important *Völkerschau* promoters. Many ethnographic performances were also organized by colonial merchants returning to Germany, who would bring a few individuals with them to promote their firm and earn extra money.[15]

Both Hagenbeck and the Castan brothers worked in close contact with Berlin anthropologists in staging and promoting these shows. This was not merely because of their own scientific interests but also because they needed anthropologists to attest to the authenticity of their performers and to legitimate them to the police.[16] These shows brought non-Europeans into Germany, sometimes violated child labor laws, often included more sexualized nudity than the law generally tolerated, and seemed generally weird and suspicious to the Prussian police. There was even the suggestion that the exotic performances were a cover for "a bordello of the worst sort."[17] The appearance of what was often referred to as "a certain scientific interest" behind these shows helped allay official suspicions and get the re-

FIGURE 1.3

Laplander show in Berlin, 1897. Berliners in the background peer over a fence at Laplanders performing in the foreground. The first performance of Laplanders in Germany, which initiated Hagenbeck's vigorous promotion of *Völkerschauen,* occurred in 1874. *Source: Illustrierte Chronik der Zeit* 31 (1897): 469.

quired police approval.[18] For example, the Passage-Panopticon was allowed to present "scenes from a Tunisian harem" when a police inspector concluded that it was of "solely ethnological interest."[19] Anthropologists regularly wrote professional evaluations of the displayed people, which impresarios used to promote their shows, attesting both to their authenticity and to the "high degree of interest aroused" by the performers.[20]

Performances were not merely opportunities for anthropological study: the cooperation of anthropologists was necessary if these *Völkerschauen* were to be allowed to take place.[21] Exotic shows thus required that performers satisfy anthropologists as well as popular audiences. Performers often made special appearances at the meetings of the Berlin Anthropological Society, and the anthropological society held special meetings at the zoo or the panopticons.[22] Performers had to let themselves be studied and also had to prove their authenticity to anthropologists or risk having their shows banned. For example, when a promoter refused to allow anthropologists to take measurements of a group of Abyssinians performing at Castan's Panopticon in 1906, the anthropologist Felix von Luschan considered having "the entire show forbidden as 'crude mischief' if the people are being displayed under a false flag and if a scientific examination is hindered."[23] Anthropologists played an important role in determining both the credibility and the legality of these shows.

Performers were thus expected to conform to a certain anthropological understanding of the non-European. In the next chapters, I consider in greater detail the philosophical and cultural background of this understanding. What is essential here is that anthropologists expected Africans, indigenous Americans, Pacific Islanders, and marginalized societies in Europe and Asia to be "natural peoples" (*Naturvölker*). Natural peoples supposedly lacked writing, culture, and history and thus contrasted sharply with "cultural peoples" (*Kulturvölker*), such as Europeans. Anthropologists believed that in natural peoples they would be able to glimpse human nature directly, unmasked by the complications of history or culture. Anthropologists did not communicate this theory directly to the performers, and it is often clear that the performers would not have been willing to conform to it in any case. However, these anthropological expectations shaped the interactions and mutual misunderstandings that occurred between the natives of Germany and the travelers who came from abroad. The ethnographic performances, made possible by the growth of European imperialism and mass culture, provided social, cultural, and political foundations and fault lines for the new discipline of anthropology and its challenges to humanism.

In 1878, a group of thirty-two individuals from the Sudan traveled to perform in Germany, Paris, and London, managed by an employee of Carl Hagenbeck's. They were the second group of Sudanese to travel to Germany, where they were billed as "Nubians" to suggest something more primitive and exotic than the Arabic-speaking Christian and Muslim population of the modern Sudan (cf. fig. 2.2 below). There is no record of the terms of their contract, although the fact that Hagenbeck made assurances to the Egyptian government about their eventual repatriation indicates that they were not simply abducted.[24] When the Sudanese performed for two weeks in the Berlin Zoological Garden, they became the subject of what the president of the German Anthropological Society, Johannes Ranke, called "a true paradigm of an anthropological-ethnological study."[25] It was also a paradigm of the difficulties that anthropologists and performers faced in these efforts to create natural peoples.

The study was directed by the head of the Berlin Anthropological Society, Rudolf Virchow, whose political connections had been instrumental in persuading the Egyptian government to allow the Sudanese to embark on this tour in the first place. Virchow began his studies by measuring the width (side to side), length (front to back), and height (top to bottom) of their heads, the length and breadth of their noses, the height and width of their faces, the distance from the tip of their noses to their chins, and the width of their jaws. Virchow and several colleagues used a color table to determine the hues of their skin, their finger- and toenails, and their lips and eyes. Two other anthropologists tested the color perception of the performers and recorded their color vocabulary. Three philologists specializing in Ethiopian and Egyptian languages found that they could say little about the performers because the "Nubians" did not speak an indigenous language, only Arabic.[26] Inquiries into the performers' religion also produced few results that interested anthropologists since all performers had converted to Christianity or Islam and were no longer "heathens." Before the group returned to Africa, Virchow had photographed eight individuals whom he considered typical. Another member of the society traced the outlines of the hands and feet of each performer. After some difficulty, Louis Castan convinced two performers to let him make plaster casts of their faces, hands, and feet. A sculptor made a bust of one of the performers and sold copies to members of the society, including to Virchow.[27]

During the regular meeting following its visit to the show, the Berlin Anthropological Society debated whether these so-called Nubians were more closely related to sub-Saharan Africans or to West Asians. At the time, this was one of the more important questions in the field of the anthropology of Africa.[28] Both because of their physical appearance and because of their geographic location, the people of the Sudan were considered intermediaries between Asians and Africans, and thus their ethnic makeup and origins had important implications for understanding both Africa and Asia. Members discussed the physical appearance of the performers, their customs, and their tools (which were displayed with them in the zoo). One group, led by the anatomist and North Africa specialist Robert Hartmann, believed that the Sudanese originated from sub-Saharan Africa and that they may even have exerted some influence on the Semitic population of the Arabian peninsula. This group pointed out that the Sudanese possessed tools, customs, and economic practices more similar to those of the rest of Africa than to those of the Near East. Johann Gottfried Wetzstein, a former Prussian consul to Damascus and an expert on the history and languages of Syria, cited the supposed cowardice of the Bedouins to support his claim that Arabs never could have ventured to travel to the Sudan, although others pointed out that they might have come as traders rather than warriors. They failed to reach a conclusion and looked forward to further discussions based on future Sudanese shows in Berlin. Unfortunately for the anthropologists, only one more group could be brought to Europe

before the Mahdist uprising in 1881 made it impossible to recruit any more
performers from the region.

This "paradigmatic" study of natural peoples was unable to wrest the
individuals under consideration from history, even though the lack of history was supposed to be a defining characteristic of natural peoples. The
type of information that anthropologists collected was modeled on natural
scientific data: measurements, photographs, and diagrams rather than narrative descriptions or textual evidence. The language and the religion of
the performers were of interest only insofar as these traits represented a
"natural" condition. When it was discovered that the performers spoke
Arabic and practiced Christianity and Islam, that their language and religion were historical acquisitions, these phenomena lost their significance.
The knowledge that anthropologists desired about "authentic" Nubians
had been effaced by history. Despite the mass of "natural scientific" data
that anthropologists had been able to collect, the debate about racial relations among Africans and West Asians continually returned to questions
about historical events. Virchow attempted to stifle these inquiries, insist-
ing that the participants restrict themselves to a "concentrated and deliber-
ate" course of inquiry, either to linguistics or to physical anthropology, and
eschew speculations based on history.[29] The final intervention of history
occurred in the Mahdist uprising, when the history of colonialism itself
prevented further "Nubian" performances, which, anthropologists hoped,
might have offered more conclusive evidence. This, however, did not lead
anthropologists to abandon their quest for natural peoples; they simply
looked elsewhere.

A similarly confused interaction occurred with two Inuit families who
traveled from Labrador to Germany in 1880 with Adrian Jacobsen, a collector of anthropological artifacts employed by Hagenbeck.[30] Jacobsen
could speak the language of the Inuit and served as an interpreter. While in
Berlin the Inuit performed in the zoological gardens, and, like their Sudanese predecessors, they became the subjects of an anthropological investigation. When Virchow arrived to measure the group, one family, who
had converted to Christianity, cooperated; the other family, a couple and
their fifteen-year-old daughter, resisted. The mother of this second family,
who was seriously ill at the time, refused to allow Virchow to measure her,
trembled with rage when he insisted, and threw furniture around the
room. Virchow was clearly troubled by this interaction as well as by a
newspaper article about these performers that condemned the practice of
keeping "our equals in a zoo."[31] In his presentation to the Berlin Anthro-

pological Society, he offered a defense of such ethnographic displays in the name of science. As for the woman who refused to allow Virchow to measure her, he suggested that her rage was in fact a "shamanistic state," that is, not individual resistance, but a manifestation of primitive religion. Paradoxically, the Christian family, presumably less traditional, was more useful to the anthropologists than were the "heathens," who were less willing to cooperate with Europeans.[32] Eventually, all the Inuit performers died in Germany, apparently from smallpox, which they had not been immunized against. Like so many European and non-European explorers, they had gambled their health and safety in a strange country and had lost. As was often the case, anthropologists kept their measurements, many of their performance props, and at least one of their skulls.[33] Despite the tensions with these foreign travelers, anthropologists were thus able to integrate them into their own discipline.

Like anthropologists and impresarios, performers could make clever use of their stage personae, even when those personae were imposed on them by European managers. For example, in 1886, Carl Hagenbeck sponsored a show of Duala from Cameroon, some of whom had served aboard the German navy ship HMS *Bismarck*. As often occurred in such shows, the performers did not simply appear naively before audiences but rather played roles that they and the impresarios had fabricated. To increase interest in this particular show, Hagenbeck billed one of the performers, a politically unimportant son of a local leader from the village of Bonabella, as "King Dido." Unaware that *King Dido* was merely a stage name, Crown Prince Friedrich hosted him and three of his compatriots in the New Palace in Potsdam. After their interview, a royal coach conducted the performers to a train returning to Berlin. When the governor of Cameroon, Julius Soden, learned of this meeting, he was furious. Soden believed that indigenous leaders in Cameroon regarded the people whom the crown prince had entertained as "*damned niggers* and *slaves.*" He feared that such meetings would undermine German colonists' own claim that, in comparison to "a '*German King*' or '*prince,*'" the elites of Cameroon were themselves "nothing but *damned niggers.*" Two years later, when Crown Prince Friedrich had become kaiser and king and was dying of throat cancer, King Dido wrote from Cameroon to inquire about his health. Bismarck forbade the kaiser to respond.[34] The Duala sailors did more than merely spend a pleasant afternoon at Potsdam and have an interesting chat with an exotic German ruler. They also, as Governor Soden correctly perceived, challenged the authority of European colonial rule in their home country. They thus transformed their popular representations of Africa into a kind of unauthorized political representation.

One of the greatest, and certainly the best documented, ethnographic performances took place as part of the 1896 Berlin Colonial Exhibition, when the Colonial Section of the German Imperial Foreign Office, in cooperation with a group of private financial backers, brought more than one hundred people from German colonies in Africa and the Pacific to live and perform next to a carp pond in Treptow Park (see fig. 1.4).[35] The Foreign Office requested that each colonial government organize a group of indigenous people for the exhibition. The German state tried to recruit indigenous elites as performers, hoping to bolster colonial domination by impressing them with German museums, theaters, zoos, and military parades during their stay in Berlin.[36] The German state thus conceived of the colonial exhibition as a kind of two-way *Völkerschau,* performing foreign lands for the Germans and Germany for the colonial performers: "The Exhibition Committee was careful to make life as agreeable as possible for the natives and also to impress upon them the highest possible conception of European culture. When they later returned to their homes, they would recount impressions of Berlin to their tribal comrades and thus spread respect and servility before the 'clever white man.' The blacks were thus not only shown the exhibition, they were also driven around and taken to the sights of the imperial city."[37] While the organizers could not always recruit elites, they did have some remarkable successes. It was always difficult to find suitable performers, and the selection process thus tended to favor those already occupying an intermediary position between colonizer and colonized. This, as well as the relatively high social status of many of the performers, made anthropological research especially problematic at the exhibition.

The imperial commissioner of the Marshall Islands suggested sending to the exhibition a certain Liktokwa, whom he considered one of the most influential leaders in the area. The commissioner wanted to impress the Marshall Islander with the "power and greatness of the German people." Liktokwa had been to San Francisco, and the city had apparently persuaded him that the United States was the most powerful nation in the world, an impression that the German commissioner hoped to change. The commissioner thought that he would be able to entice Liktokwa to travel to Berlin by promising to stop for dental work in Sydney along the way. However, this plan was abandoned because the Foreign Office feared that, rather than impressing him, the long ship journey and the climate of Berlin might kill Liktokwa.[38] Instead, a German commercial agent work-

FIGURE   1.4

Portrait of the 1896 Berlin Colonial Exhibition performers and managers. The photo-
graph is taken in front of the administration building on the exhibition grounds.
Source: Gustav Hermann Meinecke and Rudolf Hellgrewe, eds., *Deutschland und seine
Kolonien im Jahre 1896* (Berlin: Dietrich Reimer, 1897).

ing in the region assembled a group of eight inhabitants of New Britain, an
island in the Bismarck Archipelago, to represent Germany's Pacific
colonies at the colonial exhibition. Because the organizers assumed that Pacific Islanders would have particular difficulty adjusting to the European
climate, they sent only strong men who had already had extensive contact
with Germans. This group knew so little about the societies that it was to
represent that the commercial agent had to purchase "traditional" objects
to send with the performers, acquire the material for their "traditional"
dwellings, and explain to the natives how to set up an "ancestor house." He
even had to clarify what an ancestor house was (see fig. 1.5).[39] Like many
Völkerschauen, this was a performance by people in close contact with Germany, unfamiliar with the customs that they were to represent.

The recruitment of performers from German East Africa reflected the
colonial relations characteristic of that colony. In East Africa, Germany
had relatively good relations with the coastal Swahili speakers who had
sold slaves and ivory from the interior to the sultan of Zanzibar and who
served as workers and soldiers under the Germans. The German government in the coastal capital Dar es Salaam thus organized performers like a
labor gang for railroad building or plantation work, recruited, managed,

FIGURE   1.5
Performers from German New
Guinea in front of an "ancestral hut"
designed by a German expert for the
1896 Berlin Colonial Exhibition.
Source: Gustav Hermann Meinecke
and Rudolf Hellgrewe, eds., *Deutschland und seine Kolonien im Jahre 1896*
(Berlin: Dietrich Reimer, 1897).

and accompanied by a German commercial agent. Since the Germans had
poorer relations with societies from the interior of their colony, they could
not recruit from any of them except the Masai. Despite their long-standing
reputation as authentically primitive Africans (evinced more recently in
Leni Riefenstahl's famous photographs), like the other societies whose
members performed at the exhibition the Masai had a history of political
contact with Germany.[40] The East African government decided to supplement this rather paltry selection of East African societies by hiring Swahili
workers to dress like Wamakonde.[41] The group of forty East Africans
brought along a large number of local products and the material to build
the supposedly traditional houses in which they would live and be displayed. As with the Pacific Island performers, the East African group's
manager thought it necessary to enlist a European expert, in this case the
Berlin anthropologist Felix von Luschan, to help set up their dwellings.[42]
During their stay in Berlin, the East Africans enacted lifestyles and staged
dances and songs presumed to be characteristic of societies from their home
country. In the evenings, after the visitors had gone home and they no
longer had to perform, the East Africans amused themselves with German
folk songs and even sang "Deutschland über Alles," accompanied on the
violin by a member of the group.[43]

Like the East African government, the colonial government of Cameroon had trouble recruiting anyone other than members of a coastal society with whom it already had economic and political ties.[44] Germany's relations with the people of Cameroon had recently become particularly hostile when colonists set up rubber plantations that employed forced native labor.[45] Because of growing military tensions resulting from these labor policies, the commander of an interior station could not convince anyone to travel to the colonial exhibition. The people he asked feared that they were actually to be held as hostages to ensure the safety of the station.[46] The only people from Cameroon who performed at the colonial exhibition were Duala, including members of one of the two main Duala ruling families, the Bells. The Duala, and especially the Bell family, had been clients of European colonists for more than a century. Many of the other Duala at the exhibition were laborers, some of whom had served on German warships.[47] Like the East Africans, the Duala performers passed evenings with German songs, although they apparently chose bawdy tunes.[48] According to the anthropologist Luschan, the Duala performers got drunk during the day and offended the public.[49] They refused to play primitives, behaving perhaps more like sailors on German warships than like objects of colonial-anthropological discourse.

In Togo, German colonial rule rested on trading relations with indigenous elites, many of whom had attended German mission schools.[50] The Togolese troupe was organized by a Christian chief, J. C. Bruce, and his nephew, a shoemaker who had been trained in Berlin and spoke fluent German with a Berlin accent.[51] Both organizers seemed genuinely to want to teach Germans about Togolese cultures.[52] They hired native artisans and dancers to come to Berlin and hoped to earn additional money by selling souvenirs to the German public (see fig. 1.6).[53] The reliance of German colonialism in Togo on a cosmopolitan native political elite paralleled the almost anthropological way in which the Togolese performers presented themselves. They seem to have understood the sorts of things that Germans expected from an exotic exhibition—arts and crafts and dances—and set about meeting these demands at a profit to themselves.[54]

At his own expense, Samuel Maharero, the leader of the Herero of Southwest Africa, sent five notables, including his eldest son, Friedrich, to the colonial exhibition (see fig. 1.7).[55] Maharero's assumption of his own father's position in 1890 had been contested by other Herero leaders and had been resolved in Maharero's favor only with German assistance. Maharero thought of the people he sent to the colonial exhibition as a diplomatic party. He arranged for this party to meet with Kaiser Wilhelm after the exhibition to confirm the loyalty of the Herero to Germany and to support the

FIGURE   1.6
The Togolese performers at the 1896 Berlin Colonial Exhibition. The organizer and man-
ager of the group, J. C. Bruce, sits on the left.
Source: Gustav Hermann Meinecke and Rudolf Hellgrewe, eds., *Deutschland und seine
Kolonien im Jahre 1896* (Berlin: Dietrich Reimer, 1897).

current governor of Southwest Africa against criticisms that he ruled too
leniently.[56] In their performances, the Hereros did not attempt to disguise
their relation to European culture. They dressed like European colonists in
Southwest Africa, and their only regular act was to drive around the performance grounds in a type of oxcart used by both white and black farmers
in their home country. However, to the dismay of a visiting missionary,
whose interests differed from those of anthropologists and the exhibition
promoters, the Herero performers once exchanged their dresses, jackets,
and ties for old-fashioned costumes to perform what they took to be traditional Herero rituals. They wanted to show the public, one later explained,
what "heathens" back in Southwest Africa did.[57]

The managers of the exhibition made a point of strictly regulating the
lives of the performers. A volume commemorating the exhibition described this discipline in detail. Performers had to rise each morning at six
to wash themselves, which must have been miserable in the unusually cold
summer of 1896. They were then required to clean their living spaces, after
which they carried out supposedly traditional tasks, such as grinding meal

FIGURE 1.7
Friedrich Maharero, eldest son of Samuel Maharero, king of the Herero. Samuel used the occasion of the performance at the 1896 Berlin Colonial Exhibition to arrange a diplomatic meeting with the German Kaiser.
Source: Gustav Hermann Meinecke and Rudolf Hellgrewe, eds., *Deutschland und seine Kolonien im Jahre 1896* (Berlin: Dietrich Reimer, 1897).

or weaving. They were given a midday break until three o'clock, when their performances began. Except for the Herero, most performed dances, although the Duala also rowed boats around the carp pond. At ten in the evening (which would have been just after nightfall in Berlin summers), the performers were required to retire to their huts, where they were allowed to socialize among themselves.[58] Such discipline did not constitute merely a means of control; it was also an argument about both colonialism and anthropology. Colonialism, this well-ordered exhibition suggested, imposed a European form on a non-European content. Despite the enormous amount of power exercised by exhibition promoters as well as by the colonial state generally, the colonized, this exhibition suggested, neither shaped nor were shaped by European colonists. Such a spectacle of disciplined colonial subjects implied German control without suggesting any kind of cultural hybridity between colonizer and colonized.[59] Such hybridity might have undermined the legitimacy given to German imperialism by describing Europeans as cultural peoples and those they ruled in Africa and the Pacific as natural peoples.[60] It might also have undermined anthropologists' insistence that theirs was an objective natural science, marked by a cool distance impossible for conventional humanists to achieve.

Of course the exhibition organizers could not help but be aware that the Africans and Pacific Islanders present in Berlin had been coached by anthropologists and other European experts to perform cultures that were not their own. However, it seems to have been the general view that the authenticity of the performances was secured—not undermined—by knowledgeable European directors, including the anthropologist Luschan. Indeed, the fact that a European expert had instructed the performers from the Bismarck Archipelago on the meaning and construction of an ancestral hut was cited as evidence for its authenticity, against the criticism that it was a mere *"curiosity shop."*[61] The show's promoters evidently assumed that the European directors helped the colonial subjects represent more authentic cultures than they otherwise could have. In the very content of the show, as well as in the disciplined regime forced on the performers, European direction proved fundamental to the construction of primitive cultures but at the same time effaced itself as formal direction separate from authentic content.

Some performers did, however, resist this European direction. Their resistance is recorded especially well in a series of anthropological photographs published as "a lasting souvenir of the interesting band of blacks" at the colonial exhibition.[62] Although Africans and Pacific Islanders at the exhibition allowed photographs of their performances, many objected to having photographs taken by the anthropologist working with the exhibition, Felix von Luschan. Often they did not allow Luschan to photograph them individually at all. Even those who did let themselves be photographed often insisted on wearing European-style clothes for what they seem to have regarded as personal portraits (cf. figs. 1.8 and 1.9).[63] Evidently, many who performed at the colonial exhibition did not wish to be represented individually in what they perhaps considered to be stage costumes.[64] They preferred instead to appear dressed in a manner more appropriate to their social station.[65]

This resistance aroused the fury of Felix von Luschan. In his published account of his studies, included in the volume commemorating the exhibition, he labeled many individuals "limited," "impudent," or "ill-bred." Others, apparently those who cooperated with him, received labels such as "polite" or "peaceful."[66] He particularly despised a man named Bismarck Bell, a political leader who refused to be photographed in anything but black tie (see fig. 1.10). Like most performers, Bell appeared in public wearing what was regarded as authentic Duala clothing. However, like many of his colleagues, he refused to allow Luschan to photograph him in this costume. Although also known as Kwelle Ndumbe, the first name *Bismarck* indicates that his family had friendly relations with the German govern-

FIGURE   1.8 *(left)*
Anthropological portrait of Mschúngo, a performer from the Masai group at the 1896
Berlin Colonial Exhibition. Mschúngo wears some of his performance accessories but has
evidently refused to remove his European-style jacket for the photograph.
Source: Gustav Hermann Meinecke and Rudolf Hellgrewe, eds., *Deutschland und seine
Kolonien im Jahre 1896* (Berlin: Dietrich Reimer, 1897).

FIGURE   1.9 *(right)*
Amonin, a Togolese performer at the 1896 Berlin Colonial Exhibition. Amonin was part
of the minority of performers who agreed to let Luschan photograph them without any
European-style clothing. The Togolese generally cooperated with anthropological con-
structions at the exhibition, in part because they earned money by selling souvenirs to the
public.
Source: Gustav Hermann Meinecke and Rudolf Hellgrewe, eds., *Deutschland und seine
Kolonien im Jahre 1896* (Berlin: Dietrich Reimer, 1897).

ment. The Bell family was one of the two major Duala ruling families, who
had gained power in Cameroon in the eighteenth century by allying with
British colonists and who maintained associations with colonists when the
Germans arrived in the nineteenth century. Thus, as part of a powerful
client elite, Bismarck Bell stood in an ambiguous relation to colonial powers: on the one hand, he was subordinate to the German state; on the other
hand, he enjoyed a kind of social authority and power in his own right.

Luschan's tirade against Bell exceeds anything written about any other

FIGURE 1.10
Bismarck (Kwelle Ndumbe) Bell, a
Duala dignitary who refused to be
photographed in "native" costume.
Source: Gustav Hermann Meinecke and
Rudolf Hellgrewe, eds., *Deutschland und
seine Kolonien im Jahre 1896* (Berlin:
Dietrich Reimer, 1897).

performer at the exhibition, both in length and in venom: "A delightful
original and an incomparable mixture of idiot and 'trouser-nigger.' Of
course he would not let himself be measured, but one day he showed up before the camera *en grande tenue,* hung with cotillion or bowling-club
medals, and indicated with a graciously condescending gesture that he
wished to be photographed. Because of the strong tremors of the man, who
is a heavy drinker and suffers from delirium, the photographs could not be
exposed long enough. Still they are sufficient to give one an approximate
idea of the appearance of this 'dignified' village chief."[67] The photograph
itself gives the lie to Luschan's accusation that Bell was suffering from
delirium tremens to such an extent that he could not be photographed
clearly. Noteworthy also is Luschan's derision of Bell's clothing and decorations. Bell dressed not as an uncivilized colonial subject but rather in
black tie hung with medals, a style of dress favored by European colonists.
Perhaps to differentiate themselves from the indigenous population as
"civilized" cultural peoples, Europeans in the colonies conducted their social life, in general, much more formally than they did at home in Europe.
It was much more common for Europeans to wear black tie in the colonies,
with which it would be appropriate to wear medals and ribbons (which
were often awarded to German civilians in the nineteenth century).[68]

   Bell challenged the boundary between the cultural peoples and the
natural peoples, the colonizer and the colonized, the European and the

non-European. Bell dressed, not as a "traditional" Duala, but rather, in Luschan's mind, as a European colonist. By wearing black tie and medals, by preparing himself for a photograph in the way a European would, Bell challenged these binary oppositions. African elites who adapted European styles of dress, as well as other symbols of European cultures, constituted an important basis for European colonial rule, and Bell may have dressed as he did to signify his membership in the comprador classes of Cameroon. While his intention may have been to display his cooperation with European colonists, Bell's dress also represented a challenge to the asymmetry between European "cultural peoples" and colonized "natural peoples." By wearing trousers, Bell disrupted the binary oppositions that underwrote anthropology, colonialism, and, indeed, the very idea of Europe. Instead of representing natural humanity unconcealed by culture and history, Bell played the role of an anthropologist, revealing and disrupting the workings of the social and cultural system of imperialism.[69]

By refusing to be photographed in their costumes, Bismarck Bell and other performers threatened to transform Luschan's anthropological images into demonstrations of the fabricated nature of primitive culture (which is, indeed, how I use them). Luschan dealt with this threat to his own discourse by describing, in the volume commemorating the exhibition, those who openly refused to cooperate with this ethnic construction as "trouser-niggers" (*Hosennigger*).[70] This was apparently a common colonial epithet, applied especially in Cameroon, meaning a non-European who took on certain reputedly European habits (such as wearing trousers).[71] Instead of allowing the uncooperative individuals to destabilize the performance of colonial culture, Luschan transformed them into object lessons in the undesirability of colonial subjects adopting the culture of European colonists. Luschan was thus able to publish the volume of commemorative portraits without undermining the discourse of primitive natural peoples and advanced cultural peoples, even though many of the photographs show Africans wearing European clothes. Luschan transformed into a derogatory slur a description of the cultural hybridity involved in any colonial project. While anthropology depended on a clean separation between colonizer and colonized, the very practices of colonialism depended on constant transgressions of that separation. The "trouser-nigger" was in fact a key persona of colonialism, reviled for the very multicultural fluencies on which European hegemony depended.[72] The performers at the colonial exhibition were themselves perfect illustrations of this phenomenon: they were employed as illustrations of authentic, primitive culture, but they could be recruited only from groups with extensive political, economic, and cultural contact with Germany. Some performers were able to create

counterhegemonic representations in the portrait photographs, but, ultimately, Germans were able to subordinate this resistance to a colonialist
discourse.

In the 1896 Berlin Colonial Exhibition, as well as in the earlier "Nubian"
and Inuit shows, when anthropologists found that performers challenged
their conceptions of cultural and natural peoples, they restricted their studies to physical anthropology.[73] Luschan reckoned that, since bodies do not
depend on clothes or culture, he might yet acquire valuable scientific data
at the exhibition, even from the "trouser-niggers." He enlisted the help
of his spouse, Emma von Hochstetter, and seven of his students to go out to
the village by the carp pond early each morning, before the exhibition
opened to the public, and measure the performers. However, it was particularly difficult to secure voluntary cooperation because nineteenth-century
anthropological measurements were often painful. In order to measure the
dimensions of the skeleton of living people, anthropologists tightened their
calipers until the flesh was pinched to a negligible thinness.[74] Furthermore,
many people displayed at the exhibition refused, in Luschan's phrase, to
"strip off their European shells," to remove their clothing to be studied.[75]
For example, the Togolese leader continually found excuses to prevent
Luschan from measuring the female performers in his group: "One day it
was too warm, another day too cold; one day the women were unwell, another day they had to bathe; once they had just sat down to eat, another
time they were cooking. . . ."[76] The cold weather of Berlin discouraged
even those performers willing to strip for Luschan's measurements. While
Luschan was able to study many performers, these measurements were of
neither the quality nor the quantity that he desired. Despite his power as a
colonial anthropologist, Luschan still had to negotiate with subjects who
were able to exercise significant resistance.

Even before any of the colonial subjects arrived in Berlin, officials worried that the colder climate would adversely affect their health. At this
time, acclimatization was an important medical theme, and, although doctors more commonly worried about the effects of tropical climates on Europeans, they seem to have presumed that people from tropical climates
would also have health problems in Germany.[77] Furthermore, although
the small area in which the 103 colonial subjects lived that summer presented both sanitation and health problems, the exhibition managers did
not want to let them spread out.[78] The summer of 1896 was unusually cold,
and the managers of the exhibition responded to this problem by giving the
performers long underwear (which in some cases was dyed to match their
skin color) and spoonfuls of rum or other spirits on particularly cold days.[79]

This response was evidently not sufficient, for some of the displayed soon began suffering from pneumonia. By the end of the summer, many had become sick and required hospitalization. One Pacific Islander was sent home because it was thought that the Berlin climate was killing him. A man from East Africa and a man from Cameroon eventually died at the exhibition.[80] For Luschan and Wilhelm Waldeyer, a fellow anthropologist, these deaths presented a good opportunity for acquiring anthropological material. Whereas they usually had to rely on partial skeletons, stripped of any perishable soft parts, acquired in various ways in the colonies by various more or less trustworthy correspondents, here they could get entire fresh corpses. Luschan planned to give Waldeyer the brains and other soft parts and keep the skeletons for himself. Apparently, he first approached the exhibition committee with this request when he learned that the Pacific Islander (who was later sent home) had become ill and might die. The committee agreed to Luschan's request, although it seems to have found it a bit grisly.[81] Although living performers destabilized static anthropological constructions, their skulls and other body parts contributed to determining the typical properties of their "races."

Non-European travelers and performers were often able to destabilize the very categories that anthropologists took them to exemplify. The societies that anthropologists studied were not, in fact, static, ahistorical, natural entities; rather, they played an active part in the processes by which they became exposed to European power and knowledge. The level of contact that anthropologists had with the individuals they held to be representatives of natural peoples was, in fact, directly proportional to the extent to which those individuals already participated in a political, economic, and cultural network comprising a range of (historical) peoples. Bismarck Bell insisted on presenting himself to Luschan's camera as an individual with a specific historical relation to Europe, symbolized by the tuxedo he chose to wear for the portrait. Luschan managed to preserve the concept of natural peoples by recategorizing the anomalous Bell as a "trouser-nigger." Bell exemplified, for Luschan, not the natural essence of humanity, but rather a degraded individual failure, a contemptible individual acting out of place.

Even while preserving the theoretical distinction between natural peoples and cultural peoples, some anthropologists began to doubt its foundation in reality.[82] The year after his encounter with Bismarck Bell, Luschan, for example, wrote to a colleague that he could no longer maintain in his own mind a clear distinction between natural peoples and cultural peoples: "How would you determine a criterion for 'savage peoples' [wilde Völker]? For twelve years I have directed the collections from Africa and Oceania

here at the museum, and I still have not been able to determine such a criterion. On the contrary, the longer I concern myself with these questions and
the closer I come to answering one of them, the clearer it becomes to me
that it is not at all possible to divide [illegible] natural peoples and cultural
peoples."[83] Despite these doubts, Luschan, like most anthropologists of his
generation, preserved the terminology. When he failed to find authentic
nature in Bismarck Bell and the other Duala performers, for example, he
maintained his belief that there were "upstanding people from the hinter-
land," still safe from European influences and corruptions.[84] While anthropologists became increasingly aware of cases contradicting the very
foundation of their theory, for decades they were able to marginalize these
cases as anomalies.

Anthropological interest in exotic performances continued well into the
twentieth century, until they were banned by the National Socialists.[85] In
1939, the head of the newly revived Colonial Office, the former governor of
Southwest Africa, Friedrich von Lindequist, prevented a show of Abyssinians proposed by the late Carl Hagenbeck's firm. He disapproved of
such shows, he wrote, because in the past they had led to "intimate contact
with German girls and women, in which not the colored man but the white
women, forgetting their duty and honor, sought the contact."[86] The intimacy between self and other, on which earlier German anthropology had
thrived, was anathema to the fanatic racism of National Socialism. Before
this time, however, German anthropology benefited from travelers from
abroad, especially those who staged popular ethnographic performances.
While the knowledge that anthropologists gained from these shows may
today seem quite limited, at the time the performers provided a comparatively good source of anthropological information. The president of the
German Anthropological Society, who had called the investigations of the
Sudanese show a "paradigmatic" anthropological study, explained the importance of these shows for anthropologists. European travelers, he noted,
rarely had the opportunity to make measurements and observations, and,
even when they did, the data that they produced were seldom reliable. It
was methodologically more sound, he claimed, for anthropologists to study
"representatives of foreign nations" in Germany, where one had, and could
use comfortably, all the instruments that one might need.[87] The field
would not become a privileged site of research in German anthropology for
decades, and European experiences abroad were viewed with greater suspicion than were the direct observations that anthropologists conducted in
Berlin shows. Understanding the history of anthropology in relation only
to the history of European travel has masked the international character of

the discipline, even in its early stages. Anthropological knowledge was a coproduction of European anthropologists and the people they studied. Ultimately, anthropology would develop in Germany as a one-sided discussion by European scientists about non-Europeans, based primarily on dead bodies and objects. However, the social basis of anthropology was global, and, even if non-European voices were suppressed, they were still present, at least as traces.

CHAPTER 2

🕸

Kultur and *Kulturkampf:* The *Studia Humanitas* and the People without History

When ethnographic performers arrived in Germany, the success of their shows depended in part on their ability to accommodate the anthropological search for "natural peoples." They thus stepped into a controversy about the methods of the human sciences as well as a broader discussion about the role and meaning of *Kultur* in German social and political life. For most of the nineteenth century, historicism had dominated the human sciences in Germany, setting the goals and methods of the study of humankind and offering a cultural and political identity based on the interpretation of textual sources of the European and classical past.[1] For German historians, "culture" involved the European self interpreting what was conceived as its own past, a practice that necessarily excluded all those perceived as "others," especially non-Europeans. Anthropologists proposed an inversion of this humanist historicism, arguing that to understand humanity scholars should look, not at European and classical "cultural peoples" (*Kulturvölker*), but rather at non-Europeans who possessed neither culture nor history and who were therefore "natural peoples" (*Naturvölker*).[2] Anthropology was thus conceived as a natural science of natural peoples, which eschewed what practitioners held to be "subjective" historical narratives in favor of "objective" observations of people uncomplicated by culture and historical development.

This challenge to humanism was part of a larger reconstruction of *Kultur* in Imperial Germany that found its most important political manifestation in the Prussian anti-Catholic laws of the 1870s, dubbed the *Kulturkampf* (struggle for culture) by none other than Rudolf Virchow, the

liberal parliamentarian and head of the German and Berlin Anthropological Societies. The *Kulturkampf* was designed to further political, social,
and scientific progress against what its advocates presented as Catholic
backwardness. Anthropologists similarly sought to displace academic humanism as a privileged form of education and ideology with their own
natural scientific study of humankind. In rejecting humanism, anthropologists did not abandon the social and political project of the human sciences
but rather transformed notions of culture to create both a new science and
a new civic identity for a German polity marked by mass culture, imperialism, and natural science.

Since the late eighteenth century, humanist scholarship in Germany explicitly rejected the historical study of most of humanity. German historicism,
from Herder to Ranke to Droysen, made a point of selecting from the
earth's peoples certain groups exclusively worthy of admiration and, with
the exception of Herder, of study. This rejection of those perceived as other
was not merely an accident of the Eurocentric predilections of German intellectuals but rather an essential feature of humanist historicism. The fundamental structure of humanism was that of self studying self, of an
intersubjectivity between the scholar and the object of study.[3] This was not
merely the basis of a peculiarly German humanism but also a fundamental
assumption of humanist inquiry since the Renaissance. Indeed, the very
idea of a Renaissance, of a rebirth of classical antiquity through its study,
implied a potential identification between scholars and their subjects. The
project of history involved the self explicating the self and therefore required a narrative at least potentially culminating in its own author. This is
made quite explicit in Hegel's philosophy of history, and it was presupposed by subsequent German historiography. Excluding non-Europeans
became a conventional feature of history writing in nineteenth-century
Germany, at least in part as a way to establish a self by excluding an other.
This exclusion of non-Europeans became more and more difficult as the
intensification of imperialist networks made the boundaries between Europe and the rest of the world more permeable, but it was an exclusion to
which historians tenaciously clung.

   The disqualification of non-Europeans from historical inquiry emerged
in the philosophy of Herder, Kant, and Hegel even before Ranke founded
the historiographic tradition that would be an important interlocutor for
anthropology. Johann Gottfried von Herder, often cited as a forerunner of
modern cultural anthropology and cultural relativism, clearly considered
most non-Europeans inferior to Europeans.[4] He did express what he called
an "anthropological wish" to "give humanity a gallery of drawn forms and

shapes of its brethren on the earth" and included the indigenous inhabitants of the Arctic, Asia, Africa, and America in his 1784 *Reflections on the Philosophy of the History of Mankind.*[5] His supposed relativism, however, amounts to little more than attributing his mostly negative evaluations of non-European ethnic groups to the climate they inhabit rather than to inherent spiritual flaws. His recommendation to "pity" (*bedauern*) rather than to "despise" (*verachten*) sub-Saharan Africans is hardly relativist.[6] In the earlier, even more pluralist conception of culture that Herder presented in his 1774 *Another Philosophy of History concerning the Development of Mankind,* he did not consider all peoples of the globe but rather only ancient Hebrews, Egyptians, Greeks, Romans, and modern Europeans, whom he united in a single narrative of cultural progress.[7] In the *Reflections,* Herder tempered this relativism because he dealt with a greater range of societies, including groups that he did not consider equals of those that he discussed in *Another Philosophy of History.* The tension that Isaiah Berlin notes between the cultural pluralism of Herder's *Another Philosophy of History* and his normative concept of *Humanität* in the *Reflections* can be resolved by recognizing the ethnic differentiation in his relativism.[8] Even for Herder, the concept of humanity was essentially normative and depended on excluding others.

Despite his well-known differences with Herder, Kant displayed a similar attitude to cultural difference in the ethnographic section of his otherwise psychological 1800 *Anthropologie in pragmatischer Hinsicht.* He discussed only the *Volkscharakter* of the French, the English, the Spanish, the Italians, and the Germans, he explained, because Russia, Poland, and European Turkey (and presumably all other nations as well) did not have what was necessary to develop a *Volkscharakter.* While Kant did not specify what a nation needed to have a *Volkscharakter,* he did explain that Turkey never had it and never would have it.[9] In his 1784 essay "Idea for a Universal History with a Cosmopolitan Intent," Kant argued that the possibility for writing world history that was more than the "senseless course of human affairs" depended on the nations of the world becoming connected to European history. For the present, such a universal history could be a hope only for a more cosmopolitan future.[10] This tendency to exclude most of the world from historical interpretation prevailed throughout the nineteenth century and into the twentieth.[11] In general, German academics seemed to be willing to apply a pluralist or relativist notion of culture only to themselves and a few other societies.

The emergence of history as a fundamental category of German thought in the nineteenth century only increased the exclusivity of the humanities. Hegel's interest in development led him, in his lectures on the philosophy of history in the 1820s, to declare most societies not worthy of study. Spirit, the development of which Hegel's lectures would trace, "appears in reality as a series of external forms, each one of which announces itself as an actually existing people." Only certain societies, that is, embodied spirit and became relevant to world history. The inhabitants, and even the physical geography, of the Americas and the Pacific Islands were "inferior," and their destruction by Europeans only further demonstrated their irrelevance to considerations of world history. The inhabitants of sub-Saharan Africa, according to Hegel, lack consciousness of any universal, from God, to law, to humanity, as suggested, for example, by what Hegel believed to be the widespread practice of cannibalism. Hegel concluded his discussion of Africa by definitively barring it from world history: "With this we leave Africa, never to mention it again. For it is not an historical part of the world, it exhibits no movement or development. What has happened in Africa, which is to say, in its northern part, belongs to the Asiatic and European world. . . . What is properly understood by Africa is without history and closed within itself, it is still entirely trapped in the natural spirit. It had to be presented here only on the threshold of world history."[12] History, for Hegel, represented a divergence from the natural. African societies had not separated from nature to become historical and thus stood merely at history's "threshold." In his lectures, Hegel presented the history of the world spirit as it developed from its ahistorical beginnings in China, through its middle stages in the Near East, to its highest stages in Europe. Hegel's exclusion of Africans, Americans, and Pacific Islanders was not merely the result of the prejudices of a philosopher who happened also to be ethnocentric. Rather, his discussion of a single course of development in history demanded that he regard only certain peoples as bearers of this idea. If development were merely a standard course repeated in many societies, Hegel's model would not take account of the specific but be merely a kind of grim deductive dogmatism. To identify the rational and the real, and to understand the rational as development, Hegel had necessarily to limit the real to a history that he believed led to his own society.

Although Leopold von Ranke was in many ways methodologically opposed to Hegel, he followed his philosophical predecessor in explicitly excluding non-Europeans from consideration. In a lecture on "the idea of universal history" from the 1830–31 academic year, Ranke explained that world history consists of "spiritual forms . . . full of inner truth, necessity, and energy, in whose succession lies an immeasurable progress, in whose center we ourselves still stand." Those with no connection to the progressive narrative that Ranke wished to create were irrelevant, even as evidence of "prehistoric" humans: "It is impossible to proceed from the peoples of an eternal stagnation to an understanding of the inner movement of world history."[13] Ranke's model of world history clearly relied on a Hegelian notion of history as a single, unified progression, and, indeed, the historian explained: "History is not a challenge to, but a fulfillment of, philosophy."[14] For Ranke, like Hegel, this understanding of history required excluding a large portion of humanity. Ranke often pointed to a lack of written sources when he excluded non-European societies from history. "One must," he wrote, exclude questions about societies from which we possess no written documents and leave their study "to natural science and to religious viewpoints."[15] However, for Ranke, a lack of written documents was not all that excluded societies from history: "We can give only a small amount of attention to those peoples who even today remain in a kind of natural condition and who appear to have conserved in themselves the condition of the primitive world [*Urwelt*]. India and China appear quite old and have a far-reaching chronology, in which even the most clever chronologists get lost. Their antiquity is a fable [*fabelhaft*]. They belong more to natural history."[16] Ranke's dismissal of India and China stood for an exclusion of all non-European societies, as the subjects covered by his *World History* make clear. Even though India and China both, Ranke must have known, possessed well-documented, ancient histories, they, like other non-European societies, still belonged to natural history rather than to history. Societies became historical only once they had removed themselves from the realm of nature.[17] Chronology alone did not, Ranke implied, make a nation historical. To be a subject of historical inquiry, a society had to have writing, appear to be progressing, and possess some fundamental connection to the narrative of European history.

The Göttingen historian Georg Gottfried Gervinus followed Ranke in excluding non-Europeans on both philosophical and methodological grounds. In the late 1830s, Gervinus attacked his colleague A. H. L. Heeren for including Carthage, Ethiopia, and Nubia in his study of the western trade system in ancient times.[18] Gervinus was further outraged that Heeren relativized the moral faults of the inhabitants of the Near East and Africa, comparing them to the populations of Sparta and Rome, rather than simply dismissing them as inherently flawed. Gervinus claimed that the peoples of the "Orient"—that is, North Africa and the Near East— should be explained by their natural, psychological, and physiological characteristics, rather, presumably, than by their histories. For Gervinus, these people belonged in the realm of natural science rather than history.[19] Only Europeans were historical, and only Europeans have historical documents: this double emphasis on writing and history was endemic to German thinking about humanity.

Excluding non-Europeans became a canonical gesture in German history writing. Johann Gustav Droysen, whose *Historik* constituted perhaps the most programmatic statement of German historiography in the second half of the nineteenth century, was typically discriminating in his choice of objects for historical inquiry. In his lectures on historical methods, he argued that most societies are not only of no interest to historians but also irrelevant to knowledge of the nature of humanity: "Knowledge of all peoples and their conditions is of ethnographic interest, and if the human race were simply like other creatures, then that would be enough. But the human race is in its nature progress, it is history. History is the concept of the human race, and history deals with restless upward motion, with the leading zenith." Droysen rejected the historical value of "complete collections of ethnographic peculiarities," which, he held, simply reveal "not-culture" (*nichtkultur*). He dismissed the anthropologist Adolf Bastian as "schematic, doctrinaire, unhistorical." Anthropology, for Droysen, was fundamentally opposed to history because anthropology studied not individuals and change but groups and stasis. Societies "change insofar as they have history and have history insofar as they change."[20]

The historian Ottakar Lorenz went so far as to deem politically subversive the desire to "monistically grasp humanity in all its expressions." Lorenz warned that such an approach, which he called "natural scientific," might weaken the "feeling for the state."[21] Elsewhere, in a book on historical methodology, Lorenz traced the progress of the discipline from attempts by historians such as Heeren to write universal history to Ranke's more narrow definition of world history. Lorenz assured his readers that even the most universalistic historians in fact rarely allowed their narratives to wander east of the Indus River (that is, the extent of Alexander's conquests). For Lorenz, the Göttingen historian and 1848 revolutionary Friedrich Christoph Dahlmann had rightly focused history on European politics. Ranke's great achievement was to finally set to rest the confusion about the goals of history and show that history emerged "not from Schlosser's idea of universal history, not from the philosophical presuppositions of certain intentions . . . but rather from the real connection [*Zusammenhang*] of certain nations, which have developed historically in certain parts of the earth."[22]

Eduard Meyer, the great historian of Near Eastern and classical antiquity, included a section called "Elements of Anthropology" at the beginning of his great *History of Antiquity,* a section he expanded to over 250 pages in the 1907 edition. Meyer's anthropology, however, was a general theory of the development of humankind from the family to the state, rather than the study of actual, non-European societies. Meyer thus hearkened back to an earlier tradition of philosophical anthropology, a general science that he contrasted with history as a study of the unique and specific. Very few societies, he argued, reach the point where they have a high culture and an important historical role.[23] Most societies are "history-less" (*geschichtslos*), not only because they themselves do not record history, but also because even when they do undergo change it is merely a typical, rather than a unique, development.[24] For Meyer, only certain societies deserved to be "released" (*enthoben*) from the "realm of ethnology" to claim for their "fate" "the name of history." Meyer did not exclude Africa from history merely because of a lack of sources, for he denied the applicability of history even to those "Negro tribes" about which Europeans possessed "exact knowledge."[25] For Meyer, the historicity of a society had less to do with a lack of writing than with what he perceived to be a lack of individuality.

This distinction between societies without history or culture and societies with history and culture was also drawn by cultural scientists, who themselves attacked the narrow focus of mainstream historians.[26] Both Karl Lamprecht and Wilhelm Wundt, for example, distinguished their own studies of culture from the study of people supposedly without culture. Thus, Karl Lamprecht regarded his own cultural history as fundamentally different from anthropology because anthropology dealt with the "primitive factors" of humanity as exhibited by people without history, while cultural history dealt with the "development of regular, national life" in its highest cultural institutions, such as art, law, and morality. Lamprecht dismissed artifact-based studies such as anthropology as the "archaeology of bric-a-brac."[27] Wilhelm Wundt regarded the aspects of anthropology that focused on the psychological features of societies, especially on "language, myth, and morality [*Sitte*]," as a source of raw material for his own *Völkerpsychologie*. However, as Wundt himself noted, these psychological features formed only part of the study of anthropology. Anthropologists themselves, he explained, concentrated on more tangible aspects of the people they studied, especially on artifacts, daily lives, and bodies.[28] Like Lamprecht, Wundt saw anthropology as a source of raw material for studies of culture, not as a cultural science in its own right.

Although many of the leading anthropologists were university faculty members, only a small number were employed as anthropologists or taught anthropology. Courses called "Anthropologie" or "Anthropologie und Psychologie" were common offerings at the University of Berlin throughout the nineteenth century, but they consisted of a speculative inquiry into human nature that had little to do with the interests of the German Anthropological Society.[29] Most academics who studied natural peoples were professors of medicine or the natural sciences who pursued anthropology only in their leisure hours. Even the anthropologists who eventually did get positions on the philosophy faculty were so outnumbered that they could do little to promote their subject. The University of Berlin did not offer a doctorate in physical anthropology until 1915 and in ethnology until 1922, although students could study anthropology as part of geography.[30] Like the philosophy faculty, the Prussian Academy of Sciences had little sympathy for, or interest in, anthropology and found that the discipline lacked "a secure basis and a certain goal."[31] The Seminar for Oriental Languages, a colonial training academy that opened in Berlin in 1887, focused on language instruction and thus had only a marginal effect on the institutional prestige of anthropologists.[32]

Franz Boas's brief employment in Germany illustrates the dismissive attitude of traditional academicians toward anthropology. In 1886, at the age of twenty-eight, Boas applied to teach physical geography as a private docent at the University of Berlin. He presented a number of published articles in support of his application, mostly about the Inuit he had encountered during his travels on Baffin Island in 1884 and 1885. While the faculty committee thought Boas a promising lecturer, its members were perplexed about the significance of his investigations. The first evaluator, the meteorologist Wilhelm von Bezold, wrote: "This research deals with a region far removed from the centers of human culture and can by its very nature arouse little general interest." The geographer Heinrich Kiepert had similar difficulties comprehending the significance of studies of "a small region far removed from areas of general interest." Boas's writings, declared Kiepert, consisted of "observations hardly differing from those that we already possess about the same region made by practical though uneducated sailors." The first evaluator, Bezold, allowed that Boas's research on "that inhospitable region" might help scientists at meteorological and magnetic stations in the Arctic avoid problems with the indigenous population. Because Boas's trial lectures reflected his competence in physical geography, the university hired him for the 1886–87 academic year, despite the lack of interest in his anthropological research.[33] The following year, Boas left Germany for the United States, where he became one of that country's great anthropologists. Boas's habilitation evaluators neither welcomed his studies of the Inuit as important monographs on a previously neglected subject nor reacted against the challenge that they posed to the ethnocentrism of the university. These academics simply could not comprehend the scholarly interest of Boas's anthropological work.

Adolf Bastian (1826–1905) was one of a small number of professional anthropologists who could negotiate a place for themselves in the German academy. Like most anthropologists of the period, Bastian had been trained as a physician. He spent most of the 1850s traveling around the world as a ship's doctor and, shortly after his return, published his three-volume *The Human in History (Der Mensch in der Geschichte)*.[34] This work seemed legitimate to the philosophy faculty in a way that Boas's would not because Bastian cast it in the traditional form of philosophical *Anthropologie und Psychologie*. In 1866, the University of Berlin awarded him an honorary doctor of philosophy for his "research on humans and human life in its totality" so that he might offer courses on "general ethnology and anthropology," comparative mythology, and the history of colonialism.[35] Apparently, his courses were poorly attended and often had to be canceled for a lack of students.[36] Still, Bastian was one of the most important figures in institutionalizing anthropology. In addition to holding the first academic post in the subject, he also directed the ethnographic collection in the royal museums from 1869 and the independent Royal Museum of Ethnology (Königliches Museum für Völkerkunde) when it opened in 1886. He was a leading member of the Berlin Geographic Society (Gesellschaft für Erdkunde) and one of the founding members, in 1869, of the Berlin Society for Anthropology, Ethnology, and Prehistory.

In 1889, Bastian was joined at the university by the Austrian anthropologist Felix von Luschan (1854–1924). Luschan, who had studied anthropology in Paris and had lectured on anthropology at the University of Vienna, had come to work in the Berlin museum of ethnology three years earlier to direct the sections for Africa and Oceania. As head curator of the anthropology of areas that had recently become German colonies, Luschan took an active role in using colonialism to promote anthropology and developed close relations with the colonial civil service and with the military. Luschan taught physical anthropology, anthropological methods, and the anthropology of Germany's colonies. In 1905, he began teaching "social anthropology," which in Germany meant anthropology applied to eugenic questions.

In 1900, Bastian and Luschan acquired two new colleagues, Paul Ehrenreich (1855–1914) and Karl von den Steinen (1855–1929). Steinen had been one of the editors of the geographic monthly *Das Ausland* and had lectured briefly at the university in 1889. Both Ehrenreich and Steinen were specialists in Latin America and had made names for themselves exploring Brazil. Steinen taught courses on the anthropology of South America and Polynesia, while Ehrenreich concentrated his teaching on North America. Although Eduard Seler (1849–1922), a fifth colleague at the university since 1894, was also employed as curator of ancient American artifacts in the museum of ethnology, he focused on the cultural peoples of ancient America and was therefore regarded at the university as a philologist rather than an anthropologist.[37] He taught courses on ancient Mexican and Mayan history, languages, and archaeology, which were listed with philology courses.

Anthropology emerged in an institutional context only peripherally related to the university, in large part because it fit poorly in the traditions of humanism on which the university had been founded. Anthropologists probably would have been delighted to accept academic humanists into their ranks, but, for the most part, the challenge of anthropology dissuaded those committed to the traditional disciplines. As Bastian wrote to Virchow just after the founding of the German Anthropological Society, "In the philosophical-historical realm we will not be able to count on much sympathy for the time being, and the reasons for this are clear."[38] In the growing public sphere of the later nineteenth century, however, the reticence of academic humanists to accept anthropology was by no means fatal for the discipline. More significant than the few anthropologists who were able to make careers on the periphery of the academic human sciences were the hundreds of middle-class amateurs who flocked to the meetings of the German Anthropological Society and its local branches. This new social and institutional configuration allowed—indeed required—anthropologists to ground their new human science as a challenge to traditional humanism.

Adolf Bastian was the greatest spokesman of the anthropological critique of humanism. Bastian criticized historians for studying only the "highest points" of history, concerning themselves with "quality" and missing the "quantity" of world history, the whole range of less-edifying phenomena.[39] "The human qua human," Bastian explained, "does not live only in Europe and part of Asia." Anthropology would expand world history to include not just each individual cultural people as an "unconnected fragment, ripped from its context," but rather the "unified, living whole," the "*humanitas.*"[40] The "stately building in which the honored discipline of history was enthroned" admitted few "newcomers among the carefully ordered, stately row of historical peoples." Even if it could be shown that the range of peoples should be expanded to include other Eurasian societies relevant to Europe's development, the indigenous populations of the Americas, Africa, and the Pacific would still not be allowed into the "temple of history." To include these societies would require a revision of the conception of world history as the text-based study of elite societies. Anthropology offered such a revision by placing the study of humans on an inclusive, inductive basis, considering the simplest societies, "the lowest organisms of human society," and thereby deriving the laws that determined even the "cultural creations of higher levels."[41] Bastian thus proposed that anthropology rectify the narrow range of historical enquiry to create a discipline that would truly fulfill the goal of the humanities. As Ranke had argued that history was "a fulfillment of . . . philosophy," Bastian argued that anthropology was a fulfillment of history.

For Bastian, however, anthropology did not merely realize the goal of history as a *studia humanitas* but also, as a natural scientific inquiry, realized this goal in a superior way. Bastian explained that history had usurped its current position as "queen of the sciences" through illegitimately "subjective" methods: "Since history must constantly orbit in narrow . . . circles around the center of its own national consciousness [*Volksbewusstseins*]—in that it thereby raises itself to a queen of the sciences because it comprehends national life in its realizations—it can never escape subjectivity, neither in its subject matter nor in relation to the historian himself." History was entrapped in subjectivity, both because it dealt with the national self and because it had necessarily to describe the subjective experiences of the period that it portrayed. Because ethnology, however, was unrelated to the national self, and because it disregarded motivations, it was not merely a supplement to history but a superior alternative to history: "Ethnology maintains a standpoint of pure objective observation, sharply distinguished from history, which cannot rid itself of a subjective coloration because, even when kept free from calculating or doctrinaire positions, it is nevertheless based on 'research into motives.'"[42] Anthropology did not, for Bastian, merely provide additional information to make a more complete world history, but offered a superior route to understanding *humanitas*.

Anthropologists employed a conventional opposition between words and things to suggest that humanists studied not reality but only the language used to describe reality.[43] Robert Hartmann, writing in 1869, opposed his own anthropological method to the "historical method," which, he complained, relied on accounts that societies wrote about themselves. The sources of history, he suggested, contained self-congratulatory exaggerations or even lies. Hartmann maintained that historians and linguists should abandon their "blind preference" for textual exegesis and consider instead "the physical properties of people." By *physical properties* Hartmann understood not just biological characteristics but also artifacts and observable customs. For Hartmann, historical-philological textual interpretation was "blind": only "physical" things, things that can be seen, counted as certain knowledge.[44] Bastian similarly cautioned against using any single factor to characterize ethnic groups, although he proclaimed that, if one had to focus on a single factor to classify humans, "much better the round skull of craniology than some philological tailbone."[45] Virchow referred to collections of anthropological artifacts as "a factual, objective archive, on which every researcher can independently draw," and contrasted these collections to the "printed" archives "that historians can provide."[46] In contrast to texts, objects, for Virchow, were "objective." Objects existed independently of historians, on whom scholars using textual sources had to rely. In the collection of objects, Virchow suggested, the researcher encountered reality directly, while in the "printed," textual archive, the researcher depended on the mediation of the historian. Anthropologists' faith in objects and mistrust of narrative and language determined nearly all the practices of anthropology, which centered almost exclusively on collecting, measuring, depicting, describing, and displaying objects.

So fundamentally did German anthropologists reject narrative that they eschewed even the evolutionist schemas that allowed their British colleagues to connect prehistorical Europeans with contemporary non-European "primitives." British evolutionists, such as E. B. Tylor and John Lubbock, held that, since contemporary primitives and ancient Europeans were essentially identical, reports of various contemporary societies believed to be at different stages of progress could be used to reconstruct the general development of humankind.[47] German anthropologists also studied Europeans prior to Roman contact, who they believed were natural peoples, much like contemporary colonized societies. This pursuit they referred to as *Urgeschichte*. Several German anthropologists compared both ancient European and contemporary non-European natural peoples to children, who formed a mute part of the history of cultural peoples. Since these "children" did not produce written documents, they were inaccessible to historians and could be studied only by natural scientists, who considered their tools, bodies, and behavior.[48] However, German anthropologists refused to specify an evolutionist narrative that might connect ancient and modern natural peoples.[49]

German discussions of British evolutionists applauded their well-organized presentation of anthropological facts but generally remained silent about their theories of human development. In his preface to the German translation of Lubbock's *Prehistoric Times,* for example, Virchow paid little attention to the author's evolutionist argument and instead praised the book for its careful presentation of information gleaned from travel accounts and anthropological collections.[50] In a review of Tylor's *Primitive Culture,* Adolf Bastian praised the author's overview of ethnographic information but did not so much as mention his evolutionist theory.[51] Another reviewer of Tylor's work declared that he agreed with the author's "polemic" but treated only what he called its "actual object," the detailed descriptions of various societies.[52]

While the German term *Naturvölker* referred to roughly the same societies as the English term *primitives,* the two terms had fundamentally different meanings.[53] Whereas primitives were the earliest actors in a
narrative that also included Europeans, *Naturvölker* were, by definition,
excluded from the narrative of progress central to German self-understandings. Indeed, German anthropologists appeared reluctant to identify
their own ancient forebears with contemporary non-European societies,
despite their view that both groups were essentially identical natural peoples (cf. figs. 2.1 and 2.2). In Germany, both historians and anthropologists

FIGURE 2.1
Robert Hartmann, daily life in a prehistoric Swiss lake dwelling. In 1853–54, as the result
of a drought, the level of Lake Zurich dropped to reveal the tips of ancient pilings jutting
above the lake's surface. It was assumed that these were the foundation of elevated houses
in which the prehistoric inhabitants of Europe had dwelt. Houses on pilings (*Pfahlbauten*)
were also known to exist in New Guinea and thus suggested a connection between Europe's ancient inhabitants and the contemporary, non-European "natural peoples." In this
drawing, however, these prehistoric European natural peoples appear extraordinarily civilized. Their lake dwelling is a veritable International Sanatorium Berghof, laid out in
a careful grid amid tranquil natural beauty. Although the inhabitants ostensibly lack culture, history, and writing, they clearly display conversation, family, and economy. They
may be natural peoples, but the artist foreshadows their destiny as a modern *Kulturvolk*.
Source: Robert Hartmann, "Ueber Pfahlbauten, namentlich in der Schweiz, sowie, über
noch einige andere, die Alterthumskunde Europa's betreffende Gegenstände," *ZfE* 2
(1870): 1–30.

FIGURE 2.2

Robert Hartmann, Sudanese photomontage. The silent chaos of this group gives a much clearer impression of a people without history, writing, or culture than does the drawing of the Swiss lake-dwelling community (see fig. 2.1). As Hartmann explained, he distorted the perspective to make every individual figure clearly visible. Thus, except for the children making bread in the center, the individual figures have no relation to each other, and, indeed, the two in the right foreground seem strangely unaware of their imminent collision. The ancient Nubian structure in the background associates these individuals with the autochthonous "Nubians" anthropologists hoped to separate out from the modern, Arabic-speaking, Muslim and Christian Sudan. In his illustration of the "natural peoples" of ancient Switzerland, Hartmann had rendered people supposedly without history and culture as modern Europeans; in this representation, he transformed modern Sudanese society into an aggregate of natural individuals, without history or culture.
Source: ZfE 5 (1873).

viewed nature—and therefore natural peoples—as fundamentally separate from history, narrative, evolution, and even time. Bastian asked about natural peoples: "What would be old here? What young? In the eternally old or eternally young of nature?"[54] Conceptually connected to cultural peoples but simultaneously part of nature, natural peoples provided what German anthropologists hoped would be a position outside the historicity in which traditional humanists had trapped themselves. While temporality divided nature and culture, the idea of natural peoples allowed anthropologists, like no other German human scientists, to scuttle back and forth across this divide, bringing knowledge about nature to bear on all humans. The gaps in German humanism between self and other, Europe and the rest of the world, and history and nature created a space in which anthropology could create a counterhumanism.

Two brave humanists, Heymann Steinthal (1823–1899) and Moritz Lazarus (1824–1903), did in fact join the Berlin Anthropological Society and became involved in a controversy that further emphasized the rejection of academic humanism in German anthropology. Steinthal and Lazarus were both professors on the philosophy faculty at the University of Berlin and in 1860 founded the *Zeitschrift für Völkerpsychologie und Sprachwissenschaft*.[55] They inaugurated the discipline of *Völkerpsychologie* (the "psychology of peoples," or "ethnic psychology") to correct what they regarded as the narrow focus of anthropology, which prevented it from explaining the "*Volksgeist* with all its psychic facts."[56] *Völkerpsychologie* privileged general questions, for example, about art, religion, and morality, rather than the more microscopic studies favored by anthropologists.[57] Steinthal was likely attracted to the Berlin Anthropological Society because he shared its interest in expanding the purview of the humanities. In his work on the Mande languages of Africa, Steinthal urged philologists to also consider languages as dissimilar to their own "more highly organized Indo-European languages" as "an insect to a mammal." Despite these more cosmopolitan interests, however, Steinthal remained true to the basic worldview of academic humanism and rejected the anthropological concept of natural peoples: "It seems to me a remnant of Rousseau's romanticism to call these savages [*Wilden*] 'natural peoples' [*Naturvölker*]. Only the educated [*gebildete*] human is the natural human, and human savagery is unnatural."[58] Steinthal shared the empirical interests of German anthropology but remained philosophically committed to humanist conceptions of culture and education. His marginalization from mainstream anthropology would represent a decisive shedding of the last vestiges of humanism within the discipline.

In an 1872 lecture to the Berlin Anthropological Society, Steinthal attacked the antilinguistic tone of most German anthropologists. He agreed with Bastian and Hartmann that language alone should not be used to characterize ethnic groups and endorsed their recommendation that both customs and physical characteristics also be taken into account. However, Steinthal then redefined the nature of language so that linguistics would provide the key to all aspects of humanity, including customs and physical characteristics. First, Steinthal suggested, language is not merely a single aspect of human mental activity but also a "means of representation" (*Darstellungsmittel*), inseparable from what it represents. Thus, for Steinthal, to study a language required knowledge of "the spiritual content of the national consciousness [*Volksbewusstsein*], its views, how it feels and judges." Furthermore, this "spiritual content" was determined by the "surrounding nature and the bodily condition of the people." Steinthal did not allow the existence of these nonverbal determinants to undermine his belief that the study of humans should focus on language. Instead, he presented the social and bodily context of language as a reason to privilege linguistics as an inquiry into the nucleus of humanity in all its aspects: "In it [language] the whole person, body and soul, is reflected. It belongs to both and emerges from both, specifically from their cooperation and their influence on each other."[59] Although Steinthal opposed the narrow interests of philologists in language, he preserved the privileged position of language in the study of humanity. Rather than using anthropological critiques of humanism to marginalize the study of language, Steinthal employed anthropology to increase the domain of humanist linguistics.

Both Bastian and Hartmann responded to Steinthal's lecture by reiterating their view that language was an unacceptably subjective and mutable source of knowledge. Since a social group could learn new languages, language represented, in Bastian's words, "only an uncertain measurement" for characterizing ethnic groups. "Philosophical" characterizations of peoples, such as those based solely on language, Bastian threatened, "will have difficulty passing the test of induction after sufficient material has been collected."[60] Hartmann also defended a natural scientific, anti-interpretive understanding of anthropology against Steinthal's philology. Because people could learn new languages, he cautioned, their language illustrates not their true nature but only their subjective responses to historical circumstances. In contrast to language, "material" would provide a source of knowledge more secure than, because independent from, these historical and subjective factors.[61]

Two years later, Steinthal and Lazarus were again put on the defensive when, during a debate on aphasia and the localization of brain functions, the Berlin Anthropological Society took an even more antilinguistic and antihumanist turn. Eduard Hitzig reported to the society in 1874 on the famous experiments that he and Gustav Fritsch had conducted in 1870 on the localization of brain function.[62] Hitzig and Fritsch had shown that electricity applied to various parts of a dog's brain could trigger specific motions in its limbs. Hitzig suggested that this experiment, as well as animal experiments conducted by other researchers, called into question previous

notions about the relation of body and mind and presented the possibility
of "a new kind of phrenology." Indeed, the phenomenon of aphasia in humans, in which specific brain injuries damaged speech in specific ways,
suggested that even language, the medium of the human spirit, the *Geist,*
had a physiological basis. While earlier understandings of phrenology,
Hitzig admitted, had erred in denying free will and giving too much importance to correlations between skull shape and mental functions, these
new experiments did suggest that certain functions, such as bodily motion
and even speech, were controlled not exclusively by the mind but also by
the body.

Steinthal responded to Hitzig's lecture as an attack on the notion of human "freedom" on which his own linguistic *Völkerpsychologie* depended.
Steinthal insisted that Hitzig had merely demonstrated that physical motions could be instigated through electrical stimuli and had shown nothing
about language or the psyche. Virchow interjected that, while Hitzig's report did not do away with psychology altogether, "such studies did nonetheless win a definite piece of the psychic life for physiology."[63] The debate
around Hitzig's experiments continued in the next month's meeting, and,
while the majority of the discussants exercised more caution than Hitzig
did in reducing human language to physiology, they were more sympathetic to such scientific materialism than to Steinthal's humanistic defense
of the freedom of the human mind as expressed in language.[64] Steinthal
and Lazarus remained members of the Berlin Anthropological Society after these discussions, but they became much less active, focusing instead on
their own *Zeitschrift für Völkerpsychologie und Sprachwissenschaft.* While
German anthropologists were rarely radical materialists, they proved
themselves adamantly opposed to the humanist complex of *Geist,* language, and free will as the primary focus of the study of humanity.[65]

The focus on objects as an alternative to narrative made writing problematic for anthropologists. The most important genre of anthropological
writing at this time was the questionnaire, an essential tool for anthropologists of all nations who wanted reliable information from untrained amateur travelers.[66] As Virchow explained, a well-constructed questionnaire
might allow otherwise untrustworthy observers—"an ordinary ship's captain" and, indeed, "every simple, sober observer"—not only to collect
objects, but also "to secure a piece of the mental and spiritual life" of the
people they encountered.[67] Anthropologists hoped that these questionnaires would make words as reliable as they believed things to be.

By the turn of the century, Luschan had produced a questionnaire that
perfected the antinarrative techniques of the genre, which he distributed to

Germans living or traveling in Africa and the Pacific. The questionnaire was bound, and alternate pages were left blank so that the observer could take notes directly in the book. Luschan promised that, by filling out the book, a person could become an anthropological author: "Even an approximately complete response to all the demands given here would produce a particularly valuable monograph on a specific tribe, which, provided with the necessary illustrations, could be printed immediately, and give its author lasting honor."[68] Luschan sought to transform anthropological authorship from subjective narration to obedient observation. Through the questionnaire, he tried to prevent ethnographic writing from slipping into the narrative that discredited witnesses and threatened anthropological understandings of static nature. By continually stopping and starting with each new question, by having to answer specific questions briefly rather than spinning a yarn to connect the details, the author was prevented from narrating. Writing ethnography became more like filling out a form than like writing history. Indeed, the role of the professional anthropologist was, in this case, not to write about humanity, but rather to write the questions that others would answer about humanity.

The kinds of information that Luschan requested similarly undermined attempts at narration. For the most part, the questions demanded very specific, observable information about the people under consideration: Where do they live? What is their population? What do they eat? What tools do they use? What weapons do they use? The questions continually exhort the writer to collect physical objects to corroborate the answers, even requesting that information about circumcision practices be supplemented with a severed penis—if it could be taken "without giving offense." Questions about religion posed particular problems, for it would be nearly impossible to present religious beliefs without resorting to interpretation and narrative. Luschan particularly emphasized the need to collect religious objects and cautioned that "ambiguous words such as *fetish, idol,* etc. are best avoided completely."[69] By abandoning such "ambiguous words," Luschan made impossible any kind of interpretation of religion or any kind of meaningful contextualization of the phenomena under observation. Even in the case of religion, Luschan broke down narrative into nonnarrative bits, connected only as individual items in a questionnaire. The questionnaire reduced ethnographic writing to a mere accompaniment to anthropological collecting and was itself modeled on the collection of objects.[70]

Bastian conducted even more radical antinarrative experiments in his own writing, which was, as most reviewers remarked, surely as unreadable as anything ever published in the German language. Even his colleague and coeditor of the *Zeitschrift für Ethnologie,* Robert Hartmann, privately referred to him as "unspeakably confused."[71] Bastian, however, understood his writing as an attempt to revolutionize the language of anthropology.[72] As he wrote to a publisher, "A popular presentation is not intended and cannot therefore be delivered."[73] Seeking to create an alternative to the selective, interpretive, subjective narratives that he associated with humanism, he packed as much as he could into every sentence, relying on the German language's liberal construal of proper sentence length and free employment of relative clauses as well as a use of parentheses not customary in German (perhaps he learned it from English). For example, in an article on "the priestly function among the natural tribes," Bastian, typically, did not try to make any general argument about priests in various societies but rather structured his analysis, with predictable results, around the thesis that anthropological questions could be answered only by considering "the mass of details."[74] The following sentence exemplifies his experimental writing and the challenges that it presented to his readers: "In the sign language (of the American Indians) the mime speaks (in 'mimetic dance') as a translator (in the time of Nero), and as the King of Dahomey receives his guests dancing, the art of dancing was so highly regarded in Thessalonia that the leading men in the state and the champions in battle were even called head dancers (see Lucian) = Meoh in Indonesia."[75] In a single sentence, Bastian juxtaposes languages, continents, and historical epochs. He obscures and subverts the basic subject-verb structure that makes ordinary sentences essentially narrative and seeks instead a new language commensurate with anthropological counterhumanism. His writing was a modernist experiment in the nonnarrative modes of perception sought by anthropologists.

Bastian's texts struck contemporary German speakers as at odds with ordinary uses of their language, and they were not enthusiastic about its literary merits. Karl von den Steinen, a younger colleague of Bastian's at the Royal Museum of Ethnology, characterized Bastian's style in a particularly frank way: "The countless parentheses made for a labyrinthine construction rather than for clear [*übersichtlich*] divisions. The reader was beset by names, key words, jargon, sentences of such a kind that he was overcome by vertigo. On the one hand, the Greek-Roman, medieval, Egyptian, Indian, Chinese, Mexican philosophies of religion as well as the mythology of all the natural peoples, whether Negro or Eskimo, American Indian or Polynesian or Siberian; on the other hand citations, oblique references to the entire historical, sociological, natural scientific world literature. This flood of thoughts waltzed through hundreds of pages, branching out without order."[76] The anthropologist Carl Vogt was even more blunt: "Surely one cannot expect any rational person to swallow these endless so-called ethnological tapeworms of Don Bombastian. . . . They grow gracelessly into infinity [and have no] guts and no sexual organs!"[77] Although no one expressed the thought as colorfully or with such vitriol as Vogt, Bastian's readers seemed to have agreed that his writings could not be comprehended as a narrative, with beginning, middle, and end. As one contemporary German described Bastian's works, they were "not written in a flowing style and are to be comprehended only as a presentation of collections of material for the study of humankind."[78] Other reviews also indicate that readers used Bastian's books as reference works. Instead of reading the books as narratives with beginnings, middles, and ends, the reader would use the index to find information on a specific topic in the text.[79] Bastian had successfully created a language that allowed him to avoid the interpretive pitfalls of narrative.

One of the key issues in the division between Steinthal and Lazarus's *Völkerpsychologie* and anthropology had been the centrality of language to the study of humankind. Because they did not reject language and narrative, practitioners of *Völkerpsychologie* could present more readable texts than anthropologists could. In 1887, one newspaper, calling Bastian a "miserable writer," contrasted anthropological writing with *Völkerpsychologie:* "Bastian's *Zeitschrift für Ethnologie* is too hard and coy to find love outside the most narrow circles of specialized colleagues. In contrast, the *Zeitschrift für Völkerpsychologie und Sprachwissenschaft,* edited by Steinthal and Lazarus, presents itself as a scientific journal of the most noble style, which combines complete thoroughness with a pleasing form, and makes entering ethnology a joyful pleasure for the layperson."[80] The rejection of language as a source of truth prevented anthropologists from expounding their knowledge in a way that was comprehensible and interesting to nonspecialists. Anthropologists may have escaped the problems of narrative, but they did so at the expense of their ability to communicate with a broad audience. This was especially ironic because anthropologists thought that their discipline was less elitist than the academic humanities. They could not present meaningful accounts of humanity to readers, only chaotic, endless, dry collections of material. In a sense, anthropologists became a natural people, without narrative or writing.

The anthropological critique of humanism not only attacked the dominant academic disciplines of the nineteenth century but also sought to transform the vocabulary of ideology and education in Imperial Germany. Anthropology was a central part of a larger move to redefine *culture* during the *Kaiserreich* by giving the term progressive, modernizing connotations

associated with natural science, quite different from what is often understood as the German idea of *Kultur*.[81] The most important political expression of this redefinition of culture was what Virchow led his fellow liberals
in calling the *Kulturkampf* (struggle for culture), an anti-Catholic campaign of the 1870s. After 1871, Bismarck passed, with the support of both
Progressives and National Liberals, a series of Prussian laws designed to
curb what was perceived as the power of Catholicism over politics, society,
and education. *Kultur* signified the political, economic, and intellectual
progress that German liberals such as Virchow wanted to bring to their
"late nation" after 1870, and fighting Catholicism seemed like a good way
to do it.[82] In the Prussian House of Deputies, Virchow used a highly normative notion of *Kultur* to defend the anti-Catholic laws of the early 1870s:
"The modern [Catholic] orders, since the time they became subservient to
the Jesuit spirit, are absolutely incompatible with the *Kultur* whose bearers
we believe ourselves to be."[83] *Kultur* constituted a polemical concept favoring what its proponents understood to be progress, not a relativist understanding of human difference. The term appeared again in this context in
the so-called culture exam in history, philosophy, and German literature
that an 1873 Prussian law required all clergy to pass.[84] Virchow denounced
Catholics as opponents of Germany and the Hohenzollern monarchy and
lauded Bismarck, Wilhelm I, and the Prussian state as progressive and liberal, partly because of their support of the anti-Catholic measures. "The
national thought," Virchow proclaimed, "is a liberal thought."[85] The *Kulturkampf* reconciled liberals such as Virchow to the Bismarck state, not because they abandoned their principles, but rather because the state realized
a progressive notion of culture that they themselves helped create and that
anthropology both depended on and fostered.

The notion of culture realized in the *Kulturkampf* implied not the humanist project of *Bildung* but rather a modernizing project emphasizing
natural science and progress. In the Prussian parliament, Virchow chided
members of the Catholic Center Party about the thirteenth-century ban by
Parisian clergy against the natural scientific writings of Aristotle: "Thence
came that system, which later poisoned the political development of all Roman peoples and in part that of the Teutonic peoples too. There is where
the inquisition begins, there begins censorship. There begins scholastic
philosophy with its opposition to natural science, with its formalism and its
oppression of every free direction of the spirit. There, gentlemen, begins
the opposition of papism and the modern world."[86] Virchow employs here
a stock image of a dangerously reactionary medieval Catholicism to promote in the newly founded German Empire what he identifies as "the
modern world." *Kultur,* for Virchow, represented all that he imagined that

Catholicism opposed: the strength of the nation, freedom of thought, and the progress of natural science.

The study of culture in the traditional humanities had bound scholars and their community to the past, which was, anthropologists held, inconsistent with the modern culture that they desired. The Greeks, Virchow pointed out in an 1868 speech to the Prussian parliament, did not make the ancient Egyptian language the basis of their education, nor should modern Germany make "the old classical languages" the basis of its education.[87] Anthropology proposed a reinterpretation of the relation of time to the human sciences.[88] Humanistic scholarship has traditionally been understood as a revival of the past in the present, an understanding that presupposes a model of time that connects past and present as a continuum.[89] This model of the humanities was particularly important in nineteenth-century Germany, where schoolchildren, for example, spent more time learning classical Greek and Latin than studying any other single subject. This classical learning formed the basis for the culture of the German educated middle classes, the *Bildungsbürgertum,* who defined themselves more by their humanist education than by their wealth or a particular relation to the means of production.[90] Anthropology represented part of a larger challenge to this humanistic understanding of modernity as a culmination of the past and presented modernity instead as a break with the past. History as it was understood by anthropologists and historians alike was not merely a past but a past related to the historian: historical time connected self and other. This was why, for Bastian, history would always be "subjective." Anthropology was a natural science because of a radical disjunction between anthropologists and the societies they studied. Anthropologists were part of time; the people they studied were not. Claiming that the natural people were out of time (and not merely from an earlier time) meant a fundamental reconceptualization of the human sciences and thus their relation to the present.

This modernist notion of culture was realized in anthropology not by studying those with culture—the *Kulturvölker*—but rather by studying the *Naturvölker,* who had no culture at all. Perhaps paradoxically, anthropologists suggested that, the more Germans learned about *Naturvölker,* the more they studied those without *Kultur,* the more cultured Germany would became. In this, they gave an optimistic, positivist twist to Rousseau's worries that "since all the progress of the human species continually moves it away from its primitive state . . . it is by dint of studying man that we have rendered ourselves incapable of knowing him."[91] Anthropologists would have agreed that the more they studied humans they deemed "natural," the less like natural humans they became. However, this meant only that they became more cultured through natural scientific progress.[92] When anthropologists studied those they believed to lack culture, they felt themselves culturally elevated. German anthropologists sang of this elevation at a typically festive annual congress, recalling their prehistoric ancestors and

How they . . . gnashed prognathic jaws	Wie sie endlich mit prognathen
With roasted mammoth in their maws.—	Kiefern aßen Mammuthbraten—
Ach, then one feels all the more,	Ach dann fühlt man sich nachher
A cultured person to the core. . . .	Als Culturmensch um so mehr. . . .[93]

By using natural scientific methods to study people without culture, anthropology would create culture. Historians such as Droysen might write about the "leading zenith"; anthropologists, by studying those without culture, became this zenith. Anthropology, not humanism, brought culture in this new sense.

Anthropology attacked humanism both as scholarly pursuit and as political education for citizens. Bastian often denounced the "'dogmatism of classicism,' which looks back on two small peninsulas." He argued that anthropology was a more relevant source of political education than classicist humanism was: "Through its strict maintenance of the consensus, classical learning has a beneficial influence in the education of impressionable youths, but it remains insufficient for the mature man, who finds himself up against more powerful and far-reaching problems in contemporary political life." According to Bastian, classical learning, the foundation of traditional humanist education in Germany, was a doctrine perhaps for socializing children but no longer suitable for educating German citizens. Traditional humanist education had become insufficient, he went on to explain, "since the horizon has broadened to include the entire space of the globe." Humanism, conceived as Europe's autobiography, had become too narrow a basis for education. Anthropology, however, could provide a basis for a new national education, much as German humanists had in the late eighteenth century: "In ethnoanthropology . . . there is already a pronounced popularization, as in the time of the 'popular philosophy' that emerged from the . . . *Sturm und Drang* period, in the sense of Möser's *Patriotic Fantasies,* supposed to lead youths from the "Latin cattle stocks.'"[94] Bastian's reference to this early attempt to "lead youths from the 'Latin cattle stocks'" indicates the extent to which anthropology's counterhumanism rested on the venerable ancients/moderns conflict within humanism. This attack on humanism depended on a humanist conception of scholarship as a source of political virtue and moral education for citizens. Bastian radicalized the modern position by rejecting the Eurocentrism and the focus on history, writing, and interpretation that had characterized all humanism.

Anthropologists created an innovative *studia humanitas* that they hoped would provide a new civic education and a scientific project to update what they regarded as outdated historicist humanism. However, their position between history and nature proved to be more precarious than they had expected. Natural science is, of course, no fixed doctrine, and their model of a timeless, unchanging nature placed anthropologists in direct conflict with the evolutionary theory then gaining ground in Germany. Furthermore, their conception of natural peoples—so powerful because it fused the binary poles of humans and nature—proved to be theoretically monstrous. Fixing their new humanism on a concept of nature only led anthropologists into further practical difficulties and conceptual adventures.

CHAPTER 3

⊠⊠

Nature and the Boundaries of the Human:
Monkeys, Monsters, and Natural Peoples

German anthropologists understood nature as a static system of categories that allowed them, in their study of "natural peoples," to grasp an unchanging essence of humanity, rather than the ephemeral changes that historians recorded. However, the concept of nature was anything but stable in nineteenth-century Germany. Since the early part of the century there had been a deep tension between Kantian models of natural science and idealist *Naturphilosophie,* conflicts in which many anthropologists were themselves active participants. Furthermore, in nature anthropologists sought a realm free from historical change just as Darwinians began asserting that nature, like humans, did, in fact, change over time. The boundary between history and nature, which formed an important basis for both humanism and anthropology, came to appear more unstable than ever. Some of the most important sites of this new Darwinian challenge were freak shows, which anthropologists attended as eagerly as they did ethnographic performances. In these shows, various deformed individuals were presented as missing links between monkeys and men or as monstrous hybrids of humans and animals. Anthropologists attempted to normalize these "monsters" by declaring them individual pathologies unrelated to questions of human nature or biological evolution. Paradoxically, their own concept of natural peoples was itself monstrous, for, like the "freaks" that anthropologists debunked as pathological, natural peoples transgressed the boundaries between the cultural and the natural, the historical and the eternal, the human and the nonhuman. The paradox of the natural person made German anthropology a powerful response to humanism, but it also made the discipline radically unstable.

The idea of nature and natural science that informed German anthropology was based on elements from two conflicting approaches, conventionally associated with Immanuel Kant and Friedrich Schelling.[1] The founders of German anthropology belonged to a generation of natural scientists who, in the second half of the nineteenth century, rejected Schelling's romantic *Naturphilosophie* in favor of a return to Kant's more secular and rationalist notion of nature and natural science.[2] As is the case with so many philosophical rejections, however, anthropologists preserved as much *Naturphilosophie* as they cast off, and their understanding of nature was really a synthesis of the two philosophers' approaches.[3]

From Kant anthropologists took an idea of nature as a static and objective system that could be conclusively known by scientists.[4] In his *Metaphysical Basis of Natural Science,* Kant had maintained that an "authentic natural science" consisted exclusively of a priori deductions of necessary laws. He thus applauded a version of Newtonian mechanics based solely on mathematics as a perfect natural science and dismissed chemistry as a "systematic art" rather than a science because its laws were derived from sensory experience of "given facts."[5] Unlike Newton, Kant excluded theological considerations from natural science, founding a tradition in Germany of strictly separating natural science and religion, a tradition sharply distinct from British natural theology.[6] While this law-based, objective, totally secular, and perfectly knowable nature would have appealed to anthropologists, they would not have subscribed to the Kantian notion of science as the a priori deduction of mathematical laws. Indeed, anthropology was above all a science of the given facts, which Kant had rejected as a source of natural scientific knowledge.

It was precisely over this issue of the empirical that Schelling had originally broken with Kant, and it was in their empiricist approach to nature that anthropologists retained their allegiance to Schelling. Schelling had justified experience and empirical knowledge of nature against Kant's insistence that true knowledge of nature had to be deductive, a priori, and law-like. Thus, a science of qualities, such as chemistry with its qualitatively different elements, could count as a science for Schelling but not for Kant. For Schelling, the rehabilitation of the empirical in natural knowledge was part of an idealist project to overcome the difference between theological and natural knowledge, mind and nature, and speculation and experience.[7] When anthropologists denounced *Naturphilosophie,* it was not for its empiricism. Worse than the idealism of *Naturphilosophie* was, for anthropologists, its view of nature as becoming rather than being, a view antithetical to the concept of nature that anthropologists wanted to use against historicist humanism.[8] Thus, Virchow asserted that, "while the facts teach that the races of humans and the species of animals are immutable," *Naturphilosophie* (wrongly, in Virchow's view) teaches that they can change.[9] Furthermore, anthropologists separated religious and scientific questions, following Kant's rather than Schelling's understanding of the relation of natural and theological knowledge. Allowing theology and development to enter into discussions of nature would undermine the basic project of anthropology as an antihumanist science of natural peoples outside history. When they spoke of *Naturphilosophie,* anthropologists thus thought as much about Darwinism as about the philosophical writings of Schelling and his followers.

Anthropologists saw in the science of botany a model for their own antievolutionist synthesis of Kant's systematizing with Schelling's empiricism. There were a number of botanists active in the Berlin Anthropological Society, including the great latter-day *Naturphilosoph,* Alexander Braun.[10] Braun argued that the study of plants allowed one to observe the essence of nature relatively directly because plants do not disguise themselves with culture, as humans do.[11] Adolf Bastian extended Braun's understanding of plants to natural peoples, whom he compared to cryptogams, flowerless plants such as algae, mosses, and ferns. As botanists had gained general knowledge about plants by studying the flowerless cryptogams, which had previously been "despised and crushed under foot," so too would anthropologists solve the "highest questions of culture" by considering natural peoples, who lack the "flowers of culture."[12] Bastian proclaimed that the goal of anthropology was to attain a "total impression" (*Total-Eindruck*) of humanity in all its variations.[13] He explained that the botanist took from the multiplicity of plants the general idea of the plant, the so-called *Urpflanze.* Rudolf Virchow similarly compared anthropology's attempts to grasp the idea of the human in the variety of empirically given natural humans to Goethe's attempt to know the *Urpflanze* in the variety of empirically given plants. Virchow was careful to point out that this *Urpflanze* was no actual plant, no ancestor or "missing link," but rather a concept derived from wide-ranging observations, or what was known as a "total impression."[14] This "total impression" would also allow the anthropologist, like the botanist, to develop a classificatory schema based on a "natural system" rather than on arbitrary distinctions. Whereas anthropologists' understanding of a natural system owed perhaps more to Kant than to Schelling, knowing this system through an inductive total impression that gave insight into a general idea—the human equivalent of the *Ur-pflanze*—was *Naturphilosophie* pure and simple.

The understanding of nature as radically separate from time and narrative rested also on a distinctly German understanding of the relation of theology, nature, and history. In England and France, geologists appropriated and applied scriptural traditions of viewing the creation of the earth as part of a single narrative that also included human history.[15] While in one sense historical treatments of the earth broke with scriptural accounts of Creation, in a more fundamental sense they continued biblical traditions of historicizing nature.[16] In Germany, by contrast, geologists do not appear to have focused as closely as their English or French counterparts on comprehending the earth as a historical entity. German earth scientists divided what English and French speakers called *geology* into *Geognosie* and *Geologie*. *Geognosie* was the study of geological features of the present earth, while *Geologie* attempted to account for the historical development of the earth. Most Germans regarded *Geognosie* as the primary task of earth scientists and viewed the reconstruction of the chronological development of the earth as primarily of speculative rather than scientific interest.[17] While humanist scholars and philosophers in Germany radically historicized human society, knowledge, and experience, German natural scientists were unusually hesitant to apply historicist modes of understanding to nature. Although in England and France all reality, both natural and human, could be comprehended historically—indeed, as a single historical narrative—in Germany nature existed primarily in a permanent present tense.

This radical separation of nature from history was made possible by the wide acceptance in Germany of historical criticism of the Bible. The idea that nature can be comprehended as historical development of the kind conventionally seen in human societies finds an origin in the biblical account of Creation. Genesis models divine creation on human actions and thus presents nature as the historical product of an anthropomorphic God. This allows for a narrative about the emergence of the earth that blends smoothly into the rest of the Bible, which centers on human action. However, this biblical historicizing of nature did not have the same meaning in Germany as it did, for example, in England. The historical criticism of the Bible, developed and made widely known by German theologians in the late eighteenth and the nineteenth centuries, rendered the Bible a product of human history, a document authored by humans. For these theologians, the Bible did not stand outside history and thereby establish humanity and nature as parts of a single narrative whole. Johann Gottfried Eichhorn's seminal *Einleitung in das Alte Testament* argued against such a "merely theological use" of the Hebrew Bible, which would read it simply for "religious ideas," as if it had been written in the present and were not a "work of gray antiquity."[18] For Eichhorn, and for the ensuing tradition of historical-philological criticism of the Bible, biblical interpretation became a variant of historical philology, and the positivity, or historical truth, of biblical events became a question of secondary importance. German theologians practicing this historical criticism in the nineteenth century did not take their work to imply a deistic devaluation of Scripture, and, by the second half of the nineteenth century, the historical criticism of the Bible became an accepted part of theology in Germany.[19] Indeed, in one of his *Kulturkampf* diatribes, Virchow demanded that Catholics abandon "their stiff traditions" and accept as valid the philological-historical criticism of the Bible.[20] Liberal Protestants in Germany could not look to nature for outside confirmation or elaboration of scriptural truth, as, for example, British and French geologists did with regard to the account of Creation and the Flood. While in Britain time united nature and human history, a presupposition authorized by Scripture as well as by modern geology and Darwinism, in Germany time served as a radical division between nature and history.[21]

Most anthropologists viewed Darwinism as unfounded speculation about the origin of humans, differing little from religious explanations of the origins of humans.[22] For example, Gustav Fritsch, one of Germany's leading anthropologists, did not consider questions about the origin of the human species to be scientific questions. He viewed the question of the origin of humans as primarily of religious rather than of scientific significance. In his paradigmatic 1872 *The Natives of South Africa,* Fritsch wrote that the question "ape, or no ape?" had as much place in his book as "information on the number of paradises."[23] German anthropologists displayed little interest in the religious implications of their discipline, in contrast to British anthropologists such as Tylor and Lubbock, who presented their narratives of human evolution from original savagery as alternatives to the biblical narrative of the Fall. Although in Britain both evolutionist anthropology and Darwinism might have seemed like challenges to revealed religion, in Germany such doctrines seeking narrative development in the timeless realm of nature appeared as irrelevant, and even backward, religious questions.

German anthropologists sought to work out a natural system that would describe the static typology of nature. Their understanding of race illustrates particularly well this typological understanding of nature. Anthropologists believed that, like the borders among species, the borders among the human races were absolute. Anthropologists were not, however, polygenists and believed that even though the various human races were absolutely distinct, they were also part of a single species. Individuals themselves could vary widely, and only a few individuals counted as "typical representatives" of a species or a race. Most individuals, Virchow and others admitted, varied from the species type. These atypical individuals, they maintained, gave some observers the illusion that species were continuous with one another. This was especially apparent, Virchow argued, in deviants from racial types who looked like intermediary stages between races, thus giving the sense that races were continuous rather than absolute categories. Anthropologists sometimes alluded to a climatic origin for racial variations among humans, although they ultimately remained agnostic about the origin of the natural system of human types that they described.[24] Virchow claimed that the question of the origin of racial variations was not for "natural scientists" but rather only for "speculative men of letters."[25] Although racial characteristics might have originated in climatic conditions, they became permanent, and questions of natural history and natural origins were therefore separated from understandings of nature, which was conceived as an achronological system of absolute categories.

The classification of the human was not an end in itself, however, but a step toward understanding the fundamental idea of humanity. Although physical, racial properties were the paradigmatic instance of natural typology, the types to be described by anthropology's natural system were to account for both the mind and the body. Anthropologists ultimately rejected both humanistic and biologistic reductions of the human and proclaimed their discipline a study of "the whole, the person with body and soul."[26] The physical and mental diversity that did exist among humans anthropologists explained as results of geographic and climatic differences. Thus, while humans were fundamentally all the same, they had to make their tools from different materials and fashion their ideas in relation to different environmental conditions, depending on their geographic location. Similarly, their differences in appearance probably found a similar origin in geography.[27] However, anthropologists were not interested in explaining geographic variation as much as they were in using geography as a means of canceling out the variations that might otherwise have made a unified understanding of all humanity an impossible goal. Beneath the variety of empirical humans was the idea of the human, corresponding to the *Urpflanze* sought by botanists through the total impression. Nature thus provided the basis for a totalizing science that could both classify humans on the basis of all aspects of their physical, mental, and social lives and derive a general theory of all humanity. This was to be achieved through a totalizing empiricism, the total impression, whose possibility rested on this very concept of nature.

Darwinism was diametrically opposed to the conception of nature fundamental to anthropology, for it replaced the absolute, static differences among natural types with narrative continuity. Particularly threatening to anthropology was the implication that the human could not be understood as a single idea but rather was part of a continuum that also included animals. For this reason, anthropologists often referred to Darwinism derisively as the "monkey doctrine" (*Affenlehre*) (see fig. 3.1).[28] They attacked what they called "transformationism," the belief in the very possibility of the development of one species from another (such as humans from monkeys). Bastian compared species to chemical elements and thus related the assertion that one species could become another to alchemical arguments that lead could become gold. He likened the monkey doctrine to the myths of certain natural peoples that humans originated from animals, such as a Polynesian story of the development of humans from worms.[29] Vir-

FIGURE 3.1
Girl and monkey. This photograph formed part of the collection of the Berlin Anthropological Society. Although no commentary about the photograph survives, it likely was understood as an illustration of the Darwinian "monkey doctrine." While Berlin anthropologists rejected Darwinism because it blurred the boundary between humans and animals, they devoted much time to transgressing and defending this boundary. This photograph gives a humorous rendition of the monkey doctrine.
Source: ABGAEU, P. 1646. Reproduced courtesy of Berliner Gesellschaft für Anthropologie, Ethnologie und Urgeschichte.

chow also rejected the idea that one species could transform into another and regarded all deviations within a species—even racial variations—as pathological.[30] He similarly viewed artificially bred varieties of domestic animals as pathologies, exceptional in that their traits could be inherited by their offspring. The understanding of species by German anthropologists could not have varied to a greater extent from the Darwinian understanding: whereas for Darwin *species* was a fuzzy concept, for most German anthropologists it was absolute.

A number of prominent German anthropologists did indeed embrace biological evolution, although it did not fit well into the mainstream disciplinary goals of anthropology. Darwinist anthropologists tended to adjust their views to fit with antievolutionist anthropology, in part because of the enormous power wielded by Rudolf Virchow in the German Anthropological Society.[31] Hermann Schaaffhausen of Bonn, the most important Darwinist anthropologist in Germany, limited the role of evolutionism in his explanations of humans so that his subscription to the monkey doctrine did not prevent him from cooperating with the German Anthropological Society. For Schaaffhausen, the discipline of anthropology was made possible only when it was realized that humans had descended from apes and were, therefore, subject to natural scientific analysis rather than philosophical inquiry, which had, he ventured, made no progress since antiquity.[32] That the *studia humanitas* should be the province of natural scientists rather than humanists was a point made by nearly all German anthropologists, Darwinist or not.

The problem that evolution posed to German anthropology was that it made the static categories of human nature into a fluid continuum with no more conceptual clarity than historical narrative. Schaaffhausen arrived at a compromise Darwinism that allowed him to exempt the categories of anthropology from the murkiness of evolution. In the 1868 article "The Doctrine of Darwin's and Anthropology," he cautioned that the "mental activity" of humans is a "new force" that distinguishes humans from plants and animals. Also, natural selection could not explain many human racial characteristics, such as skin, hair, and eye color, as well as the size and build of the body, which, according to Schaaffhausen, were caused by the climate. Races do not struggle with each other for survival, for nearly all conflict occurs within, rather than among, racial groups. Furthermore, once acquired, racial characteristics become hereditary, and racial types would therefore become permanent. Thus, according to Schaaffhausen, the Inuit had dark skin, supposedly a characteristic caused by warm climates, because they had originally migrated from a warmer area and retained this trait long after its external cause had been removed.[33] Racial characteristics

were not the arbitrary outcomes of a struggle for survival but rather fixed
types of a distant origin. Schaaffhausen was able to remain an adherent of
the Darwinian monkey doctrine without challenging the understanding of
nature and humanity fundamental to German anthropology.

The most important criticisms of the monkey doctrine in German anthropology took the form of demonstrating and debunking what appeared to
be evidence for the descent of humans from apes.[34] Fossil finds supposedly
representing extinct intermediary species between humans and apes constituted the most rare type of evidence for the monkey doctrine. These included the skull fragment found in the Neanderthal (the Neander Valley)
near Düsseldorf in 1856, the similar bones found in Spy, Belgium, in 1886,
and the fossil remains found in Java in 1891–92. Virchow's discussion of
the Neanderthal skull fragment is a paradigm of the way in which he recast
as pathological individual cases that appeared to support the evolution of
humans from apes. *Globus,* one of nineteenth-century Germany's equiva-
lents to *National Geographic,* referred to Virchow's study of the Neanderthal fragment as an "incomparable example of scientific treatment of
material in contrast to the superficial drivel of others."[35] At an 1872 Berlin
Anthropological Society meeting, Virchow presented a plaster cast of the
Neanderthal fragment, the crown of the skull, and reinterpreted its supposed ape-like characteristics as pathological (see fig. 3.2).[36] Virchow argued that the individual it came from suffered from two separate head
injuries, one of which led to decay of the bone. The skull also indicated that
the individual suffered from an atrophied brain, which led to the growth of
additional bone matter around the forehead and fusion of the sutures,
which further deformed the skull. Additionally, the skull exhibited general atrophy due to old age. Other bone fragments accompanying the find
indicated that, as a child, the individual had suffered from rickets and that,
when he died, he was severely crippled by arthritis. If these pathological
characteristics were taken into account, Virchow argued, the skull's dimensions fell "within quite tolerable boundaries": an unfortunate individual, no doubt, but hardly a missing link between man and monkey.[37]
    As more skulls and skull fragments resembling the one found in the
Neander Valley turned up throughout Europe, Virchow maintained his
resistance to identifying them either as representatives of a race or as ape-
like. Since the skulls resembling the Neanderthal fragment were found in
different locations and were from different time periods, they did not suggest the existence of a single race of Neanderthal-like individuals. Indeed,
Virchow offered, the inhabitants of the Frisian Islands off the coast of Hol-
land also resembled the Neanderthal, although they were neither a sepa-

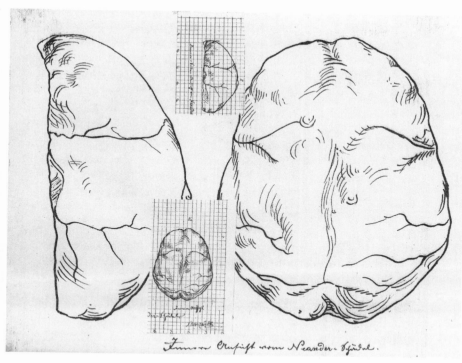

FIGURE 3.2
"Interior View of the Neanderthal Skull." Sketch by Rudolf Virchow, 1872.
Source: ABGAEU, Sig.: NSRV 68. Reproduced courtesy of Berliner Gesellschaft für Anthropologie, Ethnologie und Urgeschichte.

rate race nor particularly ape-like.[38] In 1895, the Berlin Anthropological Society gave a similarly skeptical reception to the Java ape-man, which one member declared to be a man with the head of an ape, a freak even more interesting than the dog-headed and cat-headed men known to pathology (and circuses).[39] When, later that year, the society brought Eugène Dubois, the Dutch discoverer of Java man, to Berlin to present his findings, Virchow conceded that the skull fragment did appear to belong to an ape resembling a human. However, Virchow pointed out, the resemblance between apes and humans was already well-known; what still had not been proved was that this resemblance indicated descent.[40] Because he refused to understand nature as a connected narrative but rather grasped it as a system of static classifications, Virchow made impossible the easy slip from resemblance to descent, a slip on which the theory of the evolution of species depended.

FIGURE 3.3

Front (*top*) and back (*bottom*) of an advertising leaflet for performances of "the Two-Headed Nightingale." The text of the front reads: "This new wonder of the world, Misses Christine-Millie, will be shown every afternoon from 2:30 to 4:30 in the concert hall of the 'Passage.'... Misses Christine-Millie, a highly interesting and appealing appearance, will dance, sing, and speak with her admirers. Professor Dr. A. Berger will be present and offer a complete explanation three times a day...." The text of the back reads: "The under-signed examined the so-called Two-Headed Nightingale (Misses Christine-Millie) in the

Anthropologists encountered Darwinism most directly in freak shows, which often occurred in the same venues as ethnographic spectacles. These shows employed Darwinism to bill various deformed humans as atavisms, individuals whose development had somehow been arrested and thus who shared characteristics with their animal ancestors. As a professor of pathology and director of the pathological institute in the Charité hospital in Berlin, Virchow kept anthropologists informed of any potential atavisms he came across in his work. A network of correspondents around the world also sent photographs and descriptions of deformed people they encountered. Additionally, Louis Castan, one of the owners of Castan's Panopticon in Berlin, often presented his freak-show performers at the meetings of the Berlin Anthropological Society. The interest of anthropologists in these shows legitimated them in the eyes of the police, as it did the ethnographic performances. Anthropologists also offered public testimonial to the authenticity of freak-show performers (see figs. 3.3 and 3.4).

For Virchow personally, and for the educated public of Imperial Germany generally, birth defects, especially those in which the victim resembled something other than a human, seem to have been extraordinarily amusing.[41] In 1899, Virchow gave a speech at the opening ceremonies of the Pathology Museum in Berlin in which he spent much of his time joking to a clearly amused audience of invited dignitaries about various deformed babies preserved in jars of alcohol. For example, when presenting a series of fetal conjoined (Siamese) twins, Virchow remarked:

> Since we have so many great statesmen among us, I allow myself to remark that this group here is the first group of *Terata* [monsters] ever to conduct a peace conference. (Laughter.) It is a group in which two fetuses become such close brothers that they meld into each other. (Laughter.) This turns out to produce a monster. (Much laughter.) This monster was so important to the ancients that the Romans took it into their temples. It is Janus, the god of war and peace. Janus is of course for the most part not quite as soundly formed (laughter) as the Romans imagined him to be.[42]

Hôtel de Rome today. They hereby declare that the connection of the two sisters is original and natural, that its appearance is extremely interesting and appealing, and that, apart from the general rarity of such arrangements, the present case distinguishes itself by the entirely new fact that there is common feeling in the lower extremities. Berlin, 5 February 1873. Rud. Virchow, B. v. Langenbeck, Dr. B. Fränkel."
Source: ABGAEU, Sig.: Ver 40. Reproduced courtesy of Berliner Gesellschaft für Anthropologie, Ethnologie und Urgeschichte.

FIGURE   3.4
"The Tallest Man in the
World: The Giant Mach-
now Introduces Himself to
Professor Dr. von Luschan
in the Berlin Museum of
Ethnology." Feodor Mach-
now was a performer in
Castan's Panopticon, and
this photograph, published
in a popular weekly, sug-
gested that his perfor-
mances possessed scientific
legitimacy and interest.
Source: Die Woche 5, no. 2
(1903): 789. (The photo-
graph stands on its own
but is implicitly associated
with Felix von Luschan,
"Der Riesenwuchs," *Die
Woche* 5, no. 2 [1903]: 777–
78.)

While Virchow himself was well-known for the peculiar intensity of his
interest in deformed individuals, the frequent laughter from the audience
indicates that such pathologies were also generally held to be interesting
and funny. While today we might imagine laughing at birth defects as
something low and undignified, in Imperial Germany they appear to have
been a legitimate source of amusement for social, academic, and political
elites.

Anthropologists' accounts of freaks as pathologies rather than atavisms competed with the popular Darwinism that framed the shows in
which they encountered these unfortunate individuals.[43] Performers were
often touted as missing links between apes and humans in order to make
their deformities even more thrilling to the public. For example, an American touring Europe in 1894 put on a show in which he lectured on Darwinism before a cage containing a severely retarded and extraordinarily

hairy man, with the stage name "Ram-a-Samy," who the impresario claimed was a missing link discovered by British soldiers in India.[44] While this seems to have been an important selling point for extremely hairy individuals, the names given to other performers also often stressed their status as intermediaries between humans and animals. Examples include the "Stork Boy," an extraordinarily skinny man who put on a false beak and danced on stage, or the "Bear Lady," an American woman with deformed limbs who wrapped herself in a bear skin and roared at the audience from within an artificial cave. Both these individuals performed for the Berlin Anthropological Society, the latter several times.[45] Members of the society, including Virchow and Bastian, regularly denounced as misleading "humbug" claims of impresarios that deformed performers represented missing links or were part animal.[46] Still, despite his disagreements with impresarios, Virchow encouraged anthropologists to visit what he considered to be particularly interesting shows and often convinced impresarios to stage special performances for the society's meetings. Anthropologists regularly had the opportunity to observe as Virchow demonstrated that individuals who appeared to bridge the gap between humans and animals were in fact merely pathological. While anthropologists were not excessively discriminating about what human oddities they would view and discuss, they were especially interested in microcephalics (people born with unusually small skulls and brains, sometimes called *pinheads*), people with tails, and extraordinarily hairy people.

Microcephalics became a privileged case for discussions of the relations between humans and monkeys as a result of studies conducted by the Swiss zoologist Carl Vogt (see fig. 3.5). Vogt published articles in both French and German in the late 1860s claiming that microcephalics represented an atavistic recollection of a missing link between apes and humans. He cited the supposed similarity in both size and convolutions between the brains of microcephalics and the brains of spider monkeys. He further noted the unusual agility of microcephalics as well as their predilection for climbing.[47] Darwin himself agreed that all Vogt's conclusions about microcephalics lent credibility to his own theory, adding that "idiots" were also often unusually hairy.[48] Virchow criticized Vogt for placing pathological deviations from normal humans in a single "series" (*Reihe*) and for drawing conclusions about the evolution of healthy individuals from this misconstrual.[49] Although it was quite difficult to recruit microcephalics for study, Virchow did succeed in 1872 in getting a guest from St. Petersburg to bring several plaster casts and the brain, hardened in alcohol, of a microcephalic named Mottey who had died in a madhouse in Voronezh, Russia. The Russian lecturer demonstrated that Mottey's brain did not resemble a monkey's

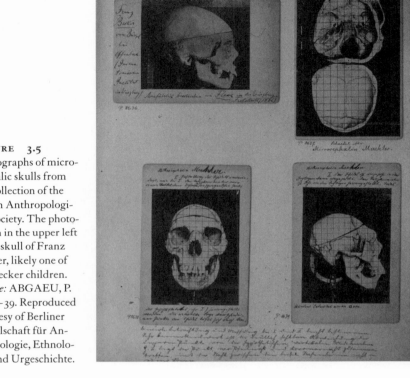

FIGURE 3.5
Photographs of micro-
cephalic skulls from
the collection of the
Berlin Anthropologi-
cal Society. The photo-
graph in the upper left
is the skull of Franz
Becker, likely one of
the Becker children.
Source: ABGAEU, P.
8636–39. Reproduced
courtesy of Berliner
Gesellschaft für An-
thropologie, Ethnolo-
gie und Urgeschichte.

brain and described the subject's general apathy and obesity as well as his
limited ability to speak or to understand space, time, and music. He also reported that Mottey had feminine breasts and described in detail his genitals.[50] Mottey's mental disabilities, as well as the implication that he was a
hermaphrodite, seem to have strengthened the conclusion that microcephaly constituted a pathology rather than an atavism.

German anthropology benefited greatly from a certain Frau Becker, a
poverty-stricken mother who supplemented her income by charging anthropologists to study her three microcephalic children.[51] Virchow's studies of the Becker children, published in 1877 and 1878, argued conclusively
that microcephaly was not an atavistic characteristic but rather an individual pathology. While microcephaly could be hereditary, Virchow admitted, it was not hereditary enough to characterize a species. Furthermore,
since most microcephalics were sterile, an "originary race of pure micro-

cephalics" would be impossible.[52] Although most anthropologists seem to have favored Virchow's interpretation of microcephalics as merely pathological, the German Anthropological Society continued to discuss the meaning of microcephaly, listing it as one of the most important topics for the discipline in 1879.[53] German and Berlin Anthropological Society meetings continued to feature occasional microcephalic performances, in part, it seems, because anthropologists found them so entertaining.

People with tails (*Schwanzmenschen*) and extraordinarily hairy people (*Haarmenschen*) constituted another potential transgression of the border between humans and animals. In two Berlin Anthropology Society meetings in 1875, Virchow read letters sent to him by Bernard Ornstein, a corresponding member of the Berlin society and the chief doctor of the Greek army. Ornstein had included in his letters a photograph and a report of a patient with an unusually hairy patch at the base of his back (see fig. 3.6).

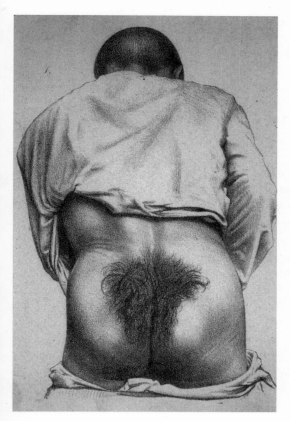

FIGURE 3.6
Is the hairy patch at the base of this man's spine a tail? Bernhard Ornstein, the chief surgeon of the Greek army, thought that it was. He sent this image to Virchow, arguing that it represented an atavism and therefore supported Darwinism. Virchow dismissed this hairy patch as a mere pathology. Arguments about whether phenomena such as this one were pathological or atavistic were some of the most important early debates about Darwinism in Germany.
Source: Bernard Ornstein, "Ungewöhnliche Haarbildung in der Sacralgegend eines Griechen," *VBGAEU* 7 (1875): 91–92.

Virchow cautioned against understanding this pathology as an atavistic characteristic, noting that this patch of hair could not be considered a tail unless it protruded from the body. He did, however, allow that such pathologies might account for the ancient Greek belief in satyrs.[54] Four years later, in 1879, Ornstein reported a case that seemed to meet Virchow's criteria for an atavistic human tail, a man with a small protuberance on his lower back (see fig. 3.7). He wrote that he expected the society to view the picture as an "illusion" or as "blasphemy" against their own "religious and philosophical dogmatism" (that is, their opposition to the theory of evolution). He recommended that the Berlin society read writings by the evolutionists Lamarck and Haeckel.[55] The Society's *Transactions* do not record any response to this report, but Virchow did respond to a similar report from Ornstein six years later. Virchow warned against taking the protuberance for a tail, since it did not contain extra vertebrae. It was, he concluded, a protruding, but otherwise normal, spine. Virchow once again reinterpreted a potential atavism as a individual pathology.[56]

Individuals suffering from a disease called hypertrichosis, a condition in which a person grows an extraordinary amount of hair over part or all of the body, were another important topic of debate for anthropologists (see figs. 3.8–3.10). Perhaps the most important of these so-called hair people were the Russian father and son pair Andrian (1818–ca. 1884) and Fedor Schaafjew (1870–?). The Schaafjews interested anthropologists particularly because their unusual hairiness appeared to be a trait passed from father to son and thus seemed to be a kind of racial characteristic. The animal-like appearance of this supposed racial characteristic implied that hair people represented a kind of intermediary species between animals and people. Virchow cautioned that, even if Fedor had inherited his condition from his father, this unusual hairiness would still constitute a pathology rather than a species. Some varieties of domestic animals, such as bulldogs, he pointed out, represent long lines of inherited pathologies.[57]

One of the more hermeneutically interesting cases of the interpretation of potential atavisms as pathologies was a series of articles on abnormal hair growth in humans published by Max Bartels, a Berlin physician who later became an editor of the Berlin society's journal.[58] Although Bartels never advocated viewing apparent atavisms as anything but pathologies and elsewhere argued against the very possibility of atavisms,[59] he did preserve a kind of continuity between humans and animals: "Through pathological processes, all possible animal forms can appear in humans, including feathers, which according to Elbe have been observed in at least two cases."[60] Bartels noted that the most common of the "animal forms" to appear in humans is whisker-like hair growing out of warts and birth-

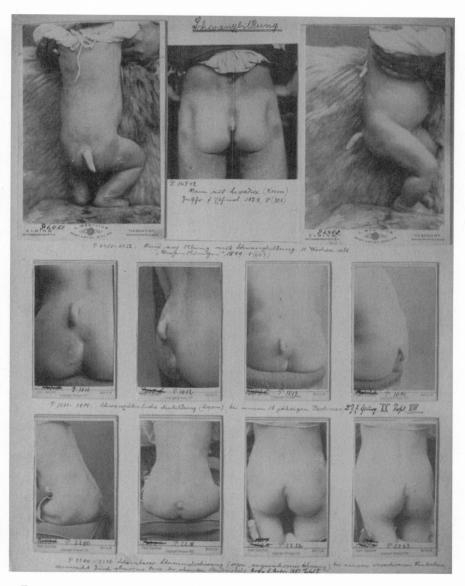

FIGURE 3.7

"Tail Formation." Photographs from the collection of the Berlin Anthropological Society. The photograph sent by Ornstein to Virchow in 1879 is the center one in the top row. The debate about whether such formations were atavistic tails or pathological protuberances continued for at least a decade.

Source: ABGAEU, P. 6451, 14742, 6452, 1011–14, 2280–83. Reproduced courtesy of Berliner Gesellschaft für Anthropologie, Ethnologie und Urgeschichte.

FIGURE   3.8

"Abnormal Hair Growth." Assemblage of photographs from the collection of the Berlin
Anthropological Society. The individuals depicted here were some of the most important
"hair people" of nineteenth-century Europe. In the upper-left corner is six-year-old
Stephan Bebrowsky (see fig. 3.10). In the top center is Krao. The eight-year-old daughter
of a Siamese official, she was billed in Berlin as a "missing link" (an appellation that Virchow dismissed as "idle Humbug") (Rudolf Virchow, comment on "Affenmensch und
Bärenmensch," *VBGAEU* 16 [1884]: 106–13, 111). The police forbid the Berlin Aquarium
from displaying her with apes. In the center are Andrian Schaafjew and his son Fedor.
In the upper right is Ram-a-Samy, a severely retarded man, billed as a missing link discov-

FIGURE 3.9

Hirsute family from Burma. The arrangement of these individuals followed the conventions of a family portrait, suggesting that they were related to each other. The possibility that such characteristics could be inherited lent credence to the idea that they were atavisms rather than individual pathologies.

Source: ABGAEU, P. 3724. Reproduced courtesy of Berliner Gesellschaft für Anthropologie, Ethnologie und Urgeschichte.

ered by British troops in India. In the lower left and center are two members of the hirsute family pictured in fig. 3.9. In the lower right is a bearded woman, photographed in Berlin in 1891.

Source: ABGAEU, P. 3400, 3171, 8690, 4624, 1916, 1917, 8200. Reproduced courtesy of Berliner Gesellschaft für Anthropologie, Ethnologie und Urgeschichte.

FIGURE 3.10
Stephan Bebrowsky (b. 1890).
A particularly extraordinary
case of hypertrichosis. He
was likely a circus performer,
and his hair has been arranged
to emphasize his startling appearance. A younger Be-
browsky appears in the
upper-left photograph in fig.
3.8. He performed for the
Berlin Anthropological Society in 1896 and 1907.
Source: ABGAEU, P. 9315.
Reproduced courtesy of
Berliner Gesellschaft für Anthropologie, Ethnologie und
Urgeschichte.

marks. Bartels thus suggested that every human body was a potential source of atavisms, and one can imagine the readers of the *Zeitschrift für Ethnologie* glancing uneasily at their own hairy warts and birthmarks, sud-denly viewing them as traces of animal ancestors. Although Bartels seems to have agreed with Virchow that unusual hair was pathological rather than atavistic, he still devoted much of his anthropological career to the study of the hirsute.

The practice of interpreting monsters as signs of something beyond themselves (which is what an atavism is: a sign pointing to a supposed bio-logical past of humans) can be traced back to antiquity. The word *monster* itself comes from the Latin *monstrare*, "to show," for monsters were origi-nally understood as signs sent from the gods to humans. In this sense, mon-sters are things to be interpreted; they are hermeneutic problems.[61] Indeed, monsters and hermeneutics are linked originally: monsters are messages from the gods; hermeneutics derives from the name of Hermes, the mes-senger of the gods. Max Bartels proclaimed that "nothing in nature is insignificant and beside the point"; there is even a "casuistry of the birth-mark."[62] However, even Bartels, who was unusually willing to admit parallels between humans and animals, did not assert that birthmarks (or rather the thick hairs that often grow out of them) pointed to a real animal past for humans.

Paradoxically, the interest of German anthropologists in freaks seems to have been in declaring them uninteresting. If monsters were signs, they were not signs pointing beyond themselves to an animal past but rather signs of individual pathologies, signs pointing merely to themselves. Virchow's discussion of the Neanderthal skull fragment is a good example of this: the characteristics of the fragment pointed not to characteristics of an intermediate race or species between human and ape but rather to pathologies of the individual from which the skull came. Tails found on humans pointed not to a common animal ancestry that reappeared in an individual but rather merely to pathological disturbances of the spine.

One is tempted to say, especially with regard to such monsters as the Stork Boy or the Bear Lady, that anthropologists were interested in freaks merely because they found them entertaining. However, looking at freaks and being merely entertained itself constituted a scientific argument. For anthropologists, these monsters were, in fact, not monsters at all: they did not represent a message from the gods or from humanity's past. By being merely entertained, anthropologists reaffirmed the boundaries between humans and animals. The assertion that circus freaks fit soundly within the range of the human species struck at one of the principal sources of Darwinist argument. Freaks could be interesting, even hilarious, but they could not represent anything more than themselves.

Anthropology was made possible by the extraordinary individuals who appeared on the popular stages of late nineteenth- and early twentieth-century Europe. The ethnographic performers and the freaks played complementary roles in elaborating the theoretical foundations of anthropology. In studies of deformed men and women often performing in the same venues as ethnographic shows, anthropologists elaborated their understandings of nature and their opposition to Darwinism. Whereas the freaks were demonstrated to be atypical (that is, neither belonging to nor indicative of a type), ethnographic performers were valued precisely because, and only if, they were determined to be typical. Thus, in his study of Hagenbeck's "Nubian" show, Virchow focused on several individuals whom he considered to be peculiarly typical. In his study of the Neanderthal skull, he asserted that it was merely an individual pathology and therefore did not represent a type. Because nature itself in Germany was a system of types, the supposedly typical performers in exotic shows illuminated nature, while the atypical monsters lay outside nature and were interesting merely as individuals. Anthropologists thus presented and elaborated a metaphysics of type in the arena of exotic and freak shows.

The concept grounding German anthropology, the *Naturvölker,* was itself a paradox, a monster crossing the boundaries that anthropologists used to delineate their study in the first place. On the one hand, natural peoples undid the humanist assumption that culture and history distinguished humans from nature. All humans, anthropologists offered, were fundamentally "natural," although only the natural peoples exhibited this nature clearly. Natural peoples, not cultural peoples, thus embodied the human universality also sought by historians and other scholars. Natural peoples crossed—and thus allowed anthropologists to cross—the boundary between what were conventionally understood as the human and the nonhuman. Natural peoples were monsters in precisely the sense that circus freaks were not. They were things to be shown, things that indicated something about the nature of humanity, things that really crossed the border between the human as historical being and nature as static grid. Natural peoples sat squarely on an otherwise absolute border between humanity and nature, a border that German humanism, and especially the historical criticism of the Bible, had allowed to exist in a way that both the natural theology and the Darwinism of England did not. It was precisely their ambivalent position on this border between humans and nature that made natural peoples so interesting, so good to think with.

Even while anthropologists broke down one kind of distinction between the human and the nonhuman, they preserved another: that between humans and animals, a distinction threatened by Darwinism and especially by freaks. Unlike natural peoples, freaks were not allowed to cross the boundary between the human and the nonhuman because this threatened the integrity of the human, the object that defined anthropology. While anthropologists generalized human nature to include all humans, even those supposedly without history and culture, they did not want to abandon the timeless, qualitative distinctions within nature, which made anthropology a powerful alternative to humanism. Darwinism, especially Darwinian interpretations of freaks and of human evolution, threatened to make ephemeral the categories of nature, much as anthropology had made ephemeral the categories of culture and history. Thus, anthropologists made biological distinctions, including racial distinctions, absolute: nature was timeless, and any change in nature was merely pathological. This notion of nature provided anthropologists with a resource to undermine the legitimacy of history as the premiere human science. Anthropology was in constant danger, however, of succumbing to its own ruse, that of arguing that what others saw as fundamental and essential (for historians, history and culture) was in fact only ephemeral and accidental. By demonstrating that freaks were not signs of humanity's past, they assured that there existed a realm of fundamental natural categories to be carefully described and cataloged.

The contradiction in German anthropology between the role of freaks and the role of ethnographic performers points toward a larger contradiction in a discourse based on the concept of natural peoples. Anthropologists attempted to study humans as if they were not human. Of course *human* is no transhistorical verity but rather a historically specific construct, elaborated in nineteenth-century Germany above all by the discourse of historicism. The human was understood as a historically active subject, comprehensible through the interpretive work of scholars participating in a common narrative with the individuals they studied. This understanding of the human was implicit in all historical scholarship, but it was explicated precisely in the period and place where anthropology emerged, for example, in the philosophical hermeneutics of Wilhelm Dilthey. Anthropologists rejected both the methods and the subjects of inquiry of humanism but attempted to preserve its goal: knowing the human. They hoped that by using "objective," natural scientific methods on natural peoples they could know the human better than humanists could. To make this move, they had simultaneously to collapse the distinction between nature and humans on which humanism was founded and to preserve this distinction from the monsters of the freak show and from the Darwinist monkey doctrine. Rather than placing the *human,* as an object of inquiry, on a firmer basis than previous traditions of scholarship had, anthropology wrenched the concept of the human apart. In the next chapter, I turn from the end of the human as object of scholarly inquiry to the end of the human subject, the humanist scholar, in anthropological practice.

CHAPTER 4

≋

Measuring Skulls: The Social Role
of the Antihumanist

Alas, poor Yorick! I knew him, Horatio: a fellow of infinite jest, of most
excellent fancy: he hath borne me on his back a thousand times; and
now, how abhorred in my imagination it is! my gorge rims at it. Here
hung those lips that I have kissed I know not how oft. Where be your
gibes now? your gambols? your songs? your flashes of merriment, that
were wont to set the table on a roar? Not one now, to mock your own
grinning?

—*Hamlet,* act 5, scene 1

What so dismayed Hamlet about Yorick's skull was precisely what
made the skull the paradigmatic object of anthropology. The skull
lacks "gibes," "gambols," "songs," "flashes of merriment": it is absolutely
naked, unconcealed by culture. The absence of flesh, which makes Hamlet's "gorge rim," meant for anthropologists a human body without the
subjective history of tissue, whose thickness depends in part on eating
habits and other behaviors. More than any ethnographic artifact, the skull
presented anthropologists with an object that could be studied in a way
fundamentally different from the interpretive methods of the humanities.
Studies of skulls were based on quantitative measurement and precise
comparison and were thus totally devoid of what anthropologists regarded
as subjectivity—either in the researcher or in the object under consideration. This "objectivity" was the goal of all German anthropology, so, while
the skull was a paradigm for the discipline, anthropology was by no means

merely an anatomical science. Because of the precise quantitative and comparative methods of German craniometry, anthropologists had to work out explicit standards for every aspect of this part of their science that they could only strive to approach in their studies of other objects. In craniometry, therefore, the ideal of the individual anthropologist and of the scientific community appears as in no other subspecialty of the discipline. In agreeing on conventions to measure and represent skulls, anthropologists worked out a new social and epistemological role: the antihumanist scientist.

Anthropological studies of the skull were not merely anatomical, nor were they based on a kind of latter-day phrenology that would read the characteristics of individuals or social groups from cranial size or shape. Anthropologists' view of nature as timeless and of race as immutable allowed for a nonevolutionary physical anthropology that focused on physical traits as ethnological characteristics, characteristics that shed light on the relations among various populations in an area. This was the focus, for example, of the study of racial data collected from the Sudanese show at the zoo, discussed in the first chapter, where anthropologists tried to determine whether "Nubians" were more related to the inhabitants of sub-Saharan Africa or those of West Asia. Anthropologists understood the skull as an arbitrarily chosen body part that they used to characterize human races. They hoped that, by taking certain standardized measurements of skulls from a given population, they could mathematically calculate the typical skull form of that group. These types could in turn be compared with each other to determine patterns of migration and other racial relations around the world. Today, we are more attuned to the arbitrary nature of constructions of races. The fallacy of assuming that there is, for example, a "West Asian" type and then averaging skull measurements to determine the nature of that type is now obvious in a way in which it was not in earlier decades. Measuring any "race" made it appear to be a category of nature.[1]

Anthropologists desired more craniometric data than could be collected by a single scientist or even by a single local group of scientists. They opposed the notion that a racial type could be identified by measuring a supposedly typical individual member of a race. Because of a dearth of craniological material, earlier anthropologists, such as the eighteenth-century Göttingen professor Johann Friedrich Blumenbach, had relied on studies of what they assumed to be typical individuals to characterize entire races. The anthropologist Robert Hartmann mocked the lone scholar who takes "this or that cranium" and "measures, describes, draws, and with childish joy catalogs it in one of the usual craniological categories."[2] The new anthropologists advocated measuring large numbers of individuals, using increasingly complex statistical methods to compare the data, from simple averaging in the late 1860s and 1870s to more complex tests of statistical inference around the turn of the century.[3] The anthropologist Hermann Welcker wrote that, "because a single case can never contain the whole truth, one uses statistics."[4] The requirement that anthropological knowledge be based on large samples meant that only an organized group, such as the German Anthropological Society, could make convincing conclusions about race. The methods of craniometry helped define the identity of both the individual expert and the social group of anthropologists.

Throughout the 1870s, German anthropologists devoted much energy to working out a uniform procedure for craniometric studies of race. In doing so, they institutionalized their own methods and created the technical basis for a community of natural scientific human scientists. The craniometric methods that anthropologists adopted represented a commitment to collaborative work among a wide range of amateurs and professionals and further institutionalized anthropologists' rejection of Darwinism. When, in 1883, German anthropologists settled on a common method for measuring skulls, the so-called Frankfurt Agreement, they worked out a collective identity as natural scientists of humanity.

Agreeing to study race by measuring skulls left open a range of methodological questions. The skull is an irregularly shaped object, and there are any number of linear measurements that can be taken of it. The first craniometric agreement in Germany was signed in Göttingen in 1861, although, by the mid-1870s, few anthropologists actually followed it.[5] In 1873, the Göttingen zoologist Hermann von Jhering proposed a standardized schema for skull measurement that established many of the conventions that would eventually be taken up by all German anthropologists.[6] Most agreed with Jhering that the most important measurement of a skull was the cephalic index, the ratio of the length of the skull to its breadth, expressed as a percentage. Using ratios allowed anthropologists to study skull shape rather than skull size. Skulls that were proportionately long according to this scheme were termed *dolichocephalic,* and skulls that were proportionately wide were termed *brachycephalic.*[7] Other measurements of the skull were also calculated as proportions of a horizontal line passing through the length of the skull and were based on lines perpendicular or parallel to this horizontal. Anthropologists also measured various angles on the skull, again in relation to this horizontal. The horizontal line running through the length of the skull was thus the key to the whole system. Although anthropologists disagreed about which craniometric measurements were most important, they shared Jhering's view that defining generally accepted craniometric procedures was more important than the details of those procedures. However, every anthropologist had an interest in preserving as much of his own measuring schema as possible, for the more of his own methods the German Anthropological Society declared standard, the more his past work would be considered relevant to future anthropological research.[8] Anthropologists tried and failed nearly every year at the German Anthropological Society conference to achieve "clarity and unity" in craniometry.[9]

To make matters worse, throughout the 1870s some anthropologists disagreed not only about what measurements to take but also, even more fundamentally, about how to determine the horizontal to which all craniometric measurements were related. The most significant resistance to Jhering's scheme came from the Darwinist Hermann Schaaffhausen (1816–93), an anthropologist and professor of physiology from Bonn. Schaaffhausen objected to all proposals that placed the all-important horizontal through arbitrary points on the skull. Instead, Schaaffhausen suggested determining the horizontal by imagining how the living individual would have normally held his or her own head. Thus, while most anthropologists wanted to set this horizontal by drawing a line passing through the bottom of the eye socket and the top of the ear hole, Schaaffhausen wanted to determine the horizontal by setting the skull so that the individual would be looking straight ahead. Schaaffhausen maintained that skulls should be measured in this supposedly natural position.

While discussions about the craniometric horizontal were always expressed as the driest negotiations over conventions of measurement, it is clear that Schaaffhausen's interest in the horizontal stems from his Darwinism and from his peculiar desire to differentiate races hierarchically. Schaaffhausen hoped to observe both physical and psychic differences between supposedly higher and lower races in the structure of the skull, especially in the degree of prognathy. The degree of prognathy described the amount a person's mouth jutted forward and was calculated by measuring the angle between the horizontal line of the skull and a line passing over the bridge of the nose and the front of the upper jaw. Darwinist anthropologists, such as Schaaffhausen, associated a high degree of prognathy in a group of humans with a close relation to apes. Even non-Darwinists regarded prognathism as the factor responsible for the supposedly savage appearance of certain groups of people.[10] Schaaffhausen held that, when placed on the Jhering horizontal, skulls, especially those "of the lower races," often looked down.[11] A skull looking down would have a significantly lesser degree of prognathy than a skull looking forward, and thus Jhering's method would make Schaaffhausen's assertions about prog-

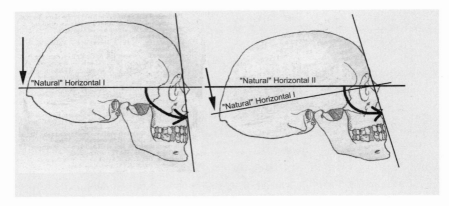

FIGURE   4.1

Tilting the skull backward increases the angle of prognathism. Since the "natural" horizontal was determined by setting the skull so that it seemed to the anthropologist
to look straight ahead, anthropologists were relatively free in setting the angle of prognathism. If an anthropologist expected a skull to be prognathous, it would appear
to look straight ahead when it was tilted backward. Most anthropologists rejected this
"natural" horizontal in favor of the "German" horizontal, illustrated in fig. 4.2.

nathism more difficult to support with craniometric data. As the chin de-
scends toward the chest, the bridge of the nose comes forward, and the jaw
recedes, thus decreasing the angle of prognathy. Likewise, if the head is
tilted backward, the forehead recedes, and the jaw juts forward, thus increasing the angle of prognathy (see fig. 4.1).

The real advantage of Schaaffhausen's system was that it allowed the
anthropologist to fix the skull more or less arbitrarily, according to his own
predilections. The "natural" horizontal of the skull was determined by
placing the skull such that a line passing through the center of the eyes
sockets ran parallel to the floor. Since an infinite number of lines run
through a single point, an anthropologist could essentially place the skull at
whatever angle he preferred. Jhering's system did not allow the measurer
the same liberty in determining the skull's horizontal because, in it, the
horizontal was determined by a line running through two well-defined
points on the skull.[12] The kind of craniometry that Schaaffhausen advocated was a far cry from the classificatory work based on the cephalic index
advocated by most German anthropologists. For Schaaffhausen, "The
skull presents to us a small version of the whole human" and could be used
to make judgments about both the body and the psyche of its possessor.
Prognathism, for Schaaffhausen, represented the most important cultural
indicator provided by the skull: "A prime indicator of the development

[*Bildungsstufe*] of a skull is its prognathism. . . . When the jaws push forward, the forehead remains behind. Where the urge to eat prevails, thinking is less developed. This indicator of low cultural development [*Bildung*] is not made less valuable by the observation that Parisians are also prognathous. A European never exhibits the prognathism of a Negro."[13] What most German anthropologists would have objected to in this statement was not the racism, for few would have disagreed that a "Negro" was less "culturally developed" than a "European." Rather, the element in this passage that contradicted most German anthropology was the assertion that physical anthropological characteristics indicated the psychic properties of races.[14]

That Schaaffhausen was wrong mattered less to most anthropologists than that his methods differed from their own. Rather than excluding Schaaffhausen, anthropologists sought to integrate the eminent craniologist. Schaaffhausen had been placed in charge of cataloging all the skull collections in Germany, and, even as he rendered this valuable service, he made his own scheme more ingrained in the practice of anthropology. To use one of Schaaffhausen's catalogs was to accept, at least as practicable, Schaaffhausen's heterodox craniometric methods.[15] By 1880, the negotiations between Schaaffhausen and mainstream German anthropologists appear to have reached a crisis point. After the particularly tense negotiations at the German Anthropological Society's yearly convention, anthropologists proposed methods that would simply exclude Schaaffhausen from the community of German anthropologists, a proposal that Virchow rejected.[16] They concluded their long afternoon with an amusing performance, a presentation of one of the microcephalic Becker children.[17]

Finally, at the 1883 meeting of the German Anthropological Society in Frankfurt, after more than a decade of attempts, German anthropologists followed Virchow in adopting most of Jhering's method. Johannes Ranke, a leading anthropologist from Munich, had asked Virchow to end the controversy by expounding a craniometric methodology. "We others," he promised, "will then all gladly take your side."[18] Virchow's adaptation of Jhering's craniometric schema, which came to be known as the "Frankfurt Agreement" (Frankfurter Verständigung), recognized Schaaffhausen's "natural" horizontal, but only as a secondary measurement of little significance for the other measurements of the skull; the principal dimension that determined most other measurements was Jhering's, which came to be known as the "German horizontal" (*deutsche Horizontalebene*) (see fig. 4.2).[19] In a ritual perhaps borrowed from the framing of constitutions, anthropologists were asked to sign their names to the text of the Frankfurt Agreement, to signify that they accepted it. To sign the Frankfurt Agree-

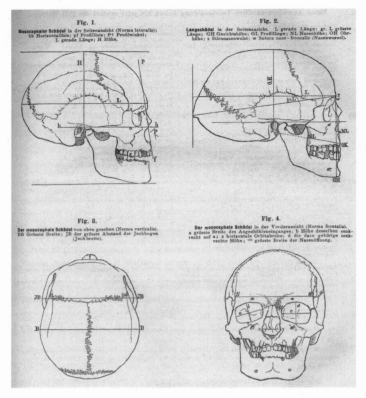

FIGURE   4.2

The Frankfurt Agreement: diagram (*above*) and table (*facing*) explaining the principal dimensions and indices for the skull. The "German" horizontal is the line running above the ear hole and beneath the eye socket, marked "h" on this diagram.

Source: Julius Kollmann, Johannes Ranke, and Rudolf Virchow, "Verständigung über ein gemeinsames craniometrisches Verfahren," *AA* 15 (1884): 1–8.

ment was to affirm one's membership in the community of German anthropologists and to commit oneself to following the methods of that community, even if one personally disagreed with aspects of those methods. Even Schaaffhausen signed the Frankfurt Agreement and thus bound himself to follow a method that was fundamentally at odds with his own theoretical position. German anthropologists were willing to compromise on theoretical questions to get a regular format for their data collecting that would allow them to work together on the great inductive project of anthropological knowledge.

Tabelle der Hauptmaasse und Indices für Schädelmessungen.

Schädel-Nummer	Herkunft, Geschlecht, Alter.	Hirnschädel										Gesichtschädel											Index								Bemerkungen:
		Capacität	Länge	Breite	Stirnbreite	Höhe	Ohrhöhe	Länge der Schädelbasis	Horizontalumfang	Sagittalumfang	Querumfang	Gesichtslänge	Obergesichtshöhe	Gesichtsbreite	Jochbreite	Höhe der Nase	Breite der Nase	Breite der Orbita	Höhe	Länge des Gaumens	Breite	Profilwinkel	Längenbreiten-	Längenhöhen-	Breitenhöhen-	Gesichts-(GH:GB)	Obergesichts-(GH:GB)	Nasen-(NH:NB)	Augenhöhlen-(O₁:O₂)	Gaumen-(G:G')	
		C	L	B	B'	H	OH	LB	U	S	Q	GH	GH'	GB	J	NH	NB	O₁	O₂	G₁	G₂	Pc	LB	LH	BH						

Anthropologists agreed on the German horizontal at Frankfurt also because it unified both a wide range of inquires and a wide range of expertise. The points used to determine the German horizontal, the bottom of the eye socket and the top of the ear hole, were relatively easy to find for those with little training. Furthermore, these points on the skull are covered by very little flesh in the living. The method could, therefore, be used to measure, in Virchow's words, "every head, be it living or dead, be it covered with skin and hair or be it naked." Individuals with access to anatomical collections or dead bodies could measure them, while those who wanted to measure people living around them could also practice craniometry. Virchow admitted that the German horizontal was an arbitrary line and that, "if someone were solely a professor of anthropology," he might want to continue to argue about the best skull measurements. However, the majority of those wishing to conduct craniometric measurements decided simply to settle on a specific scheme and follow it.[20] By choosing the Frankfurt line, German anthropologists defined the boundaries of their own discipline. The community of anthropologists would not consist exclusively of professors of the subject (of which there were, in any case, precious few) but rather would also include amateurs who needed little more than a practical agreement to start working. The Frankfurt Agreement thus represented a commitment among anthropologists to a relatively open discipline and, indeed, by choosing a flexible and easy-to-use method, provided the very basis for this broad community.

The controversy over adopting Schaaffhausen's natural or Jhering's arbitrary horizontal illustrates the mutually constitutive relation among theoretical presuppositions, methodological questions, and social solidarity.[21] By arriving at something as arbitrary, conventional, and apparently uninteresting as the German horizontal, anthropologists not only made a judgment that determined the direction of their inquiries and reinforced an antibiologistic and anti-Darwinist bias in their science but also created a sign of their solidarity. The Frankfurt Agreement both depended on and created a kind of cooperation that anthropology itself in turn both depended on and created. By focusing on their interactions with a single object—the human skull—a group of anthropologists did more than just determine what they could learn from that object and how they could learn it. They also, through their negotiations, forged a community of interpreters. They agreed on a craniometric method that defined a broadly inclusive community of participants. This community constituted itself by making a mutual commitment to working together, a commitment that they later codified in their Frankfurt "constitution."

Anthropologists had to agree on conventional standards, not only for measuring, but also for representing skulls. As one anthropologist wrote, the "tasks of scientific craniometry" were, "on the one hand, to perfect the methods of measurement and, on the other hand, to make the results of these measurements as readily visible [*anschaulich*] as possible."[22] In making these results "readily visible," anthropologists had further to explicate their own understandings about the ways in which they did and should see and about their own roles as natural scientists of humanity. While many anthropologists were avid practitioners of photography, they were skeptical about the realism of photographic representations. They preferred drawing because it avoided what they considered to be the pitfalls of photography. To avoid what they feared would be the arbitrary sketching of objects, they designed machines to automate and standardize aspects of drawing. Their discussions of vision and their technological innovations shed further light on their assumptions about the type of vision that they applied to many areas of anthropological inquiry and about the role of the knowing subject in anthropology.[23]

The methods that anthropologists used to produce what they regarded as realistic images reveal the kind of vision that they hoped to achieve. Anthropologists were anything but naive realists, and their own discussions of representational practices, especially of photography and drawing, provide insight into their understandings of vision and realism.[24] What makes the anthropological aesthetic so interesting is that it rejected a tradition of realism based on linear perspective that emerged in the Renaissance.[25] Drawings based on linear perspective were held to be realistic because they distorted objects in a way supposedly similar to the way the human eye distorts them. They thus represented not only a set of objects but also a vanishing point, which indicated the human perspective from which these objects were seen. Linear perspective was therefore a representation of human vision and an attempt to equate reality with the way humans perceived it.[26] The realism of camera images became a possibility only after pictures with elements such as linear perspective and a uniformly sharp focus were deemed realistic. The camera was designed as an imitation of a type of painting that, through a specific understanding of vision, posited itself as realistic. The introduction of photographic film in the nineteenth century as a means of reproducing images from cameras only further automated the ability of the camera to imitate painting.[27] While photography may have solved the problem of objectivity by making available a mechanical rhetoric for photographic images, it merely continued the problem of the realism of linear perspective.

Anthropologists welcomed photography only cautiously. The most enthusiastic advocate of photography was Gustav Fritsch, who recommended it as a way to overcome the arbitrary nature of artistic representation. Fritsch's competence with the camera was recognized at least since 1869, when he participated as a photographer in an astronomical expedition to Aden. It was partially in recognition of the advantages of having an experienced photographer on the medical faculty that the University of Berlin hired Fritsch as a lecturer in anatomy in 1872.[28] Fritsch hoped that photography would check the "free hand" that had introduced inaccuracies into the representations of earlier anthropologists such as Johann Friedrich Blumenbach.[29] He promised that photography would prevent the kind of gross distortions perpetrated by Ernst Haeckel in his infamous illustration of the progression of the races in his *Die Anthropogenie*.[30]

Anthropologists recommended specific techniques for taking photographs of maximum scientific value. They divided photographs into physical anthropological images, designed to show corporal characteristics, and ethnographic images, which represented the customs of their subjects. Anthropologists wanted measurements of individuals in various photographs that could be compared with each other as well as with measurements taken from living individuals and skeletons. This required precise standardization. In physical anthropological photographs, the subject

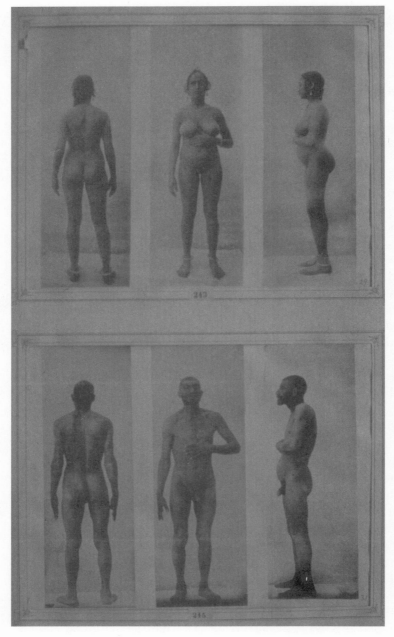

FIGURE 4.3
Anthropological nudes. The pose illustrated in these photographs from the collection of the Berlin Anthropological Society was the preferred stance for anthropological nudes.

should remove as much clothing as possible for photographs in both front and side view. The lighting should be simple and clear, and the subject should stand before a light-colored background so that the outline of the figure appeared clearly (see fig. 4.3). The photographer should make images to a standard scale and take at least one measurement of the subject's body to check the accuracy of the dimensions of the photograph. If such calibration was not possible, the photographer should at least photograph the subject standing next to a ruler. If the photographer wanted to take the whole figure rather than just the face, the subject should stand erect, with one arm hanging naturally and one hand placed with the palm on the center of the torso, just below the chest. In contrast to these physical anthropological images, ethnographic photographs gave the "artistic tendencies of the photographer more room." Ethnographic photographs were not designed to allow physical comparisons among individuals, but rather to represent scenes of daily life and characteristic costumes. Of course even in ethnographic images "artistic tendencies" would be checked by the precision of the camera.[31] Photography thus provided a way to create observations free from the distorting effects of artistry and other arbitrary intrusions of the illustrator into the representation.[32]

The very lack of individual control that made photography a good antidote to art created other representational problems for anthropologists. Anthropologists were well aware of the distortions caused by transforming a three-dimensional, full-size, full-color, real object into a two-dimensional, scaled-down, black-and-white representation (see fig. 4.4). They recognized that the transformation of three dimensions into two caused distortions of scale because portions of an object farther from the camera lens appear smaller in the photograph than do the portions nearer to the lens. Fritsch recommended increasing the distance from the camera to the object and decreasing the opening of the lens to reduce this "perspectival shortening." He recognized, however, that some perspectival shortening would inevitably occur and recommended that photographers familiarize themselves with their lenses so that they would at least be aware of, and could communicate, the extent to which a given photograph suffered from this distortion.[33]

The hand placed just below the chest allowed the viewer to consider the hand shape. The hand left hanging at the side of the subject allows the viewer to consider the length of the arm.
Source: ABGAEU, P. 243, 245. Reproduced courtesy of Berliner Gesellschaft für Anthropologie, Ethnologie und Urgeschichte.

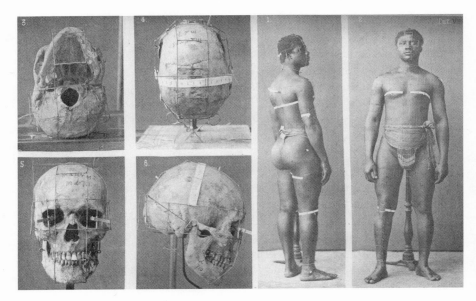

FIGURE   4.4
Wire measuring frames on a skull and on a living person. The Würzburg anthropologist
M. Gottschau proposed using wire frames such as these so that the dimensions of objects
could be determined in photographs despite perspectival distortion. While this method
was never widely used by anthropologists, it does illustrate the problems that they identified with photography and some of the reasons that they normally preferred drawings for
anthropometric purposes.
Source: M. Gottschau, "Neuer Messapparat für photographische Aufnahmen von Leben-
den und von Schädeln oder Skeletten," *AA* 12 (1880): 235–49.

In this early stage of its history, photography did not yet appear as a
perfect, unproblematic rendering of reality. Rather, conventions of viewing
and making photographs were still very much up for grabs.[34] Anthropologists perceived two major problems with photographs. First, variations in
the color of an object often appeared in a photograph as shadows and therefore incorrectly indicated depressions. Thus, for example, a dark spot on a
skull might appear indistinguishable from a shadow caused by a depression in the skull.[35] Second, photographs did not discriminate between relevant and irrelevant detail. Although photographs themselves were poor
means of communicating visual information, an anthropologist could use
them to direct an illustrator to make unambiguous pictures. Fritsch suggested that an anthropologist experienced in viewing photographs inter-
pret an image for an illustrator, who could then draw what the photograph
represented as the anthropologist knew it really to be, rather than as the

photograph rendered it.[36] As Fritsch wrote elsewhere, a good illustrator could learn to make photographs intelligible to lay viewers: "Long observations have taught me that it is in no way easy for all people to see photography correctly [*richtig zu sehen*], in that darknesses caused by certain local tones, especially by yellowish ones, appear to many as the effects of shadows. It requires a certain amount of study to avoid these illusions. A sketch-artist, however, who has worked his way into the 'manner' of photography, finds in [photographs] a quite clear pattern to translate the forms into another, generally understandable mode of representation."[37] In our contemporary, photo-literate society, it is difficult to appreciate Fritsch's concern that the lay could not "see photography correctly." Fritsch warns that the tones reproduced on photographic film cause "illusions" that only those trained in the "'manner' of photography" can see through. Even in the nineteenth century, as the passage from Fritsch illustrates, the realism of photographs was not apparent to audiences untrained in this special type of vision. Photographs were not as widely consumed as drawings, which newspapers and scientific journals used to present realistic illustrations. As Fritsch points out, drawings represent "in a clear manner many of the parts that, in the photograph, are more difficult to see."[38] Drawings, for Fritsch, represented a clearer, more legible, and therefore more realistic medium of illustration than photographs.

Anthropologists generally accepted that drawing, rather than photography, was the most accurate means of representing skulls, precisely because it allowed the expert to control the representation. Photography automated representation so that images were free of much personal influence but at the same time made it difficult for anthropologists to control the representation, to ensure its correspondence to reality. The photographer exercised control over lighting, focus, camera angle, and composition; the illustrator could exercise even more control over the representation and could thus make it more like reality, more realistic. The principal issue about drawing for anthropologists was precisely the type of control that they should exercise over their representations.

One of the most novel proposals was to use drawing machines to standardize much of the discretion of the drawer, the most famous of which was the "Lucaesian apparatus," a device invented by the Frankfurt anthropologist and instrument enthusiast Gustav Lucae (see figs. 4.5 and 4.6).[39] The skull was fixed in relation to a glass plate and viewed through a lens, or diopter. The diopter assured that the anthropologist's gaze always followed a line perpendicular to the glass plate passing through the point that he drew. The skull was drawn in ink directly on the glass plate through which the anthropologist viewed the object. A piece of paper was then pressed to

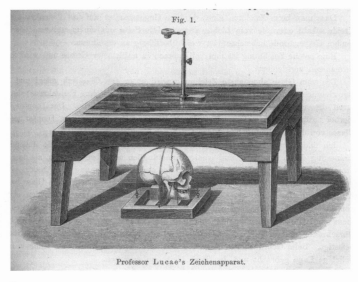

FIGURE 4.5
The Lucaesian apparatus.
Source: Theodor Landzert, "Welche Art bildlicher Darstellung braucht der Naturforscher? Beitrag zur Kenntnis der verschiedenen Darstellungweisen vom Standpunkte
des Naturforschers und Künstlers," *AA* 2 (1867): 1–16, 3.

the glass and the ink transferred onto the paper. Unlike both photographs
and conventionally realistic drawings and paintings, which use a perspectival projection to represent objects as they appear to the human eye, the Lucaesian apparatus produced a geometric projection, in which all points in
the drawing were taken from lines intersecting the plane of representation
at right angles, opposite the object (see figs. 4.7 and 4.8).

The Lucaesian apparatus became the conventional means of craniological representation only after considerable debate among anthropologists. In the late 1860s, before the German and the Berlin Anthropological
Societies were founded, anthropologists debated the advantages of the
kind of geometric projection produced by the device. All agreed on basic
assumptions about geometric and perspectival projections. Humans see the
world not as geometric projections represent it but rather only from a specific perspective, as artists and photographers depict it. Geometric projection represents an object from a moving perspective that is always directly
opposite the point that it draws along a perpendicular line. A perspectival
projection represents every point on an object from a single, stationary
standpoint opposite that object, a point that signifies the eye of the viewer

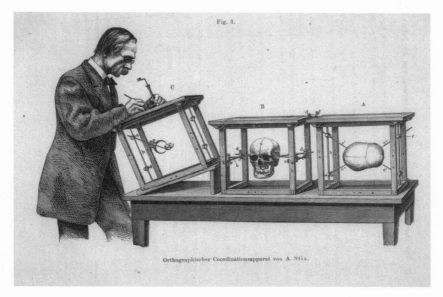

FIGURE   4.6
Using a drawing machine to represent a skull. The illustrator has a small skull, perhaps
from a bird, fixed in a wooden frame. He uses a diopter (held in his left hand) to keep an
exact, perpendicular perspective on the object. He draws the object on a glass plate. The
ink on the glass will then be transferred onto paper. The result will be a geometric projection.
Source: Gustav Lucae, "Noch einiges zum Zeichnen naturhistorischer Gegenstände,"
AA 6 (1873): 1–12, 5.

standing outside the picture (see figs. 4.9 and 4.10). Geometric projections
reproduced the proportions of the outline of the object but did not reproduce how the object appeared to the human eye. Perspectival projections
reproduced how the real object appeared to the human eye but distorted
the dimensions.

When anthropologists resolved this debate in favor of geometric projection, they rejected the privileged role of appearance as a key to reality. As
the advocate of perspectival projection, Hermann Welcker, argued, geometric projection distorted certain aspects of the skull that he deemed significant: "The physiognomy of the skull, like that of the living head, as well
as a good portion of other significant aspects of form, is reproduced in the
most clear and striking way through the kind of projection that painters
have always chosen."[40] Perspectival projections, the technique of artists,
allow people to be represented in pictures as they appear and thus, as
Welcker noted, allow scientists to make physiognomic judgments based

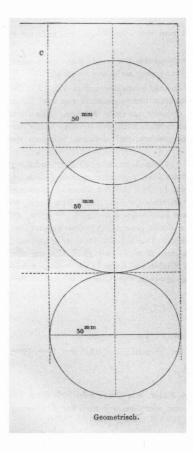

FIGURE 4.7
Geometric projection.
Source: Theodor Landzert, "Welche Art bildlicher
Darstellung braucht der Naturforscher? Beitrag zur
Kenntnis der verschiedenen Darstellungweisen vom
Standpunkte des Naturforschers und Künstlers," *AA*
2 (1867): 1–16, 8.

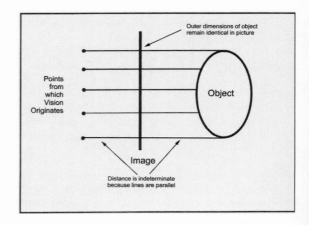

FIGURE 4.8
Geometric projection gives accurate external dimensions and
indicates no position for the
viewer.

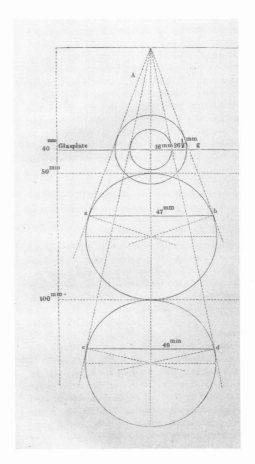

FIGURE   4.9
Perspectival projection.
Source: Theodor Landzert, "Welche Art
bildlicher Darstellung braucht der Natur-
forscher? Beitrag zur Kenntnis der ver-
schiedenen Darstellungweisen vom
Standpunkte des Naturforschers und
Künstlers," *AA* 2 (1867): 1–16, 6.

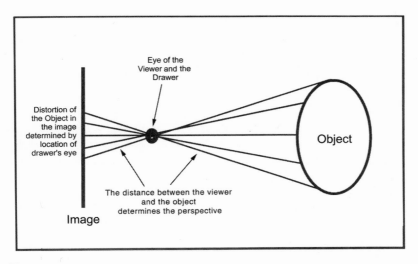

FIGURE   4.10
Perspectival projection distorts the dimensions of an object to a greater extent than geometric projection does and indicates the position of the viewer.

only on visual representations. While anthropologists opposing this artistic type of representation admitted that geometric projection did not reproduce objects the way humans saw them, they held that reproducing the dimensions of a skull was more important than reproducing its appearance.[41] Since anthropologists were especially interested in the so-called cephalic index, which is based on the ratio of the length of a skull to its width, geometric projections from the front and from the side would allow for the most important anthropological measurements. Choosing geometric projection as a mode of representation thus represented a paradoxical loss of realism in the name of exactitude. In the early 1870s, anthropologists settled on geometric over perspectival projection for representing skulls. The Lucaesian apparatus thus became one of the central pieces of anthropological equipment. Even while anthropologists argued about how to measure skulls, they agreed that the Lucaesian apparatus was the best way to draw them.[42] By rejecting perspectival projections in favor of geometric projections, German anthropologists rejected venerable traditions of realism. That anthropologists could regard linear perspective as an aesthetic choice rather than an immutable feature of realism was perhaps enabled by Helmholtz's work on the psychology of spatial perception, especially his argument that the geometry of perception was learned rather than innate.[43] In geometric projection, its proponents believed, things were shown, paradoxically, as they were rather than as they appeared.

Geometric projections, however, not only made drawings that anthropologists could measure, but also helped define the role of the subject in anthropological knowledge. A comparison of figures 4.8 and 4.10 illustrates how the viewer posited by geometric projection and the viewer posited by perspectival projection differ. In perspectival projection, the object is reduced to a single point in either the eye of the illustrator or the lens of the camera and is then reprojected onto a two-dimensional surface. Perspectival distortion transforms the proportions of the object to an extent that varies with the distance of the lens or the viewer from the object. While the relation of the two proportions also varies with the shape of the lens— something that figure 4.10 does not take into account—what is essential here is that the variations in the image and its relation to reality are a function of the perspective of the viewing subject. The picture thus represents, not only an object, but also the specific location of the viewer of that object. It implies the location of an eye and an "I" outside the image, which represents an object and for whom the object is represented. Perspectival projection represents the viewing subject with the viewed object by transforming the appearance of the object to mimic the perspective of the subject.

By contrast, geometric projections do not represent the viewing subject. The points on the image are always directly opposite points on the object; the image represents no viewer's eye or I. The points from which vision emanate could be at any distance from the skull and in any case cannot be unified as a single perspective or subject position. Indeed, a geometric projection can be taken only along a plane opposite its object, not from a single point. Geometric projections show, not things as they appear to the human eye, but rather things in their real proportion, things as, in a purely metric sense, they really are. They achieve this authenticity by dispensing with the subject position given by perspectival projections and having the anthropologist draw as if he were in no specific place. The Lucaesian apparatus allowed the anthropologist to make drawings that did not rely on a human perspective, for geometric projection dispensed with the subject.[44] As Nietzsche would have said: "Here we are asked to think an eye which cannot be thought at all, an eye turned in no direction at all, an eye where the active and interpretative powers are to be suppressed, absent, but through which seeing still becomes a seeing-something, so it is an absurdity and non-concept of eye that is demanded."[45] It is precisely this "non-concept of the eye" that anthropologists produced with the Lucaesian apparatus.

Anthropologists succeeded in grasping their subjects as objects but in doing so had to constrain their own subjectivity within narrow bounds and even, in the case of geometric projections, efface this subjectivity. By *subjectivity* I do not mean anything psychological but rather a specific viewing position that is included in certain types of representation. Anthropologists gained what they regarded as natural scientific objectivity at the price of their own subjectivity. They bound themselves to drawing machines and sought knowledge by becoming a mere appendage to an already-existing material condition of production. The Lucaesian apparatus allowed anthropologists to alienate their vision and to achieve a kind of perspectiveless knowledge. Did they really achieve objectivity? They did achieve a particular optic affect that for them was more true than appearance and allowed them to create a social role fundamentally different from the humanist historian. The anthropologist using the Lucaesian apparatus could not have been more distant from the historian described by Wilhelm von Humboldt: "The more deeply the historian comprehends, through genius and study, humanity and its deeds, or the more humane he is made by his circumstances, and the more purely he lets his own humanity reign, the more completely he fulfills the task of his profession."[46] For Humboldt, history both required and encouraged the humanity and individuality of the scholar, attributes that anthropology sought to efface. Wilhelm Dilthey described humanist modes of knowledge in visual terms that contrast nicely with the practice of the anthropologist when he described knowledge in the humanities as based on "inspired insight" (*geniale Anschauung*).[47] Anthropologists consciously avoided such subjective experience to achieve a new mode of knowledge, the perspectiveless vision that they regarded as a hallmark of natural scientific truth. Anthropology made this erasure of the subject into a basic technique and a technology embodied in the Lucaesian apparatus. In the optics of anthropology we see man—not as object of inquiry but rather as knowing subject—"erased, like a face drawn in sand at the edge of the sea."[48]

Skulls were paradigmatic objects for German anthropologists both because they were perfect examples of the kind of data that they sought in all their studies and because their study required precise standardization. In reaching agreements about apparently mundane issues such as how to measure and how to draw a picture of a skull, anthropologists achieved consensus both about major theoretical issues and about their own social and epistemological identity. When anthropologists signed the Frankfurt Agreement, they obliged themselves to avoid the Darwinian questions of racial hierarchy associated with Schaaffhausen's interest in prognathism. Furthermore, by choosing a horizontal line that was easy to determine on both living humans and bare skulls, they enabled individuals of varying expertise with access to a wide range of anthropological materials to participate in their project. In the Frankfurt Agreement, anthropologists thus determined the direction of their inquiries and defined the social composition of their discipline. When anthropologists agreed to represent skulls using the Lucaesian apparatus, they similarly worked out broad questions both about the nature of truth in their discipline and about the social identity of the anthropologist. Anthropological knowledge would be based not on the common appearance of objects, but rather on knowledge separated from perspective of the individual. The geometric perspective of the Lucaesian apparatus minimized the role of the knowing subject by avoiding the vanishing point of linear perspective. The subject posited by this vanishing point was, not incidentally, itself part of a humanist tradition dating back to the Renaissance and an important feature of the self-understanding of humanist historicism from Humboldt to Dilthey. The Lucaesian apparatus provided an epistemological role for anthropologists radically different from that of the traditional humanities. Their studies of the skull allowed them to escape their own subjectivity and to avoid the subjectivity of the people they studied. Skulls, however, were an easy case for anthropological knowledge. As the epigraph to this chapter indicates, the skull itself had long been a conventional representation of absent subjectivity. Creating antihumanist knowledge that went beyond mere craniometry inspired further flights of the theoretical, social, and technological fancy that marked anthropology in Imperial Germany.

PART II

CHAPTER 5

🔃🔃

A German Republic of Science and a German Idea of Truth: Empiricism and Sociability in Anthropology

Potsherds, bones, glass, and wood—	Scherben, Knochen, Glas und Holz—
We dig them up, and that is good.	Alles buddeln wir mit Stolz
Hurrah, hurrah, hurrah,	Juchheidi, heidi, heida,
Hurrah, hurrah,	Juchheidi, juchheida
Hurrah, hurrah, hurrah,	Juchheidi, heidi, heida,
Hurrah, hurrah!	Juchheidi, heida!
	—"Urfideles Buddellied"

The German Anthropological Society and its local branches were not merely institutions in which anthropologists conducted their new science but also organizations realizing political goals that had been thwarted in the founding of the German Empire in 1871.[1] This was true above all for Rudolf Virchow, the leader of the German and the Berlin Anthropological Societies, who had been directly involved in the Prussian parliament during the constitutional crisis that had defined the structures of German politics in the last third of the nineteenth century. The comparative, empiricist project of anthropology fragmented the autonomous knowing subject and provided an antiauthoritarian model of knowledge and politics. Anthropologists contrasted their own empiricist, social forms of knowledge with what they perceived to be the authoritarian structure of philosophy, in which, they imagined, a lone thinker issued dictates unchecked by facts. A tradition of associating natural scientific empiricism and political liberalism informed the project of the founders of German anthropology. However, the "facts" presupposed by empiricism and the free society presupposed by liberalism are both historically specific cultural constructs based not simply on lofty ideals but also on everyday practices and sociability.[2] The politics of German anthropology consisted not just in ideologies that inhered in the discipline, but also, more importantly, in its construction of new sources of legitimate authority specific to the context of Imperial Germany.

The 1860s must have been disorienting years for Rudolf Virchow. He had been among the liberals who, dissatisfied with the slow pace of administrative reform in Prussia, had founded the German Progressive Party (Deutsche Fortschrittspartei) in 1861. The Progressives hoped to encourage Prince Wilhelm to make the "moral conquests in Germany" of which he had spoken on becoming regent to the Prussian throne in 1858. At the time, such allusions to German unification implied a commitment to liberal reform since creating a national German government would require sweeping away the political and economic systems of the states that made up the German Confederation. In 1862, a year after founding the party, Virchow, along with over one hundred other Progressive deputies, was elected to the Prussian parliament. As the largest party, the Progressives appeared to have brought Prussia to the brink of a republican form of government, which would have had ministers responsible to elected representatives rather than to the king. Wilhelm, by then king of Prussia, briefly considered abdicating. Instead, at the last minute, he appointed Otto von Bismarck minister-president of Prussia to bully the liberal parliament into submission.[3]

On assuming office, Bismarck, as is well known, informed parliament that "the great questions of the day" would not be decided "by speeches and majorities . . . but by iron and blood."[4] In an 1865 attempt to use "iron and blood" to circumvent the routines of parliamentary business, Bismarck challenged Deputy Virchow to a duel. German duelists at this time employed accurate, reliable pistols at close range, which often meant death for at least one of the parties. In parliament, Virchow had accused Bismarck of misrepresenting the truth, and, as was the customary response to such imputations of lying, Bismarck demanded satisfaction from the forty-one-year-old medical school professor.[5] Virchow opted to apologize publicly to Bismarck rather than fight the duel.

In addition to this minor victory by "iron and blood," Bismarck achieved more internationally visible conquests. In 1864, he rallied liberal support by conquering the Danish provinces of Schleswig and Holstein, thus "liberating" the German-speaking populations formerly under the Danish crown. In 1866, Bismarck used the occasion of a war against Austria, Prussia's former ally from the Danish war, to subjugate all Germany militarily. With the help of bribes to local monarchs and assurances that their power would be preserved, he set up the institutional structures of a unified Germany. A final war against France in 1870–71 allowed Bismarck to complete the process of German unification under Prussian domination. By appealing to the nationalism so characteristic of German liberals and the fear of republican forms of government equally characteristic of conservatives, Bismarck managed not only to keep Wilhelm on the throne of Prussia, but also, in 1871, to elevate him to the role of emperor of a unified Germany.

Bismarck's new methods of governing and the splintering of Prussian liberalism after 1866 must have disappointed Deputy Virchow. It was not merely that his party lost the parliamentary majority that it had held a few years earlier but that the meaning of those seats had fundamentally changed. Bismarck had characteristically exaggerated when he remarked that "speeches and majorities" would be replaced by "iron and blood" as a means of government. However, the physical intimidation and humiliation that Virchow had personally suffered as a result of Bismarck's challenge to him could not have made clearer that the Prussian parliament would not be a place where norms of rational discussion would rule. In 1867, Virchow wrote to a fellow medical doctor that, as a result of recent events, he preferred to "work for the future" through science rather than in politics: "I'm not yet sure whether I'll step out of politics altogether or at least for a long time, but I certainly wish to. Since I do not feel any temptation to work for the revolution, I view my role under the government of King Wilhelm as more or less finished. To the National Liberals I am a has-been, and if I must work for the future, I'd rather do it through science than in pseudoparliaments."[6] Virchow never stepped out of politics and continued to represent the Progressives in the Prussian "pseudoparliament" until his death in 1902.[7] He also sat in the Reichstag, the German national parliament, from 1880 to 1893. Virchow's party refused to compromise with the state to the extent that the National Liberals did. At the same time, Virchow was no revolutionary and, with his party, feared socialism as much as absolutism as a threat to the liberal political and economic order that he desired. The Prussian program of modernizing society by persecuting Catholics would, during the 1870s, bind Virchow more firmly to the Prussian state. In these unhappy years before the *Kulturkampf,* however, he redirected his political energies toward founding an anthropological society.

Two years after being humiliated and squeezed out of German politics by Bismarck, Virchow became a virtual Bismarck in the German Anthropological Society. He usually headed, and always at least informally directed, both the German Anthropological Society and its Berlin branch from their founding in 1869 until his death. He created an ersatz Germany in the anthropological society, organized federalistically and dominated from Berlin. The German Anthropological Society even excluded the Viennese branch at least in part because members believed that the German Anthropological Society should follow the German Empire in excluding Austria.[8] Like Bismarck, who combined the offices of minister-president of Prussia and of imperial German chancellor, Virchow lead both the most powerful local anthropological society in Berlin and the national umbrella group.

Virchow's *Reich* was a scientific polity whose political structure was co-produced with its epistemological practices. Anthropologists were committed empiricists, following a tradition of associating empiricism and republicanism that emerged after the English Civil War in the Royal Society. As the great promoter of the Royal Society, Thomas Sprat, had explained in 1667, the empiricist, experimental natural philosophy practiced by the Royal Society allowed for discussions free from the religious and political enthusiasm that had characterized the civil war. By focusing on things rather than on words, by conducting experiments and collecting observations rather than philosophizing or interpreting texts, the society would foster a discourse free from religious and political ideas. The Royal Society offered itself as a model for the rest of English society, demonstrating how one might solve disputes through calm discussion about things rather than through ideological and military combat.[9] "Solutions to the problem of knowledge are," as Steven Shapin and Simon Schaffer put it in their study of Restoration experimentalism, "solutions to the problem of social order."[10] Both knowledge and the social order require specific configurations of authority, legitimacy, and power. Thus, political arrangements imply epistemological arrangements, and epistemological arrangements imply political arrangements. Founding scientific societies has long constituted a response to crises in the political order, from the classic exemplar of Restoration England to Prussia in the 1860s and 1870s.

The tradition of associating republicanism and Baconian empiricism was taken up in the twentieth century by sociologists of science, hoping to find in science a political resource against the challenges of fascism. Baconian science focuses on commonly verifiable data and is relatively modest about proposing theories. It is a type of inquiry often regarded by its practitioners as inductive rather than deductive and is informed by an epistemology fundamentally opposed to theorizing, an epistemology that privileges what its practitioners regard as specifics rather than generalities.[11] The sociologist Joseph Ben-David argued that Baconian science, especially insofar as it differed from philosophical doctrines, allowed for social cohesion among scientists, even in—indeed because of—the absence of widely accepted conclusions: "Baconism . . . opposed . . . a closure of the scientific outlook by creating the blueprint of an ever-expanding and changing, yet regularly functioning scientific community. The experimental doctrine was not a theory, but it was a valid strategy of conduct for scientists. For those who adopted it, it became a medium of unequivocal communication, a way of reasoning and of refutation in limited fields of common interest. By sticking to empirically verified facts (preferably by controlled experiment), the method enabled its practitioners to feel like members of the same 'community,' even in the absence of a commonly accepted theory."[12] For Ben-David, scientific communities are communities not because of shared beliefs or ideas but rather because their members are committed to a method of limited, empirical inquiry.[13] Robert Merton, Edward Shils, and Joseph Needham have all seen in the communication and community required by experimental science a guarantee of democracy. Science would not—these sociologists argued—allow the authority of privileged, esoteric doctrines or of arbitrarily privileged individuals to reign supreme.[14] While sociologists and historians have cast doubt on the extent to which science and democracy actually presuppose each other, the connections between science and democracy have often been important to scientists' own understanding of their enterprise.[15] The German Anthropological Society participated in the tradition of republican Baconism that also includes Sprat, Ben-David, Merton, Shils, and Needham. By eschewing grand theorizing and focusing on what were understood to be the facts, a wide range of anthropological practitioners could organize themselves as a republic of science that fostered democratic participation.

Anthropologists in Imperial Germany were especially radical in their antitheoretical empiricism. They almost never felt that they (or anyone else) had enough of what they recognized as facts to make generalizations with sufficient certainty.[16] This skepticism led anthropologists to withhold definite conclusions about issues ranging from the biological origin of humans to the ethnic composition of the Sudan to the use of rattles among non-European and prehistoric societies. Nothing beyond the most basic there-ness of an empirical observation or an artifact counted as certain anthropological knowledge. Anthropologists went so far as to maintain that they could collect facts without actually producing knowledge. As one anthropologist bluntly put it: "We do not know anything yet, we cannot know anything yet, and are not yet permitted to know anything. . . . To the united natural scientists . . . can simply be reported the facts that we have collected so far."[17] The writer evidently assumed that it was possible to "collect" (*ansammeln*) "facts" and yet not to "know anything" (*gar nichts wissen*). He implied that anthropology consisted of collecting facts that were so free of theory that no prejudice or preunderstanding came into play in data gathering.

Anthropologists presented their radically empirical project as an alternative to philosophy. By *philosophy,* anthropologists meant not a specific philosophical school but rather speculation based on a priori assumptions rather than on what were understood to be facts. In one of the more specific of his numerous denunciations of philosophy, Bastian, for example, criticized Kant's preference for a priori deductions over empirical knowledge. Bastian argued that education and language gave a philosopher so many presuppositions that much of what appeared a priori to him was in fact a posteriori. What philosophers thought must be true about all people, Bastian warned, was often true only about philosophers. Philosophers could not, therefore, use "self-observation" to get to the "roots of the primitive elements" of the human mind. Rather, he wrote, certain knowledge about humans would come only from collecting facts about people from all over the world and especially from "the simplest natural peoples": "Only the facts supplied by ethnology, . . . observations of the simplest natural peoples and their methods of thinking, can provide for an objectively correct relation to this problem [of the 'primitive elements' of thought]. The sooner philosophy decides to use these observations, the better for it."[18] Bastian did not want to invalidate the project of philosophy, which he conceived here as a project of constructing general knowledge about human thought. Rather, he wanted to replace what he viewed as the speculative and introspective methods of philosophy with the empirical, inductive methods of anthropology as well as with anthropology's focus on the supposedly primitive.

Anthropologists employed empiricism not only as a check on their own knowledge but also as a means of criticizing the theories and the knowledge of others. Rudolf Virchow spoke of the "shocking power" (*erschütternde Macht*) of anthropology to undermine both "basic views" and "arbitrary and adventurous speculations, which have done harm not only to science but also to morality."[19] Anthropologists' arguments against Darwinism in the 1870s and 1880s utilized this antispeculative stance, claiming that the "monkey doctrine" (*Affenlehre*) was mere fancy unfounded in empirical reality. Virchow presented anthropologists' critique of Darwinism as a struggle of "serious positive research against merely deductive and speculative construction."[20] In his review of *The Descent of Man,* Bastian dismissed Darwin's theory and proclaimed: "The method of induction has ended the empire of theories."[21] Later, in the 1890s and after, German anthropologists rejected racist anthropologists and fanatics for things Aryan (who were also mostly Darwinists) as similarly unscientific. Thus, in a 1903 German Anthropological Society meeting, when the Germanophilic Ludwig Wilser enthused about the racial characteristics of ancient Teutons, a leading member of that organization was nominated by the rest of his colleagues to "protest publicly against such a lecture, which diminishes the dignity of science." "The lecture," he continued, "was a mass of inaccuracies that could hardly be corrected; it was simply guesses." The chair of the meeting refused to allow Wilser to defend himself against this diatribe, maintaining that such a defense would itself be "too far away from scientific topics."[22] German anthropologists held an extraordinarily modest opinion of the competence of their judgments. Far from being a body of certain knowledge, anthropological science involved collecting facts before which all knowledge appeared uncertain.

As their empiricism weakened the ability of anthropologists (and those against whom they argued) to claim certain knowledge, it strengthened their group cohesion. Baconianism dissolves knowledge as a set of doctrines held by individuals and reconstitutes it as the collective work of a community. Empiricist methods allowed anthropologists working on widely disparate topics to participate in what all regarded as a common enterprise. During a speech to the German Anthropological Society, Wilhelm von Gossler of the Ministry of Culture remarked on the unusually wide range of inquiries that could be united within the discipline: "Graves have been exhumed, caves stripped of their secrets, skulls of the oldest corpses and the youngest newborns completely measured—hardly a Nubian or a Laplander can set foot on German soil without being measured. . . . Distant natural peoples have to report on their sense of color and their propensity to make ceramics. [Prehistoric] reindeer men must tell us about their artifacts, and flint has become an important bearer of culture. Psychology, comparative linguistics, everything is drawn into your efforts."[23] The idea that anthropology brought together disparate studies and disciplines was common even into the twentieth century. Virchow expressed this view well when he wrote that prehistory was not a discipline (*Fach*) but that, "on the contrary, all disciplines participate in it."[24] Not only were studies of physical anthropology, ethnology, and prehistory united in anthropology, but these subdisciplines themselves incorporated numerous natural scientific and humanistic disciplines.

Anthropologists viewed their discipline as a collective project undertaken by people with various levels and types of expertise. They contrasted this aspect of their science with what they held to be the solitary nature of philosophy in order to mount a political critique of philosophizing. They not only rejected the claims of philosophers to knowledge through theorizing but also disparaged what they saw as the individualistic nature of philosophy. Ben-David's view that philosophical doctrines do not promote cooperative work surely would have found sympathy among anthropologists, who often contrasted their own collective methods with the individualist methods of philosophers:[25] "We hope . . . that in philosophy the age of the system will soon be over and that all the men of this discipline will in the future decide to work together [*in Eintracht*] on the same building."[26] The building metaphor in this passage emphasizes the cooperation that anthropologists and others attributed to Baconian science: a building stands as a sign of the collective work of its builders. There were as many systems, anthropologists held, as there were philosophers to produce and defend them. Anthropology represented to its practitioners a single project on which they could all work together. A good example of this type of project is the map that the German Anthropological Society made of the prehistoric sites in Germany. Members from all over the country were asked to report to the society on prehistoric finds in their area. These reports were compiled in a map of all the finds in Germany, which was distributed to all members of the society. Individuals could each contribute a small amount of data, which, by itself, would be insignificant, and receive, in return, valuable knowledge.[27]

This cooperative and accumulative model of knowledge demanded that anthropology enlist a large and diverse range of practitioners. One of the most important avenues of recruitment was through the press. The science reporter for the *Vossische Zeitung,* August Woldt, was a member of the Berlin Anthropological Society and wrote articles that he hoped would increase the popular appeal and the membership of the society.[28] The proceedings of most meetings, if not every one, were published in the *Vossische Zeitung* and, as was then common journalistic practice, were soon reprinted by other newspapers around Germany.[29] The press seems to have agreed with Virchow that popular participation was essential to the practice of anthropology.[30] One paper even encouraged anthropologists to interest farmers in their discipline so that they might acquire valuable prehistoric material plowed up in fields.[31] While the press, perhaps under Woldt's influence, mostly praised anthropology for the broad public participation that it encouraged, there were exceptions. One paper called anthropology a "fashionable science" (*Mode Wissenschaft*) whose amateur practitioners were often gullible victims of scientific hoaxes.[32] As early as

1867, anthropologists worried about what Schaaffhausen called the "comfortable commonplace" that anthropology was little more than an "occupation for dilettantes" that "entertains the curious public with all sorts of human peculiarities."[33] However one evaluated anthropology, it was widely recognized as a science that encouraged and depended on wide public participation.

The popular character of anthropology allowed anthropologists to give their discipline a specifically political interpretation. For Adolf Bastian, the rejection of philosophy as an individualistic and dogmatic mode of knowledge in favor of a collective and empirical, natural scientific mode represented a move toward democracy: "Philosophy (*pasan technēn Sophian* [the art of wisdom]) and natural science . . . stand on the same ground and belong to the same empire. With them the issue is just their methods. Their conflict is thus a constitutional one, about whether the authority of *hate akrotatos ēdē ōn* [the thing that is already the highest], as has been the case, will continue to govern ingrained [*eingelernten*] *progymnasmata* [preparatory exercises], or if the time is now right to allow *self-government* [in English in the original] on the broad basis of natural science."[34] Evidently, Bastian held a view similar to Virchow's of anthropology as a liberal science. For Bastian, philosophy and natural science occupied the same "ground" or "empire": they were competing "constitutional" systems within a single country. Bastian appears to gesture here toward the constitutional conflict of the Prussian parliament with Bismarck and the Hohenzollern monarchy. The resolution of that conflict in the 1866 Indemnity Bill established the subordination of parliament to the monarch and the executive, a solution that Virchow and other Left liberals opposed. Bastian superimposes the opposition between anthropology and philosophy on the Prussian constitutional conflict in order to renegotiate in epistemological terms a political conflict whose outcome was unfavorable to German liberalism.

Philosophy, in Bastian's interpretation, represented monarchical absolutism, the "authority of [the thing that is already the highest]." This view certainly had some basis in the history of academic philosophy in Germany. While, by the time Bastian was writing, history had become the discipline most associated with legitimating ideology for the Prussian monarchic state, before 1840 philosophy had played this role. Hegel and Hegelians at the University of Berlin had supported the Carlsbad decrees of 1819, which had sought to undo the liberalization that had occurred in Prussia and Germany as a result of the occupation by Napoleon's forces and the Prussian reform movement. These Right Hegelians had lent their support to the neoabsolutist state and had benefited from its patronage.[35] Natural sciences, such as anthropology, offered, according to Bastian, an alternative to this rule by "ingrained [preparatory exercises]." Philosophy, Bastian implied, had taken more authority than was warranted and should remain a "preparatory exercise" for other, presumably more valuable, studies. Natural science, by contrast, would provide a "broad basis" for "self-government," a term that Bastian gave in English, likely to indicate his desire for an English- or American-style system with a government responsible to elected officials. This type of government was the hope of the Progressive Party, a hope that had been dashed by the Indemnity Bill. It was disappointment over precisely this issue that had led Virchow to turn to "science" to "work for the future." Bastian apparently held similar hopes for the republic of science represented by the German Anthropological Society.

An organic connection between empiricism and republicanism held great appeal to German anthropologists, just as it did to the founders of the Royal Society and to twentieth-century sociologists of science. However, there is far more, theoretically, epistemologically, and socially, to this Baconian science than democracy and cooperation based on empiricism. Absolute empiricism would be an impossible mode of knowledge for any community. The antitheoretical empiricism advocated by anthropologists would preclude any kind of inferential knowledge and, indeed, perhaps even the possibility of language itself. In its most extreme form, empiricism would require that objects be referred to only with specific proper names since even the theoretical work necessary to refer to types of things would be discounted. The inductive definition of a word would always be deferred since its definition would have to await its last use. Bastian, for example, criticizing Kant's argument that time is an a priori concept, presented such a radical theory of language, maintaining that humans learn language only through inductive inference from empirical observations of the world: "The concept of time appears in humans like every other concept does. The concept of the tree comes from the trees that one sees, the concept of color comes from the various colors, and so forth."[36] If this were the case, then one would have to see, for example, every tree or every color before one could properly use the concept *tree* or *color*. An accurate language would be possible only after an impossible amount of experience. Bastian made precisely this argument in his methodological call for a "natural system in ethnology."[37] He asserted that there would never be an accurate classification of ethnic groups until anatomical, psychological, and social data about all societies on the planet had been collected and compared. Until a perfectly referential language had been achieved through such a massive induction, Bastian maintained, people could speak only an inaccurate language that would not allow for certain knowledge.[38] In this radically empiricist understanding, knowledge remained unstable since even the secure connection between words and things would be deferred until the last thing was known. This presented an epistemological catch-22: one would have to have a perfect language to have knowledge, but to have a perfect language one would have to know everything already. If this empiricism really accounted for anthropological practice, then anthropologists would hardly have been able to use language: the theorizing involved in giving a thing a name, in ordering it in a category, would not have been permitted.

In fact, anthropologists did use concepts despite their unwillingness to account for this theorizing in their self-presentations. Facts could be neither known nor spoken about without theorizing them at least in some crude way.[39] On the most basic level, the presupposition of anthropology, as the name of the discipline itself implied, was the existence of the human as a distinct and unique category. As we have seen, anthropologists rejected Darwinism because it undermined the difference between human and beast; they similarly rejected humanistic modes of knowledge because nineteenth-century German humanism privileged certain humans (especially ancient Greeks and modern Germans) as more nobly human than others. All the modern human sciences presuppose the concept of the human, as Foucault has demonstrated. Ethnology, Foucault argues, deals with "the historical *a priori* of all the sciences of man—those great caesuras, furrows, and dividing-lines which traced man's outline in the Western *episteme* and made him a possible area of knowledge."[40] Anthropology assumed the existence of the human, perhaps at a level far more fundamental than other human sciences.

While more medical anthropologists such as Virchow grounded the unity of the concept of humans biologically, Bastian justified this concept psychologically and idealistically. According to Bastian, all humans embody the same "basic ideas" (*Grundideen*), which are manifested variously among various peoples as "ethnic thoughts" (*Völkergedanken*). Bastian plays on an ambiguity in the word *Idee*. On the one hand, the word can mean "idea" in an ordinary sense: a mental phenomenon that is often a more general version of a "thought" (*Gedanke*). Thus, the transition from specific ethnic thoughts to more general basic ideas initially seems unproblematic. On the other hand, the term *Idee* invokes an idealist tradition that views the idea not as a mental concept, as a general thought, but rather as a form (*eidos*), the ideal reality behind specific appearances. This understanding of the idea became especially important in German philosophy with Hegel as well as in early German natural science with such *Natur-philosophen* as Goethe, Oken, and Schelling. While Bastian's anthropology appears psychologistic because of its references to thoughts and ideas, its resonances with idealism allowed for the study of all human phenomena, including the nonpsychological. By couching his idealism in psychological terms, Bastian presents a rhetorical tool for connecting disparate bits of information about various societies to a unified concept of the human.

Among the supposedly primitive societies that anthropologists studied, ethnic thoughts were, in Bastian's words, the "immediate expression [*Abdruck*] of their geographic province."[41] "Cultural peoples," societies that have developed historically, exhibited, according to Bastian, less clear relations between their geographic province and their ethnic thoughts. Furthermore, the ethnic thoughts of cultural peoples had more obscure relations to the basic ideas common to all humanity. According to Bastian, anthropology should exhaustively study all natural peoples to understand their ethnic thoughts. These ethnic thoughts could themselves in turn be interpreted to grasp the basic ideas of which they were a manifestation.[42] These basic ideas were common to all humanity, both cultural peoples and natural peoples. The presupposition of the existence of an eventually knowable essence common to all humanity, as well as the presupposition of the physical unity of humans, underwrote the anthropological project and guaranteed that all the details collected by individual anthropologists could be understood as parts of a meaningful whole.

This understanding of the human as a unified concept behind all anthropological facts allowed for a practical hermeneutics in which various members could work together on a common problem by presenting empirical data deemed relevant to it. For example, after an 1872 lecture on prehistoric artifacts found outside Berlin, discussion among members of the Berlin Anthropological Society turned to what appeared to be a rattle. One member, the *Gymnasium* director Wilhelm Schwartz, assumed that it was a toy since that was the European use for rattles. Bastian pointed out that rattles were not always used simply as toys and that, among the Egyptians and the indigenous populations of Brazil and Australia, rattles had ritual significance. Schwartz countered that the small size of the particular rattle in question indicated that it had been used as a toy. Another member added that, in children's graves in Greece, one often found rattles in the shape of deer, pigs, and other animals, thus supporting Schwartz's claim that rattles were toys rather than Bastian's claim that they were religious objects. Bastian retorted that their presence in children's graves did not prove that the rattle in question was a toy rather than a religious object since the Eskimos put dog skulls in children's graves. Bastian reckoned that dog skulls were not used as toys but were intended to guard the dead child. Instead of the issue developing into a scientific duel between Bastian and Schwartz, a third member interjected that the rattles might be neither religious objects nor toys and that the natives of Siberia, with whom he was familiar, used rattles to drive their sled dogs. The controversy did not continue, and, as in countless other similar episodes, the society simply moved on to its next topic.[43]

All discussants evidently assumed that a rattle possessed a single universal function apart from its individual applications among various peoples but that these applications were the only way to understand this universal function. Thus, what native Siberians did with rattles shed light on what Greeks, Brazilians, Egyptians, Australians, and prehistoric Germans did with rattles. The assumption of the homogeneity of the human was not just some vague monogenetic intuition but rather a real belief that all humans were the same in very specific ways—even in their use of rattles. Equally noteworthy is that the contemporary European use of rattles as children's toys, which clearly informed Schwartz's initial interpretation, had no bearing on the universal function of rattles. As highly developed cultural peoples, contemporary Europeans were less significant than primitive natural peoples, who displayed most immediately the basic ideas of humanity. Finally, understanding the basic idea of a rattle amounted to more than just an exercise in induction. Rather, if anthropologists could grasp what a rattle was for various natural people, then they could extend this knowledge to what a rattle was for a long-extinct natural people, the ancient Germans whose rattle had initiated the discussion. This discussion presupposed the possibility that one could say something about rattles in general, a possibility grounded on an understanding of the human as a unified idea. Such a concept of the human thus provided a theoretical ground for the empiricism of German anthropology.

Clearly, Baconianism, understood as an empirical, inductive approach to knowledge, does not adequately characterize the activities of German anthropologists. Susan Cannon has encouraged historians of nineteenth-century science to drop the concept of Baconian science in favor of that of Humboldtian science.[44] By this shift in terms, Cannon indicates that nineteenth-century empiricist scientists, even those who themselves believed that they were following Baconian methods, were doing more than mindlessly collecting facts and were doing so not simply because they were amateurs inept at mathematics or other, more theoretical, pursuits. Rather, these scientists followed the model established by Alexander von Humboldt in his journey to South America. Humboldt, Cannon points out, did not go to South America to make uninformed empirical observations: explorers had, after all, done that already. Rather, Humboldt explicitly differentiated himself from these earlier explorers, distinguishing himself as a "scientific traveler." Humboldt was interested not simply in facts but rather in facts measured and recorded in such a way that they could be compared and that theories could emerge from them. Cannon thus rightly points out that even—or perhaps above all—nineteenth-century empiricists had to worry about method and concern themselves with the theory that their enterprises were meant to produce.

Humboldt's distinction, however, between the irregular observations of the explorer and his own scientific observations obscures the most basic problem of empiricism: the facts themselves. No example better illustrates the problematic nature of facts than the debates around standardizing craniometry discussed in the previous chapter. The point of those discussions was that how one determined facts (in that case, the significant dimensions of a skull, especially its horizontal) both presupposed and reinforced conceptions of science and of the community of scientists. For the "German horizontal" to become an empirical fact, anthropologists had to agree that questions of prognathism, evolution, and racial hierarchy were irrelevant to their science. The horizontal itself also implied a wide community of practitioners since it was relatively easy to determine and could be found on living humans as well as on skulls. Accounts of Baconianism or Humboldtianism that presuppose the existence of facts and then proceed to analyze a method and sometimes its social or political implications are starting from the wrong end. The case of German craniometry suggests that accounts of Baconianism such as Ben-David's, or Virchow's and Bastian's, do not give adequate attention to the mutually constitutive relation of facts and sociability. These accounts argue that "sticking to the facts" allows for community consensus and cohesion. However, at the same time, community cohesion allows for people to agree on a specific identification of the facts. The appearance of sticking to the facts is both artifact and precondition of the cohesive community of Baconian or Humboldtian science. It is not merely that facts are pretheorized but also that they are presocialized, that they are the product of a definite social organization. Not only does sticking to the facts allow for social consensus, but social consensus also allows for facts—to which the community is therefore already stuck.

The scientific practice and the forms of truth of German anthropology depended on specific traditions of sociability available in Germany in the nineteenth century. If the characteristic middle-class public institution was in England the coffeehouse and in France the salon, in Germany the voluntary association (*Verein*) provided the central institution of the public sphere. At least since the eighteenth century, middle-class German men had organized themselves into clubs for various purposes. Some of the most popular types of associations were for gymnastics and sharpshooting, although clubs could also be organized around more intellectual pursuits, from butterfly collecting to studying anthropology. As Thomas Nipperdey has argued, these associations played a triple role in the history of the German bourgeoisie. First, they allowed the bourgeoisie, freed from the feudal society of orders, to organize and mobilize itself. Second, associations both helped the process of specialization and professionalization in bourgeois society and prevented this specialization from leading to social fragmentation. Finally, associations represented a forum in which bourgeois society could challenge the aristocratic state and an organization that could compete with the state in matters of authority and ideology.[45]

Club members often conceived of their organizations as republics in miniature.[46] After 1848, and to an even greater extent after 1871, the German bourgeoisie and their associations became less revolutionary and more patriotic. Indeed, in the 1880s and after, many associations became important forums in which bourgeois nationalism asserted itself. In his account of the Pan-German League, Roger Chickering shows the important role that middle-class rituals of masculine solidarity—drinking, making toasts, and singing—played in constructing socially unified political organizations and a basis for promoting new forms of German nationalism.[47] The experience of being a bourgeois male member of German political society took place in, and took its structure from, these organizations. While one could surely find similar types of associational life in Britain, France, or nearly anywhere else, the political nature of clubs and the clubby nature of politics was perhaps unique in Germany. Clubs might become explicitly political, as in 1848, when so many participated in the revolution, or in the 1880s and after, when large pressure groups pushed German policy toward a militarist, right-wing fervor. They also could be only implicitly political, as was the case with the anthropological societies in Germany.

This type of German associational life made possible and sustained epistemological forms of German anthropology.[48] The empiricism that characterized the practice of anthropology in Germany, where socially produced facts were collected and contributed to a common pool without being used by individuals as raw material for knowledge, mirrored the associational life of anthropologists. No anthropologist could know anything without taking part in a community of anthropologists whose collective knowledge made sense only in terms of its socially embodied entirety. If German anthropology was a republic of science, then it was a peculiarly German republic of science whose inhabitants appeared neither as autonomous individuals nor as political parties representing individual interests but rather as mass associations that coordinated individuals in a common project.[49] The republic of science for anthropology was based not on the equality of humans before the truth of nature but rather on the coordination of humans with the goal of producing truth.

This coordination was achieved in large part through quite ordinary clubby sociability. This ranged from large, raucous celebrations to more ordinary social events (see fig. 5.1). Members of the German Anthropological Society belted out songs such as the one that forms the epigraph of this chapter during meals, outings, and other revelries at their annual conferences.[50] Members strove to be as cordial and sociable as possible, making numerous toasts, and drinking prodigious quantities.[51] Excursions, usually to a local archaeological site, formed the social centerpiece of the meetings for members and their spouses. A day trip to an ancient Roman burial site during the 1889 Mainz festival, for example, began with a journey down the Rhine aboard a festively decorated steamship. The conferees brought along a small canon, from which they fired blanks, and they were entertained by a brass band, which they had hired for the duration of the conference. When the boat docked at a town near the dig site, the mayor met the anthropologists on the shore to deliver a welcoming address. The anthropologists completed the final half mile to the site in a procession led by the band, trailed by curious villagers. When nothing spectacular or supernatural emerged from the graves, the inquisitive villagers wandered away, disappointed. Before steaming back to Mainz, the conferees held another feast. During the return trip, fireworks were shot from the banks, while anthropologists cheered and returned fire from the ship's cannon. The Berlin branch of the society similarly, if less extravagantly, undertook excursions several times a year and made a point of socializing after each of their monthly meetings over food and drink at a nearby restaurant (see fig. 5.2).[52]

The sociability of German anthropologists rested on an understanding of themselves as an exclusively male leisure organization, that is, as a typical German club. The following song from an 1892 German Anthropological Society meeting, in which the singers imagine that they are prehistoric men, reveals much about anthropologists' understandings of gender, science, and sociability:

FIGURE 5.1

Flyer for the 1880 German Anthropological Society meeting in Berlin. Represented, roughly from top to bottom, are the following: Adolf Bastian is seated in the clouds; Ernst Friedel, director of the Berlin Provincial Museum, offers tea to the Berlin bear; an anthropologist, possibly Rudolf Virchow, measures a skull; another examines the tail of a possible missing link; a linguistically inclined colleague consults a "Nubian Lexicon" with a horseman; Hermann Schaaffhausen balances a monkey on his chin; and Heinrich Schliemann runs away in the lower left corner. The whole scene is illuminated by the figure of Germania. This combination of the carnivalesque and the patriotic characterized German anthropology in this period.

Source: ABGAEU. Reproduced courtesy of Berliner Gesellschaft für Anthropologie, Ethnologie und Urgeschichte.

FIGURE   5.2
Outing of the Berlin Anthropological Society in 1885. Virchow leans against the tree, wearing a straw hat.
Source: ABGAEU, P. 2079. Reproduced courtesy of Berliner Gesellschaft für Anthropologie, Ethnologie und Urgeschichte.

Toil and sweat didn't plague my life,	Von Arbeit war ein Freund ich nicht,
I left that to my loyal wife.	Die war des braven Weibes Pflicht.
I lay about on cave bear fur,	Ich lag meist auf der Bärenhaut
Drinking beer that was brewed by her.	Und trank das Bier, das sie gebraut.
From bison horns I gulped my brew,	Trank süssen Meth aus Büffelhorn
An old school man, tried and true.	Als Mann von altem Schrott und Korn.[53]

While the humor of the song rests on the dissonance between the modern, cultivated singer and the crude caveman narrator, the song also invites identification between the two. The imaginary exclusion of women from anthropology was quite serious, and such songs would have reminded the husbands and wives attending the banquet of the special, excluded status of women in the society. Anthropologists were expected to bring their wives to the meetings, and the festive banquets always included an extended toast "to the ladies." The songs, however, do not allow for a female singer. Thus, in a room full of both men and women, the male anthropologists would sing songs while their wives listened and watched. These songs reaffirmed the solidarity on which their science depended, a solidarity based on traditions of German masculinity and male bonding. Furthermore, like the caveman narrator, the anthropologists self-consciously disassociated their roles from work. Anthropology at this time was a leisure pursuit, one carried out in the inclusive and sociable atmosphere of clubs rather than in the exclusive atmosphere of the professional workplace. Anthropologists thus emphasized their sociability, which demanded that they follow prehistoric men in considering their activity a masculine leisure pursuit.

This self-conception of anthropologists as exclusively male is particularly striking because anthropologists were not exclusively male. It is not clear, for example, what Johanna Mestorf, one of the most important German experts in prehistory, did during these songs. Johanna Mestorf (1829–1909) was born in the Danish and German duchy of Schleswig-Holstein before it was annexed by Prussia. She had been involved in the discipline of anthropology at least since 1871, and her ability to speak Danish and Swedish gave her additional expertise on developments in Scandinavian prehistoric archaeology. By 1880, she had become a director of the prehistory museum in Kiel, and, in 1899, she became the first woman in Germany to receive the title *professor*. She advised both Virchow and the Ministry of Culture on employment decisions for the Royal Museum of Ethnology. Virchow and other anthropologists considered her help necessary for setting up an 1880 Berlin prehistory exhibition and persuaded the minister of culture to grant her an extended leave of absence from her position in Kiel for this purpose.[54] Mestorf was probably as successful as a woman could be in the sciences in nineteenth-century Germany. While she surely was not allowed to play as active a role as she would have had she been a man, she also was central enough to German anthropology at a time when women were regularly excluded from science that the male identity presented by German anthropology cannot be viewed as a mere reflection of reality.

The spouse of the Berlin anthropologist Felix von Luschan, Emma von Hochstetter, was another woman who participated in German anthropology. At a time when women were routinely excluded from universities, she managed to obtain an informal education in natural science, probably from her father, the great Viennese naturalist Ferdinand von Hochstetter. Despite contemporary beliefs about the danger to women of traveling outside Europe, Hochstetter accompanied her husband on his travels and contributed significantly to his photographic and anthropometric work. Although she did not appear as the author of any anthropological publications and Luschan always presented her contributions simply as menial, although useful, assistance, it is clear from Luschan's own descriptions that Hochstetter did significant anthropological work.[55] While Johanna Mestorf and Emma von Hochstetter are the only two women whose participation in nineteenth-century German anthropology has left traces, there likely were others. Still, anthropologists imagined their society as a masculine club. By explicitly gendering their identity, they were able to use models of social interaction conventional in Germany to sustain the scientific interaction that their discipline required.

Virchow used the homosocial identity of the anthropological society to recast it as a republic of science. Just as French revolutionary republicanism had depended on images of manly virtue and self-government by men, so too did Virchow imagine German anthropology as a masculine republic.[56] For Virchow, this republicanism evidently implied consensus as much as diversity of opinion:

> The men who are interested in the many varieties of anthropological projects belong to such varying social groups [*Gesellschaftskreise*], so many different political parties, so many different religions and confessions, that if one wanted to focus on these aspects one could organize permanent war in the society. We have managed never to have such a war. The aristocrats and the democrats, the blacks [Catholics] and the reds [socialists], have all remained equally peaceful under our banner. They have always pursued only those tasks that interested the whole society. We have set ourselves up quite convivially [*menschlich*]: that I can say with complete certainty.[57]

In the craniometric controversies and their resolution we saw how social unity among scientists (the assumption that they should work together despite intellectual differences) led to scientific agreement (the ratification of the Frankfurt Agreement). Virchow suggests that scientific agreement on the common pursuit of anthropology led to social and political concord, the ability of the whole political spectrum in Germany to put aside their differences and work together.

Anthropologists regarded the state as a guarantor of the social order that was fundamental to their scientific practice. The idea that the state guaranteed the freedom of civil society, rather than being an institution from which civil society had to be protected, rests on long-standing traditions of German liberal theory.[58] In the 1880s, the Berlin Anthropological Society made itself a juristic person, a social body recognized by the state as having a legal existence apart from its individual members. Becoming a juristic person meant that the library, the photography collection, and the funds of the society were owned by the group itself rather than by the persons who composed that group.[59] Berlin anthropologists attempted to increase the involvement of the state in their organization to make permanent the social organization that they had until then founded on an informal, interpersonal basis. Bastian explained that "the state affords in its institutions a permanent guarantee of the kind that could not be offered in fluctuating societies with changing leadership."[60] The state, for Bastian, was a system of stable institutions, which themselves functioned as a source of stability in human affairs and supplied a secure basis for the reproduction of the social practices of anthropology.

The concept of truth acted as a further check on the caprice of the individual members of the society. This was recognized explicitly by the Prussian police when they considered an application by the Berlin Anthropological Society to become what was known as a "juristic person." A juristic person was a social body having a legal existence apart from its individual members so that, in the case of the anthropological society, it could hold its library, collections, and funds as group rather than as individual property. There was initially some concern about granting the status of a juristic person to a group that did not have a property restriction for voting members. In the end, however, the police decided that such formal limitations of the franchise were unnecessary in a scientific society because science itself appeared as an authority independent of, and having precedence over, the will of individual members.[61] Thus, the statutes of the German Anthropological Society, which all its local chapters were also obliged to follow, cautioned that, although members elected their leaders, "scientific questions cannot be decided by voting."[62] Virchow himself seems to have viewed expert knowledge as a legitimate check on democracy. For example, when the Prussian parliament had to select a sewage system for Berlin, Virchow argued that an expert commission rather than a vote of the representatives should determine the outcome.[63] He also advocated forbidding the teaching of Darwinism in secondary schools, which he regarded as a "too broad use of the freedom" that the sciences had achieved in Germany in the nineteenth century. Not only, Virchow warned, was Darwinism an unscientific hypothesis, but it also encouraged socialism.[64] Virchow viewed science in this case as a check on the freedom of opinion and as a defender of the political status quo, especially against socialism and Darwinism.

In anthropology meetings, there always existed a sharp distinction between people recognized as experts, with a right to speak on scientific questions, and laypeople, who could elect the leadership of the society and contribute empirical data but not participate in deciding scientific questions. When theoretical disputes arose in the otherwise Baconian discussions in anthropology society meetings, the leaders would appoint a commission of experts to decide the issue without democratic influence. This occurred, for example, in 1879, when the Berlin society received a package of fossil bones from northern Germany relevant to the question of the antiquity of humans in Europe. The bones were found near prehistoric artifacts, and several bore traces of having been used as tools by humans. These artifacts suggested that humans inhabited northern Germany at a time much earlier than had previously been thought. The interpretation of these bones thus had serious consequences for the future study of prehistory. Instead of openly discussing the issue, the society appointed an expert commission, made up of Virchow and other leading anthropologists. The commission met in private and reported to the whole society the following month, announcing that the find did indeed indicate evidence that humans lived in Germany at the time of prehistoric mammals. The membership seems to have accepted this expert report, which thereby became scientific knowledge, a truth claim both supported by and making sense of conventionally agreed on facts. In this case, there did not occur the kind of democratic Baconian inquiry that characterized so many of the public discussions in the Berlin Anthropological Society. When a commission of experts made decisions, these seem to have been accorded a level of certainty usually unattainable in public meetings. Speaking in the third person, as "die Commission," the esoteric group had a kind of authority that no member speaking in the first person in a public meeting ever had.[65] Experts produced knowledge that checked the opinions and actions of all. Their authority was therefore simultaneously scientific and social.

There were two factors allowing for the appearance of unproblematic and untheorized facts in German anthropology. One of these factors was a theoretical presupposition, the concept of the human, that gave meaning and purpose to the detailed work of anthropology, that transformed acts such as digging, collecting, sorting, and reporting into "induction" or "data gathering." The other factor was a broad sociability common to German bourgeois male society. This sociability created the solidarity that any notion of unproblematic facts presupposes. The operations of the "Commission," the social embodiment of the theory underwriting empirical anthropology, suggest that these two factors were in fact part of a single, social, whole. As the sociability rested on relations of homosocial republican equality within the society, the theoretical foundation rested on authoritarian relations between the experts in the society and the rank-and-file members. Rank-and-

file members could not successfully propose theories; they could only collect and present facts, which the society would eventually, it was claimed,
combine to inductively derive theories. This exoteric uncertainty contrasted sharply with the certainty that elite members of the society could
achieve esoterically, when they formed private *Commissionen,* whose discussions were not reported in the society's *Transactions.* The esoteric elite
spoke as an impersonal authority when they reported their findings to the
entire society. Indeed, despite the democratic and broadly participatory
impulse in much of the institutionalization of anthropology, there existed
also a strong elitism among many leading German anthropologists. For
example, one anthropologist suggested to Virchow, who usually chaired
German Anthropological Society meetings, that, when there were no specialists (*Fachmänner*) present at a meeting, discussion should be prevented.
Without the specialists, the anthropologist wrote, the society was no more
than a group of *Dilettanten* whose discussions were "only a waste of
time."[66]

As most anthropologists were aware, this combination of expert and
amateur in anthropology gave the discipline its unique character. Some
outside observers even ridiculed anthropology because of its popular and
dilettantish character.[67] While anthropologists themselves distinguished
between *Dilettanten* and *Fachmänner,* they saw an important role for both.
The *Fachmänner,* they believed, should guide the *Dilettanten,* who would
participate by collecting anthropological knowledge.[68] Bastian revealed
his view of the relation between expert and lay anthropologists when rejecting an article for publication that he considered too theoretical: "My ob-
jections [to publishing the article] spring from the view that such general
conjectures (which in oral presentations are justified and can be clarified
. . .) become, when published, disproportionately valued and thereby mislead the eyes of the laypeople. . . . Objective research is hindered when one
privileges a single direction over many possible others by giving it general
attention. . . . It would be . . . a shame to cut short the many interesting contributions that could eventually be won through objective observation by
one-sidedly favoring a specific approach."[69] Public discussions, Bastian
suggested, had protocols of knowledge and authority different from those
of published journal articles. Public assertions were subject to the qualifica-
tions of all present and thus, Bastian reckoned, could not favor certain di-
rections for research or shut out others. Public lectures, as we have seen,
provided an occasion for members to contribute details, and, indeed, as
Bastian elsewhere observed, the discussions after the lectures were more
important than the lectures themselves.[70] Published articles, on the other
hand, stood as fairly solid truths, at least for the lay members. If Bastian and

others were to continue to encourage the "eyes of the laypeople" to focus on as wide a spectrum of "objective observations" as possible, then they had to avoid shutting off valuable discussions by publishing premature conclusions.[71] *Fachmänner* could produce knowledge or theory, while *Dilettanten* could contribute only what were commonly regarded as facts.

Anthropologists broke apart knowledge as an individual cognitive project so that they might reconstruct it in a collectivity, embodied not in any single person but rather in the social body of the voluntary association. They understood truth not as the outcome of rational debate among individuals but rather as the product of the coordinated interaction of the group. While many imagined this group as a democratic republic of science, it rested on a collective epistemological and social subordination of *Dilettanten* to *Fachmänner*. The practice of anthropology was understood as a collective working toward the truth. In reality, the truths accepted by anthropologists were not the products of democratic Baconian empiricism but rather the conclusions of esoteric and impersonal *Commissionen*. Truth thus acted as a check on the freedom of individuals. This notion of truth as an authority reflected the peculiarities of nineteenth-century German liberalism, which rested not on the freedom of the individual against the state, but rather on the freedom of the individual created and protected by the state. The homosocial rituals of German voluntary associations rested as much on the controlled unity of group songs as on the individualism of open debates. Perhaps, as Ralf Dahrendorf has suggested, one can speak of national styles of truth, much as one can speak of national styles of liberalism. In any case, anthropology offered itself as a social and scientific form that participated in the development of a political culture in Imperial Germany.

CHAPTER 6

⧓

Anthropological Patriotism: The *Schulstatistik* and the Racial Composition of Germany

In addition to presenting a model for political and intellectual culture in the *Kaiserreich,* anthropology contributed to a reconstruction of German nationalism. In the 1870s, the German Anthropological Society persuaded the German states to record the hair, eye, and skin color of over 6 million German schoolchildren to determine the fate of the fair-skinned, blond, blue-eyed "classic Teutons" (*classische Erscheinungen des Germanen*) described by Tacitus and the origins of the brown-skinned, brown-haired, brown-eyed individuals who had become so preponderant in Germany.[1] The survey produced important anthropological knowledge about the nation, particularly that Germans were a blond, blue-eyed, and white-skinned "race," which was contrasted to brunet "races," particularly Jews. Perhaps even more importantly, it taught the more than 6 million students whom it studied, as well as the teachers who collected the data, that Germanness could be perceived through "racial" characteristics that were publicly perceivable by any layperson. Anthropologists thus made their notions of race, which they had developed in studies of non-Europeans, relevant also to European identity. Instead of Humboldt's nation of scholars or Fichte's linguistic notion of Germanness, anthropologists disseminated a biological national identity, one that would have momentous importance for subsequent developments in German history.[2]

Rudolf Virchow headed the commission in charge of what was initially conceived as a "statistical study of skull form in all of Germany."[3] The focus on skull form soon had to be abandoned, however, because anthropologists wanted to conduct the survey on a scale so grand that they would have to rely on totally untrained observers to collect data. They hoped to get schoolteachers to survey their pupils and military officers to survey new recruits. While anthropologists had formulated craniometric procedures that they thought would be suitable for amateurs, they evidently did not trust the thousands of teachers and officers who would carry out this survey to measure skulls accurately. Instead of craniometric dimensions, anthropologists decided to consider, in Virchow's words, some "external characteristics of living humans" that untrained observers could measure.[4] The commission settled on eye, hair, and skin color as such "external characteristics." Instead of dividing Germans into dolichocephalic and brachycephalic groups, German anthropologists intended to use these color data to divide them into a "blond type" (der blonde Typus) and a "brunet type" (der brünette Typus).[5]

The German Anthropological Society did not merely want disaggregated numbers of, for example, how many pairs of blue eyes or how many heads of blond hair existed in a given region. Anthropologists wanted to determine the distribution of various combinations of hair, eye, and skin color because they associated these combinations with racial types. They held that there were just two pure physical types and that all others were a mixture of these two types. One of these pure types, they assumed, was the blond type, the classic Teutons described by Tacitus, with blond hair, blue eyes, and white skin.[6] The other type, the brunet type, they seem to have derived simply by taking the opposite of the blond type: the brunet type had brown hair, brown eyes, and brown skin. All other combinations of hair, eye, and skin color, anthropologists argued, resulted from various mixtures of the two pure types. The blond type was associated with the "German race" and the brown type with a number of other races, including Czechs, Walloons, Slavs, Franks, and, most importantly for the present discussion, Jews. Thus, while not themselves races, blond and brown types were the physical markers that defined the races inhabiting Germany. By grouping their color data to reflect the distribution of two distinct types, anthropologists ensured that their study would produce information analogous to more esoteric studies of the distribution of dolichocephaly and brachycephaly.[7]

Although these race-defining types were named by hair color—blond and brunet—the architects of the study associated them with skin color, white or brown. They valued data on eye and hair color because "the color of the hair and the eyes stands in a certain relation" to the color of the skin. The color of the skin, they now argued, constituted a racial marker and thus corresponded more directly than eye or hair color to skull form, the true racial marker. Skin color, anthropologists admitted, would be difficult to measure accurately since, to the untrained eye, Germans had more or less the same skin color. They asked for data on eye and hair color because they perceived a strong correlation between these more easily differentiable colors and skin color. Thus, they included in the pure brunet type those Germans reported to have brown eyes, brown hair, and white skin since they assumed that the untrained data collector had mistakenly recorded brown skin as white. Anthropologists hoped that this notion of race based on skin color would ultimately correlate with notions of race based on skull form, although they left this final correlation to an unspecified future date.[8]

An assumption of racial difference between non-Jewish and Jewish Germans was incorporated into the study almost from the beginning. When Virchow proposed the method of the study at the society's yearly congress in 1873, a member, whose name has not been recorded, called out: "Herr Dr. Virchow will perhaps also have the confession [of the subjects] recorded. There are many regions with a large population of Jews, and the data from these regions would lead to false conclusions."[9] Members of the assembly agreed that Jewish subjects could distort the data about "German" racial characteristics, and, by the next meeting, Virchow had adjusted his methodology accordingly.[10] Unlike foreign populations living in Germany, such as those of French or English descent, who were excluded from the survey altogether, racial data were to be taken from Jews and listed separately. Virchow had initially decided to record the confession of every subject but was reportedly accused in the press of wanting to use such data to begin an "inquisition" against Catholics. Virchow's interest in confession must have seemed particularly ominous to Catholics because of his prominent support for the anti-Catholic *Kulturkampf*.[11]

A well-known opponent of political anti-Semitism, Virchow maintained that his separate tabulation of racial data about Jews did not constitute a negative evaluation of that group.[12] He separated Jews from Germans in the study not for religious considerations, he offered, but rather because Jews belong, "according to their origin, to a different nation." Thus, Virchow explained, he was not carrying out a new anti-Semitic "inquisition."[13] He clearly conceived of anti-Semitism primarily as a religious prejudice so that a purely racial understanding of Jews could not be considered anti-Semitic. At this early stage of the project, Jews represented a group of indeterminate racial characteristics that posed a threat to the purity of the data to be collected. The role of the Jews changed markedly over the course of the study, as the Jewish racial data moved from the periphery to the center of the inquiry.

The military and public schools, the commission decided, contained populations that were representative of German society and subject to authorities that could conduct the study. While the military declined to participate, the German states agreed to have teachers collect the data from their classrooms, although many governments did not recognize the scientific value of such data.[14] The Prussian minister of culture also doubted the ability of rural schoolteachers to carry out the study with sufficient accuracy.[15] To help persuade the state governments to support the study, Virchow emphasized that the statistics would have political value, for they would provide "exact knowledge of the entire people and the individual tribes [*Stämme*], especially their particular physical and mental capabilities."[16]

While the potential political uses of the *Schulstatistik* (school statistics), as the project came to be known, made state governments more cooperative, the politics of the survey only alarmed the subjects of the study and their parents. People in southern Germany apparently did not want to make information about their color available to Prussia because they feared that it would be used to levy some new tax.[17] In Prussia, too, especially among the Catholic population in the eastern half of the monarchy, there were revolts, reportedly led by women who feared that the statistics would be used to further the *Kulturkampf*.[18] A rather incredible, but often-repeated, account has it that many feared that the survey would be used to select children of particular complexions to be sent either to Russia or to Turkey (the latter to pay off a gambling debt that Kaiser Wilhelm owed to the sultan).[19] Be that as it may, it seems clear enough that at least a portion of the people studied did not comprehend the purpose of the study and were suspicious about its possible political uses.

To secure the cooperation of the teachers who would gather the data, the German Anthropological Society distributed a pamphlet explaining the purposes of the survey and the methods that teachers should use to determine eye, hair, and skin color.[20] The pamphlet appealed to the humanistic bent of the German school system, explaining that the study of the racial composition of Europe "is a necessary prerequisite for the study of the cultural history of humanity in general and the prehistory of each country in particular." Determining the geographic distribution of the blond type and the brunet type in Germany would help anthropologists reconstruct the prehistory of Germany, when one or more original populations in Europe were joined by a later "Aryan (Indo-Germanic)" migration. Even in this pamphlet, anthropologists admitted that the question of German races would finally be settled only by determining the distribution of dolichocephalic and brachycephalic skull types. Until anthropologists could gather enough craniological data, however, this survey of the distribution of eye, hair, and skin color would have to suffice for studying the race of Germans. "Well-known scientists hold the opinion," the pamphlet assured the teachers, "that the long-headed population is blond and light-colored, the short-headed population brunet and dark-colored." Reconstructing this prehistory by tabulating the racial makeup of their classrooms would, the anthropologists promised the teachers, "lead finally to the same goal toward which the school also strives: self-knowledge." The school survey was a grand attempt to disseminate anthropology as the basis for a new civic humanism.

In addition to explaining the purposes of the study, the pamphlet also imparted to teachers and students the skills necessary to undertake a study of race. The procedural recommendations given in the pamphlet, as well as layout of the table distributed to teachers to record the data, suggest the methods that teachers might have used to conduct the study (see fig. 6.1).

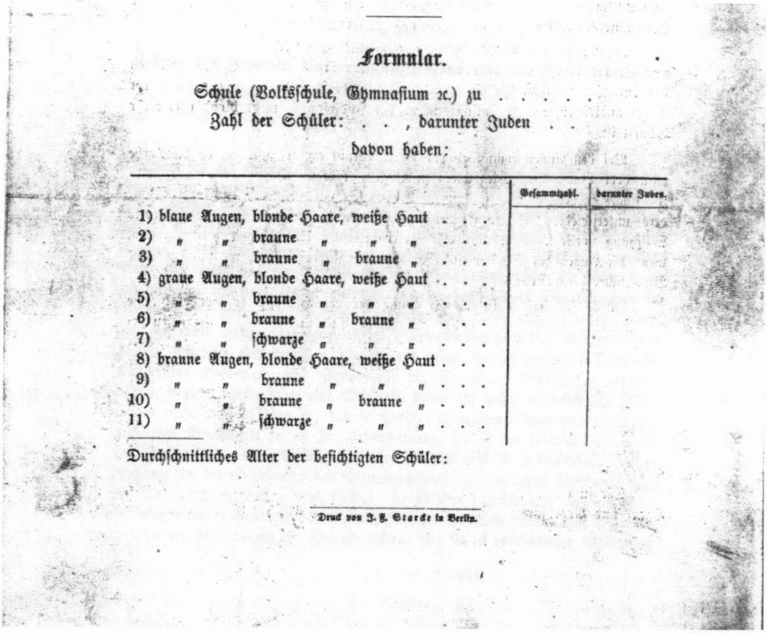

Formular.

Schule (Volksschule, Gymnasium x.) zu . . . . .

Zahl der Schüler: . . . , darunter Juden . .

davon haben:

	Gesammtzahl.	darunter Juden.
1) blaue Augen, blonde Haare, weiße Haut . . .		
2) " " braune " " " . . .		
3) " " braune " braune " . . .		
4) graue Augen, blonde Haare, weiße Haut . . .		
5) " " braune " " " . . .		
6) " " braune " braune " . . .		
7) " " schwarze " " " . . .		
8) braune Augen, blonde Haare, weiße Haut . . .		
9) " " braune " " " . . .		
10) " " braune " braune " . . .		
11) " " schwarze " " " . . .		

Durchschnittliches Alter der besichtigten Schüler:

Druck von J. F. Starcke in Berlin.

FIGURE 6.1
Table on which teachers recorded the hair, eye, and skin color of their students. Note the separate column for Jewish students.
Source: Rudolf Virchow, "Gesammtbericht über die von der deutschen anthropologischen Gesellschaft veranlassten Erhebungen über die Farbe der Haut, der Haare und der Augen der Schulkinder in Deutschland," *AA* 16 (1886): 275–475.

The teachers would have taken the form and entered the type of school and its location at the top. They then would have lined up all the students in their classes, excluding any of foreign parentage, as the pamphlet recommended. The students would then be counted and the number entered at the top of the form. If the teachers did not already know which children were Jewish, they would have had to find out so that the number of Jewish students could also be entered at the top of the form. The line of students would then be arranged according to eye color, with the lightest blue eyes at one end and the darkest brown or black eyes at the other.[21] The students would be required to remove their jackets and roll up the sleeves of their shirts to expose their forearms, which were normally covered and thus not tanned by the sun. The teachers could then proceed down the row of children, beginning at the end with the student with the lightest blue eyes. They would first examine the student's hair, determining whether it was blond or brown. If it was blond, the only option on the table was that the student's skin was white. All blond, blue-eyed German children were thus counted as white. Students with gray eyes and blond hair were similarly automatically listed as white, whereas students with gray eyes and black hair were automatically listed as brown. If a blue-eyed child's hair was brown, the teacher would have to examine the student's exposed forearm to determine whether the student was white skinned or brown skinned.

Teachers were to note separately the total number of students who fit into each of the eleven types and the number from each type who were Jewish. This division of the types into Jewish and non-Jewish could have taken place in two different ways. Teachers could have determined the type of the student and, if the student was not Jewish, made a mark in the *Gesammtzahl* (total number) column or, if the student was Jewish, made a mark in the *darunter Juden* (Jews among them) column. After finishing with all the students, the teacher would then have had to add the number from the *darunter Juden* column to that from the *Gesammtzahl* column. Alternatively, teachers could have taken the students successively out of line and grouped them according to which of the eleven types they belonged to. They would have then simply counted the total number in each group, entering those numbers into the *Gesammtzahl* column, and the number of Jews in each group, entering that number into the *darunter Juden* column. In either case, conducting the survey entailed a precise arrangement of students according to race.

The survey constituted a ritual in which students were arranged, not just as a way to *express* anthropological notions of race, but actually as a way to *experience* those notions of race. As is clear from the pamphlet that the anthropologists wrote for schoolteachers as well as from the initial resistance to the survey by the parents of its subjects, the idea that Germans were made up of separate, discernible races was by no means obvious to ordinary Germans. The initial lineup required by the measurement, in which students were arranged on a continuum from the lightest-blue to the darkest-brown eyes, would have taught the students and the teachers—not theoretically, but practically, with their bodies—that one's own body and the bodies of others could be experienced and ranked according to regular racial differences. From this initial, perhaps simpler arrangement, the teachers then taught themselves and their students more subtle distinctions and arrangements. They learned that bodies could be arranged, not only according to eye color, but also according to hair color. They also learned—if not through a second spatial arrangement, then at least through the physical gestures of pointing and counting—that two far more difficult-to-discern properties, skin color and Jewishness, could also be used as principles of arrangement and treated as somatic phenomena.[22] The form itself reproduced this physical ordering in the classroom; from the simple gesture of lining up according to eye color, students learned spatial divisions between white and non-white Germans, between non-Jewish and Jewish Germans. The process of filling out the form distributed by the German Anthropological Society taught both students and teachers to perceive and judge an individual's race on the basis of simple observations of eye and hair color and to relate these racial observations to whether a person was Jewish. Just as a dance, or the layout of a village, or a parade, can produce, concretize, and reproduce cosmologies, world orders, so too did the spatial arrangement both in the classroom and on the survey form produce an order of races—an order that did not exist before.[23]

As the hundreds of thousands of forms came in from all parts of the Reich, the German Anthropological Society rendered the classification of races on the form (which itself represented an arrangement of races in the classroom) as a spatial ordering on a map of Germany. In 1875, the anthropological society hired the Royal Statistical Bureau in Prussia to compile the statistics, which took two years to collect.[24] Other state statistical bureaus also tabulated local results. From the single surviving tabulation, it appears that state statistical bureaus filled out forms of the kind used by individual teachers with the collected results for each county.[25] These forms were then sent to Berlin, where anthropologists, including Virchow, transferred the data onto simple black-and-white maps of Germany marked off into squares, each representing a county.[26] The anthropologists made a separate map for each trait and colored each square varying shades of green according to the prevalence of a given trait. They also made maps giving the prevalence of the blond type and the brunet type throughout Germany.

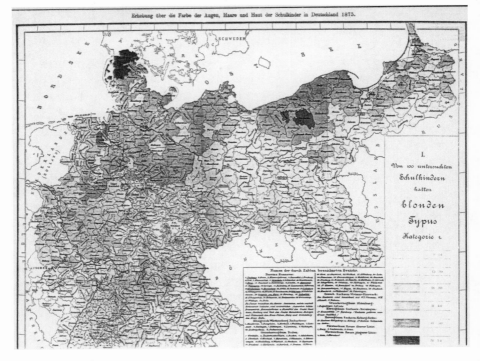

FIGURE   6.2
Map showing the geographic distribution of the "blond type." Titled "Survey of the Color of Eyes, Hair, and Skin of Schoolchildren in Germany, 1875. I. Of 100 Schoolchildren Examined, the Following were of the Blond Type."
Source: Rudolf Virchow, "Gesammtbericht über die von der deutschen anthropologischen Gesellschaft veranlassten Erhebungen über die Farbe der Haut, der Haare und der Augen der Schulkinder in Deutschland," *AA* 16 (1886): 275–475.

These schematic maps were then used to draw more realistic maps, presenting the geography of Germany in terms of the distribution of the two German types (see fig. 6.2).[27] As the initial data collecting involved a spatializing ritual in which teachers arranged children to racialize them, this map-coloring process did the same on a larger scale for the nation. Germany itself was pictured as a racially differentiated space.

As early as 1876, even before the results of the school statistics were complete, Virchow concluded from the data that Jews formed "a quite respectable contrast to the real Teutons."[28] The process of conducting the survey had taught Virchow to view Jews as a separate race. Virchow himself recognized this process, noting that the "children of Jewish confession" were originally considered separately only because it was thought that they might cause a "disturbance in the summation" of the data. Although, as it turned out, the data from Jewish students would not have affected the statistical analysis, the separate study did lead to an unexpected conclusion: "From the separated survey it became clear . . . that certain very sharp oppositions exist between the races (*Rassen*). While, of the total number of German schoolchildren, calculated together, almost 32 percent were blond, among the Jewish schoolchildren only 11 percent were counted [as blond]. Brunets occurred among all the schoolchildren a bit more than 14 percent; among the Jews it was 42 percent."[29] While today one might regard the same data as evidence of a lack of racial uniformity among Jews or Germans, when Virchow and his contemporaries considered the data, their conclusion was unequivocal: Jews were a separate race from Germans. While not all individuals of the brunet type were Jewish, Jews were racially distinct from the blond type, which was largely made up of Germans.

Virchow was able to maintain the idea of a single Jewish race despite the obvious variations in the statistics of Jewish hair, eye, and skin color. Anthropologists had been aware of the existence of blond Jews before the survey discovered them. There were three prevalent explanations for blond Jews: Jews came to look like the surrounding population as they became assimilated; Jews mixed with the surrounding population as they became assimilated; and there were two Jewish types, a common dark type and a rarer blond type.[30] Against the first two arguments Virchow pointed to his statistics: Jews did not look like the surrounding population into which they had, supposedly, been assimilated, and they did not mix with the surrounding population to a significant extent. The statistics show that 54 percent of non-Jews were mixed form while only 47 percent of Jews were mixed form. Thus, the "first cardinal phenomenon" discovered by the survey was that "it is precisely among the Jews that the smallest number of mixed types appear."[31] Virchow further noted that blond Jews rarely had blue eyes and that they were thus actually mixed types. He held that an inclination of Jews to marry among themselves meant that these mixed types would soon be eliminated: "Finally, through new pure Jewish marriages, the old blood will be freshened up again."[32] Virchow concluded that there was a single brown Jewish racial type that, despite variations, would always be kept pure because the Jewish race remained separate. Data on Jews had originally been marginalized simply to preserve the purity of data about Germans; Virchow later drew the Jewish data into the center of the study and transformed the school statistic into a racial study, and a mass racialization, of Jews.

The second "cardinal phenomenon" discovered by Virchow's study was that Germans were of the blond type, that they were white rather than brown.[33] While more than half the students measured were of the mixed type, two-thirds of the pure were of the blond type and only one-third of the brown type. The study did find that the north of Germany was more blond than the south. However, while the brunet type was only 27 percent more prevalent in the south than in the north, the blond type was 47 percent more prevalent in the north than in the south. Virchow concluded that, because the blond type varies more from north to south, and, presumably, because there are more pure blonds than pure brunets in Germany, the blond type was "the dominant type" (*der herrschende Typus*). The brunet type, in contrast, was a "secondary type" (*Nebentypus*). The two "cardinal phenomena" that Virchow derived from the study were that, despite variation, Jews were a single brown racial type and that Germans were predominantly a single blond (and therefore white) racial type. Far from overturning scientific racism, the German Anthropological Society's study, even as interpreted by Virchow, gave racism a new statistical, scientific, and practical basis.

In his methodological discussions, Virchow also drew the Jews from the periphery of the school statistic to its center. Indeed, Virchow legitimized the very value of the data on skin color with reference to a specific racial characterization of Jewish Germans. While the study was primarily concerned with skin color as a racial characteristic possibly related to skull form, the measurement of skin color, to a greater extent even than the measurement of eye and hair color, seemed highly arbitrary. It would be difficult, Virchow feared, to rely on the regularity of teachers' judgments about the whiteness or brownness of their students' skin, for skin that looks brown to one teacher might look white to another. In a final step, closing the circle of the argument, Virchow used the two cardinal phenomena to justify the data from which these phenomena themselves had been derived. That teachers recorded white skin for 91.5 percent of the non-Jewish children but only for 74.37 percent of the Jewish children indicated, for Virchow, that the measurements of skin color were done relatively accurately and reliably. Virchow supposed that both these figures for the whiteness of skin were higher than they should be because teachers had not yet learned to discriminate between whiteness and brownness in German children.[34] That teachers correctly identified Jews as less likely to be white than non-Jews also indicates, however, that they had already begun to acquire the discriminating eye that Virchow's study demanded.

The school statistics had a discernible, if difficult-to-measure, effect on the German public. Although Virchow's conclusions were not officially published for ten years, local newspapers reported the findings for their region as soon as they were calculated.[35] Almost immediately, the color of the Jewish and the non-Jewish students, as well as the number of Jews in a given area, became public knowledge. That the findings were published in newspapers along with other items of public interest must have given them a significance that they did not necessarily already possess. The political controversies surrounding the study and the initial popular resistance to it, as well as the apparent newsworthiness of the results, likely imprinted it in the memories of students, teachers, and parents.[36] The experience was in any case a common one for nearly an entire age cohort of Germans.[37] The study was not only an important event in the history of scientific racism; it was also a broad dissemination of anthropological skills and practices.[38]

In addition to the popularization of anthropology, the study provided the basis for a range of anthropological theorizing. The Munich anthropologist Johannes Ranke cited Virchow's survey as the greatest anthropological study ever and viewed it as establishing the blond type as a particularly German racial type.[39] Julius Kollmann, a Swiss anthropologist and professor of medicine, used Virchow's findings immediately after they were published to argue that races were permanent types that could be changed neither by climate nor by crossbreeding. Individuals born of parents of different races would appear as a cross between the two races, but they would not themselves constitute a new racial type. Racial characteristics could also not be changed by migrating to new climates. This constituted an important argument against evolution, for, if types were perfectly passed on from parent to child, then there would be no means by which evolutionary transformation could happen.[40] Virchow agreed with these views on the permanence of race, which he regarded not only as an argument against Darwinism, but also as support of German eastward colonization. The permanence of racial types meant for Virchow that Germans in Eastern Europe would remain German rather than being transformed by the local environment.[41]

Friedrich Nietzsche used the German Anthropological Society study in his 1887 *On the Genealogy of Morals* to differentiate "a blond race," which he called "the conqueror and *master race,* the Aryan," from an inferior race, which he characterized by its peculiar "coloring" and "shortness of skull." On the basis of this distinction, Nietzsche suggested that socialism represented a primitive, pre-Aryan social form, a "monstrous *atavism [ungeheuern Nachschlag]*," and an attempt of brown people to rule the blond.[42] The anthropologist Otto Ammon cautioned that Nietzsche did not grasp the details of Virchow's study and used it unfairly as an argument against socialism. He did, however, applaud Nietzsche for being "completely conscious of the meaning of race for culture."[43]

With the school survey, anthropologists began a process of reconfiguring the basis of German identity on an antihumanist basis. The survey was perhaps the most important means by which anthropology as a mode of perceiving, and engaging with, the world was propagated in nineteenth-century Germany. Publications, as well as museum and other exhibitions, certainly also provided important means of popularizing anthropology. However, the school survey was unique in its massive scale, its systematic application, and its dissemination of anthropological skills, rather than just theories.[44] The survey taught an enormous number of ordinary Germans to perceive nationality in their own bodies and in the bodies of others. It transformed the publicly visible traits of hair and eye color into signs of more abstract qualities—skin color and nationality. Furthermore, it taught participants to perceive Jewish Germans as racially different from non-Jewish Germans. German anthropologists did not participate significantly in the anti-Semitic movements of the later nineteenth century, and the point of their study was not to exclude Jews from German citizenship or any other aspect of national life. Indeed, before the survey, Virchow himself explicitly denied that race should have anything to do with citizenship in the German state.[45] However, anthropologists did make available the categories and skills of their science to a public that they could not control. The study was thus an unintended contribution to a restructuring of discourse about German nationality that would result in the Nazi "racial state."[46] The anthropological critique of humanism had a multitude of potentials, and Nazism was only one of them. What is essential here is that anthropology represented an attempt to displace—or at least supplement—the humanist political traditions of Imperial Germany with a culture of natural science in which concepts of race played an important role.

PART III

CHAPTER 7

The Secret of Primitive Accumulation:
The Political Economy of Anthropological Objects

The transition from a human science of subjects and texts to one of observation and objects was part of a larger reorientation of nineteenth-century European urban culture toward things as a source of
meaning.[1] From the Crystal Palace, which opened in 1851, to the glass and
iron commercial arcades that sprung up in Paris, Berlin, and other urban
centers, Europe saw the emergence of a mass commercial culture based on
industrial goods marketed to a broad range of urban consumers.[2] It is no
accident that anthropology developed in Germany in nearly the same historical moment that Marx published his analysis of the commodity and
commodity fetishism in the first volume of *Capital*. Just as, in Marx's view,
consumers believed that commodities contained value in themselves, apart
from the society and culture that produced and consumed them, so too did
anthropologists believe that the objects in their collections contained truth
in themselves, apart from the global political economy in which they were
enmeshed. For anthropologists, objects spoke for themselves and therefore
did not require the uncertain, subjective interpretation that texts demanded. Indeed, "natural peoples" themselves were conceived as objects,
devoid of history and part of a static, objective realm of nature. However,
much as the "facts" analyzed in chapter 5 turned out to be inseparable from
the social relations among anthropologists, so too were these objects themselves radically entangled in (subjective) human history. Despite the empiricist and objectivist hopes that anthropologists pinned on artifacts, these
objects did not contain truth in themselves but rather gained meaning
from the social worlds that produced, circulated, and consumed them.[3]

The objects that anthropologists studied were purchased, received as gifts, or taken as booty in the everyday course of colonial rule. They often resulted from interactions subordinating the colonized, as, for example, when they were taken as part of a "punitive expedition" or received as tribute signifying the allegiance of a local ruler to the German flag. When colonizers sent these objects to anthropologists, colonial rule gained significance as a contribution to science, to *Kultur* in the modernizing sense expounded by anthropologists. Stripped of their connection to the individuals who produced and formerly owned them, the objects themselves embodied the absence of *Kultur* in colonized societies. These objects were thus preinterpreted as embodying a fundamental difference between colonizer and colonized: the colonized were passive and ruled, the colonizers active and ruling. Colonial rule depended on denying the colonized an active history and thus paralleled anthropologists' own division of the earth's peoples into *Kulturvölker* and *Naturvölker*. The collection of anthropological objects was one of the ways in which Europeans were able to present themselves as *Kulturvölker* and their colonial subjects as *Naturvölker*. Anthropologists participated in imperialism by stabilizing the interpretation given by Europeans to the objects that they acquired from the colonized. The attempt to amass a complete collection of the objects of natural peoples was part of a larger project of denying the colonized an autonomous history while simultaneously extolling the historical mission of Europeans.

Like all aspects of colonial rule, colonial exchanges were often vigorously contested by the colonized, and the meaning that colonists gave to these exchanges often had to compete with the intentions of colonial subjects. The anthropological and colonial interpretation of non-Europeans was at odds with the dynamic history of all human societies, both before and after European conquest. Neither colonists nor anthropologists could completely subordinate this historical reality to a culture and politics of objects. Anthropological collections thus embodied not only the ideological "cultural peoples"/"natural peoples" binary but also the very insufficiency and instability of this binary. The objects that were supposed to give direct knowledge of ahistorical, natural humans often bore indelible traces of the colonial history in which they were acquired. Like the commodity in Marx's analysis, the anthropological object presented not just the self-understanding of a cultural and economic system but also the contradictions and blind spots of that system.

The exchanges that made up colonialism—exchanges of gifts, exchanges of commodities, and even exchanges of fire—both supplied anthropologists with objects and began the process of stripping those objects of their history. Perhaps like all exchanges they introduced a moment of instability that was particularly threatening for colonists and anthropologists. Even in the face of the overwhelming power exercised by colonists, the colonized often—intentionally or unintentionally—challenged European interpretations of the exchange. Indeed, the very notion of exchanges between colonizer and colonized threatened the sharp gap between European cultural peoples and colonized natural peoples on which European understandings of both anthropology and colonial rule depended. In this chapter, I use a number of exemplary exchanges to suggest the ways in which German anthropology was an integral part of a larger colonial political economic network.

In 1909, King Kabua of the Marshall Islands honored the fiftieth birthday of Kaiser Wilhelm II with a day of celebrations. Nearly three decades earlier, the Germans had named Kabua king and assisted him in prevailing over a major political rival. As in many colonies, Germans lent military support to a single leader to simplify administration. (The same, of course, could be said of the elevation of the Prussian king to German kaiser in 1871.) Since becoming king, Kabua had grown wealthy selling to German firms the coconut meat and oil (copra) that his subjects harvested and gave to him as tribute.[4] The birthday party began with a sermon at the Protestant mission based on the passage from Paul's letter to the Romans: "Let every person be subject to the governing authorities. For there is no authority except from God, and those that exist have been instituted by God" (Rom. 13:1). This sermon was followed by boat races between Germans and the indigenous people. After a reception for the local European and indigenous political elites, Kabua's subjects performed dances. As souvenirs of the celebrations, Kabua sent the kaiser a drum, a spear shaft used in the dances, and two sleeping mats. Kabua also sent the kaiser a handwritten letter, which a local missionary translated into ungrammatical German. Kabua's letter described the ceremonies and expressed the desire that the two rulers might someday meet and chat.[5]

Despite what might at first appear to be groveling collaboration with German authority, Kabua actually used the kaiser's birthday party to challenge colonial rule. The German government of the Marshall Islands had, of course, cast the celebration of the kaiser's birthday as a ritual of submission, as the sermon indicated. By sending Wilhelm gifts and a birthday letter, however, Kabua did not make himself "subject to the governing authorities," as Paul's letter recommended, but rather presented himself as an equal to the kaiser. Kaiser Wilhelm was thus obliged by a venerable norm of reciprocity to give his fellow monarch equivalent gifts, including a handwritten letter. This exchange of gifts embodied the mutual obligations of the two leaders and reaffirmed their political alliances. It further signified their common superiority to their subjects: only they, as rulers, were worthy of exchanging equivalent gifts.

The kaiser nearly accepted Kabua's rendering of the celebrations, which would have diminished the authority of the German administrators in the Marshall Islands. King Kabua would have appeared as a monarch equal in status to Wilhelm and thus superior, by implication, to German colonial officials, who were themselves subjects of the kaiser. The colonists thwarted Kabua's efforts by preventing the kaiser from reciprocating. The reciprocity with which Wilhelm wished to respond to Kabua was, at the insistence of the Colonial Office, replaced with the condescension with which a monarch appropriately responds to his subjects. The Colonial Office objected that Kabua did not merit a handwritten letter from the kaiser and that his "level of culture" (*Bildungsgrad*) would not allow him to properly appreciate the honor of receiving one. The kaiser agreed instead to have a picture of himself that already hung in a district office in the Marshall Islands given to Kabua. By giving him an inferior gift and withholding a handwritten letter, Wilhelm suggested that Kabua was a lesser subject rather than an equal monarch. The gifts were thus altered, under the direction of the German Colonial Office, from a sign of mutual respect to a sign of submission of the colonized to the colonizers. Finally, the kaiser deposited the birthday presents that Kabua gave him in the Royal Museum of Ethnology, and thus this colonial tribute was transformed into anthropological objects.[6]

The collection of anthropological objects depended on, and was a constituent part of, a broader system of colonial exchanges. The objects clearly had an important function in the establishment of German colonial rule, both defining and representing the political relations between colonizer and colonized. Both Kabua and Wilhelm initially understood the objects as part of a reciprocal interaction among (equally historical) individuals. This understanding was subverted by colonists who correctly perceived such an interpretation as an attack on their own claims to authority in the Marshall Islands. An important part of the colonists' interpretation was placing the objects in the museum of ethnology. In the museum, they were made to represent natural peoples, who stood across an unbridgeable gap from German cultural peoples. Anthropologists thus collaborated with, and benefited from, the colonial interpretation by taking Kabua's birthday presents for their museum.

Because Berlin was the "intellectual-spiritual center" (*geistige Mittelpunkt*), as well as the political capital, of Germany, anthropologists in the imperial metropolis were given special access to the international networks of the German state.[7] Even before Germany took colonies of its own, anthropologists worked with diplomats and the navy to acquire artifacts and to recruit Germans living abroad as collectors. After the acquisition of German colonies in 1884, colonial military and civilian officials also sent anthropological objects to Berlin. An imperial law in effect from 1889 to 1914 intensified the relation between Berlin anthropology and the German state, requiring that all collections acquired by Germans traveling or living abroad on Reich business be offered to the Berlin museum of ethnology before being sold or donated to any other museum.[8] The Berlin museum of ethnology thus sat, like a spider, at the center of a web of collectors spanning the globe. As a result of this special relation to the state, the anthropology museum in Berlin was able to acquire an average of more than two thousand artifacts per year between 1895 and 1907.[9] By the turn of the century, the Berlin museum possessed the largest anthropology collection in the world.[10]

In exchange for this government assistance, Berlin anthropologists occasionally used the international relations that they cultivated to further the state's foreign policy objectives. Thus, when Ladislau Netto, the director of the Brazilian National Museum, attended a congress of ancient American archaeologists in Berlin in 1888, the Foreign Office asked Berlin anthropologists to treat him particularly well. Netto was an influential man, who, the German ambassador to Brazil explained, might persuade the Brazilian government to make decisions favorable to German immigrants. The foreign office hoped that anthropologists would arrange to offer Netto better treatment than the other foreign guests at the congress and that Netto could perhaps be given a medal for donations to the museum. Netto was made vice president of the congress, and, although his donations to the museum were not enough to warrant nomination to a Prussian order, he was given a portrait of the kaiser.[11]

The exchange in artifacts could itself become a part of German foreign policy. During his 1881 visit to Berlin, the Siamese prince Chau Prisdang toured the museum of ethnology. Bastian used this opportunity to slip him a memorandum about ethnographic objects that he would like to acquire from Siam. He also had a copy of the memorandum sent directly to King Chulalongkorn of Siam, whom he believed could give the museum of ethnology objects that no foreign traveler could purchase for any price. The next year the king of Siam sent jeweled gold cases as gifts to three Hohenzollern princesses, for which the kaiser sent two large vases bearing his own portrait in return. Bastian saw the possibility of continued gift exchange between the Prussian and the Siamese royal households as a rare opportunity for ethnological acquisitions. The museum offered to pay for infantry weapons, artillery pieces, and other military equipment as counter gifts to the king of Siam from the kaiser, an arrangement that Kaiser Wilhelm accepted. King Chulalongkorn may have regarded German weapons as a way to further his well-known project of modernizing the Siamese military and resisting European hegemony. This exchange was not merely an adventuresome museum acquisition policy; it was also a bold colonial political move, both establishing a relationship between Germany and Siam and helping Chulalongkorn check the authority of other European powers in Asia. Indeed, these colonial-political implications may explain why the exchange of weapons was ultimately rejected. King Chulalongkorn sent a final shipment of Buddhist antiquities in 1886 but then dropped the relationship.[12] The political economy of anthropological objects was not merely a parasite on but rather a constituent element of a larger global network.

The German military collected so many artifacts that Felix von Luschan once referred to the Berlin museum of ethnology as "the greatest monument to our colonial troops."[13] Shortly after it was founded, the Berlin Anthropological Society turned to the German navy for assistance in collecting artifacts. In 1872, the society produced a pamphlet of "Suggestions for Anthropological Investigations on Navy Expeditions," which the Imperial Admiralty forwarded to ships in foreign waters and placed in the navy's libraries at Kiel and Wilhelmshaven.[14] Anthropologists thought that the navy did not spend long enough in a single place to "psychologically penetrate" the natives, but they did hope that officers would use stops in foreign ports to trade European goods for local products.[15] They also hoped that officers would encourage Germans living abroad to collect artifacts and to donate their collections to the Berlin museum. The pamphlet further explained how navy doctors could take reliable anthropometric measurements using only a tape measure and obstetric calipers.[16] Much of the hope that anthropologists had at this stage for the assistance of navy officers rested on the assumption that, while zoology, botany, mineralogy, and geology required special training, anthropology and ethnology could be done by any educated person.[17]

Anthropologists presented their discipline as a virtuous activity for individual officers and for the navy as a whole. In 1874, a local philosophy professor gave a lecture at the navy officer's club in Kiel deeming anthropology one of the navy's "ideal," "culture historical" tasks.[18] Perhaps the navy complied with the wishes of anthropologists to gain social prestige at a time when it played second fiddle to the army and did not yet have the place in the popular imagination that it would acquire at the turn of the

THE SECRET OF PRIMITIVE ACCUMULATION

century. Furthermore, doing science made routine colonial administration into a sign of *Kultur*—which was itself an important colonial ideology.

The navy's collecting duties developed from an occasional activity for officers during their leisure time to an integral part of its operations.[19] In 1874, Bastian persuaded the navy to order the surveying ship HMS *Gazelle,* bound for the South Pacific, to acquire "everything collectible" from ports of call.[20] A Lieutenant Franz Strauch assigned to the *Gazelle* did much ethnographic collecting for the museum and developed a lifelong interest in anthropology. He eventually rose to the rank of rear-admiral and acted as a key intermediary between the navy and the museum of ethnology.[21] By 1882, the navy had become so involved with anthropology that it informed the museum of an expedition that it thought might provide opportunities for anthropological collecting and inquired if anthropologists had any specific requests from the area.[22] Beginning in 1897, the navy allowed Luschan to place one thousand marks per year at the disposal of the surveying ship HMS *Seagull* for the purpose of acquiring anthropological collections.[23] A lower paymaster was placed in charge of purchasing objects, while a more senior officer, given instruction at the Berlin museum, conducted ethnographic observations.[24] The first officer on the *Seagull* with anthropological duties, Lieutenant Kuthe, was instructed at the museum in techniques of ethnographic and anthropological observation and also in photography.[25] Luschan sent Kuthe numerous requests for specific information and artifacts from the region.[26] Although Kuthe's poor health had him back in Berlin after less than a year on the *Seagull,* he did manage to write a report on the customs of northwestern New Mecklenburg, based partly on his own observations and partly on "credible information from trustworthy Europeans."[27] The following year, the museum employed Kuthe as an assistant in their East Asian Section. Other officers took Kuthe's place as the museum's agent aboard the *Seagull,* and the *Seagull* itself was eventually replaced with the HMS *Planet,* but this close relation between the navy and the museum continued into the twentieth century.[28]

The military not only provided huge numbers of artifacts but also made objects available to anthropologists that they otherwise never could have obtained. As Luschan explained, military operations involved a different kind of acquisition than the civilian trade in artifacts: "It is in the nature of the situation that a warship often finds itself in a position to collect large wood carvings or entire series of important objects at little or no cost, whereas a private man, despite all his scientific knowledge and personal contacts, can get such things only at a price so high, if at all, that the museum would not easily be able to make any more purchases."[29] Luschan's point was not simply that it was cheaper to steal than to buy but also that the navy could take objects that could not be purchased at any price. The societies colonized by Europeans did not produce their everyday objects in surplus in order to sell to curious foreigners. Those societies that did sell to Europeans often made objects especially for the tourist trade and the European exotic art market, which anthropologists regarded as inauthentic.[30] By forcibly taking the property of indigenous societies rather than purchasing it, the navy could deliver what anthropologists considered to be more authentic goods. As Adolf Bastian, head of the museum of ethnology in Berlin, wrote in 1900: "From military expeditions undertaken for colonial political purposes the ethnological collections of the royal museums have been valuably enriched at various times. . . . In punitive expeditions the property of the guilty, instead of being destroyed, is preserved for the scientific study . . . of wild tribes."[31] Colonial governing strategies, involving as they did the intimidation and expropriation of indigenous people, produced collections of anthropological objects.

Even the threat of military force could invite donations of anthropological objects. In 1887, Herr Schulle, a commercial agent in one of Germany's protectorates in the South Pacific, reported to the colonial government that, despite many warnings, the natives in his region continued to practice cannibalism. Schulle also complained that difficult relations with the indigenous population had recently disrupted his business. Perhaps Schulle made false accusations to encourage vigorous action by the navy, which might bolster his own authority on the island and help restore trade. The navy agreed to send the cruiser *Albatross* to the area, and the ship's commanding officer, Lieutenant Commander von Frantzius, delivered a "punitive speech" (*Strafrede*) to a group of local leaders assembled for the purpose. Herr Schulle, the commercial agent, translated Frantzius's speech into the local language, after which the leaders, at least according to Schulle's account, promised to stop eating people. Since all communication between Captain von Frantzius and the indigenous people occurred only as translated by Schulle, it is not clear what the indigenous leaders believed the navy demands to be or how they really responded to those demands. Later, the chastised leaders paddled out to the *Albatross* to present Frantzius with gifts, which, Schulle explained, indicated the gravity of their promise to renounce cannibalism. Before the *Albatross* sailed away, Herr Schulle claimed that a leader on another part of the island had threatened his life. Schulle induced Frantzius to deliver another "punitive speech," also translated by Herr Schulle. Frantzius had a group of local inhabitants brought on board the warship and demanded that they promise never to kill any Europeans and to respect European property rights. These natives also presented Frantzius with gifts to emphasize their sincerity. Frantzius later sent these gifts to the Admiralty in Berlin, which in turn gave them to the museum of ethnology.[32] Such transformations of the local products of an indigenous South Pacific society into anthropological evidence were facilitated by an intermediary stage as colonial booty.

Luschan became quite adept at acquiring anthropological material from colonial governments in Africa as well as the Pacific.[33] The navy enforced German rule in the South Pacific colonies, so Luschan could work directly with the Imperial Navy Office in Berlin to recruit anthropological collectors for that region. The African colonies, however, were policed by army units, known as *Schutztruppen,* under the command of the governors of each individual colony.[34] Luschan established direct contact with each of the colonial governments of Africa to acquire anthropological materials and kept the governments informed of activities in their own colonies likely to provide opportunities for anthropological collecting.[35] Luschan also corresponded with individual officers of the *Schutztruppen,* perhaps those with whom he had become acquainted in his anthropology courses in Berlin. Colonial wars presented particularly good opportunities for collecting, although they also made collecting haphazard and chaotic.

The East African Maji Maji uprising illustrates the close and contradictory relation between anthropological collecting and colonial warfare.[36] In 1905, societies in the south of German East Africa united under Kinjikitile Ngwala, a charismatic religious leader of the Matumbi society. A Matumbi clan would often employ particular war medicines that it believed would protect its members against the weapons of a particular enemy or make them invisible to that enemy. Kinjikitile revolutionized warfare and colonial resistance by making a war medicine, called *Maji* (Swahili for "water"), that assisted all Africans, not just a particular clan or even just the Matumbi. *Maji* was supposed to turn German bullets into water or make them flow off the body like water from an oiled object. United by a common belief in this war medicine, and motivated by common resistance to German exploitation, East African societies in the south of the colony rebelled against German colonists, especially against the recruitment of forced labor for cotton farming. To put down the rebellion, the German government brought in German military units as well as units made up of Papuans and mercenaries from the Sudan, Somaliland, and Zululand. While the Maji Maji enjoyed some initial victories, their spears, arrows, and muzzle-loading rifles were no match for German machine guns. The Germans defeated them by 1907, at the cost of fifteen European lives and the lives of several hundred of their African soldiers. The Maji Maji lost seventy-five thousand in the fighting, and a further one to two hundred thousand Africans died as a result of a scorched-earth policy that the Germans adopted to deny the rebels food.

In 1906, Luschan received a report from the government of East Africa in Dar es Salaam, informing him that, in the course of the war, the German army had captured hundreds of muzzle loaders, spears, bows, arrows, and other objects.[37] The colonial government sent the more than four thousand pounds of booty to the Berlin museum, as the 1889 law required. When the objects arrived in Berlin, Luschan was disappointed to find that the spears, which formed the bulk of the collection, were mostly not traditional native handiwork but rather weapons improvised for war on a scale that no society in Africa could have experienced before Europeans arrived. The colonial contact that initially made it possible for an academic in Berlin to acquire more than twelve hundred spears had also initiated war on a scale requiring the people producing those spears to adopt techniques of mass production. Anthropologists thus obtained an enormous number of objects, but those objects had little scientific value because they were regarded as artifacts of colonial warfare rather than of a traditional African society. Colonial warfare both enabled and distorted the kind of large-scale collecting that the inductive natural science of humanity demanded. Luschan could not get rid of the objects. The arrows had poisoned tips, so they were unsuited for donation to secondary schools.[38] Luschan thought that he might return the objects to East Africa, where they might be sold to tourists in order to recover the original shipping costs. Finally, he obtained permission to burn them.[39]

The imperialist networks that supplied anthropologists with ethnographic artifacts also provided them with body parts of the colonized, especially, although not exclusively, their skulls. Although the political economy of body parts is in many ways similar to that of ethnographic artifacts, it presented peculiar problems because the body is not alienable property. Individuals cannot give up their own skulls in the same way they give up their possessions. Colonial warfare and administration often resulted in the deaths of individuals whose bodies anthropologists wished to study, and colonial administrators were often able to mail corpses much as they mailed clothing, tools, and other objects. Virchow recommended that travelers bring back, in addition to bones and hair, salted skin and dried hands, which he suggested might be collected at public executions, prisons, hospitals, and battlefields.[40] Luschan was less specific about where he wanted body parts collected and later worried that his requests to colonial police officers and medical doctors for corpses would encourage them to murder people.[41] Skulls were, as we have seen, the most important physical

FIGURE 7.1
Virchow poses with part of his physical anthropological collection. Former medical students and other doctors working in European colonies sent Virchow body parts that they collected from the indigenous population.
Source: Die Woche 3, no. 4 (1901): 1792.

anthropological object, and they were the most commonly collected (see figs. 7.1–7.3). Anthropologists also developed means of acquiring bodily objects without killing individuals, such as taking hair samples, measurements, and plaster casts. Like ethnographic artifacts, body parts could be acquired from the normal course of colonial rule.

For Luschan, the Maji Maji rebellion in East Africa presented a particularly good occasion for collecting physical anthropological objects. In 1906, Luschan read in the newspaper that an *akida,* an African official of the German government, had presented the governor of East Africa with the severed heads of three Mwera rebels, which the governor had then buried. Luschan wrote to the governor: "I devotedly allow myself to

FIGURE   7.2
Skull from the collection of the Berlin Anthropological Society. After the skulls arrived in Berlin, their measurements were entered in a card catalog, and a serial number was written on the skull. The sex and origin of this skull's former owner have also been written on it.
Source: Photograph by the author.

FIGURE   7.3
Skulls from the collection of the Berlin Anthropological Society. The skulls pictured here are only a small portion of the more than six thousand objects currently possessed by the Berlin Museum of Natural History, which holds both Virchow's collection and a portion of Luschan's.
Source: Photograph by the author.

inquire if there exists any possibility that the skulls might be dug up and sent to Berlin. If the opportunity to rescue for science a freshly severed head ever presents itself again, I would be most grateful if these heads would be treated with formaldehyde or in another appropriate way and sent to the Royal Museum. It would be of very great scientific value if soft parts, especially with various tattoos, could be saved for posterity in a secure and unproblematic way."[42] Luschan was also particularly interested in obtaining body parts of soldiers from New Guinea recruited to fight in East Africa, since it was very difficult to take such material from people living in New Guinea. Luschan hoped to acquire not just the skeletons but also the flesh of these Papuan soldiers: "If it can be done without upsetting the survivors, the brains should be removed and treated according to one of the familiar methods of preservation. Otherwise I would at least request that the corpses of the Melanesians be interred in a separate part of the graveyard and that each individual be buried with a well-sealed bottle that contains the exact nationality [of the corpse]. It would then be easy to dig up and identify the skeletons in several years, after the survivors have already been repatriated."[43] Luschan made contact with the army doctor assigned to the New Guinea troops, but the doctor could not succeed in acquiring any soft parts. Luschan had to content himself with just two skeletons.[44] Still, war allowed corpses to be taken from societies that refused to cooperate with anthropological collectors.[45]

Even in times of peace, however, anthropological collections could be acquired by robbing graves. This was a common practice among travelers collecting for anthropologists, who would often covertly exhume corpses and ship them to Berlin. For example, in an article about the Coroados of Brazil, the anthropologist Rheinhold Hensel expressed regret that he could collect only the skulls, and not the entire skeletons, from graves that he opened. "There was no time to collect the skeletons as well," he explained, "since I was afraid I would be surprised by the Indians."[46] The traveler and later museum director A. B. Meyer attempted to purchase skulls from Pacific Islanders, but, when he could not, he simply stole them.[47] Often, depending on local circumstances, anthropological collectors could hire indigenous laborers to rob graves. Luschan, for example, commented that, in parts of German East Africa, one could get a skeleton dug up for "a bright cloth or a piece of soap" but that, in other regions, grave robbers required a full day's wages or even "quite considerable sums of cash to appease any scruples."[48] Grave robbing thus often involved the cooperation of indigenous groups, who were also sometimes able to successfully deny anthropologists the corpses of their compatriots. For example, in 1911, residents of German Samoa learned that a number of their skulls had been stolen for anthropology collections in Berlin. They claimed that this would cause them misfortune, and, when a dysentery outbreak occurred among them, they blamed it on the German official who took the skulls. The official asked Luschan to return the skulls so that they might be reinterred. Luschan did so but warned that the official should inquire first about what skulls they thought were missing since, if more were returned than the Samoans believed to be missing in the first place, they might become suspicious.[49]

Collectors abroad occasionally found it impossible to preserve or to remove the flesh from the parts before putting them in the mail, which could have loathsome results. As a woman named Anneli Yaam, a contact of Luschan's in Bangkok, explained in a letter accompanying a shipment of a dozen severed heads: "Many of them were still very fresh, but preparing them would have hardly been possible since bringing pieces of corpses back into the city is punished with imprisonment. It is my view that you must prepare the bones there yourself since it can be done here only with the greatest inconvenience and at a very high cost. I would have to rent a house outside the city wall and could hire people only at great cost and with great difficulty since the fear of spirits, corpses, and body parts is quite abnormal here."[50] Yaam demanded more money for the heads than Luschan wanted to pay, and, as Luschan soon learned, many of the heads were from children and were therefore useless for the kind of physical anthropology undertaken by Berlin anthropologists. Luschan insisted that Yaam either accept a lower price for the "stinking inferior things" or pay to ship the decomposing heads back to Siam. Luschan and Yaam must have settled their differences, for less than a year later Yaam sent him several locks of hair— carefully labeled with the ethnicities of the people from whom they were taken.[51]

Because of the ease of collecting hair, it became an important anthropological object. Hair can be acquired from the living, does not decompose, and is relatively easy to ship. In the collection of the Berlin Anthropological Society, there were envelopes, test tubes, and cigar boxes full of hair, all labeled according to origin (see fig. 7.4).[52] Because of the relative ease with which a person could acquire a lock of hair and mail it to Berlin, hair was sometimes used in deciding racial questions.[53] Hair played a particularly significant role in the *Negritofrage* of the early 1870s, the question of the origin of the dark-skinned inhabitants of the Pacific, especially of the interior of the Philippines and New Guinea. While cranial evidence ultimately allowed anthropologists to conclude that these "Negritos" were unrelated to sub-Saharan Africans, at first Berlin anthropologists had so few skeletons that they also collected and described "Negrito" hair.[54]

To avoid the troubles of collecting and shipping body parts, anthropological collectors could send various more portable representations of bodies from the colonies to Berlin. Anthropometric measurements were especially easy to ship. If informants had the training and the instruments to make measurements trustworthy, they could simply write down the numbers and send them to anthropologists in Germany. However, measurers had problems getting people to submit to the lengthy and often uncomfortable procedures associated with anthropological measurement. Anthropologists were interested in the dimensions of the skeleton

FIGURE 7.4
Hair samples from the collection of the Berlin Anthropological Society. Currently stored in the Berlin Museum of Natural History.
Source: Photographs by the author.

exclusive of the flesh since the amount of flesh on a body reflected what a particular individual ate rather than supposedly objective racial character-istics. To take skeletal measurements of living individuals, one had to squeeze the calipers until they came as close to the bone as possible.[55] In his attempts to measure performers at the 1896 colonial exhibition, Luschan had found that "a general difficulty . . . lay in the great aversion of most people to letting themselves be measured and in the complete impossibility of exercising any coercion over them."[56] He felt that very good measure-ments could be obtained only from slaves, who had no choice but to accept the pain of accurate measurement, or from corpses.[57] However, most mea-surers did not have the luxury of dealing only with slaves and corpses, and they therefore had to make compromises with living humans. For exam-ple, Luschan recommended avoiding measurements that required the sub-jects to remove all their clothes since many people would refuse to be measured if they had to be naked.[58] One of Virchow's contacts refused to take a certain measurement because it involved sticking metal rods in the ears of people who already resisted cooperating.[59] Luschan advised his cor-respondents abroad to measure the strength of people in addition to their physical dimensions only because subjects would often submit to a whole battery of procedures just so that they could test their strength on a dy-namometer.[60]

Despite such tempting incentives, few people volunteered to be mea-sured, and most anthropometric data were taken from soldiers or other people already subjugated to an authority willing and competent to mea-sure them. For example, when Luschan himself traveled to South Africa in 1905, he visited a prison, where he found "perhaps a greater number of Bushmen, Hottentots, and Griqua . . . than had ever before been placed at the comfortable disposal of a scientific traveler."[61] Colonial prison hospitals provided frequent occasions for measuring and collecting, and Virchow and other professors of medicine who were interested in anthropology steered their students toward the colonial service to take advantage of this opportunity.[62] Data gatherers measured not the people they wanted to measure but those whose social position required obedience. What mea-surements they took depended both on the amount of time that they could demand from a subject and on which parts they could expose and touch. The accuracy of those measurements depended on how forcefully they could pinch a particular person with calipers.

One way in which to avoid the exigencies of craniometry in the field was to send representations of people for anthropologists to measure in Berlin. While it might seem that photography would provide a convenient means of representation, anthropologists felt that, despite their efforts at standardization, they still could not take satisfactory measurements from photographs. One of the more novel solutions to transforming people from around the world into data for anthropologists was to take a plaster cast of an individual's face, hands, and feet or even of the whole body (see fig. 7.5). Anthropologists were particularly interested in the face, hands, and feet for two reasons. First, they believed that these were the most distinctively human parts of the body. The face was linked to human appearance and thought. The hands and feet were unique because their functions differed more from each other in humans than in any other animal. Furthermore, the feet were associated with the erect posture of humans, and the hands represented human art and skill. Also, anthropologists believed that the face, hands, and feet differed regularly among races and that one could therefore use the shape of these parts to characterize different populations.[63]

Making a plaster cast of a face took about forty minutes, during which time even pure gypsum plaster often began to irritate the skin. If the plaster

FIGURE 7.5
Virchow discusses a plaster cast of a human foot with colleagues. On the wall behind them hang casts of faces and hands. Anthropologists collected plaster casts of faces, hands, and feet because they believed that these body parts presented particularly significant racial characteristics.
Source: *Die Woche* 3, no. 4 (1901): 1791.

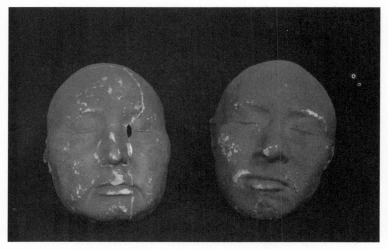

FIGURE   7.6

Plaster casts of the faces of two Inuit, Joe and Hanna. Such casts took forty minutes to
make and sometimes caused a great deal of discomfort to the subject. These casts were
made in 1880 by a Herr Dr. Bessels and are currently in the Berlin Museum of Natural
History. See [?] Bessels, "Abgüsse von Eskimo," *VBGAEU* 12 (1880): 133.
Source: Photograph by the author.

was adulterated with lime, as it occasionally was, the process could cause
serious burns.[64] Some favored putting pieces of straw or rubber tubes in the
nose of the subject to assist breathing, although others thought that this was
not necessary and distorted the face too much.[65] It is not surprising to learn
that Otto Finsch, the most famous anthropological plaster caster, found
that "in general a strong dislike prevails against the process of having a cast
taken," making it expensive and occasionally dangerous for the collector.[66]
Although plaster did not give anthropologists direct access to the dimensions of a person's bones, it did give them a virtual human body, which
could be studied at will (see figs. 7.6 and 7.7). Also, plaster casts of human
faces formed impressive displays in museums and curiosity shows, especially when painted (see fig. 7.8). Plaster casts could be infinitely reproduced and sold, which made them important sources of income at a time
when scientific travelers had few funding opportunities. Moreover, museums and collectors could copy plaster casts and trade them with each
other.[67]

    Like the political-economic system that transferred the possessions of
colonized people to anthropologists in Berlin, the system bringing in pieces
and representations of their bodies was, despite some difficulties, enor-

mously successful. Today, the physical anthropology collection of the Berlin Anthropological Society can be found in the attic and the cellar of the Berlin Museum of Natural History. The collection consists of over six thousand skulls as well as dried skin, hair, plaster casts of faces, heads, hands, and feet, postcranial skeletons, and perhaps even other parts that

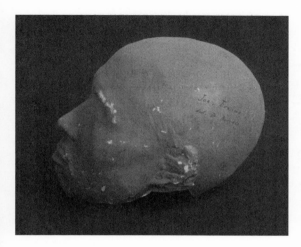

FIGURE 7.7

"Joe, Eskimo." Plaster cast of the entire head of an Inuit sent to Berlin (see fig. 7.6). Herr Dr. Bessels, who made the cast, placed a leather cap on Joe's head to keep his hair out of the plaster. See [?] Bessels, "Abgüsse von Eskimo," *VBGAEU* 12 (1880): 133.
Source: Photograph by the author.

FIGURE 7.8

Plaster cast of a face for museum display. Unlike casts such as those in figs. 7.6 and 7.7, this cast was made into a display piece, perhaps for the Royal Museum of Ethnology. It was painted, and an earring has been added. The object has been recently restored by the Berlin Museum of Natural History.
Source: Photograph by the author.

have remained packed in boxes since the Second World War. The cooperation between Berlin anthropologists and the German colonial state transformed administrators and soldiers into anthropological collectors and colonial raids and massacres into scientific expeditions.

One of the most important motivations for colonists to collect anthropological objects for the Berlin museum was the hope of being named to the Prussian Royal Order of the Crown or the Royal Order of the Red Eagle.[68] Because the museum of ethnology was a royal museum, retaining traces of its origin as the king's cabinet of curiosities, donations of artifacts could be interpreted as service to the Prussian monarch.[69] Royal orders conferred prestige on their members and gave them the privilege of wearing ribbons and medals with formal attire. Outward signs of social status such as royal orders were particularly important to European colonials. Perhaps to differentiate themselves from the indigenous population as "civilized," Europeans in general conducted their social life in the colonies much more elaborately than they did in Europe. In the colonies, formal evening wear, with which it would be appropriate to wear medals and ribbons, was worn at private parties, in clubs, and sometimes even at lunches in restaurants. Even more so than in Germany, orders would have been a daily and obvious part of life for Europeans in the colonies.[70] As Adolf Bastian observed while traveling in Batavia (present-day Jakarta) to collect artifacts for the museum: "Decorations are a strong impetus, especially among the doubtful mixtures of yellow and brown-black who adorn themselves with all kinds of medals from Austria, Italy, the Netherlands, Saxony, etc., which they were given for small collections from one place or another that they donated to museums. Since they show off these decorations constantly on their breast, on their visiting cards, on their stationary, etc., it is easy to spot someone with the kind of personality easily impressed by high decorations."[71] Bastian regarded these Europeans, greedy for medals, as a bit less than civilized and characterized them as racially other to indicate this.[72] European colonials found these medals extremely important to their social life and soon came to expect nomination to orders as a routine price for their collections. Indeed, one German living in Batavia demanded the return of his collection when it was deemed too small to merit an order.[73]

Colonists could thus exchange relatively cheap trade goods for the possessions of indigenous groups and then trade those objects for royal orders. A good example of this type of exchange occurred in German New Guinea in May 1898, when Lower Paymaster Max Braun of the HMS *Seagull* purchased objects for the Berlin museum of ethnology. Braun gave an indigenous leader a hatchet, a carpenter's plane, and four packets of tobacco in

THE SECRET OF PRIMITIVE ACCUMULATION

exchange for a wooden figure used to protect coconut trees from thieves.[74] Even this exchange, which went quite smoothly, illustrates the work required to fix such encounters as culture collecting nature. One might at first be tempted either to applaud or to denounce this exchange as a form of modernization. The Papuan, one might claim, abandoned traditional economic practices based on the magical manipulation of the world, represented by the wooden figure, in favor of modern economic practices based on technological intervention in the world, represented by the hatchet and the carpenter's plane. One might also point to the integration of the Papuan into a system of commodity exchange and away from a gift economy. However, rather than "modernizing" the supposedly primitive, the moment of exchange actually destabilized the distinction between the modern and the primitive. After all, the transaction between Lower Paymaster Braun and the Papuan leader concluded with a "natural person" holding a metal hatchet and a carpenter's plane and a "cultural person" holding a wooden statue supposedly having occult powers. Even more significantly, for collectors like Lower Paymaster Braun, this exchange was a step toward initiation into the Prussian Order of the Red Eagle or the Order of the Crown, groups centered around totems that transferred royal aura to their members. At the point of exchange, these objects had a number of ambiguous meanings in precisely the "subjective," historical sense that anthropologists hoped to eliminate from their study. Only when the objects were placed in an anthropology museum was the exchange stabilized as a contribution to science rather, for example, than as an exchange of one kind of magic for another.

Anthropologists were themselves troubled by the instabilities that accompanied nearly all contact between cultural peoples and natural peoples. The possibility that individuals like the Papuan leader lived on, with hatchet, carpenter's plane, and tobacco, was unsettling to anthropologists because it undermined their conception of ahistorical natural peoples. Rather than accepting historical change among natural peoples, anthropologists imagined that such exchanges destroyed indigenous populations. Bastian is reported to have often quipped that "the first ray of light that falls on a previously unknown tribe is often also the last."[75] Anthropologists believed that the first contact with a "previously unknown" social group would not only permanently alter its natural, ahistorical character but might even condemn it to physical extinction.[76] Anthropologists thus maintained that the conditions that allowed Europeans to encounter and collect from a society were also the conditions that would ultimately destroy that society. Shortly after Germany took its first colonies, Bastian wrote that he expected that most of the people colonized would "succumb to a quick physical decline and die out."[77] He meant not to criticize colonialism but rather to convey the urgency of the need to collect anthropological material as quickly as possible.[78] The death of natural peoples was conceptually preferable to the melding of scientist and subject that characterized "subjective" history writing. Anthropologists regarded historical change in natural peoples as a pathological phenomenon. Indeed, this was one of the reasons that anthropologists generally preferred to deal with objects rather than with people, for, as we have seen, the natural peoples they supposed they would encounter rarely appeared without traces of history, whether in the form of European clothes or more "culture" and less "nature" than anthropologists expected.

This ambiguous relation of savagery and civilization appears particularly clearly in the collection occasioned by the international suppression of the Boxer uprising in 1900. Kaiser Wilhelm encouraged German troops bound for China with his infamous "Hunenrede," the speech that inspired the First World War epithet for German soldiers: "When you meet the enemy, he will be defeated. Pardon will not be given; prisoners will not be taken. Those who fall into your hands are in your hands. As a thousand years ago the Huns under King Etzel [Attila] made a name for themselves that allows them still to appear mighty in tradition, so let the name Germany be known in China in such a way that never again will a Chinese dare even to look askance at a German."[79] German soldiers thus enforced colonial rule in China by acting like Huns, like barbarians. It may even have been the peculiar brutality of German rule in the Shandong peninsula, the geographic origin of the Boxers, that provoked the uprising in the first place.[80] After the uprising was put down, Bastian persuaded the German government to use the postwar plundering opportunities to collect for the museum of ethnology. While he could not persuade the German government to demand war reparations in the form of artifacts, he did arrange to have a museum employee sent to China to collect under the favorable conditions of the European occupation. As Bastian wrote: "If the basis of a lasting scientific monument can be laid during the horrors of war and despite its destruction, the war will appear in a gentler light to the eyes of civilization."[81] Bastian offered that collecting anthropological artifacts in China would give a civilized appearance to a war in which Germans behaved like "Huns" fighting *against* civilization. He suggested that "civilization" would view this destruction of civilization favorably if it were used as an occasion to collect museum pieces. Bastian's attempts to gain artifacts from German military involvement in China illustrates the unstable nature of the distinction between civilization and barbarism, a distinction on which both anthropology and colonialism nonetheless depended.

The anthropological critique of humanism participated in a larger transformation of the meaning of the human and of *Kultur* in the colonies. Both anthropology and colonialism were understood, and legitimized, as active, historical culture collecting (and ruling) passive nature. However, *nature* and *culture* were fragile constructions, for the colonial exchanges that created this binary simultaneously threatened to undermine it. The exchange of objects presupposed a great deal of historical, intersubjective interaction between *Kultur* and *Natur,* interactions that threatened the definition of *Natur* as passive and ahistorical. Furthermore, the violence that Europeans exercised in the colonies—which Kaiser Wilhelm himself compared to the violence of Huns—threatened the identity of Europeans as *Kulturvölker*. By collecting anthropological objects in the course of colonial rule, European domination—even in its most Hun-like forms—could, as Bastian recognized, present itself as *Kultur*. If colonialism was not *Kultur* ruling *Natur,* then the binary opposition that structured anthropology—*Naturvölker* versus *Kulturvölker*—was also no longer valid. Anthropology helped colonialism preserve the nature/culture binary, and, in doing so, the discipline picked itself up, so to speak, by its own ideological bootstraps.

By historicizing the objects of anthropology, I have, in a sense, undone the nature/culture binary. When anthropological objects arrived in Berlin, they bore traces of the colonial history that had brought them to the imperial metropolis. "The 'development' of a thing," as Nietzsche argued, "is a succession of more or less profound, more or less mutually independent processes of subjugation exacted on the thing, added to this the resistances encountered every time, the attempted transformations for the purpose of defense and reaction, and the results, too, of successful countermeasures. The form is fluid, the 'meaning' even more so."[82] Anthropological objects were heterogeneous in precisely the sense described by Nietzsche. Colonial rulers had "exacted" "a process of subjugation" on the bodies and possessions of indigenous populations and thus partly transformed them into artifacts of natural peoples collected by "cultural peoples. Many of these objects, such as the Maji Maji spears or King Kabua's birthday presents, also bore traces of what Nietzsche described as "successful countermeasures," various forms of resistance to colonial rule. Anthropological collections were to complete and stabilize the reinterpretation of the objects of the colonized as the artifacts of natural peoples, separated from the global history that made them available to anthropologists in the first place. Instead, these collections strengthened the connection of anthropology to colonial rule by further embroiling the discipline in the agonistic politics of taking, and giving meaning to, the possessions and the bodies of the colonized.

🗿🗿

CHAPTER 8

Commodities, Curiosities, and the Display
of Anthropological Objects

The Royal Museum of Ethnology (Königliches Museum für Völkerkunde), which opened in 1886 in Berlin, was intended to stabilize the bodies and the possessions of the colonized as natural scientific objects. However, the moment curators broke open the shipping crates packed with scientific cargo from every part of the globe, these objects became enmeshed in new interpretive struggles within the urban culture of Berlin. To retain the bodies and possessions of the colonized for their science, anthropologists had to prevent them from entering the popular European culture of exotic spectacles, a culture that had claimed these objects long before the opening of the museum. Presenting colonial objects to the public gaze, however, also placed these museum pieces in an uneasy relation with the burgeoning consumer culture of Berlin. Even though museum curators dismissed this culture of commodities and curiosities as "mere voyeurism" (bloße Schaulust), fundamentally different from their own scientific interests, the very idea that humans could be known by the objects that they possessed was informed by commodity fetishism. Indeed, anthropologists even borrowed technologies of display from the glass and iron commercial arcades that sprang up in Berlin and elsewhere in Europe. The museum sought to stabilize oppositions between science and mass culture, museum objects and consumer goods, and anthropology and the humanistic disciplines. However, the very success of the museum made it an arena in which these oppositions, as well as the basic project of anthropology, could be challenged by its visitors, its political patrons, and by a new generation of anthropologists, trained in the museum.[1]

Anthropologists exhibited conventional anxieties about the market, which offered new objects but also presented new threats to what was perceived to be a traditional order prior to the market, an order that anthropologists wished to study.[2] They were aware that the political economic system that made their study possible was based on a global intensification of commercial capitalism. Indeed, promoters of the discipline promised that it would improve the performance of German merchants in the world market, for example, by providing information on the fashions and tastes of areas in which they wished to conduct business.[3] However, anthropologists also realized that "international-cosmopolitan world trade" would change forever the "natural" character of the societies that they studied.[4] Particularly troublesome to anthropologists was the possibility that anthropological objects had been produced only to be sold to European collectors.[5] Indeed, this was one of the reasons that military expeditions were such valued sources of artifacts, for they took things not meant for Europeans. Luschan expressed typical anxieties about the commodification of anthropological objects in the Admiralty Islands: "What we have recently received from there is all absolutely inferior, often even intentionally 'slapped together' for export; it does not even remotely compare to our own older pieces. It is possible that one still might find some 'curiosities' in the interior, but I would not expect large, valuable series or significant museum acquisitions from the Admiralty Is[lands]."[6] Anthropological objects differed not only from commodities made for export but also from curiosities. Anthropologists regarded a single object by itself as a mere "curiosity."[7] As Bastian explained, since anthropology was an inductive science, it required "comparative series that are as complete as possible."[8] An anthropological object could be neither a commodity, made only to be sold, nor a curiosity, a unique object separated out from a series of other, similar objects.

Anthropologists described individual curiosities as the province of the general public's "voyeurism" or "lust for a show" (*Schaulust*). The distinction between anthropological ways of collecting and observing objects and *Schaulust* was especially urgent because, as we have seen, anthropologists often looked at the same things that titillated the audiences of popular exotic shows. Anthropologists spent considerable energy distinguishing their own projects from what they called varyingly a "cabinet of curiosities," a "panopticon," or "black vaudeville" (*schwarzes Tingl-Tangl*).[9] Differentiating themselves from these popular phenomena was particularly difficult because, even after the Royal Museum of Ethnology opened in 1886, anthropologists continued to conduct research in cabinets of curiosities, panopticons, and exotic vaudeville shows. Anthropologists believed that they could utilize these shows without suffering from the taint of mass culture because they differentiated the way in which they viewed them from the way in which ordinary people viewed them. Anthropologists asserted that, while others visited the panopticons simply to satisfy their "desire for the new" or their "simple lust for a show," they themselves attended these performances in a scientific way for scientific purposes.[10] They supposed that they had a special way of observing the bodies and possessions of the colonized, one that allowed them to obtain knowledge rather than mere entertainment.

Indeed, the anthropological gaze—at least according to its practitioners—transformed the commodities and curiosities of the metropolis, even pornography, into scientific evidence. In the first edition of a book describing his expedition to Brazil in 1887–88, the anthropologist Karl von den Steinen included as a frontispiece a photograph of a nude Brazilian whose penis was clearly visible. Apparently, Steinen received criticism for this photograph, which was not reproduced in a popular *Volks-Ausgabe* of the book. In the preface to this popular edition, Steinen challenged those who, in his words, had suggested "that we can regard [*anschauen*] valuable pictures only with the same eyes with which we regard piquant photographs from European metropolises." According to Steinen, pornography demanded a different way of seeing, different "eyes" than the eyes required for anthropological photographs. To the uninitiated, all nude photographs might appear pornographic, but anthropological modes of vision canceled the "piquant" element of the images. Steinen encouraged the readers of his popular book to "learn to grasp the naked body anthropologically and culture-historically, as in art they had learned to enjoy it aesthetically."[11]

Anthropologists made liberal use of their purported ability to see nudes anthropologically rather than pornographically. Indeed, the Berlin Anthropological Society's collection "Nude Studies of Races" contains numerous pornographic images, many of which depart widely from the conventions of anthropological photography (see fig. 4.3 above).[12] Twenty-one images in this collection are pornographic in the most literal sense, representing prostitutes (Greek: *pornē*), mostly from Egypt and Japan. The collection also included prints from Wilhelm von Gloedden's famous nineteenth-century erotic photographs of young men and adolescent boys in classical settings, categorized as anthropological studies of the Sicilian race and sometimes, because they were often posed with sea creatures, as zoological, too (see fig. 8.1). Other "racial nudes" are labeled "female American," "female European," "female Berliner," "Else Breipöhler," "Hilda Breipöhler," "male model, name unknown," "Lionel Strongart, German-American" (fig. 8.2), "L. Strongart as Boxer," "L. Strongart as Theseus in the battle with the Amazons" (fig. 8.3). The photographs of

FIGURE 8.1
A representative of the Sicilian race. Prints of Wilhelm von Gloedden's collection of erotic photographs were categorized as racial studies in the collection of the Berlin Anthropological Society. The catalog of the photography collection noted that this image was also of zoological interest (presumably because of the eel the model holds). Anthropologists professed that they could make use of such "piquant" images without tainting their scientific gaze with a pornographic leer.
Source: ABGAEU, P. 11463. Reproduced courtesy of Berliner Gesellschaft für Anthropologie, Ethnologie und Urgeschichte.

men followed contemporary conventions of erotic nude photography, casting the models as classical figures or as athletes.[13] While it may be tempting to expose anthropology as a cover for the sexual pursuits of bourgeois men (much like Kingsley Amis's *Egyptologists*), in fact the scientific perusal of pornography was one aspect of a larger attempt to reclassify the commodities and curiosities of the modern metropolis as natural scientific objects.

In contrast to popular *Schaulust,* anthropologists defined their way of seeing as a gaze that would take in all anthropological facts in a single, summarizing glance. This anthropological gaze also provided, as we have seen, an alternative to the "inspired insight" (*geniale Anschauung*) that Dilthey attributed to humanists. Anthropologists sought to achieve what Bastian called a "total impression" of the variety of empirically given "natural peoples." Anthropologists hoped that this method would allow them, as it had allowed botanists, to create a "natural system," a classification of their objects of study based on their true nature. They opposed this natural system, based on a total impression, both to historicist methods of interpretation and narrative and to the popular curiosity and to the commodity. From the beginning, Bastian recognized the amount of work that gaining an anthropological total impression would demand.[14] At the most basic level, it required simultaneously viewing people spread all over the globe, a feat that would have been physically impossible for an unassisted individual. It

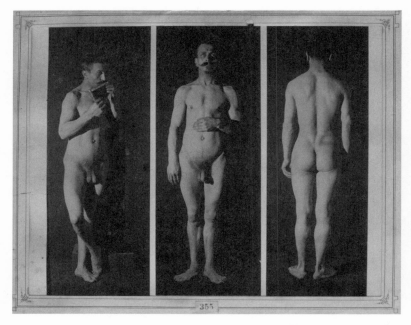

FIGURE   8.2

"Lionel Strongart, German-American." The use of conventions of anthropological photography in the middle image suggests that an anthropologist took these images. Placing
one hand just below the chest and leaving the other at the side allowed anthropologists to
consider hand form and measure arm length (see fig. 4.3 above). The photographer has
combined this standard anthropological format with the classical motifs traditional in photographs of nude men. The photograph on the left has Strongart in a very unscientific pose
playing a pan flute.

Source: ABGAEU, P. 355. Reproduced courtesy of Berliner Gesellschaft für Anthropologie, Ethnologie und Urgeschichte.

would also have been impossible for an individual in the field, who could
consider only one particular society. A complete collection of anthropological objects displayed in a museum, it was hoped, would allow an individual to achieve the anthropological total impression. One of the most
important practical tasks of anthropology was creating a mode of vision
that posited the objects of the colonized as natural rather than historical
and as the objects of science rather than of *Schaulust.*

The Royal Museum of Ethnology was to institutionalize this anthropological mode of vision. It was designed in consultation with anthropologists to
house both the royal anthropological collections as well as the collections of

FIGURE 8.3

"L. Strongart as Theseus in the Battle with the Amazons." This photograph of Lionel Strongart was likely also taken by one of the photographers in the Berlin Anthropological Society. In this image, the model has abandoned all anthropological convention and assumed a classical role typical in this period for erotic photographs of males.

Source: ABGAEU, P. 357. Reproduced courtesy of Berliner Gesellschaft für Anthropologie, Ethnologie und Urgeschichte.

the Berlin Anthropological Society. Bastian and others spent much time planning the new structure, for they hoped that it would become a model for all future anthropology museums.[15] As Bastian explained to Virchow: "Before now ethnological museums were sometimes natural scientific museums, sometimes art museums, and sometimes a kind of . . . chamber of horrors, and now we have reached the time to build the first ethnological museum as it should be."[16] There was a self-consciously utopian aspect to the museum construction, as anthropologists hoped to spread their own understanding of their discipline through this visual technology. The defining feature of the Berlin museum was to be its completeness. As Adolf Bastian wrote to the minister of culture in one of his early memorandums on the museum, it would bring together "the monstrous mass . . . necessary to sufficiently represent in a systematic, methodological order the ethnological provinces of the earth in their full extent."[17] The museum was designed as an apparatus that allowed an individual to view all humanity simultaneously by surveying the totality of the artifacts of humanity's natural representatives, the natural peoples.

The anthropologists who designed the Berlin museum took much inspiration, ironically, from the very commercial arcades from which they sought to differentiate themselves, for they found the glass and iron constructions used to display commodities ideal for displaying anthropological objects. Berlin anthropologists would have been especially familiar with this type of construction, for the panopticons that they frequented for ethnographic performers and freak shows were located in commercial arcades, great structures with roofs of iron and glass that allowed sunlight to illuminate the commodities offered inside to the consumer-*flâneur*.[18] The combination of glass and iron, which revolutionized interior urban space in late nineteenth-century Europe, allowed for a new kind of museum display. Glass and iron had made it possible to bring the brilliance of sunlight into

FIGURE 8.4
The Royal Museum of Ethnology in Berlin. Adolf Bastian, the director of the museum, had hoped to build a "system of pavilions of glass and iron." The state, however, demanded a monumental exterior.
Source: Sigrid Westphal-Hellbusch, "Zur Geschichte des Museums," *Baessler-Archiv* 21 (1973): 1–99, 14. Original in the archive of the Museum of Ethnology, Berlin (MfV).

enclosed areas, such as the Crystal Palace or the numerous commercial arcades in European cities. Reportedly, Bastian's initial plan modeled the
museum directly on these commercial structures, as a "system of pavilions
made from glass and iron."[19] The state, however, demanded a monumental construction and thus rejected this plan in favor of a building with a
more conventional exterior (see fig. 8.4).

The advantages of glass and iron construction, however, were realized
in the display cases designed in part by one of the museum's curators, Albert Voss. By the turn of the century, this type of cabinet came to be known
as "the Berlin iron case" and was also used in other anthropological museums.[20] Previous museum cabinets had consisted of wood frames supporting glass panes. Voss used iron frames instead of wooden ones because iron
frames could support much larger pieces of glass (see figs. 8.5 and 8.6).[21]
Despite their distaste for the public's *Schaulust* and the threat that they perceived in the commodification of the objects of the colonized, anthropologists found in the technologies of commercial mass society a means for

FIGURE   8.5
Advertisement for the type of cabinet
designed for the Royal Museum of Ethnology in Berlin (1914). This image emphasizes what anthropologists liked
most about the case: the narrow support
frame makes the case itself nearly invisible. A large number of artifacts would,
they hoped, become simultaneously visible when displayed in such cabinets.
The copy reads: "Museum Cabinets.
Dust-proof iron cabinets. Cabinets for
all sorts of collections and instruments.
Unsurpassed specialty / H. C. E. Eggers
& Co., Inc. Hamburg. Supplier to state
and city museums."
Source: Anzeigen zu der Museumskunde
10, no. 3 (1914) (unnumbered pages).

Eiserne Museumsschränke im Museum für Völkerkunde, Berlin

Lieferant:

PANZER A-G., BERLIN N. 20

FIGURE 8.6
Advertisement for the Berlin iron case. The photograph shows an ideal arrangement for the case, in which the artifacts are well illuminated and easily visible through the large glass panes.
Source: Anzeigen zu der Museum-skunde 10, no. 3 (1914) (unnumbered pages).

achieving the total impression that they believed to be the mark of their science.

Anthropologists hoped that these glass cases would distract viewers as little as possible from the artifacts on display. Because only the thin iron frame could be seen, the case itself became relatively invisible. The cases were made to identical specifications so that, in Bastian's words, "heterogeneously diverse cabinet forms" would not cause an "interruption of the evenly measured impression" of the collection or disturb "the view given to the public" (see figs. 8.7 and 8.8).[22] The regularity of the cases, it was hoped, would make them invisible to the visitor, who would notice only the displayed objects. The cases created the illusion that their contents floated in space and allowed the museum setting to retreat into the background. They maximized an individual's ability to view a large number of anthropological objects simultaneously.

The arrangement of the cases in parallel rows in large halls compounded their visual effects by allowing the museum visitor to consider the

FIGURE 8.7
Display of Indonesian artifacts in the Royal Museum of Ethnology, Berlin. The photograph shows how the Berlin iron cases made a large number of artifacts simultaneously visible and allowed a great deal of light to fall on objects. The tall object in the foreground indicates that curators did not always follow the antimonumental aesthetic of the museum. The object is, in any case, too large to fit into the cases. *Source:* MfV. Reproduced courtesy of the Museum für Völkerkunde, Berlin.

contents of a number of cases simultaneously (see figs. 8.9–8.11).[23] From almost any position, the viewer's gaze had to pass through multiple cases, thus giving the visitor a total impression of the artifacts. Because there were no visual barriers between the displays, the visitor would be pushed to compare the artifacts in adjacent cases. This, anthropologists hoped, would allow the eye to compare and generalize from the artifacts of different natural peoples and thus encourage anthropological induction. The total impression of anthropological artifacts was thus to follow from the organization of the cases. Furthermore, this arrangement prevented other types of looking. Viewers could not allow their vision to tarry on any single artifact; the cases forced the eye to leap from thing to thing. In the museum, no object could be singled out; all were forcibly combined into a totality. The closed space of academic history writing was replaced with the brilliant openness and plenitude of the commercial arcades.

The museum resisted interpretive language by eschewing written explanations of its displays in both labels and guidebooks. The guidebooks to the museum were remarkably reticent about the objects on display, although they did include general information about the regions from which

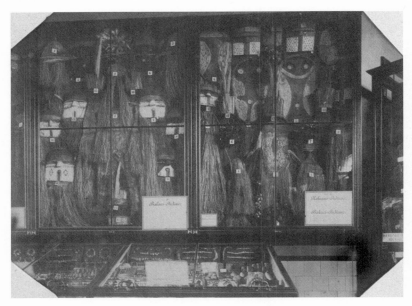

FIGURE   8.8
Display of North American masks in the Royal Museum of Ethnology, Berlin. Again, the
large panes of glass made possible by the use of iron frames allow a large number of objects
to be simultaneously visible. This, the museum designers hoped, would allow the visitor to
achieve the "total impression" that Bastian advocated as an anthropological method.
Source: MfV. Reproduced courtesy of the Museum für Völkerkunde, Berlin.

the artifacts originated. Alfred Grünwedel, one of the section directors,
explained this lack of written explanation as a result of the methods of anthropology: "Since they [conventional museum guides] mostly treat questions of general ... interest, they preclude that great quantity of detail
work that forms the primary activity of each section. They are simply neglected insofar as they do not find expression here and there in the labeling
of the cases."[24] For Grünwedel, museum work focused so exclusively on
specific objects that handbooks, which treat broad questions, would have
no place. Should visitors want some sort of text explaining the objects on
display, Grünwedel suggested that they turn to the labels identifying the
objects. These labels, however, were themselves extraordinarily spare, con-
sisting of the type and geographic origin of an object, with the occasional
addition of the name of its collector or donor.[25] Some of the displays had
photographs, maps, and charts to complement these labels, although this
seems to have been more the exception than the rule.[26] The museum had
no general introductory information posted in the halls.[27] Curators re-

FIGURE   8.9

Parallel arrangement of cases in the ethnographic museum in Dresden. Oswald Richter, trained in the Dresden museum, worked in the Berlin museum from 1904 until his premature death in 1908 from a poisoned arrow in a museum. He used this image as a positive example of the traditional methods used in the Berlin museum. The image demonstrates the effect that anthropologists desired from what they called the "fish-bone system": as a visitor peers through rows of parallel cases, a large number of artifacts become simultaneously visible. This was designed to compound the visual effects of the Berlin iron cases themselves.

Source: Oswald Richter, "Über die Idealen und Praktischen Aufgaben der Ethnographischen Museen," *Museumskunde* 4 (1908): 224–35, 224.

stricted the role of words in the museum to the terse labels. The knowledge acquired in the museum was to be based on looking at objects rather than reading texts.

This simple idea in architecture, based on commercial arcades, presented the possibility of a nonnarrative, natural science of humanity. By

FIGURE 8.10
Parallel cases in the Royal Museum of Ethnology, Berlin. Parallel rows of glass cases make
the contents of several displays visible at once. While the cases do make a large number of
objects visible, it is also apparent that viewers could not see the complete collection at once,
as the museum's designers had hoped might be possible.
Source: MfV. Reproduced courtesy of the Museum für Völkerkunde, Berlin.

displaying objects in the museum's cases, anthropologists transformed
them into artifacts of "natural" humanity. The "nature" in which objects
were fixed in the museum was a non-Darwinian fixed system of categories.
Berlin anthropologists disapproved of evolutionist anthropology museums, which sought to display artifacts in the context of the development of
human culture, such as the Pitt-Rivers Museum in Oxford or Gustav
Klemm's anthropological collection in Leipzig. One anthropologist de-
rided the Pitt-Rivers Museum and others that tried to order their collection

FIGURE 8.11

Display in the Royal Museum of Ethnology, Berlin. Parallel cases are visible in the background. Ideally, this arrangement would allow the visitor to view the numerous pots displayed in both cases simultaneously. The photographer overexposed the portions of the photograph near the window so that the cases farther from the window would be visible in the image. This suggests that the museum displays were not as well lighted as they appear in this photograph.

Source: MfV. Reproduced courtesy of the Museum für Völkerkunde, Berlin.

according to the development of types as "creations of enthusiastic private persons."[28] Like Pitt-Rivers, Gustav Klemm had ordered his collection in Leipzig according to developmental series, which he meant to illustrate an evolutionist narrative. Another anthropologist dismissed such narrative orderings of artifacts as "merely a doctrinaire interpretation [*Auffassung*], but no real understanding through viewing [*Anschauung*]."[29] The Berlin curators rejected displays arranged to illustrate narratives. Narrative was contrary to their preference for the visual and also to their understanding of nature as a static grid. To enter the museum of ethnology was, anthropologists hoped, to enter a world in which an antihistorical natural science of humanity was possible.

The display of artifacts in the Berlin museum of ethnology constituted an argument about how an observer should think about the collections and the people they represented. As Lee Rust Brown has shown, classification in the non-Darwinian natural history museum presented both the meaning of nature and the technique by which that meaning could be grasped.[30] Rather than presenting a more or less stable system of categories, as natural history museums could, the Berlin museum of ethnology presented only the potential for a stable system of categories. As Bastian repeatedly insisted, and as most acknowledged, anthropology had not yet found a natural system; the classifications of humanity would be the result rather than the foundation of the discipline and the museum. The museum was arranged according to the geographic origins of the artifacts simply because this seemed like the most neutral arrangement, not because the curators held each geographic region to constitute a unique cultural entity, comprehensible only in its own terms. The expectation that a total impression would lead an individual viewer almost intuitively to comprehend the underlying order of the collection authorized the apparent lack of order in the museum. Rather than displaying objects to illustrate a known order, the Berlin museum displayed them in the hope that an order would emerge.

The museum of ethnology thus presented not so much a specific classification of humans as a method by which humans could be classified and known. Humans, or at least natural humans, could, the museum sought to demonstrate, be subject to the same kind of classification as the rest of nature. Understanding humans was therefore, the museum offered, the province not of the humanist historian, who fit individuals into narratives, but rather of the natural scientist, who fit specimens into display cases and classifications. The relation of human scientist to human, the museum encouraged the visitor to accept, was one based not on the hermeneutic intersubjectivity of reading and interpretation but rather on the distant objectivity of vision. Anthropologists were not always sure what they were looking at and never found categories that they trusted. This, however, had less significance than the very fact that they were looking (rather than reading or interpreting). Their immense collection, anthropologists hoped, would be given order when it was seen simultaneously, in the total impression. Like the Paris natural history museum, described by Brown, the Berlin museum of ethnology identified the meaning of humanity with the technology for grasping that meaning. Anthropologists were not entirely disingenuous when then claimed to have no specific doctrines about human nature but only an empiricist methodology for approaching their subject. However, this methodology itself constituted a particular way of seeing, a particular theory of nature, and a particular understanding of humanity.

Curators carefully framed these modernist museum displays to situate anthropology in relation to other human sciences, please their political pa-

FIGURE 8.12

The foyer of the Royal Museum of Ethnology, Berlin. On entering, the visitor faced a statue of the Buddha beneath a classical ceiling. This recalled to the visitors their status as "cultural peoples" before they ventured into a museum dedicated to natural scientific knowledge of "natural peoples."

Source: MfV. Reproduced courtesy of the Museum für Völkerkunde, Berlin.

trons, and accommodate even those parts of their collection that did not fit into their schema, especially the "cultural peoples" of Asia and ancient America. After leaving the crowded street just off Potsdamerplatz in the center of Berlin, museum visitors found themselves face to face with a statue of the Buddha, a relatively familiar figure in a Germany enthusiastic for Indian culture (see fig. 8.12). Bastian believed that the late eighteenth- and early nineteenth-century European reception of Buddhist writings amounted to a second Renaissance, both extending and superseding the revival of classical Greek and Roman letters in the fourteenth and fifteenth centuries.[31] The figure of the Buddha—which had also appeared on the cover of the *Zeitschrift für Ethnologie* since its first issue in 1869—was no museum artifact but rather was meant to suggest that anthropology had progressed beyond the conventional academic humanities with their outmoded fixation on Greek and Latin antiquity.

The ceiling mosaic above the Buddha made clear, however, that anthropology did not reject the tradition of classical humanism but had rather extended it into the modern world of natural science and global colonialism. In the center of the mosaic was a representation of the heavens, depicting both astronomical bodies and classical divinities. Around the heavens, seven female figures represented the achievements of civilization: trade, science, art, religion, law giving, agriculture, and industry. Between each of these images of civilization were vignettes of important moments in human life, including travel, birth, death, and education.[32] The ceiling mosaic emphasized both familiar aspects of life for Europeans and conventional markers of civilization and *Kultur*. This room was not an anthropological display but rather a representation of anthropology's self-appointed role as modernizing *Kultur* and the human sciences beyond the confines of traditional academic humanism. It prepared visitors for their role as cultural peoples observing objective natural peoples.

The visitor unwilling to climb the museum's stairs would have come away from the museum with an impression of a monumental structure devoted to both patriotic and scientific purposes. The first floor contained prehistoric German artifacts and Schliemann's collection of Trojan antiquities. The museum of ethnology housed the "treasures of Troy" because anthropologists had persuaded the state that they were "not artistic [*künstlerisch*] but rather scientific [*wissenschaftlich*]" and part of "an epoch that lies behind the development of higher art."[33] They thus acquired for their museum Schliemann's objects, which had in any case aroused only the disdain of classical philologists.[34] The prehistory curator, Albert Voss, viewed the prehistoric German collection as not only of scientific but also of patriotic importance.[35] Placing these objects on the ground floor may thus have had a strategic function, for German anthropologists emphasized their nationalistic interests in prehistory to gain the attention and support of the Prussian minister of culture.[36] The Schliemann collection also had a kind of heroic significance because of its association both with Homer's epics and with its plucky collector. It was displayed, as Schliemann required, in a way that showcased individual objects.

The monumental exterior of the museum, the Buddha foyer, and the patriotic ground floor framed the second floor, the inner core of the museum, which displayed the collections of the colonial natural peoples. Only this floor presented in a perfect form the glass and iron technologies of the total impression devised by anthropologists. This floor held the collections of the *Naturvölker* proper: Africans, Pacific Islanders, and the indigenous inhabitants of the Americas. In addition to these displays of natural peoples, the floor also exhibited the "ancient cultural nations" of South and Central America, which included many pieces too monumental to fit into the iron cases. The third floor contained collections from the cultural peoples of India, Indonesia, Southeast Asia, Japan, Korea, and other parts of Asia.[37] Visitors interested in physical anthropology could find a small collection on the fourth floor, although it was sometimes closed to the public.[38] Anthropologists had originally hoped to have a larger display of human bodies, including a gallery of statues of fully costumed human types of the sort found in Castan's Panopticon. Such figures were used throughout the collection (see fig. 8.13), but the fourth floor contained only a modest exhibit of skulls, skeletons, and plaster casts of faces.[39]

The Berlin museum was extraordinarily successful in amassing the objects that would allow for a total impression of the natural peoples. According to the American anthropologist George Dorsey, it contained "the largest amount of ethnographic material to be found in any one museum in the world" and probably, he speculated, "a greater number of specimens than any other two museums combined."[40] However, as artifacts streamed in from around the globe, it became more and more difficult to display them in such a way that they could present a total impression. The museum, as we have seen, was designed to allow the viewer to gain a clear, simultane-

FIGURE 8.13

Royal Museum of Ethnology displays contained figures such as these to illustrate the physical anthropology of a region.

Source: MfV. Reproduced courtesy of the Museum für Völkerkunde, Berlin.

ous overview of as complete a collection of objects as possible. The form of the museum, which allowed for this total impression, gave meaning to its content, the complete collection. If an overview were not possible, the completeness of the collection would be pointless. Similarly, the completeness of the collection gave content to the overview: obviously, if the display cases contained only a few objects, one could not speak of an overview as a meaningful form of empirical, inductive knowledge making. The total impression that anthropologists hoped to present in the museum was to be total in two senses: it would consist of a single glance that took in the totality of the artifacts presented, and the artifacts presented would represent the totality of the natural peoples of the world. While anthropologists hoped that the displays in the museum of ethnology would unite the two aspects of the total impression, completeness and clear overview, in practice these two aspects contradicted one another. As the collection continued to grow, thus increasing its completeness, it became less and less amenable to a clear overview. The concept of completeness itself, therefore, became meaningless, as the collection became a confusing jumble rather than an orderly, comprehensible basis for creating inductive knowledge about humanity. As Adolf Bastian complained, every advance that the museum made toward its goal of completeness was a retreat from its goal of the totalizing, summarizing gaze.[41]

Even while still merely a collection within one of the royal museums in Berlin, the number of ethnological artifacts had grown so large that it had begun, as Bastian put it, "to escape all control."[42] Museum employees were so anxious to display the collections in a larger space that, when the new museum of ethnology opened in 1886, they moved without making careful lists of what they put in each of the new Berlin iron cases.[43] Curators occasionally lost objects in the chaos of the collections. If an artifact could not be found in the proper cabinet, curators would simply have to give up the search and hope that the object would some day turn up.[44] Others, not listed in the inventory, would sometimes turn up unexpectedly. For example, while cleaning his section, Luschan discovered five fur pelts, four hippopotamus teeth, three turtle shells, and two small elephant tusks. Being unable to identify any of them as part of the ethnological collection, he gave them to the zoology museum in Berlin.[45] Indeed, the collections were in such disarray that, as one researcher found while working in the museum, curators often could not identify even those objects that did belong in their collections: "How often has it occurred that I found some highly important object and, with my heart pounding, asked 'where does it come from?' Then the *Herr Direktor* or *Konservator* would bashfully tug at his hair and claim that a few years ago he did indeed know and that it would soon occur to him again. Then he would get out a few tattered shreds of paper, which bore the high title of 'archival files,' and leaf around in them. Normally the files could give no answer because the document in question was 'misplaced.'"[46] By the turn of the century, the collections had become such a jumble that, Bastian lamented, "the cases are overfilled so that every instructive arrangement of the collection remains impossible."[47] The American anthropologist George Dorsey remarked of the Berlin museum that "a majority of the collections can leave only a feeling of confusion in the mind of even the most careful observer."[48] Because the museum made such remarkable progress in achieving the completeness that anthropologists associated with their natural scientific method, it undermined the very summarizing gaze that gave this completeness meaning (see fig. 8.14).

Many visitors, in part correctly, perceived the disorganized displays as a conscious neglect of the public by the museum's curators. Although the museum of ethnology eschewed attempts to communicate with the general public, members of the public did visit the museum and sought to appropriate it for their own purposes. The public both openly protested the museum's failure to explain its collections to the nonspecialist visitor and covertly undermined the efforts of the curators to prevent popular participation in the museum. Visitors often expressed their discontent with the museum by complaining to attendants about the uninstructive guidebooks and demanding their money back.[49] Curators recognized the museum's failure to communicate anthropological knowledge. As Luschan wrote: "The public wanders dull-wittedly around our halls, and I am positive that, of a hundred visitors, ninety-nine do not realize when they move from one ethnographic province to another."[50] The total impression for which anthropologists strove appeared to the public, according to Luschan, as an undifferentiated mass of unexplained objects.

The founders of the Berlin museum of ethnology had, however, never intended to construct an institution of popular instruction and amusement. They imagined the ideal visitor as, in the words of one anthropologist, a "knowledgeable viewer" (verständnisvollen Beschauer).[51] Visitors with no prior knowledge of anthropology were not expected. Like many anthropologists, Luschan had a low estimation of the public's ability to understand the displays in the ethnographic museum, writing, for example, that the public cared only for "'impressions of tourists' and other stupid and hateful nonsense."[52] If the museum were to educate the public, anthropologists maintained, it would be only by instructing teachers and other already-educated people who would in turn transmit this knowledge to a wider population.[53] As late as 1906, the Berlin museum employee Oswald

FIGURE   8.14

Cluttered display in the Royal Museum of Ethnology, Berlin. Although displays such as
this were apparently rarely photographed for the museum's archives, they plagued visitors
and curators alike. In an age when displaying only portions of the collection seemed anathema to scientific museums, objects simply had to be crammed into display cases. Rather
than giving visitors a "total impression" of the entire collection, the practice resulted in the
collection becoming increasing invisible in its own tangle. Practical problems with the aesthetics of the total impression encouraged curators to seek new display techniques and, ultimately, new theoretical approaches as an alternative to the methods of Bastian and his
generation.
Source: MfV. Reproduced courtesy of the Museum für Völkerkunde, Berlin.

Richter wrote that anthropology museums should be designed primarily
for the educated (*Gelehrter*), although he disagreed with those who, he
claimed, advocated keeping the public out altogether.[54]

As members of an elite scientific institution with no popularizing aspi-
rations, anthropologists did not know whether to applaud or to denounce
the popular German Colonial Museum, which opened in 1896. This pri-

vately owned museum was, according to its promoters, to provide the kind of popular ethnographic spectacle offered in the Berlin Colonial Exhibition and satisfy the "the needs of all levels of the population for recreation, pleasure, and education [*Belehrung*]."[55] Anthropologists first reacted to the colonial museum by trying, as Luschan put it, to "nip it in the bud" because they viewed it as a misleading popular institution that would compete with the museum of ethnology for artifacts.[56] Luschan termed the colonial museum "shameless mischief" and compared it derisively to a panopticon.[57] However, the very elitist self-conception that initially inspired anthropologists' outrage at the colonial museum soon led them to endorse the popular institution. Since their own institution, they now reasoned, had no interest in entertaining or educating the public, the colonial museum could not be regarded as competition. Within a decade, the colonial museum's promotional pamphlets included praise from Luschan and other anthropologists for its efforts at popular instruction. "In my view," announced Karl von den Steinen, "the state would have had to create the German Colonial Museum if it did not already exist."[58] More than the initial outrage, this new tolerance for the colonial museum emphasized the strong distinction that anthropologists sought to draw between their own museum and popular culture. Anthropologists believed that the Royal Museum of Ethnology would construct a gaze that would neither instruct nor entertain but rather assist in constructing elite knowledge about the nature of humanity.

The supposedly esoteric nature of anthropological knowledge did not dissuade the general public from visiting the Berlin museum of ethnology. (Nor, for that matter, did it spoil anthropologists' own enthusiasm for *Völkerschauen* or freak shows at Berlin's panopticons.) Children climbed on the plaster facade of the museum, designed to give the impression that the brick building was constructed of imposing blocks of stone.[59] Within the museum, they ran amok and on two occasions set off fireworks inside the building.[60] The public also undermined attempts by curators to conceal erotic representations in the museum's displays. The potential of nudity to arouse *Schaulust* had long troubled anthropologists, and many shared the concern of the museum curator Karl von den Steinen that the public could view nudity only "like piquant photographs from European metropolises." Accordingly, the curators devised various ways to cover the sexual organs of unclothed statues in the museum. On one occasion, however, a visitor removed an amulet that Luschan had fastened before the unusually large genitals of a figure on display, exposing to the public the lurid aspects that curators tried to conceal from them.[61] Members of the public pushed museum curators to present displays that would educate or titillate them rather than merely ignoring their interests, demanding the kind of presentations that they had perhaps come to expect from their visits to Berlin's panopticons.

Like the general public, the employees of the museum also suffered from the attempt to make the museum of ethnology a complete, uninterpreted overview of a massive collection of artifacts. While Bastian set the direction of the museum and conceived of its basic mode of displaying artifacts, he left the practical work of setting up such displays to the curators. Karl von den Steinen and Bernhard Ankermann, two of these curators, seem to have resented Bastian for his unwillingness to participate in the cataloging that he required of the other employees.[62] Another, Fritz Graebner, objected "that they were supposed, like handymen, to take inventory of objects as they came in from every possible part of the earth."[63] Luschan similarly complained that work in the museum had become "mechanisch," involving mostly registering objects.[64] Because of the dearth of university course offerings in anthropology, those interested in the subject learned by volunteering at the museum. These students provided senior curators such as Luschan with a source of labor on which to place some of the burden of cataloging.[65] Luschan prevented even those researchers not employed by the museum from using the museum's collections for any work other than detail studies of individual objects, as the private scholar Leo Frobenius remembered: "As soon as the young author [Frobenius] began to turn away from small monographs, the old man [Luschan] used all means available to keep him from the collections that he directed. He [Luschan] explained that for the present our task would have to be collecting and treating the collected things monographically, in the most narrow scope."[66] By keeping anthropological research as narrowly empirical as possible, Luschan ensured that all researchers in the museum contributed to the cataloging project. Although Frobenius was not employed by the museum, his resentment against the narrow empiricism of the senior curators was shared by junior employees in the museum. By institutionalizing the project developed by Adolf Bastian and others, the museum of ethnology created a crisis that brought out the implicit contradictions of the project. The tedium of the work that an empirical approach to anthropology required led junior employees to oppose the methods of their seniors.

Around the turn of the century, curators began discussing ways in which to change the type of display in the museum to better appeal to the general public. The main suggestion for reforming the museum was to divide its objects into a *Schausammlung,* or collection for display, and an *Arbeitssammlung,* or collection for scientific work. This division had first been proposed by the general museum administration soon after the museum opened.[67] It was apparently a common display technique in natural history museums, in which the public wanted to see only a small fraction of the collection, while scientists needed a much larger number of objects for their research.[68] Bastian spoke for all the museum curators when he rejected such a division of the museum of ethnology: "It would mean cutting into a powerfully growing bud to [pluck] prematurely the few leaves that have so far sprouted, young and healthy, in order to set up a *Schausammlung,* a curiosity cabinet . . . , a kind of panopticon according to modern tastes to entertain with varied showpieces the impatient curiosity [*Neugierde*] of a sensationalistic [*schaulustigen*] public. One should hardly expect a serious-minded expert [*Fachgelehrten*] to sacrifice his time and work for such a purpose."[69] Anthropology, Bastian argued here, was too new a science to make the selections necessary for a *Schausammlung.* He believed that anthropology was still at a stage in which it could only collect material but not yet draw any conclusions from it. Selecting particular objects as more important than others, he maintained, could be done only on the basis of premature judgments about the societies that those objects represented as well as about humanity in general. To make a *Schausammlung* would, in Bastian's view, not only mislead the public, but also divide the collection in a way that would prejudice future ethnological research, burdening it with incorrect conclusions based on insufficient material. Even worse, Bastian implied, such a display would undermine the distinction between the "scientific" museum of ethnology and the panopticons, a distinction that formed the foundation of anthropologists' own understanding of the museum (see fig. 8.15). Bastian, as well as most of the other curators, refused in principle to alter the displays to accommodate the thousands of artifacts that continued to arrive each year from Germany's colonies.

By 1900, the disorder in the museum had become an issue of public concern, even provoking an exchange of anonymous letters in Berlin's elite newspaper, the *Vossische Zeitung.*[70] The general museum administration responded by asking the chief curators of each section of the museum to comment on dividing the museum's collections so that a smaller number of artifacts might be displayed in a way more comprehensible to the public. Possibilities for this division included separating the museum into a collection for display and a scientific collection, dividing the artifacts of the cultural peoples (societies of Japan, China, India, and ancient America) from those of the natural peoples (indigenous societies of Africa, Oceania, and modern America), and removing the physical anthropology displays on the top floor of the museum to a different museum altogether.[71] While the positions of each of the museum's curators differed on these various divisions, they appealed to a common structure of norms and understandings.[72] Curators expressed varying degrees of enthusiasm about keeping

FIGURE 8.15
"Counterexample": a display in
the colonial museum in Haar-
lem. The curator Oswald
Richter cited this image as an instance of aesthetic concerns taking precedence over scientific
concerns in an anthropology museum. In this neat arrangement
of artifacts he saw a "trophy-
like" display opposed to the "total impression" toward which
anthropology should strive. "Art
cannot be allowed to master science," Richter warned.
Source: Oswald Richter, "Über
die Idealen und Praktischen
Aufgaben der Ethnographischen
Museen," *Museumskunde* 5
(1909): 102–13, 103.

the collection of physical anthropology material in the museum of ethnology, although none wished to see the collection removed. The division of
cultural peoples and natural peoples provoked slightly more disagreement,
although all the curators shared similar fears about such a division. Separating the two would make impossible future research on the transition
from the nonhistorical cultureless state of the natural peoples to the historical and cultural state of the cultural peoples. Grünwedel and Müller, the
curators for India and China, respectively, also feared that separating
the cultural peoples out of the museum of ethnology would subordinate
their areas of specialty to the more art-historical approaches of other museums, which, they both agreed, would transform the collections into, in
Müller's words, a "scientifically worthless curiosity cabinet."[73]

The curators were too committed to the ideal of completeness to accept
any reduction in the quantity of objects exhibited in the museum, even if
this meant that the displays would be unable to instruct the public. Indeed,
they were willing to abandon the clear overview of objects in order to con-

tinue to progress toward completeness in the museum. Luschan concerned himself particularly with the tension between educating the public and providing a collection for researchers. After a group of schoolchildren visited the museum of ethnology, Luschan observed that "it would no doubt have served the interest of youth much better if they had spent their time playing ball outdoors." He recognized that most people "leave an overfilled museum as ignorant and uninstructed as when they entered it."[74] Nonetheless, Luschan privileged the scientific function over the public function of the museum, and, like the other curators, accepted its failure to communicate with the public as the price of its scientific value.[75] He did propose a complex system of sliding walls that would allow a small portion of the collection to be displayed to "the large, sensationalistic [schaulustige] public" while keeping the whole collection available to scientists, but nothing seems to have come of this project.[76] Attempts to move part of the museum to the outlying suburb of Dahlem to allow for a more spacious display also failed because of a lack of funding and a disinclination to move the museum so far from the center of Berlin.[77] While senior curators, especially Luschan, could recognize problems with the museum as it was conceived and executed, they could not successfully reform the institution that they had created.

The museum of ethnology stabilized the objects of the colonized as artifacts of natural peoples and made possible an antihumanist mode of knowledge based on natural scientific observation rather than literary interpretation. In completing the colonial interpretation of these objects, however, anthropologists entered into a problematic alliance with the culture of commercial galleries. Despite worries that anthropological objects might have been souvenirs for tourists or might become curiosities for a voyeuristic public, anthropologists relied heavily on the conventions of commercial culture. The objects themselves were part of a global commercial system that threatened their scientific status by transforming them into commodities, produced for consumption rather than simply embodying a timeless human nature. Museum curators borrowed technologies of display directly from the glass and iron construction of the commercial arcades. The shows that provided anthropologists with an important source of data were also part of the culture of the arcades. Perhaps equally inspired by the arcades, and by consumer culture generally, was the fetishistic belief that objects could contain (scientific) value in themselves, apart from the social and cultural contexts in which they were produced, circulated, and consumed. This was certainly fundamental to anthropologists' assertion that their study of objects was more reliable than historians' textual studies.

Anthropologists sought to differentiate the way in which they, as scientists, consumed these objects from the way in which objects were consumed in the popular milieu from which anthropology emerged. As the museum supported a distinction between natural peoples and cultural peoples, it also created a distinction between anthropologists as elite scientists and the uneducated public. Anthropologists maintained that their objects were not commodities or curiosities but rather constituted complete series of scientific evidence that allowed for a total impression. They further held that, when they viewed these objects, they did so as natural scientists rather than as untrained voyeurs. The museum thus allowed anthropologists to further specify their definition of German *Kultur*. Not only did they differentiate it from the unadorned *Natur* of the colonized, but they also differentiated it from the mass culture of the arcades.

In the last chapter, we saw how the natural peoples/cultural peoples distinction depended, in fact, on a dense network of interaction between the two terms of the binary. Similarly, the distinction between science and popular culture that anthropologists sought to institutionalize in the museum of ethnology belied a real interdependence. While the design of the museum originated in the arcana of anthropological theory and the utopian fantasies of anthropologists, it became a real part of the urban culture of Berlin. The public registered protests against the elitist conception of the museum, which denied it the instruction and entertainment that it had come to expect from the objects of the colonized. These protests became effective demands for change in a political context more and more attuned to integrating and educating a broad sector of the population. Curators in the museum found that their own experiences were not that different from those of the public. Like "handymen," or like clerks in commercial arcades, curators had to devote themselves to cataloging a seemingly endless inventory of products to be shown to the public. They also found the museum an uninstructive and confused jumble of artifacts and, like the public, demanded that the museum change. Of course, no anthropologist would have regarded his own demands as in any way similar to those of the public, and even the most ardent reformers rejected any kind of popularization. However, the similarities between elite and popular experiences of the museum are undeniable. The museum did not separate anthropology from mass culture, as its designers had intended, but rather opened up the discipline to the public more fundamentally than ever before. This new architectural structure did not merely undermine the most basic categories of the discipline but would also determine its theoretical development in the twentieth century.

PART IV

History without Humanism: Culture-Historical Anthropology and the Triumph of the Museum

By institutionalizing their discipline in the Royal Museum of Ethnology, anthropologists hoped to conduct their project of an inductive natural science of humanity on a more secure basis and on a grander scale. Paradoxically, the museum provided the foundation for a revolution against the very theory that it had been built to secure, for anthropologists radically altered the social milieu of their discipline by institutionalizing it. The professionals employed in the museum of ethnology faced demands that differed markedly from those of the variety of amateurs who made up the membership of various anthropological societies. These curators devoted their professional energies exclusively to the study of anthropology and, at the same time, had to engage a much broader audience than amateur anthropologists had ever addressed. In the early twentieth century, two of these museum curators, Fritz Graebner and Bernhard Ankermann, responded to their own dissatisfaction with museum work, the complaints of the public, and broader, political demands for popular education by proposing to end the radical separation between anthropology and history. They proposed to treat all societies—even those classified by their seniors as "natural peoples"—as having culture and history and thus established what came to be known as the "culture-historical method" (*kulturhistorische Methode*) in anthropology, sometimes also called "diffusionism" or the *Kulturkreislehre* (theory of culture circles).[1]

Junior curators at least partially accepted the mission of the museum as an institution of popular instruction and began offering public tours of the museum on Sundays.[2] The education reforms encouraged by Kaiser

Wilhelm II, which emphasized patriotism and general character formation over specialized philological studies of Latin and Greek in the *Gymnasium,* may have also encouraged curators in the museum of ethnology to
reach out to the public. The kaiser's demand that *Gymnasia* "educate patriotic [*nationale*] young Germans, not young Greeks and Romans," may also
have made the discipline of anthropology itself seem more relevant to public education than it had in the more classicist decades of his grandfather's
reign.[3] The culture-historical method allowed curators to select certain objects as particularly significant historical traces and place them in broad
narratives about cultural contact, thus avoiding the unexplained jumble
that had irked earlier museum visitors. The separation between expert anthropologists and the uninstructed, voyeuristic public thus began to collapse in the museum even as museum anthropologists themselves became
more professional.

While the museum foiled the original intentions of its creators, it fur-
thered the project of anthropology as a *studia humanitas* adapted to a world
of imperialism, mass culture, and natural science. Presenting anthropology
as a form of history heightened its challenge to humanism: anthropology
would be not merely a natural scientific discipline separated from history
but rather a natural scientific form of history, superior to humanist variants. Culture-historical anthropologists did not propose to follow the doc-
umentary and interpretive, "subjective" methods of traditional historians;
rather, they continued to pursue their own "objective," antihumanist
methods. Anthropologists pursuing this new direction could finally abandon the fruitless search for pristine natural peoples unaffected by history
and culture. Conceding that societies supposed to be natural had a history
also undermined the achronological and antinarrative conception of nature that had grounded the discipline in the previous century. After the
turn of the century, when they had accepted the possibility of history and
narrative in nature, German anthropologists could—and did—begin to
subscribe to doctrines of biological evolution.

That junior curators responded to crises in the Berlin museum of ethnology by reconciling the natural scientific approach of anthropology with
narrative and history stems likely from the example of the human sciences
in Leipzig, where scholars such as Wilhelm Wundt, Karl Lamprecht, and
Friedrich Ratzel had long been comfortable mixing humanistic and natural scientific disciplines.[4] The differing attitudes toward the nature/cul-
ture binary had meant that, during the nineteenth century, there had been
little mutual interest among Leipzig human science and mainstream German anthropology, which had depended on a fixed boundary between na-

ture and culture. Indeed, despite the fact that Leipzig had an important anthropology museum even before Berlin did, in 1876 Leipzig's local anthropological society dissolved, and only two members remained in the German Anthropological Society.[5] Perhaps this resulted from the disdain of Wundt, Lamprecht, and Ratzel for anthropology as it was practiced in Berlin and elsewhere in Germany.

Still, the attempt by Berlin curators in the early twentieth century to bridge the gap between anthropology and history was surely inspired by Karl Lamprecht's *Kulturgeschichte.* Although Lamprecht was no advocate of anthropology as it was practiced in Germany, anthropologists must have sympathized with his call to have a more scientific history focused on broad social and cultural processes rather than on political history and unique individuals. The vehemence with which professional historians rejected Lamprecht's position in the famous *Methodenstreit* of the 1890s must also have been familiar to anthropologists.[6] Despite his disdain for German anthropology as "purely descriptive," Lamprecht did, in the preface to the 1902 edition of his *Deutsche Geschichte,* suggest that anthropology might someday offer comparative data for the study of the "primeval Teutons."[7] Probably more important for German anthropologists than Lamprecht's own position was his exemplary attempt to move the human sciences away from the humanist historicism of earlier decades. Anthropologists just beginning their careers around the turn of the century seem to have held similar hopes for broadening anthropology to include historical development, much as Lamprecht would have liked to include anthropology in his own discussions of historical development.

The Leipzig geographer Friedrich Ratzel was perhaps the most important inspiration for the culture-historical turn in German anthropology. Ratzel had been a journalist and popularizer of Darwin before he joined the faculty at the technical university in Munich in 1875. In 1886, Ratzel became a professor at the University of Leipzig, where he remained until his death in 1904.[8] Although he had been enthusiastic about the German Anthropological Society when it had first been founded, he never joined its ranks and soon became an important critic of its ahistorical approach.[9] Ratzel's *Anthropogeographie* is often incorrectly regarded as constituting a geographic, or diffusionist, alternative to mainstream German anthropology. German anthropologists had in fact never disregarded geography, and many even accepted some notion of diffusion. The use of what were identified as racial similarities to reconstruct the migrations and interactions of societies had long been a standard anthropological practice.[10] Bastian was exceptionally adamant in his idealist notion of the uniformity of all humans, holding that, without "specific indications of

contact," one must always conclude that similarities among various societies result from "an identical course of ideas [*Ideengang*]."[11] However, Virchow was far less strict and even proposed as one of the main issues of
anthropology the question whether culture developed independently
within human groups or was passed from society to society.[12] Even if diffusionist explanations were not welcomed by anthropologists, geographic
variation was, for it explained differences among natural peoples as
regional expressions of a common human essence.[13] Ratzel's work was
threatening to German anthropologists not because of his interest in geography, but because he rejected the idea of uniform natural peoples and demanded that all societies be studied historically.[14]

Ratzel's focus on the history of geographic diffusion undermined the
assumption common to most German anthropologists that a single, ideal
essence united all humans and could be studied easily in the *Naturvölker*.
The controversy thus focused especially on cultural parallels, apparently
identical phenomena appearing in widely distant places among populations with no obvious relation to each other. German anthropologists
would most often explain such similarities as the result of the uniformity of
human nature, which produced identical phenomena in different places.
In one of his most famous criticisms of this method, Ratzel pointed out its
obvious practical and theoretical flaw, using the example of the parallel
appearance of wooden armor around the Pacific: "If wooden armor
[*Stäbchenpanzer*] came into being among the Chukchi [of Siberia], on the
Aleutian Islands, in Japan, and in Polynesia all through a *Generatio aequi-
voca* of the human intellect, it would be enough to study a single case of this
kind to understand all the others. Then the spirit of man more than the
productions of this spirit would interest ethnography, then the careful
study of the geographic distribution of an ethnographic object would have
but little value, and ethnology could do without the help of geography."[15]
Ratzel is perhaps a bit unfair here, for Bastian and others would have advocated studying all wooden armor in all its geographically determined
variations before specifying the nature of wooden armor. However, Ratzel
was right that anthropologists studied wooden armor not because the
Chukchi, the inhabitants of the Aleutian Islands, the Japanese, or the Poly-
nesians made it, but rather because humans (in general) make wooden armor (in general). In the same work, Ratzel further pointed out that
Bastian's method of seeking universal "basic thoughts" (*Grundgedanken*)
behind all particular social phenomena could explain similarities among
societies but not their differences. Ratzel thus regarded the anthropology
of natural peoples as reductionist because it treated societies merely as examples of natural humanity rather than studying them in their geographic

and historical specificity. For Ratzel, on the other hand, wooden armor was of significance, not only for humans in general, but also for the study of the cultural history and human geography of the Pacific. Ratzel was interested in the societies of the world rather than merely in "the human intellect."

Anthropologists responded to the challenge of Ratzel's method by re-asserting the distinction between the unchanging and universal natural humanity that they studied and the ephemeral particularities chronicled in historical studies. In an 1888 review of Ratzel's *Völkerkunde,* Virchow employed a Kantian distinction between the analytic and the synthetic to convey this fundamental difference: "The analytic method of ethnology can work well with the synthetic method of culture history only when the latter [that is, culture history itself] first begins, after ethnology has cre-ated a secure basis for observations. The close relation between the history of culture and the history of religion demonstrates conclusively how little the ethnological position of individual peoples means for their culture-historical and religious position in their later development, when they de-velop close relations with ever wider circles of foreign peoples."[16] Anthro-pology formed a necessary "basis" for culture history because it makes comprehensible the nature of humans prior to their historical interactions. Indeed, for Virchow, the history of religion demonstrates that these inter-actions obscure, rather than reveal, the true nature of humans. Perhaps he thought of the "Nubians" he studied at the zoo, who all turned out to be Muslims or Christians.[17]

In 1904, Ratzel attacked the separation between anthropology and history in an article for the *Historische Zeitschrift* that must have been offensive to practitioners of both disciplines.[18] Ratzel argued that there was no inher-ent difference between the societies that anthropologists studied and those studied by historians and that, out of a desire to have knowledge about all the societies around the globe, anthropologists simply investigated those groups that historians refused to consider. The distinction between "nat-ural peoples" and "cultural peoples," Ratzel suggested, had more to do with disciplinary prejudices than with inherent differences among so-cieties. Ratzel attacked the notion that only literate people could be the subjects of historical research. He reminded his readers that, before hiero-glyphs had been deciphered, historians had written about ancient Egypt solely on the basis of physical evidence, ranging from ordinary objects of daily use to great monuments, and that the study of monuments itself formed an important part of the history of every society.[19]

Ratzel further charged that the contrast between history as the study of events and individuals and anthropology as the study of static collectivities relied not on anything inherent in the subjects themselves, but rather on the distance between the scholar and the object of study. Ratzel noted that, with the passage of time, even the battles of Königgrätz and Sedan, the two most celebrated military events in the founding of the German Empire, had come to appear less and less as the achievements of individuals and more and more as manifestations of collective "peoples" (*Völker*).[20] Finally, Ratzel pointed out the obvious fault in the concept of natural peoples: the assumption that certain people living in the present represented the "primal, original condition" (*Urzustand*) of humanity, that certain people could be deemed untouched by time and history and could therefore be held to represent humans in their natural state.[21] Ratzel thus encouraged anthropology to give up its project of classification and to focus instead on history, which he envisioned as a narrative about the interaction and spreading of cultures in geographic space.[22] The role of geography in Ratzel's thought was in one sense similar to its role in Bastian's: it formed the medium or arena in which the real processes took place. For Ratzel, this process was history; for Bastian and most German anthropologists of his generation, it was the manifestation of a universal human nature.

Geographic historicist attacks on German anthropology did nothing but commit both sides more resolutely to their original positions until Leo Frobenius, a proponent of the culture-historical method, came to conduct research in the Berlin museum.[23] Frobenius, whom we encountered earlier complaining about the strict control that Luschan exercised over researchers in the museum of ethnology, was a self-taught student of African culture who in the 1890s began publishing books based on travel literature and museum collections. Although he belonged to the Berlin Anthropological Society, Frobenius rejected the highly empirical methods of Bastian and others, explaining: "They do an extraordinary amount of measuring, describing, combining, criticizing, and even microscoping. But all that represents a decline into that favorite fault of the German scholar, namely, sinking into fruitless tinkering, rather than directed, creative progress."[24] Frobenius proposed that, instead of this dry cataloging, scholars turn their attention to the "development" (*Entwickelungsgeschichte*) of cultures. He regarded cultures as "organic beings" (*organische Lebewesen*) with a life cycle of birth, maturation, and death. He thus regarded anthropology as a kind of vitalist biological science. He was particularly interested in studying cultural development, especially the "inheritance" (*Vererbung*) of culture through contact among societies.[25] Frobenius followed Ratzel in his interest in the development of cultures rather than in the classification of static natural peoples, but he rejected attempts such as Ratzel's to introduce history into anthropology and regarded the discipline as the natural scientific study of natural peoples. Like most anthropologists, Frobenius modeled anthropology on the natural sciences but relied on an evolutionary, and possibly Darwinian, model of natural science.[26]

Frobenius viewed cultures themselves as living beings independent of their individual "bearers" (*Träger*). Thus, while praising the cultures of Africa to a greater extent than perhaps any other anthropologist of his time, Frobenius expressed contempt for "Negroes" (*Neger*), the bearers of that culture: "Whether in the north or in the south, Negroes seem the same. As young peoples [*Völker*] they are brutal fellows, as old peoples cowardly and cruel lads."[27] Frobenius believed that the contrast between the praiseworthiness of African culture and the despicable nature of African people supported his argument that culture was independent from its bearers. He did not believe that African people invented their own culture; rather, he thought that it had originally spread with migrations from Asia.[28] Although culture-historical anthropologists were often racists, their views belittled colonized people no more than those of earlier German anthropologists, who denied that natural peoples had culture and history.

While conducting research in the African and Pacific section of the Berlin museum, Frobenius evidently influenced two junior curators, Fritz Graebner and Bernhard Ankermann, who would adapt the methods of Ratzel and Frobenius to mainstream German anthropology and to the requirements of museum work. Fritz Graebner had studied history at the University of Berlin, completing a dissertation on Bohemian politics in 1901. In 1899, while writing this dissertation, Graebner began working as a scientific assistant under Luschan, who had him catalog artifacts from the Pacific. Graebner's historical training gave him an unusual background for a discipline that considered itself a natural science, which surely made him more receptive to Ratzel's and Frobenius' historicism. Graebner remained an assistant under Luschan until 1906, when he moved to Cologne to help Wilhelm Foy set up an anthropology museum there.[29] Bernhard Ankermann had been hired as an assistant under Luschan two years before Graebner, in 1897, to catalog African artifacts. In 1901, he completed a dissertation on the cultural history of musical instruments and continued to work in the Berlin museum for the rest of his career.[30]

In November 1904, shortly after the *Historische Zeitschrift* published Ratzel's essay on history and anthropology, Graebner and Ankermann delivered lectures to the Berlin Anthropological Society that have rightly been remembered as the beginning of a scientific revolution in the discipline. Graebner's and Ankermann's lectures, on "cultural circles and cultural strata" (*Kulturkreise und Kulturschichten*) in Oceania and Africa, began a shift in German anthropology from ahistorical idealist empiricism to culture history. Graebner encouraged his colleagues to go beneath the superficial "appearances" (*Erscheinungen*) that they described in their work to the deeper "cultures" (*Kulturen*) that formed the "coherence" (*Zusammenhang*) among them. When Graebner spoke of "appearances," he must have thought especially of the countless artifacts that he and his colleagues at the museum "were supposed, like handymen, to take inventory of . . . as they came in from every possible part of the earth."[31] However, the concept applied equally well to the ethnographic writing of the nineteenth century, which also seemed to skim across the surface of phenomena, unwilling to give narrative or any other coherence to the natural peoples. For Graebner, every human group, not just those regarded as cultural peoples, had a culture; there were no simply natural people. The similarities among appearances in various groups of people indicated that they possessed historically related cultures and had derived from a common origin; Bastian would have argued that such similarities simply pointed to a common human nature.

Although Graebner attacked the fundamental presupposition of earlier anthropology, he was careful to maintain the importance of museum work. After all, he did not want to theorize himself out of a job. He cautioned that, since anthropologists currently possessed only "superficial" knowledge about the cultural coherence of appearances, the first task of the new culture-historical method would be determining which groups of objects belonged together as part of a single "cultural circle" (*Kulturkreis*). This would take years: "We must simply consider the possibility," Graebner advised, "that hardly a single one of our contemporary cultures has a single origin." Once the appearances of contemporary cultures were grouped together, the next task would be to determine the historical relations among these various local cultural circles.[32] Unlike Frobenius, Graebner hoped to initiate a research program in anthropology rather than simply proclaiming a solution to anthropological questions. Graebner was a professional anthropologist with interests in preserving the institution in which belonged, rather than, like Frobenius, a revolutionary outsider attempting to discredit that institution. Still, no less than Frobenius, Graebner was committed to questioning the most fundamental assumptions of the anthropology of Bastian's generation by asking "Whether the so-called people without history are not also subject to historical representation."[33]

Graebner also initially attacked anthropologists' preference for objects over written descriptions of intangible customs, although he would later modify this position. For earlier anthropologists, such subjective observations recorded by individual witnesses compared unfavorably with objects, which could not, they reckoned, lie. In his 1904 paper, Graebner not only relied on written reports but actually maintained that such information about the "social condition" (*gesellschaftlichen Zustand*) of a group provided a more secure indication of a specific culture than its "more easily and distantly transportable material culture."[34] Earlier anthropologists had privileged ethnographic artifacts and racial traits over linguistic evidence, arguing that natural peoples could learn new languages but that their possessions and bodies were the spontaneous expression of an unchanging nature, mediated only by geographic conditions. Graebner took this logic a step further, finding objects as suspect as earlier anthropologists had found language since objects too could also be transported from culture to culture. His assumption about the relation of what he called *material culture* to human groups differed fundamentally from that of earlier anthropologists since he assumed a long history of interaction and exchange among groups rather than an ahistorical world of natural peoples. Thus, although Graebner did cite objects from the museum of ethnology in his lecture, he relied especially on reports about kinship systems to describe a western and an eastern Papuan culture.[35] As Ankermann later pointed out, Graebner could rely on written reports of Pacific cultures from the famous expedition led by the British anthropologist Alfred C. Haddon to the Torres Straits in 1898, which seemed more reliable than the earlier accounts by merchants, soldiers, and administrators.[36] Graebner's earlier training as a historian was likely as important as this new high-quality data, for it gave him a greater skill than his natural scientific colleagues in evaluating and using written documents.[37]

Graebner later reasserted the primacy of objects over texts in a chapter of his 1911 *Methode der Ethnologie* titled, in a twist on the language of academic historiography, "Source Criticism" ("Quellenkritik").[38] Graebner divided sources into the "immediate" (*unmittelbar*) and the "mediate" (*mittelbar*). "Immediate sources" were artifacts, which he now followed previous anthropologists in maintaining, could not present false information. To use immediate sources, the analyst had merely to determine their age, their place of origin, and their authenticity. Graebner's practice differed from that of earlier museum anthropologists only in that, as a culture historian, he was interested in the age of an object as well as in its place of origin. Mediate sources, on the other hand, were reports written by Europeans. Anthropologists had to evaluate these reports critically before they could use them, Graebner cautioned, because such accounts always contained a subjective element. While his 1904 lecture contained a far more radical position than his later *Methode der Ethnologie,* Graebner's openness to history, language, and narrative was of the utmost significance for his new approach to anthropology.

Although the methods that Ankermann employed in his 1904 lecture were more conventional than Graebner's, his conclusions were far more radically historical. Ankermann relied exclusively on objects from the collections that he helped catalog in the museum of ethnology, explaining: "Knowledge of the social organization of the African peoples is unfortunately so fragmentary that one cannot even gain a clear approximate picture of the geographic distribution of social forms; I must therefore completely ignore this aspect."[39] While Graebner had relied on literary sources, he had shied away from making strong historical conclusions about the geographic diffusion of culture, focusing more on reconstructing the two Melanesian culture circles. He did maintain that the East Papuans had been "totally suppressed" by proto-Polynesians and cautiously intimated that further research might indicate a common Central Asian origin for East Papuans and Africans.[40] In contrast to these rather timid conclusions, Ankermann boldly proclaimed that similarities among African and Asian material cultures indicated a historical link between the two continents. Ankermann maintained that the West African culture circle shared a common origin with the East Papuan culture circle and that the East African culture circle had originated in West Asia.[41] Graebner had called for a historical treatment of people previously presumed to have no history and had advocated the use of the literary sources favored by historians and rejected by anthropologists. Ankermann actually fashioned a historical narrative about people previously relegated to ahistorical, natural scientific classification.

Historicizing the objects of anthropological study undermined the concept of natural peoples. While many anthropologists continued to use the word, the idea that natural peoples exhibited pure human nature began falling apart. A year after his 1904 lecture, Graebner explicitly challenged the assumption that natural peoples represent the original condition of all humanity, the assumption that they exist outside history and thus shed light on humanity free of historical accident. While responding to a lecture by Kurt Breysig, a supporter of Karl Lamprecht's, who wanted to use anthropological data to reconstruct a general history of humankind, Graebner proclaimed: "The view that natural peoples . . . represent the original condition [*Urzustand*] of our cultural peoples can be shared only to a limited extent. We must pay heed to the conviction that the natural peoples also did not let the centuries and millennia pass over them without a trace but rather are as distant as we cultural peoples from some common origin."[42] Graebner subverted the natural science of human nature and made anthropology, like the other humanities, a branch of history. Ankermann more baldly rejected the disciplinary boundaries between history and anthropology when he wrote: "Only the circumstance that culture historians disdained dealing . . . with the culture of the natural peoples, the 'savages,' led to the development of ethnology as a separate discipline." Anthropologists should, Ankermann maintained, study the "actual history of culture" (*tatsächlichen Geschichte der Kultur*) rather than universal human nature.[43] Similarly, in his 1911 *Methode der Ethnologie,* the most canonical statement of the culture-historical method, Graebner counseled anthropologists not merely to grasp "the pure thought of development" but to "attend to the real, individual culture-historical events."[44]

In a 1913 article in the *Zeitschrift für Ethnologie,* the Austrian anthropologist and missionary Wilhelm Schmidt approvingly proclaimed that "no one raises Bastian's hope any longer of finding the totally uninfluenced 'pure' natural soul among the natural peoples."[45] Four years earlier, Schmidt had founded the journal *Anthropos,* a new forum for the culture-historical method in anthropology.[46] The culture-historical method as introduced by Graebner and Ankermann fundamentally altered German anthropology in the twentieth century. Understanding anthropology as a historical discipline differed not only from previous German anthropology but also from British and American variants of the discipline.[47] While neither the Berlin Anthropological Society nor any other group of anthropologists became practitioners of culture history overnight, the importance of the culture-historical method did grow throughout the German-speaking world over the next decades.[48] After the First World War, functionalist anthropologists such as Richard Thurnwald and Wilhelm Mühlmann continued to oppose the historicism that Graebner had introduced into the discipline.[49] As late as 1937, a contemporary of Fritz Graebner's remarked that the culture-historical method still offered anthropology an opportunity to be integrated into "the older historical sciences," an alliance that he felt would determine the future of the discipline.[50]

Although Graebner and Ankermann did not immediately revolutionize anthropological museums, they did influence other curators and initiate transformations in their display techniques. Assistants from the Berlin museum formed an important cohort of museum curators throughout Germany, and many came to advocate a more selective system of display than Bastian's "total-impression" model. Karl Weule, a former Berlin curator who had eventually become director of the Leipzig anthropology museum, challenged the Berlin style of displaying a complete, geographically organized overview of artifacts. He instead advocated presenting

"developmental series" (*Entwicklungsreihen*) to give the public a basic understanding of the development of culture.[51] Although Konrad Theodor
Preuss, an assistant curator in the Berlin museum, denounced Weule's
plans as a "dilettantish" appeal to the public, he also advocated selective displays of objects and "development historical" (*entwickelungsgeschicht-
lichen*) arrangements in the Berlin museum.[52] In 1906, Graebner moved to
the anthropology museum in Cologne to work under Wilhelm Foy, and
the two became known and respected in Germany as the "Cologne school"
of culture-historical curators.[53] Graebner worked in the Cologne museum
until he retired in 1928, becoming, after Foy's death in 1925, director of the
museum. Graebner also began to call for a *Schausammlung* to instruct the
public, although lack of funds prevented him from realizing this plan on a
grand scale.[54] In 1917, Ankermann became a director in the African section of the Berlin museum. However, not until 1924, in the more democratic environment of the Weimar Republic (and in the year of Luschan's
death), did the museum of ethnology reorient its displays toward instructing the public.[55] While the culture-historical method can hardly be said
to have immediately solved any of the problems facing either the discipline
of anthropology or the Berlin museum of ethnology, it did begin a dialogue about anthropology and museum techniques that would continue
throughout the Weimar Republic and afterward.[56]

While the culture-historical method as presented by Graebner and
Ankermann constituted a revolution in the way in which anthropologists
thought about their work, it also provided a new theoretical grounding for
the conventional practices of anthropology. Rather than undermining anthropology, the culture-historical method lent support to the discipline at a
time of crisis. The institutionalization of the discipline as it had previously
been practiced in the museum of ethnology was undermining its own credibility with the public and with the state. The concept of natural peoples
proved inadequate to describe the individuals anthropologists studied. The
culture-historical method changed the goals of anthropology from knowing human nature by studying natural peoples to reconstructing the cultural history of those societies formerly believed to consist of natural
peoples. However, the means to these new ends did not change. The basic
practices of culture-historical anthropology remained strictly empirical,
even if its proponents did open anthropology to theory and interpretation.[57] Furthermore, with the exception of Graebner's 1904 lecture,
culture-historical anthropologists continued to privilege material objects
over texts as sources of knowledge about the people they studied.

The culture-historical method thus responded to practical problems of
museum work.[58] The new method allowed curators to situate artifacts in

historical narratives, rather than merely cataloging them, and to organize displays that communicated with the public more effectively than the simple massing of material in glass cases that Bastian had advocated. Curators could now select artifacts, tell stories about them, and present synthetic understandings of anthropological material. This satisfied their own demands for an active science that went beyond mere inventory taking and also satisfied the demands of the public and the state for more instructive and communicative displays. Ironically, the interests of the "voyeuristic [schaulustigen] public," which anthropologists imagined had no place in the museum of ethnology, helped transform anthropology from a vaguely defined discipline of collection to a directed, theorized, historical science. Anthropologists of Bastian's and Virchow's generation had believed that their science rested on excluding the general public. In fact, only when the public returned to anthropology by visiting the museum of ethnology did anthropologists receive impetus to reground their discipline and transform it from a fact-collecting to a knowledge-producing enterprise. The development of the culture-historical method represented a transition in German anthropology from an age of Völkerschauen to an age of museums.[59]

The end of the concept of Naturvölker implied also the end of the sharp distinction between history and nature fundamental to nineteenth-century German anthropology. In the title of their 1904 lectures, Graebner and Ankermann referred not only to "culture circles" (Kulturkreisen) but also to "culture strata" (Kulturschichten). Ankermann especially used the concept of culture strata in his historical account of the development of African culture and isolated six strata, from the earliest "nigritische" culture to the most recent Arabic incursions.[60] Like a geologist reconstructing the earth's history, Ankermann reconstructed African history by establishing a relative chronology of various layers. This departed not only from previous German anthropology but also from earlier German studies of the earth, which, as I discussed in chapter 2, had focused on the present structure of the planet rather than on its history. Berlin anthropologists of the 1870s echoed this atemporal understanding of nature in their concept of natural peoples. By alluding to culture strata, Ankermann and Graebner did not merely invoke a metaphor from historical geology but also evinced a transformation in the attitude of German anthropologists toward nature.

In 1908, the geography professor Albrecht Penck suggested to the members of the Berlin Anthropological Society that they correlate archaeological finds with surrounding geological evidence to fix chronologies and determine the age of humans.[61] While this coordination of human history and earth history had already become conventional outside Germany in the early part of the previous century, this method evidently struck Berlin anthropologists as a novel innovation with profound implications for their theory and practice.[62] They quickly accepted such attempts to bridge nature and history, and later lecturers routinely advocated this move without arousing any opposition.[63] When the Swedish archaeologist Oscar Montelius (1843–1921) spoke to the Berlin Anthropological Society in 1910 about his efforts to establish a chronology of European prehistory, one member of the society applauded Montelius's implication "that in principle there is no prehistory [*Prähistorie*], but only history [*Geschichte*]."[64] By extending historical time into what had previously been understood as a nonhistorical topic, anthropologists not only reconceived the culture of the colonized but also undermined the strong opposition between history and nature.

The most startling consequence of the rapprochement of history and nature was the wide acceptance of Darwinism among German anthropologists in the first decade of the twentieth century. Perhaps the most remarkable convert to Darwinism was Gustav Fritsch, who in 1872 had asserted that the Darwinian question about the origin of humans—"ape, or no ape?"—had as much place in his work as "information on the number of paradises."[65] In a 1911 lecture, by contrast, Fritsch referred derisively to the earlier years as a "pre-Darwinistic time, when systematics [*Systematik*] still had an undisturbed trust in its 'good species.'"[66] Only one member of the Berlin Anthropological Society appears to have objected to this lecture, in which Fritsch asserted that humans and apes descended from a common ancestor and that races were variations that evolved through "selection and accommodation."[67] Fritsch and Hans Friedenthal, a younger colleague on the medical faculty at the University of Berlin, became the premier proponents of Darwinism in the Berlin Anthropological Society.[68] Friedenthal also taught a course at the University of Berlin on the "natural history of humans" for students from all disciplines. Fritsch had been teaching courses devoted to "descendance theory" since 1878, although it is not clear what position he took on Darwinism in the class or how that position changed over the course of his career.[69] For better or for worse, German anthropologists embraced Darwinism and applied it to humans.

By the early twentieth century, anthropologists had come to accept Darwinism to such an extent that they rewrote their own history to explain and excuse what they came to perceive as their earlier scientific shortcomings. Julius Kollmann, who had always been sympathetic to Darwinism, claimed that Virchow had so much authority in German anthropology that he had been able to prevent any discussion supporting the "monkey doctrine." With Virchow's death in 1902, he explained, German anthropology lost its most active enforcer of its anti-Darwinist orthodoxy.[70] Felix von Luschan focused instead on the evidence available for human evolution during the nineteenth century, arguing that anthropologists accepted Darwinism as soon as there was enough evidence to support it. Luschan declared, "Twice in the last century progress in the study of humans occurred in leaps and bounds, and both times this progress was linked to fossil skull crowns."[71] Luschan likely had in mind the Neanderthal crown and the remains of the pithecanthropus from Java. Virchow, however, had used both these skull crowns to mount critiques of Darwinism for misinterpreting pathological appearances in an achronological nature as historical traces of the evolution of humans from apes. These crowns were, in fact, paradigmatic arguments against Darwinism rather than steps in the slow progress of the truth of Darwinism. Virchow's opposition to Darwinism had found wide agreement among German anthropologists, even among members who later became enthusiastic supporters of the doctrine. The opposition to Darwinism stemmed neither from a lack of evidence for the theory nor from Virchow's personal intervention. Rather, opposition to Darwinism was a theoretical necessity of German anthropology, stemming from its construction of nature, narrative, and Naturvölker.

The acceptance of Darwinism and the rejection of the strong border between humans and animals made appearances by sideshow prodigies before anthropology society meetings less conceptually significant, although not less frequent, occurrences. Virchow's son Hans (1852–1940), a professor of anatomy at the University of Berlin, inherited his father's interest in freaks, although he did not inherit Virchow senior's opposition to Darwinism or his anxieties about the border between humans and animals. Performances of non-Europeans and freaks from the panopticons continued to occur in anthropology meetings in the twentieth century much as they had in the nineteenth. While ethnographic performances continued to excite the same interest in the twentieth century as they had in the nineteenth, the style of freak performance did change. Instead of focusing on oddities that appeared to transgress the boundary between human and animal, such as hirsute or tailed people, the performances in the twentieth century focused on humans with extraordinary acquired characteristics, such as tattooed women and circus strongmen.[72] Although it might be expected that such performances would raise questions of Lamarckian inheritance, no such discussions were recorded in the society's Transactions, and their only significance seems to have been the titillation that they afforded the audience. As the philosophical foundations of German anthropology shifted away from the paradoxical concept of natural peoples and the relation between humans and nature ceased to be a tense binary opposition, the position of sideshow freaks moved to the periphery of anthropologists' intellectual universe. The theory of *Naturvölker* that anthropologists had worked out in exotic and freak shows beginning in the 1870s, and institutionalized in the Berlin museum of ethnology in the 1880s and 1890s, ended in the first decade of the twentieth century. The acceptance of Darwinism was a result of the dissolution of this theoretical construct.

This new direction in anthropology heightened the challenge that the discipline presented to history. In the nineteenth century, historians and anthropologists had accepted a division of labor whereby historians dealt with change and *Kulturvölker* while anthropologists dealt with stasis and *Naturvölker*. In the twentieth century, anthropologists asserted that nature and natural peoples were also historical, thus claiming the study of historical change for their discipline. Anthropologists preserved, however, their methodological assault on history, for they still presented themselves as natural scientists studying objective evidence, superior to humanists interpreting subjective documents. By undoing the conceptual divisions that had allowed their discipline to emerge, anthropologists pushed forward their attempt to displace the humanistic disciplines. Culture-historical anthropology allowed the discipline to exploit its massive growth and its development from an amateur hobby to a museum-based profession. Thus, while in one sense historicist anthropology and the related acceptance of Darwinism undermined nearly every theoretical position held by anthropology's nineteenth-century founders, in a more important sense it realized the project of anthropology as a posthumanist human science, suited to the conditions of mass culture and the new imperialism.

᠍

CHAPTER 10

Colonialism and the Limits of the Human:
The Failure of Fieldwork

In the first decade of the twentieth century, German anthropologists, who had previously conducted research in museums and carnivals, began to advocate stationary fieldwork. The first well-organized German anthropological field expedition, and one of the earliest such undertakings ever, was mounted in 1907–9 by the Royal Museum of Ethnology in cooperation with the German navy.[1] Contrary to the armchair-to-field narratives ubiquitous in histories of anthropology, the development of fieldwork had little to do with a desire for the kind of empathetic participant observation associated with anthropology today.[2] As long as anthropologists defined their discipline as an inductive and comparative science, they were not particularly interested in focused studies of individual societies, except insofar as they provided raw data. Whether they sought a "total impression" of "natural peoples" or reconstructed culture-historical interactions, anthropologists depended on the extensive collections of metropolitan museums. Their turn to the field was a response to their dissatisfaction with the objects brought together by amateurs in the colonies, which anthropologists often regarded as inauthentic commodities or poorly documented curiosities.

The shift from the museum to the field turned out to involve far more than an opportunity to gather superior collections, for it altered the institutional and geopolitical context of the discipline. The navy sponsored anthropological fieldwork largely because it believed that fieldwork would provide psychological and sociological information about the indigenous inhabitants of the German colonies. While at the time nobody thought that such information was directly relevant to anthropology, both the navy and the museum of ethnology thought that it would be politically advantageous to contribute information relevant to the "scientific colonization" advocated by the new colonial secretary, Bernhard Dernburg. The officer in charge of the expedition, Emil Stephan, however, soon transformed this psychological and sociological research from a colonial-political task to be pursued in conjunction with anthropology to a challenge to what he called "dry museum science." Although anthropologists would become interested in such psychological and sociological research after the First World War, fieldwork initially foundered on the fundamental contradiction of both colonialism and anthropology: the human without humanity.

By the last third of the nineteenth century, professional anthropologists rejected travel narratives as unreliable sources of knowledge.[3] Anthropologists did trust amateurs to collect material culture, skulls, and other body parts, but they did not trust their observations or experiences. Felix von Luschan was typical in his mistrust of amateur travelers: "There will always be travelers who know about African huts only whether they are easy or difficult to burn down and in their journals report more about Negroes they have 'hunted down' than about living people."[4] Richard Thurnwald, an important advocate of field anthropology, similarly rejected the observations of untrained travelers: "The globe-trotter, the rhino hunter, and the beetle collector rarely have much psychological understanding of the natives. Their knowledge usually comes from their contact with '*boys*' or young girls at ports."[5] The sort of people who traveled abroad, anthropologists maintained, were not the sort of people who could be trusted to make reliable observations. While, as these passages themselves indicate, anthropologists did not reject all travel narratives, they also did not accord them the same status as their own observations of objects.

Not only did anthropologists mistrust the sort of people who traveled the world, but they also found lengthy contact with a society in itself detrimental to anthropological knowledge. In his highly regarded *Natives of South Africa,* Gustav Fritsch argued that his account, based on his own 1863–66 travels, was superior to accounts by missionaries, which were tainted by the familiarity of the writers with the people they described. Missionaries, Fritsch maintained, "following the preference and interest they have for the tribe they just lived among, have been guilty of a certain prettification [*Schönfarberei*] in relation to it."[6] The Austrian Catholic missionary and anthropologist Wilhelm Schmidt expressed similar reservations about missionaries who became so familiar with the society in which they lived that they came to believe that there was nothing "deviant, seldom, and therefore remarkable" about it.[7] Fieldwork could have no place in the mental cosmos or in the repertoire of practices of a discipline that regarded intimate familiarity with a tribe as an epistemological liability.

Like most anthropologists, however, Fritsch considered travel an important part of his career, although this was not anthropological fieldwork in the sense in which it is understood today. Fritsch, for example, seems to have relied on informants from colonial prisons, farms, and missionary schools.[8] Nineteenth-century anthropological research would today be regarded as hasty and superficial at best. For example, one correspondent, who was trusted enough to be published in the *Zeitschrift für Ethnologie*, began a report on the Coroados of Brazil by explaining: "During a one-week stay . . . I had the time and the opportunity to get to know the Indians precisely."[9] The Berlin museum director Adolf Bastian traveled more than any other professional anthropologist in the nineteenth century. He spent approximately twenty-four years of his life touring the globe, almost exclusively in order to conduct anthropological research. Traveling was not generally considered a necessary activity for anthropologists, and Bastian had difficulties justifying his lengthy absences from the museum to the general museum administration and the Ministry of Culture. He explained that the anthropologist could "no longer spare himself the work and effort to climb upward to the sources and acquire the material for his studies from the authentic Bora."[10] What Bastian meant by "climb[ing] upward to the sources" was, for the most part, making contacts with Europeans living abroad who would later send artifacts and information to the Berlin museum.[11] Karl von den Steinen, an anthropologist of the generation after Bastian, remembered that Bastian did field research by seeking out "[European] authorities who had been familiar with the natives for years and who possessed the kind of thoroughly organized material in their manuscripts and collections that a hasty foreign visitor could never bring together."[12] While anthropologists did travel, they always relied on local Europeans to mediate between them and the people they studied. Anthropologists were, in any case, interested above all in bringing together museum collections.

Anthropologists first advocated stationary fieldwork because it would allow for more complete and well-documented collections than the earlier, hasty, collection trips had.[13] The most vocal advocate of fieldwork was Felix von Luschan, who was primarily interested in improving the network of military personnel and colonial officials that had supplied his sections of the museum with artifacts for almost two decades. As early as 1892, Luschan had complained to the navy that hasty stops to collect artifacts had produced only "single trophies" and that a longer visit would be required to assemble "the systematic collections" required by anthropology.[14] However, the regular duties of colonial officers and soldiers made it nearly impossible for them to devote as much time to collecting from a single region as Luschan now demanded.[15] Luschan still preferred to entrust the navy with anthropological collecting, rather than turning it over to nonmilitary professional anthropologists. When he finally did persuade the navy to support stationary anthropological expeditions, he demanded that an officer lead the expedition and rejected an initial proposal simply to lend naval support to a civilian expedition.[16] Even Richard Thurnwald, a professional, nonmilitary anthropologist remembered today for his pioneering efforts in the field, received less financial support from the Berlin museum than the navy expedition did.[17] Luschan later explained that the "peculiar conditions in our protectorates and our previous experiences" made it preferable to keep such expeditions under the command of the navy.[18] The military had better access to the people anthropologists wanted to study and the means to acquire collections outside normal economic routes.

It was ultimately a shift in German colonial politics that made the navy willing to devote its resources and personnel to an exclusively anthropological expedition. Major wars in German East Africa and Southwest Africa in the first years of the twentieth century had led to calls in the Reichstag for colonial reform since, as they were presently managed, the colonies were clearly a financial and moral liability for Germany. Chancellor Bülow was able to attract liberals away from the parliamentary opposition to colonialism by appointing the reforming liberal Bernhard Dernburg to the newly created Colonial Office. Dernburg promoted a program of "scientific colonization," reform based on increased scientific, social, economic, medical, and environmental research in the colonies.[19] Admiral Alfred von Tirpitz, the architect of Germany's massive naval buildup, hoped that an anthropological expedition would increase the prestige of his service branch by connecting it to Dernburg's colonial reforms.[20] Together with the Berlin museum of ethnology, the navy sponsored a two-year expedition to western New Mecklenburg (New Ireland), in the Bismarck Archipelago off the northeast coast of New Guinea. The expedition was hailed, in a journal for navy personnel, as an opportunity to gain some of the prestige that the colonial armies in Africa enjoyed, demonstrating the "silent, difficult, and nevertheless so valuable culture work [*Kulturarbeit*] achieved by small station cruisers with their surveying activities."[21]

Far from welcoming the navy's assistance in efforts at "scientific colonization," the Foreign Office discouraged this foray into colonial politics. Dernburg complained directly to Tirpitz that the expedition would only burden local colonial administrators and risked provoking further colonial scandals if it were attacked when conducting research in a poorly policed area. He warned against making any public statements relevant to the politically contentious question of labor recruitment.[22] The question of creating an indigenous proletariat was one of the most hotly debated issues of Dernburg's colonial reforms, and any statement about customs, society, or population did indeed have serious political implications.[23] As Luschan explained to the leader of the expedition: "In the Imperial Colonial Office the opinion about your expedition is, as always, absolutely bad; they are obviously jealous of the cooperation of the navy."[24] Dernburg was probably right: the expedition was, for Tirpitz, a way of meddling in colonial affairs and increasing the popular profile of the navy at the expense of the Colonial Office.

Despite Dernburg's complaints, the expedition was set up to fulfill the demands of both its sponsoring institutions: for the Berlin museum, anthropological collections; and, for the navy, practical colonial knowledge and the prestige associated with the new program of scientific colonization. Although Tirpitz had reassured Dernburg that the navy would not meddle in colonial affairs, the instructions for the expedition still included colonial policy research. Luschan instructed the expedition members to conduct anthropological research and also "insofar as it is possible to help prepare practical colonial efforts by conducting research in previously little-known or entirely unknown areas on the character and customs of the natives, the population density, [and] the possibility of labor recruitment."[25] While today such research seems obviously related to anthropology, contemporaries associated it more with practical knowledge for colonial rule. Even after Luschan accepted the advantage of having experts as collectors in the field, he still did not regard sociological or psychological observations as relevant to his discipline; rather, they were a courtesy to the navy. Anthropology was still primarily a collecting science.

The novel character of the German navy expedition owed much to the personal interests of its leader, Emil Stephan.[26] Stephan was a navy doctor who had served in the suppression of the Boxer uprising in China. He began practicing anthropology in 1905 when he became the physician on the surveying ship *Seagull,* whose duties included collecting objects for the Berlin museum of ethnology. Like his predecessors, Stephan was sent to the Berlin museum just before shipping out, to be instructed in anthropological observation, photography, measurements, and collecting. He proved to be an enthusiastic and skilled collector, soon filling all the space available for artifacts on his ship.[27] His correspondence with Luschan suggests that his collecting duties had inspired a personal interest in anthropology.[28] He would become an important liaison between the navy and the

Berlin museum, on one occasion accompanying Tirpitz and his family on a tour of the museum.[29] Stephan, however, soon developed quite heterodox interests, pursuing questions that were far from the natural scientific interests in objects promoted by the museum of ethnology.

While serving on the *Seagull,* however, Stephan acquired new teachers in the study of the inhabitants of Germany's Pacific colonies. It was customary for ships arriving in the Pacific to take on indigenous laborers to work on deck and in the engine room. The new hands on the *Seagull* included a group of young men from the Barriai society of western New Britain. The Barriai had never before been employed by Europeans and did not speak Pidgin English, a lingua franca of the Pacific. They were unaccustomed to working on a warship and had no means of communicating with the German sailors, who, Stephan reported, often struck them. According to Stephan, the Barriai, homesick and grateful for his occasional interventions on their behalf, quickly warmed up to him.

Two of the Barriai, Selin and Pore (see fig. 10.1), developed a close working relationship with Stephan, teaching him their language and explaining the art of the Bismarck Archipelago to him.[30] Pore was an especially good artist, and he, as well as other Bismarck islanders on the ship, made art for Stephan and also further decorated objects that Stephan had already collected. Selin and Pore also taught Stephan about the meaning of the art and further trained him—even if this training was not consciously pedagogical—in methods that might seem familiar to present-day anthropologists but were novel for anthropology of Stephan's time. Rather than simply demanding explanations of the work, Stephan listened to individuals talking about art: "I accepted interpretations only when they were independently confirmed at various times by various people. This procedure required significantly more effort and patience than that recommended by a good schooner captain, 'curiosity collector,' and practical supporter of anthropology: 'I ask the lads only once 'cause, when I ask 'em twice, they always tell me something different!'"[31] In his interactions with Selin and Pore, Stephan learned an interpretive, empathetic approach to anthropology uncommon to the discipline at the time. Rather than collecting objects and hastily labeling them, Stephan developed a method based on listening to indigenous artists discuss their work.

Stephan hoped to bring Selin and Pore back to Berlin to be studied by anthropologists. Luschan admitted that the museum itself did not have a great interest in bringing them to Berlin since the collections from their homeland were already well cataloged. Still, he thought that the visit of the two Melanesians might be a good chance for various colonial groups in Berlin to learn their language. Luschan, however, could not drum up

FIGURE 10.1
Selin and Pore.
Source: Emil Stephan, *Südseekunst: Beiträge zur Kunst des Bismarck-Archipels und zur Urgeschichte der Kunst überhaupt* (Berlin: Dietrich Reimer, 1907), 90.

enough support from the navy or from the Seminar for Oriental Languages, a colonial languages institute, to bring the two Barriai crew members to the German capital. It would have been conventional for Stephan to support the trip with performances in zoos and panopticons, but he apparently did not wish to play the impresario for his two informants.[32]

Stephan eventually used Pore's creations and explanations as the basis for a book titled *Südseekunst* (The art of the Pacific).[33] Stephan learned that what had previously been dismissed as mere decoration was regarded by its

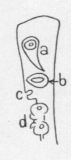

Nr. 1. VI. 23 626. 12 cm lang.
Kokos- und **Taroschaber** *āpe* der
Barriai, geschnitzt von Pore, aus
einem Schweinsknochen, der *āpe*
heißt.

a. Auge und unterer Rand der
   Augenhöhle.

b. semaña maña Ohrwurm.
   S. Taf. XII 3.

c. Mund.

d. Halsschmuck *namumuga* s. Nr. 2.

FIGURE   10.2

Coconut and taro scraper (*left*), carved from a pig bone by Pore, and Stephan's diagram
(*right*) showing how it represents a human head (a. eye and lower edge of the eye socket;
b. ear; c. mouth; d. necklace).

Source: Emil Stephan, *Südseekunst: Beiträge zur Kunst des Bismarck-Archipels und zur
Urgeschichte der Kunst überhaupt* (Berlin: Dietrich Reimer, 1907), table 5.

creators as representing animals, plants, and the human body, as Selin,
Pore, and other Bismarck islanders explained to Stephan (see figs. 10.2 and
10.3). That the work was representational meant, for Stephan, that it was
art rather than decoration. He thus dedicated his book to "the Memory
[*Manen*] of Rembrandt." Discussing the art of natural peoples distinguished Stephan from most German anthropologists, who regarded natural peoples as possessing no culture and certainly not able to produce art.
Stephan was not alone in his attempts to understand aesthetically what had
formerly been regarded as natural scientific, anthropological objects. Pablo
Picasso made his famous visit to the Trocadero in 1907, the same year
Stephan published *Südseekunst.* The expressionist Emil Nolde would soon
begin painting and sketching objects in the Berlin museum of ethnology
and working on a book celebrating the "artistic expressions (*Kunstäußerun-
gen*) of the natural peoples."[34] The question of art in the Berlin museum
had recently become especially politicized when the head of all Berlin museums, Wilhelm von Bode, suggested that objects of artistic value be removed from the Asian collections of the museum to a special museum, a
suggestion that anthropologists firmly rejected.[35] The question of the artis-

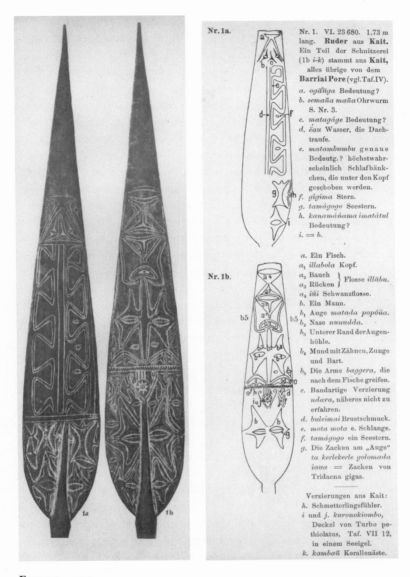

FIGURE 10.3

Both sides of an oar (*left*) from Kait with additional carvings by Pore and Stephan's explanation (*right*) of what the various figures represent.

Source: Emil Stephan, *Südseekunst: Beiträge zur Kunst des Bismarck-Archipels und zur Urgeschichte der Kunst überhaupt* (Berlin: Dietrich Reimer, 1907), table 12.

tic and cultural levels of colonized peoples had also become an issue in colonial circles, many of whom felt that the Berlin museum's presentation of
cultureless natural peoples did little to stimulate enthusiasm for colonial
expansion.[36] Stephan's *Südseekunst* was welcomed by the *Deutsche Kolonialzeitung* because the book combated the prejudice that the indigenous
inhabitants were simply "savages" (*Wilden*).[37] Stephan similarly hoped that
his expedition would change the popular view of Germany's Pacific
colonies as "dispersed islands, where murder . . . and cannibalism are the
order of the day, although in reality they are only a few days from Australia
by steamship and, in the peace that rules almost everywhere, are unmis-
takably blooming."[38] Although Stephan's interests may sound today like
forward-looking anthropological concerns, they were in fact more typical
of colonial propaganda than they were of anthropology. Stephan was able
to develop his interest in firsthand observations and interactions with Pacific Islanders, not because anthropologists came to regard his "fresh and
joyful tale" as relevant to their science, but rather because the navy decided
that such observations were relevant to colonialism. Stephan's interests,
stimulated by his discussions with Selin and Pore, fit more securely into
colonial propaganda than they did into anthropology.

Luschan was pleased when Stephan's tour on the *Seagull* ended and he
was replaced as the principal anthropologist in the German navy by the
more traditional Augustin Krämer, who focused on collecting and cataloging objects.[39] In addition to *Südseekunst,* Stephan did publish a more
conventional anthropology book, *Neu-Mecklenburg,* under the supervision
of the culture-historical museum anthropologist Fritz Graebner. In a preface, Graebner sourly explained that his role consisted mainly in ensuring
that Stephan avoided "the faults that make most travel accounts difficult to
use scientifically. Complete description of the collected material, exactitude
of information, avoidance of even the slightest generalization: all in all the
main goal of our common labor was the production of a reliable ethnographic source."[40] Stephan was still able to discuss some of his experiences
with Selin, Pore, and other New Mecklenburgers in a section on "psychological observations" but otherwise restricted himself to the object-focused
descriptions typical of conventional museum anthropology.[41]

Even before Stephan developed his arguments in *Südseekunst,* he recognized the tension between his own work and mainstream anthropology.
In a 1905 article for the popular geography journal *Globus,* Stephan wrote
a kind of schizophrenic report on his experiences, which began: "The following essay consists of two parts. The first tells a fresh and joyful tale of
my interactions with authentic natural humans under the sunny skies of
their homeland; the second breathes the camphor smell of dry museum sci-

ence." Stephan did not regard his personal experiences with Selin and Pore as relevant to anthropology, which he conceived of as a "museum science." He presented his interactions with members of the societies that he studied not as a different direction within anthropology but rather as a departure from anthropology. However, he claimed that his kind of work was superior to all previous eyewitness accounts of colonized societies, not just those by missionaries and colonial traders, but even those by the collectors who traveled for anthropologists: "Our knowledge of these distant tribes comes from traders, who want to profit from them, or from missionaries, who want to improve the heathens, or in the best case from research travelers, who mostly spend too brief a time in one place to study closely single individuals without the intervention of a translator."[42] Lest we think that Stephan was a kind of modern anthropological fieldworker, it should be remembered that nearly all the direct contact that he had with the Barriai was on the HMS *Seagull*. He gathered some additional information from a report by a 1902 navy surveying expedition that had landed briefly in the home territory of the Barriai and from a collection of artifacts that he purchased from the estate of a trader in Matupi.[43] Still, Stephan had learned a skill from Selin and Pore that allowed him to challenge the "dry museum science" of anthropology.

Even from its initial conception, the German navy expedition of 1907–9 had to contend with tensions among the very factors that made it possible. Although colonial authorities and anthropologists alike recognized that such work was important, their cooperation was marked by some discomfort. Anthropologists were uncertain of the value for their science of much of the sociological and psychological information that fieldwork promised to provide. Colonists were hesitant to allow anthropologists to involve themselves in questions related to colonial policy, especially indigenous labor recruitment. This tension with colonists was exacerbated by conflicts between the Colonial Office and the navy over who would sponsor and control research related to colonialism. Additionally, there were tensions between Stephan's personal interests in the psychology and the art of natural peoples and anthropologists' interests in preserving natural scientific objectivity. Finally, there were the practical difficulties, which no German anthropologist had ever faced, of establishing a research station in a relatively uncolonized area.

While a chance to spend a year in a single location on New Mecklenburg might seem today like the sort of thing that would interest anthropologists, Luschan in fact had difficulty convincing anyone to participate in the navy expedition. Luschan himself did not consider going, nor did he ask any of his senior colleagues. One zoologist, who had originally agreed

FIGURE 10.4
The members of the navy expedition of 1907–9 en route to the Bismarck Archipelago. *Standing, left to
right,* Emil Stephan, Otto Schlaginhaufen. *Seated, left to right,* Edgar
Walden, Richard Schilling.
Source: Otto Schlaginhaufen, *Muliama: Zwei Jahren unter Südsee-
Insulaner* (Zürich: Orell Füssli,
1959).

to serve as a physical anthropologist on the expedition, backed out, explaining that he had a large collection of butterflies to rearrange.[44] Otto
Schlaginhaufen, a former assistant of Luschan's working in the Dresden
museum, was persuaded to replace him by the promise of remaining
in New Guinea after the expedition to collect zoological specimens.[45]
Luschan also eventually got one of his own assistants, Edgar Walden, to
participate.[46] In addition to Walden and Schlaginhaufen, Stephan's expedition recruited one Richard Schilling, primarily as a photographer, but
also to oversee the practical affairs of the expedition. The expedition set sail
on 6 September 1907, arriving in early November in Rabaul, New Pomerania (see fig. 10.4). From there, the members of the expedition shipped out to
their field locations on New Mecklenburg.

  The two formally trained anthropologists, Edgar Walden and Otto
Schlaginhaufen, focused their efforts on collecting artifacts and skulls.
Edgar Walden traveled on his own to the northwestern part of New Mecklenburg (see maps, figs. 10.5 and 10.6). In this area, colonization was relatively advanced, and the roads, resthouses, farms, and trading stations

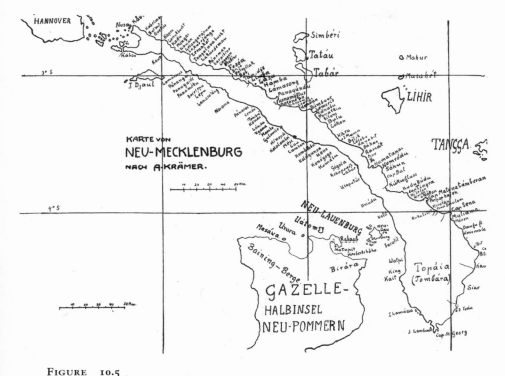

FIGURE 10.5
A map of Neu-Pommern (New Britain) and Neu-Mecklenburg (New Ireland) drawn by
Augustin Krämer.
Source: Elisabeth Krämer-Bannow, *Bei kunstsinnigen Kannibalen der Südsee: Wanderungen
auf Neu-Mecklenburg 1908–1909* (Berlin: Dietrich Reimer, 1916).

would, Walden hoped, make his research there easier.[47] Walden had never
supposed that he would be able to live alone among the indigenous population, whom he considered hostile. He did not plan to learn the native languages since, he reckoned, there were so many of them that learning one
would not help him outside a small area.[48] Walden did not get along well
with Stephan or with the German official in charge of New Mecklenburg,
and his correspondence with Luschan suggests that he needed much cheer-
ing up and encouragement. Luschan was especially interested that Walden
personally impress both the German government and the colonists in New
Mecklenburg. Making such contacts had been one of the principal tasks of
anthropological traveling for the previous half century, and recent competition from other German museums made this an especially pressing task
for the expedition from Berlin.[49] Schlaginhaufen, the other professional

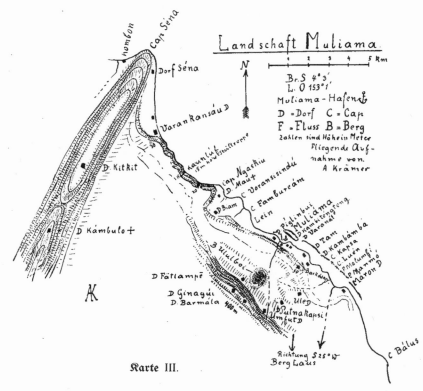

Karte III.

FIGURE   10.6

Map of the Muliama area, drawn by Augustin Krämer.
Source: Elisabeth Krämer-Bannow, *Bei kunstsinnigen Kannibalen der Südsee: Wanderungen auf Neu-Mecklenburg 1908–1909* (Berlin: Dietrich Reimer, 1916).

anthropologist, accompanied Stephan to his field location to oversee collecting. Junior curators like Schlaginhaufen often made a name for themselves by assembling collections for their museum. Thus, what might seem like a relatively menial task compared to Stephan's cultural research was in fact most attractive to the two professional anthropologists on the expedition.

The less professionally orthodox Stephan led Schlaginhaufen and Schilling to the relatively uncolonized southeastern half of New Mecklenburg. They settled on Muliama Harbor, near the southern tip of the island. Stephan chose the region because, compared to most places that anthropologists studied, it was untouched by European influence. Of course, no anthropologist had contact with societies unconnected to the global economy.

Stephan described one group as possibly "one of the most primitive tribes still living anywhere on earth" because it had acquired its European goods from other local societies, rather than directly from German colonists.[50] He placed Schilling in charge of photography and of overseeing workers and police soldiers; Schlaginhaufen conducted physical anthropological measurements and collected artifacts. Stephan devoted his time to studying the psychology and society of the local inhabitants.[51]

Stephan strictly organized the expedition and the base camp, creating a colonial order in this relatively uncolonized area. The camp was centered around a house formerly owned by two Chinese merchants, which the expedition members renamed "Castle Muliama" (see fig. 10.7).[52] Stephan and Schlaginhaufen used the merchants' house as a headquarters to write the journals that the expedition contract required them to keep (and which provide an important source for this chapter). The expedition employed nine indigenous workers, eight indigenous police soldiers, a Chinese cook, and a personal servant for each of the three researchers. The police soldiers were government employees from other parts of the island. While some of the workers and "houseboys" may have been brought from other parts of the colony, the camp also employed at least some from nearby villages.

Bild 4.   Schloß Muliama, unser Arbeitshaus in Kambitengteng.   A. B.

FIGURE   10.7
Castle Muliama. Drawing by Elizabeth Krämer-Bannow of a house taken over from Chinese merchants by Emil Stephan's expedition.
Source: Elisabeth Krämer-Bannow, *Bei kunstsinnigen Kannibalen der Südsee: Wanderungen auf Neu-Mecklenburg 1908–1909* (Berlin: Dietrich Reimer, 1916).

Adjacent to the merchants' house the workers built a vegetable garden, a chicken coop, an outbuilding for meteorological instruments, and a photographic darkroom. They also set up a parade ground with a flagpole where the police soldiers would assemble each morning for reveille. One of the workers devoted his labor entirely to keeping the ground around the camp level and free of vegetation and standing water, for reasons of health and security.

Although Stephan had led anthropologists off the deck of a ship into a relatively uncontrolled area, he did everything he could to reproduce navy discipline within his camp. Before sunrise, he would awaken the camp with a blast from his whistle. Work would continue until 11:00 A.M., when another whistle from Stephan would tell the members to break for lunch. After lunch, they worked until dark, when Stephan and Schlaginhaufen would retire to the writing house. Bedtime was around 9:00, and alcohol was strictly forbidden. It is tempting to see Stephan's Crusoe-like reproduction of his home turf as a failure of nerve. We might miss the real interest if we say, Had he had the guts of a Malinowski, he would have really gone out among the savages. Stephan, like many researchers, had obtained good results by conducting research from a warship. It was quite reasonable of him to model his land-based work on the naval practices that had previously given him such success.

Despite his organizational efforts, Stephan had trouble developing routines to interact with people and gather information from them. He complained in his journal that he did not like to ask people about their culture because it made him feel "nosy" (*hineinfragend*).[53] One of his biggest challenges, and greatest achievements, was using conventional colonial roles and modes of interaction to conduct a new kind of anthropological research.[54]

Soon after the expedition arrived in Muliama, Stephan's camp became an ethnographic performance, a *Völkerschau,* of European anthropologists. The sight of Stephan and Schlaginhaufen writing in the headquarters was apparently interesting enough to draw curious locals.[55] Stephan, who had refused to be an impresario for Selin and Pore, now himself became an ethnographic performer. Stephan and Schlaginhaufen's *Völkerschau* was, in fact, the only literally ethnographic performance, for the performers actually wrote (*graphein*) about the nation (*ethnos*) that was watching them writing. This writing performance both underscored the authority of Stephan and Schlaginhaufen by tying them to the bureaucratic administration of German New Guinea and reversed the hierarchy implicit in the anthropological gaze so that the observers became the observed. Like Stephan's expedition as a whole, this graphic performance pushed into the foreground—without overcoming—many of the oppositions that structured both anthropology and colonialism, including observing/observed, art/artifact, culture/nature, and writing/not-writing.[56] It also brought the locals into the camp, enabling Stephan and Schlaginhaufen to develop routines that established more unambiguously anthropological roles.

Stephan was able to develop these anthropological relations with the local inhabitants, who taught him their language and later became his informants, by playing three roles of colonial power: merchant, doctor, and colonial judge. Although the area at first appeared unpromising for collecting, when locals saw the enormous number of trade goods that the expedition had brought, they soon became eager assistants.[57] Stephan and Schlaginhaufen were made familiar with the commercial relations of the region by a Chinese merchant, who regularly traded with the local inhabitants.[58] Chinese merchants had been regular visitors to the Bismarck Archipelago well before Germans established dominance there. Schlaginhaufen merely had to let it be known that he wanted, for example, a basket, and he would be brought many examples of baskets from all over the area.[59] At least once, the expedition members held a kind of impromptu market in their camp, where they, local people, and visiting Chinese merchants all traded with each other.[60] On one occasion, people from several miles up the coast, perhaps given a tip by Chinese merchants, sailed to Stephan's camp to sell artifacts.[61] The camp was so economically enticing to the locals that the expedition members began to feel overwhelmed by the amount of artifacts, phonographic recordings on wax cylinders, and other observations that they had to catalog.[62] The expedition members also went to local taro and citron markets so that they could make phonographic recordings of the individuals who had gathered there.[63] While the most obvious function of these markets was to provide artifacts for Schlaginhaufen, they also gave Stephan a way to contact informants.

Stephan also employed his medical skills and played the unauthorized role of colonial judge to interact with the local population. Almost as soon as he arrived, he began treating the ailments of local chiefs, with the intention of befriending them.[64] He also conducted what he referred to as "daily polyclinics," finding many of his patients suffering from "unbelievably neglected wounds" (see fig. 10.8).[65] He also acted as the top judicial authority in the area, both within the camp and in the area surrounding it. On one occasion, a group of individuals from several villages brought in a man whom they accused of murdering someone through magic. The group asked Stephan to judge the accused sorcerer, whom they had stripped and bound. Stephan decided to keep the prisoner overnight, largely, it seems, to photograph him and to take anthropometric measurements. Stephan also

FIGURE 10.8

Stephan, seated, administers medical attention to local residents near the camp. Schlagin-
haufen observes.
Source: Otto Schlaginhaufen, *Muliama: Zwei Jahren unter Südsee-Insulaner* (Zürich: Orell
Füssli, 1959).

performed some dental work and kept the pulled teeth for his collection.
There is no record of whether the anthropologist further punished the accused sorcerer.[66] Although Stephan had no official colonial duties, he was
treated as a colonial official, which made possible interactions with the people he studied.

In addition to creating roles to routinize contact with indigenous populations, Stephan also had to invent techniques for studying social intangi-
bles, things that he could neither buy nor take but that he had to learn in
dialogue. Conventional anthropological practices gave Stephan little guid-
ance, but his earlier experiences with Selin and Pore must have been very
important. While, previously, Europeans had found pidgin to be sufficient
for communicating with people all over the Pacific, Stephan found that "in
closer dealings with the natives the insufficiency of pidgin becomes ever
more apparent. Our first concern must be to understand the language and
to speak it ourselves."[67] He determined that the language of the coastal inhabitants was close enough to the other local dialects to communicate with
members of all the societies in the area.[68] In less than a month, Stephan had

mastered the language enough to conduct studies of kinship patterns as well as of other phenomena that required discussions with locals.[69] Stephan was thus able to examine local societies from what he called a psychological and sociological perspective. He had studied trade relations, cooking, and agriculture among the various groups around his site. He also referred to "interesting observations on family, marriage classes, law, secret societies, beliefs in spirits and on the thinking and feeling of the natives."[70]

It will unfortunately never be known what Stephan planned to do with these observations because he died of blackwater fever, a deadly complication of malaria, in May 1908, about six months after setting up camp.[71] Apparently, he had refused to take quinine.[72] After Stephan's death, the expedition remained without a leader for almost six months and seems to have fallen apart for a time. Walden, who had rarely been in touch before, now fell totally out of communication with both Luschan in Berlin and the rest of the expedition.[73] Schlaginhaufen spent two extended periods in the colonial town of Herbertshöhe (Kokopo) on the Gazelle Peninsula in New Pomerania, likely enjoying the hospitality of Max Thiel, a commercial representative and enthusiastic collector of ethnographic artifacts.[74] He also undertook several trips to nearby islands to collect artifacts.[75] There is no record of how Richard Schilling, the group's photographer, spent the expedition's interregnum, but it is likely that he remained in the camp, overseeing the laborers and police soldiers. No one continued Stephan's psychological studies, and, after his death, as Schlaginhaufen reported, "the investigations of the mental [geistige] culture limit themselves mostly to recording language."[76]

Luschan decided to replace Stephan with Augustin Krämer, another navy doctor who had proved himself a reliable collector for the Berlin museum.[77] Krämer had, years earlier, replaced Stephan as chief anthropological collector on the Seagull and had done more conventional anthropology then too. Krämer had little interest in studies of indigenous mental life and viewed research into indigenous social structure as of small significance to anyone other than local colonial officials.[78] Krämer arrived in the camp with his spouse, Elisabeth Krämer-Bannow, in November of 1908. Krämer-Bannow was also an active anthropological researcher, who investigated women's lives and taro cultivation as well as making drawings and watercolors. Krämer moved the expedition location north, to a region more controlled by colonial authorities and covered by colonial roads. This can hardly have been out of a desire to protect his spouse from the trials of the field since the two of them traveled the 125 miles north on foot, through areas without roads or even the amenities of the camp.[79] Krämer lost interest in Stephan's field site because, he explained, the expedition members

had already collected information and artifacts from the southern part of
the island and should now move to the more colonized north, where it was,
in any case, easier to collect. Krämer was a fairly conventional museum anthropologist, uninterested in Stephan's type of investigation. In northern
New Mecklenburg, Krämer and his wife were joined by the other members of the group, including Edgar Walden. The expedition produced few
publications, although it did bring home large numbers of ethnographic
objects and some statistical information.

As soon as the navy expedition had drawn to a close, Krämer and his
wife took over the leadership of an expedition that the Hamburg anthropology museum had sent out the year before. Although they rejected the
social and psychological questions posed by Stephan, they did adapt the notions of fieldwork that he developed during the expedition to more immediately practical colonial goals. The first year the Hamburg researchers had
rarely left the boat and found their quick surveying method unsatisfactory.
When Krämer took charge of the expedition, he had each individual regularly leave the ship to conduct fieldwork.[80] While waiting in Palau to be
picked up by the Hamburg expedition ship, Krämer had formulated his
goals for fieldwork in a brief article that he sent to *Globus,* a popular German geographic monthly.[81] These goals would, he thought, provide colonial officials with useful information and anthropologists with something
like an "anatomical preparation" of "the social organization of the indigenous states." The four goals that Krämer proposed for field research were
(1) drawing exact maps of the settlements of an area, (2) conducting a ge-
nealogical census of the population, (3) determining the location of important public buildings, and (4) collecting information on marriage and other
family rules. Krämer argued that this information would be useful for both
short-term colonial management and long-term planning based on indigenous population trends. As an example, Krämer offered that his work in
New Mecklenburg with the Stephan expedition had allowed him to correct the figures of an official who had missed collecting taxes from 40 of 120
households in an area. In this first formulation, Krämer recommended social research as a way for anthropologists to make colonial government
more efficient. Anthropologists in the field would serve their own discipline, by contrast, primarily by collecting objects for museums.[82]

Only after the Hamburg expedition, when he returned to Berlin, did
Krämer begin to reformulate his notion of fieldwork as an anthropological
experience with which he could challenge museum anthropologists. In
Berlin, he presented "fieldwork" (*Feldarbeit*) not as a supplement to, but
as an improvement over, "museum work." The rhetoric of the field, as it
was developed by Krämer, combined colonial goals with the anthropologi-

cal insistence on objectivity and immediacy. On the one hand, fieldworkers would help colonialism with information about social structure and marriage practices. On the other, fieldworkers would continue the approach of anthropologists to immediate reality, which the discipline had initiated by rejecting subjective texts in favor of objective objects. Just as anthropological objects were preferable to historical documents, so direct collection and observation in the field was preferable to museum objects mailed by various colonial officials.

Krämer was especially critical of practitioners of the new culture-historical method. Like the earlier museum anthropology, culture-historical anthropology assumed a researcher with access to objects from many regions, gathered by others in the colonies. These researchers, Krämer suggested, often incorrectly identified the objects that they discussed, since they lacked direct experience with the areas from which they were collected.[83] He also criticized museum workers for assuming that they already knew what was "out there in the field" and rejecting information provided by fieldworkers. Instead, Krämer maintained, museum workers should use their collections to provide fieldworkers with monographs, which they would use to assist their research, much as museum workers at the time used the artifacts collected by fieldworkers to assist theirs.[84] Krämer thus proposed a reversal of the relation of field and museum. Such a transformation could never take place, however, in a discipline so fundamentally rooted in the metropolitan collection. Indeed, Krämer himself eventually became director of the anthropology museum in Stuttgart.

Although Krämer created a rhetoric of fieldwork and immediate contact, his own research did not differ from museum anthropology to the extent that Stephan's did. Stephan achieved a level of immediacy, almost intimacy, with his subjects that his contemporaries did not recognize as central to anthropology. Even if he had survived, it is unlikely that Stephan would have gained the kind of professional legitimacy that Krämer did. Stephan sought the kind of direct contact that was suggested by the empiricism of anthropological methods but that was anathema to its antihumanist understanding of objectivity and that was in fact almost impossible to achieve in colonial situations. Stephan developed such close contact with indigenous New Mecklenburgers by playing nearly every colonial role available to him: merchant, physician, and judge. He also tried to employ a kind of empathetic observation, which he had perhaps learned in his interactions with Selin and Pore. After Stephan's death, Krämer did preserve some of these methods, but he basically returned to modes of anthropology more consonant with museum work, reserving his more psychological and sociological observations for questions of local administration. The "field" had limited significance for German anthropology in this period because the discipline rejected the type of immediacy that Stephan sought.

The failure of Stephan's work to find wide acceptance among anthropologists illustrates the limits that colonialism placed on anthropology, even as it provided the preconditions for the development of the discipline. Although in one sense Stephan's attempt to "psychologically penetrate" the indigenous inhabitants around Muliama was merely a quantitative extension of anthropological empiricism and immediacy, it depended on a model of the human that had been rejected by anthropology in its study of colonized others. Anthropologists had long imagined that this failure to treat the people they studied as psychological subjects resulted primarily from a lack of data more reliable than the subjective observations of untrained witnesses. They had hoped someday to correct this omission by perfecting a questionnaire that would make psychological and sociological information as objective as they believed artifacts were. However, when anthropologists faced the possibility of reliable professionals conducting such observations, this focus on objects proved to be not a deficit but rather a fundamental aspect of their discipline. Stephan himself recognized that the "fresh and joyful tale" of his interactions with Selin and Pore aboard the *Seagull* did not fit into anthropology. Even Graebner, who made it his project to introduce historical development into anthropology, did not regard such accounts as information that anthropologists could "use scientifically." Diffusionist history was not humanist history, and, like the anthropology of ahistorical natural peoples that it was to displace, it continued to treat human subjects as natural scientific objects. While the developing needs of colonial administration created a place for "sociological" observations, especially those related to labor recruitment, colonialism did not provide the grounds for a humanist study of others. Indeed, such a recognition of natural peoples as autonomous subjects would have threatened colonial rule as much as anthropological study. Thus, even though Stephan's fieldwork was a logical extension of anthropology as a science of the new colonialism, it foundered on—and thus illuminates—the basic contradiction of both anthropology and colonialism, the concept of the human without humanity.

CONCLUSION

$\approx$

Anthropology emerged in Germany as a modernist critique of traditional academic humanism in a moment of transformation marked by the rise of imperialism, mass culture, and natural science. Throughout much of the nineteenth century, humanism had been a hegemonic discourse in Germany, shaping both scholarly knowledge and political identity. However, the end of the nineteenth century saw profound challenges to the primacy of the university as a location for producing scientific knowledge, textual interpretation as a method for creating knowledge, and the European self as an object of knowledge. Anthropology was both a product and a producer of this shift in the human sciences in Germany.

The most important determinant of this shift was the intensification of imperialism in the last third of the nineteenth century. In this moment, the people of Africa and the Pacific ruled by Europeans were simultaneously recognized as human and denied full humanity; they were understood both as human and as less than human. They were, quite literally, exotic to the European self, which was precisely what made them objects of popular fascination appropriate for the same popular venues, the panopticons, in which supposedly half-human, half-animal freaks were displayed. Whereas humanism, understood as self-cultivation through the interpretation of a historical self, rejected the exotic, anthropology, like the popular venues in which it first emerged, focused on that which was seemingly exotic to humanity.

This focus on the other also made possible a natural science of humanity, for nature, especially as nineteenth-century Germans understood that category, differed fundamentally from the *Kultur* of which they regarded themselves as bearers. Whereas humanism depended on a hermeneutic identification of scholars with their objects of study, the natural scientific methods that anthropologists applied emphasized the separation of the knowing subject from the known object. A purportedly natural scientific approach thus allowed anthropologists to answer the objection to studying "primitive humans" cited by the African linguist Carl Meinhof: "One has a feeling as when a man calls himself the friend of a child. Even while recognizing the propriety of such a friendship, one cannot rid oneself of the impression that it is really a somewhat deviant quirk that could easily become abnormal."[1] By proposing a natural scientific study of colonized societies, anthropologists avoided the impression that they had any regard for their subjects; they were not proposing an identification of European *Kulturvölker* and colonized *Naturvölker*. The very idea, common to anthropologists and their humanist critics alike, that non-Europeans were objects of natural science rather than of history was an artifact of nineteenth-century imperialism and its distinction between the humanity of the colonizers and that of the colonized.

Imperialism, however, as many scholars have recently demonstrated, was a highly contradictory, unstable process, and it not only underwrote, but also undermined, anthropology as a modern counterhumanism. The "natural peoples" that anthropologists sought among colonized societies were in fact cultural hybrids who sometimes turned anthropological examinations into occasions to resist anthropological knowledge and European rule. Also, the artifacts and body parts through which anthropologists tried to grasp natural humanity objectively and apart from history were themselves traces of a historical—and therefore radically unnatural—moment in the history of the globe. Although anthropologists themselves only rarely recognized the heteroglossic meanings of these objects, I have endeavored in this account to reactivate these objects as traces of the history of imperialism. The instabilities that imperialism introduced into anthropology were not external to the discipline, any more than anthropology was itself external to imperialism.

Yet German imperialists and anthropologists alike distanced anthropological knowledge from colonial rule. Not only did anthropologists seek to repress the history of colonialism in their efforts to create knowledge about natural peoples, but they also, as we saw in the last chapter, differentiated the kind of sociological and psychological knowledge that they thought would be useful to imperialism from their own interests. Dernburg's "scientific colonialism" did not privilege anthropology but rather a range of sciences that promoted what their practitioners called the "elevation" (*Hebung*) of the colony and its indigenous populations. Agronomy provided the model for these so-called *Kolonialwissenschaften,* which were brought together in 1908 at the Hamburg Colonial Institute. These disciplines grasped the entire space of the colony—from its soils, to its plants, to its animals, to its human inhabitants—as "nature" to be "cultivated" and made more productive. A few anthropologists, especially Georg Thilenius of the Hamburg Museum of Ethnology and the Colonial Institute and Richard Thurnwald of the Berlin museum, sought to make anthropology relevant to colonialism by claiming that it would help administrators utilize and improve indigenous labor.[2] Linguistics, law, botany, zoology, forestry, and, above all, agronomy were, however, far more successful than anthropology in offering to the colonial state strategies of colonial domination and development.

The relation of anthropology and imperialism was far more fundamental than one of providing scientific means to colonial ends. Rather, both anthropology and imperialism were phenomena of a profound shift in global politics, economics, and culture. As imperialism was the primary way in which European politics and economics attempted to come to terms with this new global order, anthropology was the way in which the human sciences attempted to come to terms with it. Despite Europe's overwhelming power, neither imperialism nor anthropology could fully master the moment in global history in which they emerged and that they helped to shape. The adaptation of the human sciences to this new global situation was thus fraught with contradictions. The old humanism did not disappear in the face of anthropology, and the conflict between the two continues to mark the human sciences even today. While politics, economics, and culture have, of course, changed fundamentally in the past century, there is no hope of restabilizing the Eurocentric provincialism that marked humanism before the nineteenth century.

Perhaps the most immediate and obvious consequence of German anthropological antihumanism was in the development of "racial hygiene" in the early twentieth century, an important inspiration for Nazi racial policy.[3] As anthropologists began to accept the Darwinian possibility that nature could develop over time, some came to the conclusion that they might help guide its development. While racial hygiene would ultimately lead to some of the worst atrocities of National Socialist Germany, in its early years it seemed vaguely reformist and left-wing. For example, Luschan recommended the *Archiv für Rassen- und Gesellschaftsbiologie* to an interested Junker correspondent with the following caveat: "You will soon see for yourself that it is edited by men quite far to the left. What one tends to call staunch conservative tendencies are totally alien to the direction of the journal."[4] Luschan himself favored the socially active role that racial hygiene gave to anthropologists, although he complained that practitioners focused too much on race and not enough on hygiene.[5] He regarded the principal task of racial hygiene as combating "the three great plagues of the people [*Volksseuche*]": syphilis, alcoholism, and tuberculosis.[6] Many anthropologists published in the two major racial hygiene journals of the early twentieth century, the *Politisch-Anthropologische Revue* and the *Archiv für Rassen- und Gesellschaftsbiologie*.[7] However, both were oriented toward broad, popular audiences and emphasized political activism, a tactic consistently eschewed by the established anthropology journals, the *Zeitschrift für Ethnologie* and the *Archiv für Anthropologie*. The *Politisch-Anthropologische Revue* incorporated as much Nietzsche and Schopenhauer as it did the more cautious writings of anthropologists.

Despite important differences from anthropology, racial hygiene did continue the critique of humanism initiated by the discipline. Like anthropology, racial hygiene stood on the boundary between the natural sciences and the humanities and promised to answer humanistic questions with natural scientific methods. One author in the *Archiv für Rassenbiologie*, chastising Max Weber and other social scientists for their neglect of race, warned his readers to learn from the example of the Chinese. The Chinese, he claimed, had fallen behind Europe after thousands of years of cultural preeminence because of "their almost exclusive cultivation of the humanistic [*geisteswissenschaftlichen*] area, especially the classical humanities: in other words, the neglect of the natural sciences."[8] While racial hygiene differed significantly from German anthropology, it continued a common natural scientific critique of the humanities and realized one of the possibilities of the rift in the human sciences signaled by the development of anthropology.

National Socialism enthusiastically embraced a racial concept of German national identity, which had first been propagated in the German Anthropological Society's statistical study of schoolchildren in the 1870s. In that study, anthropologists trained Germans to perceive themselves as racialized individuals and gave (pseudo)scientific justification to the idea of a predominantly blond German race distinct from a Jewish race. During the National Socialist period, however, anthropologists were not alone among human scientists in emphasizing race. Recent revelations about the role of historians Werner Conze and Theodor Schieder in providing information about the ethnic makeup of Eastern Europe to Nazi planners indicate how even historians embraced this type of anthropological thinking in the 1930s and 1940s.[9] Anthropologists and other social scientists also studied the racial composition of Eastern Europe and assisted the Nazi government in planning deportations and relocations to shape Europe into ethnically "pure" regions.[10]

The enthusiasm with which even those anthropologists not directly involved in ethnic cleansing in Eastern Europe supported National Socialism is well illustrated by the work of Wilhelm E. Mühlmann (1904–88). Mühlmann, a student of Richard Thurnwald's who began lecturing at the University of Berlin in 1939, enthusiastically supported National Socialism in his anthropology. Mühlmann emphasized the close relation between National Socialist ideology and anthropology in his 1938 *Methodik der Völkerkunde,* which has a preface dated "on the day of the return of Austria to the Reich." He explained that his book was designed to replace Fritz Graebner's 1911 *Methode der Ethnologie* as the definitive work on anthropological methodology. Anthropologists should, he opined, take race more seriously than they had in the early twentieth century: while Bastian had pointed to the unity among humans, it was now time to consider "the historical differentiations [of humans] on the basis of inherited differences."[11] Two years earlier, Mühlmann had lauded National Socialism for encouraging precisely the kind of natural scientistic approach to the human sciences that anthropology offered, for "the new German state" placed great value on "a biological reworking [*Durchdringung*] of the so-called humanities and social sciences [*Geistes- Sozial- und Kulturwissenschaften*]." Germany especially, Mühlmann continued, needed "orientation" in the "world of foreign races and peoples" that surrounded it. He warned against the dangers of "racial mixing" and wrote approvingly of the 1935 law against marriages between Jews and non-Jewish Germans. He applauded Germany as the first nation to recognize the Jewish problem and lamented that it would not be possible to send every Jew to Palestine.[12] After the war, Mühlmann continued as one of the leading anthropologists in Germany, authoring the well-known and widely cited *Geschichte der Anthropologie,* first published in 1948 and reprinted as recently as 1986.[13] In 1948, he became the head of the German Anthropological Association and continued to teach anthropology and sociology at the universities in Mainz and Heidelberg until he retired in 1970.

Perhaps even more striking than the theoretical continuities between German anthropology of the two imperialist periods are the practical continuities. The Holocaust made it possible for anthropologists to acquire bodies, body parts, and plaster casts of bodies from Nazi concentration camps much as they had from the institutions of the colonial state in Africa and the Pacific.[14] Anthropologists such as Eugen Fischer and Karl Seuchhardt could continue the practice, pioneered by Felix von Luschan, of soliciting body parts from the inmates of colonial prisons, hospitals, and concentration camps. Most notoriously, Josef Mengele, the infamous camp physician at Auschwitz, sent body parts from inmates to a former teacher, Otmar Freiherr von Verschuer, at the Kaiser Wilhelm Institute for Anthropology, Heredity, and Eugenics in Berlin.[15]

Such scientific exploitation of the victims of genocide had a strong precedent in the German war of extermination against the Herero of Southwest Africa.[16] In January 1904, conflicts over land ownership between German settlers and Herero led to open military conflict.[17] Dissatisfied with Governor Theodor Leutwein's attempts to negotiate with the Herero, Germany sent in General Lothar von Trotha, whose strategy against the Herero was not simply to defeat them militarily but to exterminate them as a people.[18] Trotha drove the Herero into the desert by ordering soldiers to shoot every Herero man, woman, or child not fleeing in that direction. Once in the desert, the Herero were kept from sources of water. The Herero's former rivals, the Nama, also rose against the Germans and led a successful guerilla war for years. However, they also met a fate similar to that of the Herero. While Trotha was soon recalled and his orders overturned by the government in Berlin, his campaign was brutally effective. By the time the state of war ended in 1907, there were fewer than twenty thousand Herero surviving from an original population of between sixty and eighty thousand. The Germans had also killed more than half the Nama, who had numbered twenty thousand before the war. The Germans took all collective property of the Herero and Nama and dissolved their political organizations. Those who surrendered or who could be captured were forced into concentration camps, where they continued to die in great numbers from typhus and other diseases. At the time of this writing, the Herero are attempting to get reparations from the German government.[19]

In April 1905, over a year after the war began, Luschan contacted none other than Lieutenant Ralf Zürn, the district chief of Okahandja whose paranoia and aggressive behavior toward the Herero had provoked the first shots of the war. Shortly after the fighting began, Zürn had been recalled to Germany and nearly court-martialed for his poor discipline and excessive hostility.[20] Luschan desired a Herero skull that Zürn was rumored to have brought from Africa. The anthropologist persuaded the lieutenant to donate the skull to the museum, which soon prompted a further request: "The skull you gave us corresponds so little to the picture of the Herero skull type that we have thus far been able to make from our insufficient and inferior material that it would be desirable to secure as soon as possible a larger collection of Herero skulls for scientific investigation."[21] It is unclear whether Luschan was thinking of the genocidal policy pursued in Southwest Africa or just hoped that the ordinary course of colonial war would make this "larger collection of Herero skulls" available. Just after the war, rumors did circulate among anthropologists and even in the popular press about shipments of thousands of Herero skulls.[22] In any case, Luschan posed the question to Zürn, "If you are aware of any possible way in which we might acquire a larger number of Herero skulls. . . ." Luschan was so enthusiastic that, in his initial draft of the letter, he forgot to insert his customary qualification that his request for skulls be filled only "in a loyal way"—a phrase that he inserted in the final draft of the letter.[23] Loyal or not, Zürn was optimistic about fulfilling Luschan's demands through a contact still serving in the German army near Swakopmund: "I hope that my requests will have success, since in the concentration camps taking and preserving the skulls of Herero prisoners of war will be more readily possible than in the country, where there is always a danger of offending the ritual feelings of the natives."[24] Zürn was correct in his assessment, and anthropologists were able to obtain a number of Herero corpses and skulls from the concentration camps. Germans involved in this process reported that they forced imprisoned Herero women to remove the flesh from the severed heads of their countrymen with shards of broken glass so that the skulls could be shipped to anthropologists or anatomists in Berlin.[25] The zoologist Leonard Schultze happened also to be on a collecting trip in Southwest Africa when the war broke out. He found that, although the fighting made the collection and preservation of animals difficult, it presented new opportunities for physical anthropology: "I could make use of the victims of the war and take parts from fresh native corpses, which made a welcome addition to the study of the living body (imprisoned Hottentots [Nama] were often available to me)."[26] The military doctors Dansauer, Jungels, Mayer, and Zöllner in Southwest Africa also collected Herero body parts in the concentration camps and shipped them to Berlin, where they were studied by the anthropologist Wilhelm Waldeyer and his students.[27] The Holocaust brought to Europe practices developed in colonial Africa, as the genocidal war against the Herero and the role of anthropologists in that war make all too clear.[28] Anthropologists themselves used their critique of humanism for what can only be described as antihuman purposes by justifying, and profiting from, genocide in German occupied Africa and Europe.

Emerging as it did from a colonial situation that Europeans did not completely control, anthropology also signaled an opening in the human sciences that could be turned against both the narrow Eurocentrism of earlier humanism and the antihumanism of anthropologists. Because the traditional academic humanities had more institutional power and cultural prestige in Germany than perhaps anywhere else in the world in the nineteenth century, the anthropology of that country, despite the colonialist intentions of its practitioners, gave a powerful resource to anti-imperialist intellectuals in the twentieth century. The founder of the negritude movement that emerged among students from the French colonies in interwar Paris, Léopold Sédar Senghor, cited the writings of the German anthropologist Leo Frobenius, along with "Louis Armstrong's trumpet" and "Josephine Baker's hips," as inspirations to black students in Paris that their culture was different from but no less valid than French culture. Senghor and others called for a celebration of "negritude," a culture that included blacks in Africa and in the Americas, as an alternative to both Eurocentric notions of assimilation and more narrow African or Caribbean nationalisms. *La Revue du monde noire,* a journal of the negritude movement, printed excerpts from Frobenius's works along with writings by authors of African descent from around the world. Senghor endorsed Frobenius's assertion that, for both Africans and Germans, in distinction to the French and the English, "emotion," "intuitive reason," "art," "poetry," "image," and "myth" were all important. Like German culture, African culture was ranged against the "mechanism" of the English and the French.[29] Senghor was willing to ignore Frobenius's support for German colonialism in a way unacceptable to more recent African intellectuals, including the novelist Yambo Ouologuem, who probably aimed his fictional portrayal of an anthropologist named Fritz Schrobenius at Senghor.[30] In any case, that Senghor read Frobenius profitably should not be taken to imply that the negritude movement was merely an extension of German anthropology; rather, the limitations of humanism made plain by colonialism gave rise to both negritude and anthropology as variant responses to Eurocentrism.

Aimé Césaire, cofounder with Senghor of the negritude movement, discussed the problematic relation between humanism and colonialism in his 1955 *Discourse on Colonialism.* Césaire drew parallels between National Socialist barbarism in Europe and European barbarism in the colonies, arguing that what was so shocking to Europeans about Hitler "is not *crime* in itself, *the crime against man,* it is not *the humiliation of man as such,* it is the crime against the white man, the humiliation of the white man, and the fact that he applied to Europe colonialist procedures which until then had been reserved exclusively for the Arabs of Algeria, the coolies of India and the blacks of Africa." Despite its polemic oversimplification, Césaire's comparison does draw attention to the way in which both colonialism and Nazism similarly undermined humanism. While anthropologists sought to benefit from the antihumanism of both types of barbarism, Césaire and the negritude movement sought to push forward humanism dialectically. Césaire pointed toward the utopian moment in both humanism and the critique of humanism when he proclaimed: "At the very time when it most often mouths the word, the West has never been further from being able to live a true humanism—a humanism made to the measure of the world."[31] In demanding that humanism expand to include all humans, Césaire differed from German anthropologists, who maintained that the colonized were natural peoples and thereby continued their exclusion from humanism. Césaire went beyond Bastian's observation that "the human qua human does not live only in Europe and part of Asia" to demand this "humanism made to the measure of the world." Césaire's critique of humanism has become our own, with a genealogy running roughly through Frantz Fanon and Edward Said to the most recent cultural studies of colonialism, as well as to moves to supplement or replace "Western civilization" with a more global history. I hope that the present work contributes to this tradition.

I am not arguing that recent developments in the humanities are the direct outcome of nineteenth- and early twentieth-century German anthropology. German anthropology in that period does, however, illustrate with particular clarity the interdependence of the human sciences and the global distribution of power. The current tension in the humanities and social sciences between transnationalism and a more provincial humanism is as much a product of contemporary global relations as the tension between anthropology and history in Germany was in previous centuries. By suggesting that these tensions are themselves products of international power relations, I hope that I have problematized both the Eurocentrism of the humanities and naive celebrations of global culture. By taking a global perspective on German anthropology and its critique of humanism, I have tried to show that the study of societies outside Europe was not simply the product of the good or bad intentions of European scholars but was itself the result of international cultural, economic, and political transformations. I hope that I have disrupted the impression, which anthropologists themselves were eager to give, of active Europeans choosing to study or to ignore passive non-Europeans. While this book has devoted more attention to German anthropologists than to any other group, I hope that it has also pointed to the global system in which culture and nature, colonizer and colonized, and anthropology and humanism were constructed and challenged, disrupted and defended.

NOTES

INTRODUCTION

1. The decline of German humanist, historicist, academic, and classicist cultures in the late nineteenth century has interested historians for decades. Suzanne L. Marchand has recently studied the decline of classical humanism and the development of a scientistic, object-focused antihumanism within German classical studies. My own study, I hope, complements Marchand's work by relating this antihumanism to the emergence of colonialism, mass culture, and the natural sciences. See Suzanne L. Marchand, *Down from Olympus: Archaeology and Philhellenism in Germany, 1750–1970* (Princeton, N.J.: Princeton University Press, 1996), "The Rhetoric of Artifacts and the Decline of Classical Humanism: The Case of Josef Strzygowski," *History and Theory* 33 (1994): 106–30, and "Orientalism as *Kulturpolitik:* German Archaeology and Cultural Imperialism in Asia Minor," in *Volksgeist as Method and Ethic: Essays on Boasian Ethnography and the German Anthropological Tradition,* ed. George W. Stocking Jr. (Madison: University of Wisconsin Press, 1996), 298–334. Both Marchand's work and my own continue a scholarly tradition that includes Fritz K. Ringer, *The Decline of the German Mandarins* (Cambridge, Mass.: Harvard University Press, 1969); and Georg G. Iggers, *The German Conception of History: The National Tradition of Historical Thought from Herder to the Present* (Middletown, Conn.: Wesleyan University Press, 1968). See also Rüdiger vom Bruch, *Wissenschaft, Politik und öffentliche Meinung: Gelehrtenpolitik im Wilhelminischen Deutschland (1890–1914)* (Husum: Matthiesen, 1980).

2. For an excellent history of the term *humanism,* see Vito R. Giustiniani, "Homo, Humanus, and the Meaning of 'Humanism,'" *Journal of the History of Ideas* 46 (1985): 167–95.

3. The two best accounts of German anthropology in this period are in Woodruff Smith, *Politics and the Sciences of Culture in Germany, 1840–1920* (New York: Oxford

University Press, 1991); and Paul Weindling, *Health, Race, and German Politics between National Unification and Nazism, 1870–1945* (Cambridge: Cambridge University Press, 1989). Smith and Weindling have done an excellent job of relating German anthropological theory to political ideologies, especially to liberalism in the nineteenth century and antiliberalism in the twentieth. Smith connects anthropology to a wide range of cultural sciences, while Weindling regards the discipline as a medicalization of the human sciences. In this regard, my findings correspond more to Weindling's than to Smith's. At the same time, I have tried to contextualize anthropology more broadly than Smith and Weindling do, relating to it mass culture, museums, and the global history of imperialism. This has led me to understand anthropology as an interlocutor of humanism rather than of liberalism.

4. See Fritz K. Ringer, *Fields of Knowledge: French Academic Culture in Comparative Perspective, 1890–1920* (Cambridge: Cambridge University Press, 1992).

5. Wilhelm Dilthey, *Einleitung in die Geisteswissenschaften* (1883), in *Gesammelte Schriften,* vol. 1 (Stuttgart: B. G. Teubner/Vandenhoeck & Ruprecht, 1914), xv–xx.

6. See, for example, Frederick Cooper and Ann Laura Stoler, eds., *Tensions of Empire: Colonial Cultures in a Bourgeois World* (Berkeley and Los Angeles: University of California Press, 1997); Mary Louise Pratt, *Imperial Eyes: Travel Writing and Transculturation* (London: Routledge, 1992); Ann Laura Stoler, *Race and the Education of Desire: Foucault's History of Sexuality and the Colonial Order of Things* (Durham, N.C.: Duke University Press, 1995); and Gauri Viswanathan, *Masks of Conquest: Literary Study and British Rule in India* (New York: Columbia University Press, 1989).

7. On these technologies of imperialism, see Daniel R. Headrick, *The Tools of Empire: Technology and European Imperialism in the Nineteenth Century* (New York: Oxford University Press, 1981).

8. Susanne Zantop, *Colonial Fantasies: Conquest, Family, and Nation in Precolonial Germany, 1770–1870* (Durham, N.C.: Duke University Press, 1997).

9. On this German understanding of *Bildung,* especially as it compares with education in England and France, see Ringer, *Fields of Knowledge.* See also Ringer, *The Decline of the German Mandarins;* and Ulrich Muhlack, "Bildung zwischen Neuhumanismus und Historismus," in *Bildungsbürgertum im neunzehnten Jahrhundert,* ed. Reinhardt Koselleck (Stuttgart: Klett-Cotta, 1990), 2:80–105.

10. As Jonathan Harwood has shown, natural scientists may generally have been critical of the mandarin ideology described by Ringer. See Jonathan Harwood, "Mandarins and Outsiders in the German Professoriate, 1890–1933: A Study of the Genetics Community," *European History Quarterly* 23 (1993): 485–511.

11. The Viennese organization soon left the German Anthropological Society. See Carl Vogt to Rudolf Virchow, 21 February 1870, Andree, 496–98. On the founding of local chapters of the German Anthropological Society, see "Erste Sitzung der anthropologischen Gesellschaft zu München," *CBDAG* 1 (1870): 11–12; "Erste Sitzung der Würzburger anthropologischen Gesellschaft am 14. Mai," *CBDAG* 1 (1870): 13–14; "Erste Sitzung der Gruppe Hamburg-Altona, 24. Mai 1870," *CBDAG* 1 (1870): 14; "Mitgliederverzeichnisse," *CBDAG* 1 (1870): 14–15, 23–24, 34–36; "Localverein in Leipzig," *CBDAG* 1 (1870): 46–47. Only the Berlin and the Munich An-

thropological Societies have received attention from historians. On the Berlin society, see Woodruff Smith, *Politics and the Sciences of Culture;* and Hermann Pohle and Gustav Mahr, eds., *Festschrift zum hundertjahrigen Bestehen der Berliner Gesellschaft für Anthropologie, Ethnologie und Urgeschichte, 1869–1969* (Berlin: Berliner Gesellschaft fur Anthropologie, Ethnologie und Urgeschichte, 1969), vol. 1. For a history of anthropology in Munich, see Wolfgang J. Smolka, *Völkerkunde in München: Voraussetzungen, Möglichkeiten und Entwicklungslinien ihrer Institutionalisierung ca. 1850–1933* (Berlin: Duncker & Humboldt, 1994).

12. Carl Semper, "Die Generalsecretär an die Mitglieder," *CBDAG* 1 (1870): 7–8.

13. See Julius Kollmann to Rudolf Virchow, 7 January 1875, Andree, 252–53.

14. Alexander von Frantzius to Rudolf Virchow, 3 December 1871, Andree, 148–50 (my translation). Unless otherwise specified, all subsequent translations from the German are my own.

15. Johannes Ranke, *Der Mensch* (Leipzig: Bibliographisches Institut, 1894), 1:v–vi.

16. For an excellent study of the regional museums emphasizing the interplay of localism and cosmopolitanism, see H. Glenn Penny III, "Cosmopolitan Visions and Municipal Displays: Museums, Markets, and the Ethnographic Project in Germany, 1868–1914" (Ph.D. diss., University of Illinois at Urbana-Champaign, 1999).

17. Studies of the natural sciences in Germany have generally focused on disciplines, unlike anthropology, practiced by professionals in universities or academic institutes. For a historiographic review of studies of German natural science, see R. Steven Turner, "German Science, German Universities: Historiographical Perspectives from the 1980s," in *"Einsamkeit und Freiheit" neu besichtigt,* ed. Gert Schubring (Stuttgart: Franz Steiner, 1991), 24–36. The work of Joseph Ben-David set the institutionalist and university-centered tone of much history of German science. See Joseph Ben-David, "Scientific Productivity and Academic Organization in Nineteenth-Century Medicine" (1960), in *Scientific Growth: Essays on the Social Organization and Ethos of Science,* ed. Gad Freudenthal (Berkeley and Los Angeles: University of California Press, 1991), 103–24. See also R. Steven Turner, "The Growth of Professorial Research in Prussia, 1818–1848: Causes and Context," *Historical Studies in the Physical Sciences* 3 (1971): 137–82. Recent examples of studies of science in academic institutions include David Cahan, *An Institution for an Empire: The Physikalisch-Technische Reichsanstalt, 1871–1918* (Cambridge: Cambridge University Press, 1989); Jonathan Harwood, *Styles of Scientific Thought: The German Genetics Community, 1900–1933* (Chicago: University of Chicago Press, 1993); Lynn K. Nyhart, *Biology Takes Form: Animal Morphology and the German Universities, 1800–1900* (Chicago: University of Chicago Press, 1995); and Kathryn M. Olesko, *Physics as a Calling: Discipline and Practice in the Königsberg Seminar for Physics* (Ithaca, N.Y.: Cornell University Press, 1991).

18. Adolf Bastian (Montego Bay, Jamaica) to Georg von Neumayer, 1 August 1904, ABGAEU.

19. Hermann von Helmholtz, *Ueber das Verhältniss der Naturwisenschaften zur Gesammtheit der Wissenschaften* (Heidelberg: Georg Mohr, 1862), 6.

20. Board of Directors of the Berlin Anthropological Society to Ministry of Culture, 2 July 1872. Draft: MfV, I, vol. 1, 1214/73. Final version: GStA PK, I. HA, Rep. 76Ve, Cultusministerium, Sekt. 15, Abt. XI, Nr. 2, Bd. 1, Bl. 52–60 (M).

21. One of the most important accounts of European knowledge about the colonized as ideological projection is Edward W. Said, *Orientalism* (New York: Pantheon Books, 1978). Said modifies the position that he takes in that groundbreaking work to include practice as well as projection in his "Representing the Colonized: Anthropology's Interlocutors," *Critical Inquiry* 15 (1989): 205–25, and *Culture and Imperialism* (New York: Vintage Books, 1993). John M. MacKenzie gives an excellent critique of Said's earlier position in *Orientalism: History, Theory, and the Arts* (Manchester: Manchester University Press, 1995). Most of the literature on German anthropology and colonialism has focused on the opinions and ideologies of leading anthropologists and the practical suggestions that they made for colonial administration. See Ingeburg Winkelmann, "Die bürgerliche Ethnographie im Dienste der Kolonialpolitik des Deutschen Reiches (1870–1918)" (Ph.D. diss., Humboldt-Universität zu Berlin, 1966); Manfred Gothsch, *Die deutsche Völkerkunde und ihr Verhältnis zum Kolonialismus: Ein Beitrag zur kolonialideologischen und kolonialpractischen Bedeutung der deutschen Völkerkunde in der Zeit von 1870 bis 1975* (Baden-Baden: Nomos, 1983); and Volker Harms, "Das historische Verhältnis der deutschen Ethnologie zum Kolonialismus," *Zeitschrift für Kulturaustausch* 34 (1984): 401–16. An exception to this trend is Hans Fischer, *Die Hamburger Südsee-Expedition: Über Ethnographie und Kolonialismus* (Frankfurt a.M.: Syndikat, 1981).

22. Talal Asad, introduction to *Anthropology and the Colonial Encounter,* ed. Talal Asad (New York: Humanities, 1973), 16. Other historians of anthropology have also abandoned the projectionist model in favor of accounts that consider all parties to the anthropological encounter. In addition to Fischer, *Die Hamburger Südsee-Expedition,* see Michael T. Bravo, "The Accuracy of Ethnoscience: A Study of Inuit Cartography and Cross-Cultural Commensurability," Manchester Papers in Social Anthropology, no. 2 (Manchester: University of Manchester, Department of Social Anthropology, 1996); Simon Schaffer, "From Physics to Anthropology—and Back Again," Prickly Pear Pamphlet no. 3 (Cambridge: Prickly Pear, 1994); and Lynette L. Schumaker, "The Lion in the Path: Fieldwork and Culture in the History of the Rhodes-Livingstone Institute, 1937–1964" (Ph.D. diss., University of Pennsylvania, 1994). See also Michael T. Bravo, "Ethnological Encounters," in *Cultures of Natural History,* ed. Nick Jardine, J. A. Secord, and E. C. Spary (Cambridge: Cambridge University Press, 1997), 338–57; and Henrika Kuklick, "The Politics of Perception," in *The Savage Within: The Social History of British Anthropology, 1885–1945* (Cambridge: Cambridge University Press, 1991), 279–95.

23. Richard White, *The Middle Ground: Indians, Empires, and Republics in the Great Lakes Region, 1650–1815* (Cambridge: Cambridge University Press, 1991).

24. The inability of authors to wholly master their subjects has been insightfully considered by Mikhail Bakhtin in *The Dialolgic Imagination,* ed. Michael Holquist, trans. Caryl Emerson and Michael Holquist (Austin: University of Texas Press, 1981). See also the important critique of Bakhtin's inattention to power differences in Peter Stallybrass and Allon White, *The Politics and Poetics of Transgression* (Ithaca, N.Y.:

Cornell University Press, 1986); and Allon White, "Pigs and Pierrots: Politics of Transgression in Modern Fiction," *Raritan* 2 (1982): 51–70.

25. I thus find persuasive Ranajit Guha and Gayatri Chakravorty Spivak's call for an approach to history that recognizes the agency of the "subaltern," colonized subjects accounted for neither by imperialist narratives of civilization nor by anti-imperialist narratives of national liberation. See Ranajit Guha and Gayatri Chakravorty Spivak, eds., *Selected Subaltern Studies* (New York: Oxford University Press, 1988), and Spivak, "Can the Subaltern Speak?" in *Marxism and the Interpretation of Culture,* ed. Cary Nelson and Lawrence Grossberg (Urbana: University of Illinois Press, 1988), 271–313.

26. The most important work for my approach to colonialism is Jacques Derrida, *Of Grammatology,* trans. Gayatri Chakravorty Spivak (Baltimore: Johns Hopkins University Press, 1976). In *White Mythologies: Writing History and the West* (London: Routledge, 1990), Robert Young argues persuasively that *Of Grammatology* is, in the first place, a critique of imperialism and ethnocentrism. Derrida's critique focuses above all on anthropology, especially that of Rousseau and Lévi-Strauss. Derrida rightly points out the ethnocentrism involved even in well-meaning anti-imperialist accounts of cunning Europeans and innocent colonial subjects. I have tried to show how all parties played active roles in anthropological and colonial encounters, to which there was no inside or outside, no pure *before* or fallen *after.* This view, even if not informed by a reading of Derrida, also characterizes Robert J. Gordon, *The Bushman Myth: The Making of a Namibian Underclass* (Boulder, Colo.: Westview, 1992); William Rosenberry, "European History and the Construction of Anthropological Subjects," in *Anthropologies and Histories: Essays in Culture, History, and Political Economy* (New Brunswick, N.J.: Rutgers University Press, 1989), 125–44; and Eric R. Wolf, *Europe and the People without History* (Berkeley and Los Angeles: University of California Press, 1982).

27. Previous accounts have described a cataclysmic break between the avowedly antiracist German anthropology of 1870s and 1880s and the increasingly biologistic and racist anthropology of the 1890s and after. Two excellent accounts emphasizing this break are Robert Proctor, "From *Anthropologie* to *Rassenkunde* in the German Anthropological Tradition," in *Bones, Bodies, Behavior: Essays on Biological Anthropology,* ed. George W. Stocking Jr. (Madison: University of Wisconsin Press, 1988), 138–79; and Benoit Massin, "From Virchow to Fischer: Physical Anthropology and 'Modern Race Theories' in Wilhelmine Germany," in Stocking, ed., *Volksgeist as Method and Ethic,* 79–154. I would like to give a more historically nuanced account than this castastrophist one, emphasizing continuities as well as discontinuities.

CHAPTER I

1. For ethnographic spectacles, especially in Germany, see Sierra Ann Bruckner, "The Tingle-Tangle of Modernity: Popular Anthropology and the Cultural Politics of Identity in Imperial Germany" (Ph.D. diss., University of Iowa, 1999); Stefan Goldmann, "Wilde in Europa: Aspeke und Orte ihrer Zurschaustellung," in *Wir und die Wilden: Einblick in eine kannibalische Beziehung,* ed. Thomas Theye (Hamburg: Rowohlt, 1984), 243–69; Carl Hagenbeck, *Von Tieren und Menschen: Erlebnisse und*

Erfahrungen (Berlin: Vita Deutsches, 1909); Alfred Lehmann, "Zeitgenössische Bilder der ersten Völkerschauen," in *Von fremden Völkern und Kulturen: Beiträge zur Völkerkunde,* ed. W. Lang (Düsseldorf: Droste, 1955), 31–38; Nigel T. Rothfels, "Bring 'Em Back Alive: Carl Hagenbeck and Exotic Animal and People Trades in Germany, 1848–1914" (Ph.D. diss, Harvard University, 1994); and Hilke Thode-Arora, *Für fünfzig Pfennig um die Welt: Die Hagenbeckschen Völkerschauen* (New York: Campus, 1989). Especially important for the present discussion is Timothy Mitchell, *Colonizing Egypt* (Cambridge: Cambridge University Press, 1988), and "Orientalism and the Exhibitionary Order," in *Colonialism and Culture,* ed. Nicholas B. Dirks (Ann Arbor: University of Michigan Press, 1992), 289–317. For an excellent discussion of popular performances in Berlin, see Peter Jelavich, *Berlin Cabaret* (Cambridge, Mass.: Harvard University Press, 1993). While Jelavich does not discuss displays of non-Europeans, he does address the theme of race in performances by and about African Americans and Jews.

2. On Africans in Europe, see Hans Werner Debrunner, *Presence and Prestige: Africans in Europe* (Basel: Basler Afrika Bibliographien, 1979). On African-German relations, see Renate Hücking and Ekkehard Launer, *Aus Menschen Neger Machen: Wie sich das Handelshaus Woermann in Afrika Entwickelt hat* (Hamburg: Galgenberg, 1986).

3. See "Eine Unterhaltung mit einem Togo-Häuptling," *Kölnische Zeitung,* 11 October 1896, BAP, Reichskolonialamt, 6350, Bd. 2, Bl. 47; and Colonial Exhibition to the Colonial Office, 28 October 1896, BAP, Reichskolonialamt, 6350, Bl. 50.

4. For example, the sultan of Zanzibar's cruiser *El medschidi* came to Hamburg for repairs around 1870, bringing a crew of various ethnic backgrounds. The photographer Carl Dammann brought crew members to his studio to make a volume of anthropological photographs. "Miscellen," *Mittheilungen der anthropologischen Gesellschaft in Wien* 1 (1870): 177–78.

5. Those held in a prisoner-of-war camp near Berlin were photographed and studied by anthropologists. See Robert Hartmann, lecture on the Tarcos, *VBGAEU* 3 (1871): 15–17.

6. Alfred Lehmann had a collection of advertisements for such shows that was destroyed in the Second World War. See his "Zeitgenössische Bilder der ersten Völkerschauen."

7. Stuhlmann explained that the individuals in question would have been sold to cannibals had he not bought them. See *Die Post,* 21 March 1883; Dr. Bokemeyer, "Die Pygmäen," *Berliner Börsen-Zeitung,* 22 March 1893; *National-Zeitung,* 25 March 1893; *Vossische Zeitung,* 25 March 1893; *Berliner Börsen Courier,* 28 March 1893; *Reichsboten,* 29 March 1893; and Dr. B., "Ueber die Zwergvölker Afrikas," *Neuen Preussischen Zeitung,* 23 March 1893, all in NL Virchow, 3010. On the presence of the Akas in the Berlin museum, see Adolf Bastian to Rudolf Virchow, n.d., NL Virchow, 117, pt. II, Bl. 83–84.

8. On the panopticons, see Albert Goldschmidt, *Berlin, Potsdam und Umgebungen: Praktischer Wegweiser* (Berlin: Albert Goldschmidt, 1892), 48–49, 165–66; and Peter Letkemann, "Das Berliner Panoptikum: Namen, Häuser und Schicksale," *Mitteilungen des Vereins für die Geschichte Berlins* 69 (1973): 317–26.

9. The Captain of Köpenick was Wilhelm Voigt, an ex-convict who in 1906 posed as a military officer and ordered the local government of the town of Köpenick, just outside Berlin, to hand over the treasury. The Captain of Köpenick's story is well-known from Carl Zuckmayer's 1932 play of the same name. The police prevented the Captain of Köpenick's 1908 appearances in the panopticon because they considered them politically subversive. The hunger artists who performed in the panopticons did just what Kafka described: starve themselves in public. On the Captain of Köpenick's performances in the panopticon, see *Berliner Börsen-Courier,* 20 August 1908, BLHA, Pr. Br. Rep. 30, Polizeipräsidium, Berlin C, Tit. 74, Th. 731, Bd. 6, Bl. 38. On the hunger artists, see Theodor Rosenfeld (Passage-Panopticon) to the Royal Police Headquarters, 9 January 1904, BLHA, Pr. Br. Rep. 30, Polizeipräsidium, Berlin C, Tit. 74, Th. 729, Passage-Panoptikum, Bd. 4, Bl. 6.

10. Goldschmidt, *Berlin, Potsdam und Umgebung,* 165–66.

11. BLHA, Pr. Br. Rep. 30, Polizeipräsidium, Berlin C, Tit. 74, Th. 727, Passage-Panoptikum, Bd. 2, Bl. 112–13. These medical figures, as well as the "racial busts," were, until quite recently, still on display in a Berlin establishment that had taken the name and bought many of the original figures from Castan's Panopticon. Sigfried Kracauer remembered that wax genitals were displayed separately to men and women during alternating times in the day. See Sigfried Kracauer, "Abschied von der Lindenpassage" (1930), in *Das Ornament der Masse* (Frankfurt a.M.: Suhrkamp, 1963), 326–32.

12. See Zefthe Ohaira (the performer) to the Royal Police Headquarters, 12 February 1898; and W. Meyer (Police Headquarters), memo, 17 February 1898, BLHA, Pr. Br. Rep. 30, Polizeipräsidium, Berlin C, Tit. 74, Th. 726, Passage-Panoptikum, Bd. 1, Bl. 234–35.

13. Goldschmidt, *Berlin, Potsdam und Umgebung.* On the number of visitors to the panopticon, see the brothers Castan to the Royal Police Headquarters, 1 February 1888, BLHA, Pr. Br. Rep. 30, Polizeipräsidium, Berlin C, Tit. 74, Th. 743, Castan's Panoptikum, Bd. 1, Bl. 10–11.

14. The popularity of these shows is attested to by Carl Hagenbeck, who in *Von Tieren und Menschen* recalled that he was able to cover losses in his animal importing business with profits from his human displays. On Hagenbeck, see also Rothfels, "Bring 'Em Back Alive"; and Thoda-Arora, *Für fünfzig Pfennig um die Welt.*

15. See Julius von Soden (governor of Cameroon) to Otto von Bismarck, 8 August 1885, BAP, Reichskolonialamt, 4297, Bl. 3–5. In that letter, Soden expressed concern that the popular venues in which Africans performed would leave them with a poor impression of Europe.

16. Both Castan and Hagenbeck had more than a merely cynical interest in anthropology. Hagenbeck's services to the study of anthropology were publicly recognized at the 1880 Berlin meeting of the German Anthropological Society. See the minutes of that meeting, 22, bound with *CBDAG* 12 (1881). The Castan brothers were both members of the Berlin Anthropological Society.

17. E. Schmidt to the Polizei-Präsidium, 25 May 1897, BLHA, Pr. Br. Rep. 30, Polizeipräsidium, Berlin C, Tit. 74, Th. 726. For police suspicion, investigation, and regulation of Castan's Panopticon and the Passage-Panopticon, see BLHA, Pr. Br. Rep. 30, Polizeipräsidium, Berlin C, Tit. 74, Th. 726–32, 743–45.

18. See, for example, the brothers Castan to the Royal Police Headquarters, 14 February 1884, and the brothers Castan to the Berlin City Council, 22 September 1885, BLHA, Pr. Br. Rep. 30, Polizeipräsidium, Berlin C, Tit. 74, Th. 743, Castan's Panoptikum, Bd. 1, Bl. 1–2. See also R. Neumann, E. Fiebelkorn, directors of the Passage-Panoptikum, to Polizei-Präsidium, 9 November 1890, BLHA, Pr. Br. Rep. 30, Polizeipräsidium, Berlin C, Tit. 74, Th. 726, Passage-Panoptikum, Bd. 1, Bl. 7.

19. Pröhle (presumably a policeman), memo, 30 March 1896, BLHA, Pr. Br. Rep. 30, Polizeipräsidium, Berlin C, Tit. 74, Th. 743, Castan's Panoptikum, Bd. 1, Bl. 180.

20. Max Bartels (secretary of the Berlin Anthropological Society), evaluation of a "Negress" performing in Castan's Panoptikum, 27 December 1902, ABGAEU. Rudolf Virchow also publicly attests to the "purity" of a group of "Negroes" displayed in Berlin in a printed leaflet dated 5 February 1873 in the ABGAEU. See also Virchow's testimony of 24 June 1889, reprinted in the *Deutsche Tageblatt,* 27 June 1889, NL Virchow, 3002; drafts of further anthropological evaluations of performers exist in the ABGAEU (for example, drafts by Max Bartels of 17 December 1898, 29 April 1899, and 27 December 1902). The *Berliner Volksblatt* criticized Virchow's "general willingness to support every exotic undertaking by publicizing his treasured judgments" ("Sonntagsplauderei," *Berliner Volksblatt,* 28 July 1889, NL Virchow, 3002).

21. Rudolf Virchow, the famous liberal politician and head of the German Anthropological Society and its Berlin branch, often used his political connections to help impresarios. For example, in the Sudanese performance discussed below, he had had the German foreign service persuade the Egyptian government to permit Hagenbeck to take a group of its citizens to be displayed in German zoos. Hagenbeck, in exchange, not only allowed Virchow to bring a group of anthropologists to study these "Nubians," but also had them put on a private show for the whole anthropological society. See Rudolf Virchow to Imperial German Consulate General in Alexandria, 10 October 1878, ABGAEU. Virchow helped Hagenbeck similarly with the Chilean government. See Adalbert Falk (minister of culture) to Otto von Bismarck (Foreign Office), 3 March 1879; Bismarck to Imperial Ministerial Resident Gülich (Santiago), 17 April 1879, BAP, Auswärtiges Amt, 37865, Bl. 5–6.

22. These performances and special meetings are recorded in the *VBGAEU.*

23. Felix von Luschan to Dr. Erich von Hornbostel, 10 January 1906, MfV, IB 39, vol. 1, 2405/05. See also Ernst Starbina, Castan's Panopticon, to Direction of the Royal Museum of Ethnology, 23 December 1905, and Hornbostel's initial letter to Luschan, 5 January 1906, MfV, IB 39, vol. 1, 2405.

24. Rudolf Virchow to Imperial German Consulate General in Alexandria, 10 October 1878, ABGAEU.

25. Johannes Ranke, address to the German Anthropological Society, *CBDAG* 10 (1879): 82–88, 88.

26. The philologists were Franz Praetorius, Christian Friedrich Dillmann, and Karl Lepsius.

27. On Hagenbeck's Nubian shows, see Hagenbeck, *Von Tieren und Menschen,* 83–85. On the Berlin Anthropological Society's study of the 1878 Nubian show, see Rudolf Virchow, "Nubier," *VBGAEU* 10 (1878): 333–55, 387–407. On Virchow's Nu-

bian bust, see Felix von Luschan to Rose Virchow, 19 February 1906, MfV, IB 39, vol. 1, 334/06.

28. Gustav Fritsch, for example, calls Nubia the "nodal point" of the question of the relation of western and eastern Africa. Gustav Fritsch, *Die Eingeborenen Süd-Afrika's ethnographisch und anatomisch Beschrieben* (Breslau: Ferdinand Hirt, 1872), xxii.

29. Virchow, "Nubier," 402.

30. The father of the Christian Inuit family, Abraham, kept a journal, a German translation of which is currently in the Moravian Archives in Bethlehem, Pennsylvania, and which was the source for a fascinating article on this particular *Völkerschau,* Hilke Thode-Arora's "Das Eskimo-Tagebuch von 1880: Eine Völkerschau aus der Sicht eines Teilnehmers," *Kea: Zeitschrift für Kulturwissenschaften* 2 (1991): 87–115.

31. "Die Eskimos in Zoologischen Garten in Berlin," *Magdeburger Zeitung,* 21 October 1880, cited in Rudolf Virchow, "Eskimos von Labrador," *VBGAEU* 12 (1880): 253–74.

32. See Virchow, "Eskimos von Labrador."

33. Concerns about a risk of smallpox from handling the possessions and bodies of these performers limited what could be salvaged from this show, and more objects were sent to Paris than to the Berlin museum of ethnology. Information on the death of the Inuit and the fate of their bodies and performance props comes from Thode-Arora, "Das Eskimo-Tagebuch von 1880."

34. On King Dido's visit to the crown prince and Soden's reaction, see *Norddeutsche Allgemeine Zeitung,* 28 July 1886, and Julius Soden (in Cameroon) to Otto von Bismarck, 7 September 1886, BAP, Reichskolonialamt, 4297, Bl. 26, 23–25. On King Dido's inquiry into Friedrich's health, see Prince Samson Dido (Dido Town) to Kaiser Friedrich, 8 April 1888, and Bismarck to Soden, 5 July 1888, BAP, Reichskolonialamt, 4297, Bl. 32–33. It is not clear whether King Dido really had become a prince or whether he had simply given himself another title. The italicized passages in my quotations from Soden's letter are in English in the original. Hilke Thode-Arora gives a detailed account of King Dido and this Duala show in which she claims that Dido really was a politically important figure in Cameroon. Thode-Arora's claim, however, is based on two promotional pamphlets for the show. Of course, Governor Julius Soden's understanding of King Dido was no less politically motivated than that of the show's promoters. We should not try to resolve these contradictions here since the nature of "real" nobility has plagued nobles themselves for centuries. The contrast between the interpretation that both I and Soden favor and the one put forward by Thode-Arora and the Hagenbeck impresarios indicates the way in which these *Völkerschauen* were bound up, for both promoters and performers, in the international politics of colonialism. See Hilke Thode-Arora, "'Charakteristische Gestalten des Volkslebens': Die Hagenbeckschen Südasien-, Orient-, und Afrika Völkerschauen," in *Fremde Erfahrungen: Asiaten und Afrikaner in Deutschland, Österreich und der Schweiz bis 1945,* ed. Gerhard Höpp (Berlin: Das Arabische Buch, 1996).

35. For an account of the 1896 exposition that includes a discussion of the Africans and Pacific Islanders who performed there, see Paul Thiel, "Berlin präsen-

tiert sich der Welt: Die Berliner Gewerbeausstellung 1896 in Treptow," in *Die Metropole: Industriekultur in Berlin im 20. Jahrhundert,* ed. Jochen Bobert, Tilman Fichter, and Eckhart Gillen (Munich: C. H. Beck, 1986), 16-27.

36. Eugen Neisser, "Das Leben und Treiben der Eingeborenen," in *Deutschland und seine Kolonien im Jahre 1896: Amtlicher Bericht über die erste Deutsche Kolonial-Ausstellung,* ed. Gustav Hermann Meinecke and Rudolf Hellgrewe (Berlin: Dietrich Reimer, 1897), 25-42, 42.

37. Ibid.

38. Georg Irmer (imperial commissar of the Marshall Islands, Jaluit) to Imperial Chancellor Chlodwig zu Hohenlohe-Schillingsfürst, 1 April 1895, and Foreign Office to Irmer, n.d., BAP, Reichskolonialamt, 6349, Bl. 5-7, 8.

39. Richard Parkinson to Adolf Bastian and Felix von Luschan, 6 January 1896, MfV, IB 48, vol. 1, 258/96. "Immunization List for Natives Departing on 9 March 1896 on the Imperial Postal Steamer *Admiral* to Berlin (Exhibition)," BAP, Reichskolonialamt, 6349, Bl. 43-48. G. Meinecke, "Die Eingeborenen-Dörfer," in Meinecke and Hellgrewe, eds., *Deutschland und seine Kolonien,* 13-24, 17.

40. On the Masai and German colonialism, see John Iliffe, *A Modern History of Tanganyika* (Cambridge: Cambridge University Press, 1979), 102-3, 124; and Marcia Wright, "East Africa," in *The Cambridge History of Africa,* ed. J. D. Fage and Roland Oliver (Cambridge: Cambridge University Press, 1985), 6:539-91, 545-46.

41. Hermann von Wissmann and Freiherr von Schele (imperial governor of German East Africa) to Imperial Chancellor Chlodwig zu Hohenlohe-Schillingsfürst, 17 December 1895, BAP, Reichskolonialamt, 6349, Bl. 31-32. There is no other mention of this forgery in the archival or published documents relating to the show. However, in his anthropological study of the two Wamakonde, Luschan included them in the section on the Swahili and noted that "in many dimensions and also in their entire habitus" they could be grouped with the Swahili. See Felix von Luschan, "Völkerkunde," in Meinecke and Hellgrewe, eds., *Deutschland und seine Kolonien,* 203-69, 225. Luschan's chapter was expanded and reprinted separately as *Beiträge zur Völkerkunde der Deutschen Schutzgebiete* (Berlin: Dietrich Reimer, 1897).

42. Freiherr von Schele (imperial governor of German East Africa) to Imperial Chancellor Chlodwig zu Hohenlohe-Schillingsfürst, 1 April 1895; Franz Tönnies (agent of the firm Küsel, Dar es Salaam) to Franz Stuhlmann, 8 July 1895; and Count von Schweinitz to Foreign Office, telegram, 18 April 1896, BAP, Reichskolonialamt, 6349, Bl. 3-4, 60, 9-10.

43. Neisser, "Das Leben und Treiben der Eingeborenen," 37-38.

44. Luschan, "Völkerkunde," 249.

45. See Karin Hausen, *Deutsche Kolonialherrschaften in Afrika: Wirtschaftsinteressen und Kolonialverwaltung in Kamerun vor 1914* (Zurich: Atlantis, 1970).

46. Captain von Kamptz (Station Jaunde), to Imperial Government of Cameroon, 21 March 1896, BAP, Reichskolonialamt, 6349, Bl. 90.

47. Jesco von Puttkamer (imperial governor of Cameroon) to Imperial Chancellor Chlodwig zu Hohenlohe-Schillingsfürst, 20 April 1896, BAP, Reichskolonialamt, 6349, Bl. 91.

48. Neisser, "Das Leben und Treiben der Eingeborenen," 38.

49. Luschan, *Beiträge,* 53.

50. For a history of German imperialism in Togo, see Arthur J. Knoll, *Togo under Imperial Germany, 1884–1914* (Stanford, Calif.: Hoover Institution Press, 1978).

51. Luschan, *Beiträge,* 9.

52. "Eine Unterhaltung mit einem Togo-Häuptling," *Kölnische Zeitung,* 11 October 1896, and August Köhler (Imperial Landeshauptmann of Togo) to Imperial Chancellor Chlodwig zu Hohenlohe-Schillingsfürst, 15 July 1895, BAP, Reichskolonialamt, 6349, Bl. 47, 11–13; Joseph Garber to the Foreign Office, 29 December 1905, BAP, Reichskolonialamt, 6350, Bl. 95.

53. Minutes of a meeting between J. C. Bruce and Togo Government, 4 July 1895, and August Köhler (Imperial Landeshauptmann of Togo) to Imperial Chancellor Chlodwig zu Hohenlohe-Schillingsfürst, 14 November 1895, BAP, Reichskolonialamt, 6349, Bl. 14–15, 24–26.

54. J. C. Bruce offered to set up a second exotic show from his native Togo two years later, but the German government rejected his proposal. See *Berliner Börsen Kourier,* 20 March 1898, BAP, Reichskolonialamt, 6360, Bl. 17.

55. Theodor Leutwein (imperial governor of Southwest Africa) to Imperial Chancellor Chlodwig zu Hohenlohe-Schillingsfürst, 28 March 1896, BAP, Reichskolonialamt, 6349, Bl. 77–78.

56. Friedrich von Lindequist (Imperial Landeshauptmann of Southwest Africa) to Imperial Chancellor Chlodwig zu Hohenlohe-Schillingsfürst, 26 August 1895, BAP, Reichskolonialamt, 6349, Bl. 16; Foreign Office to Office of the imperial chancellor, 12 September 1896, and Geheimes Zivilkabinett to the Foreign Office, 18 September 1896, BAP, Reichskolonialamt, 6350, Bl. 26–27, 28–29.

57. Dr. A. Schreiber (Barmen Mission House) to the Foreign Office, 12 August 1896, BAP, Reichskolonialamt, 6349, Bl. 163; Josephat Kamatoto to the Foreign Office, 18 August 1896, BAP, Reichskolonialamt, 6350, Bl. 6–7.

58. Neisser, "Das Leben und Treiben der Eingeborenen," 32–33.

59. On the problems of cultural hybridity for colonial ideologies, see Homi Bhabha, *The Location of Culture* (New York: Routledge, 1994); Akhil Gupta and James Ferguson, "Beyond 'Culture': Space, Identity, and the Politics of Difference," *Cultural Anthropology* 7 (1992): 6–23; and Robert J. C. Young, *Colonial Desire: Hybridity in Theory, Culture, and Race* (London: Routledge, 1995).

60. On the use in colonialist ideology of the distinction between historical colonizer and the ahistorical colonized, see Nicholas B. Dirks, "History as a Sign of the Modern," *Public Culture* 2 (1990): 25–32.

61. The critic of the exhibition was Otto Finsch, a former commercial agent, anthropological collector, and expert in New Guinea. Meinecke, "Die Eingeborenen-Dörfer," 17.

62. Luschan, *Beiträge,* 3.

63. Luschan published photographs of 51 of the 103 performers at the exhibition. Of those photographed, 19 (or 37 percent) appeared in exclusively European-style

clothes, 13 (or 25 percent) appeared in a mixture of European- and non-European-style clothes, and another 19 appeared in exclusively non-European clothes or with no clothes visible in the photograph at all. This means that only 18 percent of the 103 performers fully cooperated with Luschan in his anthropological project.

64. On the significance of clothing for both colonizers and colonized in British India, see Bernard S. Cohn, "Cloth, Clothes, and Colonialism: India in the Nineteenth Century," in *Colonialism and Its Forms of Knowledge: The British in India* (Princeton, N.J.: Princeton University Press, 1996), 106–62. On European clothes as form of resistance to colonialism in German Southwest Africa, see Philip Prein, "Guns and Top Hats: African Resistance in German South West Africa, 1907–1915," *Journal of Southern African Studies* 20 (1994): 99–121. On the ambiguous relation of European dress to German colonialism in Cameroon, see Christraud M. Geary, "Political Dress: German-Style Military Attire and Colonial Politics in Bamum," in *African Crossroads: Intersections between History and Anthropology in Cameroon,* ed. Ian Fowler and David Zeitlyn (Providence: Berghahn Books, 1996), 165–92.

65. Gustav Fritsch described similar problems getting his South African models to remove their European clothes for his photographs: "In the fewest cases it was the feeling of shame that one had to struggle against. However, many natives, especially the chiefs and the students of the mission schools, showed themselves to be extraordinarily proud of the not-at-all becoming rags that civilization had draped on them. Those wearing clothes [in the photographs] often appear, therefore, in European dress." Gustav Fritsch, *Die Eingeborenen Süd-Afrika's: Atlas enthaltend dreissig Tafeln Racentypen* (Breslau: Ferdinand Hirt, 1872), 4.

66. See, for example, Luschan, "Völkerkunde," 210, 217.

67. Luschan, *Beiträge,* 21.

68. Thus, a guide for scientific travelers abroad lists formal evening wear as necessary equipment, along with cigars wrapped in tinfoil and a big revolver. See Georg Wislicenus, "Einige Winke für die Ausrüstung und die Ausführung von Forschungsreisen," in *Anleitung zu Wissenschaftlichen Beobachtungen auf Reisen in Einzel-Abhandlungen,* ed. George von Neumayer, 3d ed. (Hannover: Dr. Max Jänecke, 1906), 740–62, 744.

69. For a discussion of a similar case, in which cosmopolitan non-Europeans refused to play authentic representatives of a culture, see Natalia Majluf, "'Ce n'est pas le Pérou,' or the Failure of Authenticity: Marginal Cosmopolitans at the Paris Universal Exhibition of 1855," *Critical Inquiry* 23 (1997): 818–93.

70. See, for example, Luschan, *Beiträge,* 7, 17.

71. On the term *Hosennigger,* see Hücking and Launer, *Aus Menschen Neger Machen,* 102. For an exemplary use of the term by the governor of Cameroon, Theodor Seitz, see Seitz's "Wirtschaftliche und soziale Verhältnisse der Eingeborenen Kameruns," *Koloniale Rundschau* 1 (1909): 321–36, 327–28.

72. See Homi Bhabha, "Of Mimicry and Man: The Ambivalence of Colonial Discourse," in *The Location of Culture,* 85–92.

73. Alfred Lehmann remembers this practice. See Lehmann, "Zeitgenössische Bilder der ersten Völkerschauen." This conclusion is also supported by the various

studies cited in the *Zeitschrift für Ethnologie,* including those of the Sudanese and the Inuit discussed above.

74. Felix von Luschan, "Anthropologie, Ethnologie und Urgeschichte," in Neumayer, ed., *Anleitung zu Wissenschaftlichen Beobachtungen auf Reisen* (3d ed.), 1–123, 37–38.

75. Luschan, *Beiträge,* 5–6.

76. Ibid., 12–13.

77. Foreign Office to the governors of Togo, Cameroon, East Africa, and Southwest Africa, 5 December 1895, BAP, Reichskolonialamt, 6349, 22.

78. Commercial Section of the German Colonial Exhibition to the Foreign Office, 15 May 1896, BAP, Reichskolonialamt, 6349, 81–82.

79. Neisser, "Das Leben und Treiben der Eingeborenen," 32, 45.

80. Wilhelm Gronauer, "Gesundheitszustand und Krankheiten der Eingeborenen," in Meinecke and Hellgrewe, eds., *Deutschland und seine Kolonien,* 43–51. Working Committee of the Colonial Exhibition to the Foreign Office, 31 August 1896, and Foreign Office to Baron von der Recke, 6 September 1896, BAP, Reichskolonialamt, 6350, Bl. 14, 16–17.

81. Felix von Luschan, memo, 4 June 1896, and Count von Schweinitz of the German Colonial Exhibition to Luschan, 10 June 1896, MfV, IB46, vol. 1, 711/96. Whether Luschan got the corpses of the two performers who died in Berlin is not clear. Anthropologists often did acquire corpses of ethnographic performers who died in Europe.

82. See, for example, Karl von den Steinen's account of his travels, *Unter den Naturvölkern Zentral-Brasiliens: Reiseschilderung und Ergebnisse der Zweiten Schingú-Expedition, 1887–1888,* 2d ed. (Berlin: Dietrich Reimer, 1897), vii–viii.

83. Felix von Luschan to "Hochverehrter Freund," 2 April 1897, NL Luschan, K. 21, Copie-Buch V, Bl. 292–93.

84. Luschan, *Beiträge,* 53.

85. The anthropologist Alfred Lehmann remembers going to these shows until the 1930s. See Lehmann, "Zeitgenössische Bilder der ersten Völkerschauen."

86. Friedrich von Lindequist to the Foreign Office, 29 August 1939, BAP, Reichskolonialamt, 6385, Bl. 42–44.

87. Ranke, address to the German Anthropological Society, 88. Nineteen years after this address, Ranke made the same argument about the preferability of measuring performers in exotic shows in Berlin over relying on the reports of travelers. See Johannes Ranke, review of Felix von Luschan, *Beiträge zur Völkerkunde der deutschen Schutzgebiete, CBDAG* 29 (1898): 8.

CHAPTER 2

1. On German history writing in this period, see Georg G. Iggers, "The High Point of Historical Optimism—the 'Prussian School,'" in *The German Conception of History,* 90–123. For an excellent analysis of the development of Prussian history writing in the period before 1848, see Robert Southard, *Droysen and the Prussian School of*

History (Lexington: University Press of Kentucky, 1995). See also Friedrich Jaeger and Jörn Rüsen, *Geschichte des Historismus* (Munich: C. H. Beck, 1992); and Leonard Krieger, *The German Idea of Freedom* (Boston: Beacon, 1957).

2. James Ryding discusses the opposition between anthropology and history in his excellent "Alternatives in Nineteenth-Century German Ethnology: A Case Study in the Sociology of Science," *Sociologicus* 25 (1975): 1–28. Ryding notes the hostility of historians to the study of non-European societies and explains the success of Bastian's natural scientific style of ethnology as a way to study non-Europeans without challenging the legitimacy of historical methods. James Whitman makes an equally important argument that German anthropology, especially as represented by Adolf Bastian, emerged out of a rejection of both sides of a mid-nineteenth-century controversy between philological and materialist psychology. See James Whitman, "From Philology to Anthropology in Mid-Nineteenth-Century Germany," in *Functionalism Historicized: Essays in British Social Anthropology,* ed. George W. Stocking Jr. (Madison: University of Wisconsin Press, 1984), 214–29. As we shall see below, anthropologists, including Bastian, rejected the philological side, as represented by Heymann Steinthal and Moritz Lazarus, even more firmly than the materialist side of this debate. See also Christoph Marx, *"Völker ohne Schrift und Geschichte": Zur historischen Erfassung des vorkolonialen Schwarzafrika in der deutschen Forschung des 19. und frühen 20. Jahrhunderts* (Stuttgart: Franz Steiner, 1988).

3. It was precisely in this period that Wilhelm Dilthey developed his understanding of humanism as intersubjectivity. See Dilthey, *Einleitung in die Geisteswissenschaften.* This understanding of humanism as a "melding of horizons" has been most fully expounded in Hans-Georg Gadamer, *Truth and Method* (1986), trans. Joel Weinsheimer and Donald G. Marshall (New York: Crossroad, 1990).

4. Anthropology is most often presented as a continuation of, rather than, as I argue, a reaction against, German humanism and historicism. The best version of this thesis is Matti Bunzl's "Franz Boas and the Humboldtian Tradition: From *Volksgeist* and *Nationalcharakter* to an Anthropological Concept of Culture," in Stocking, ed., *Volksgeist as Method and Ethic,* 17–78. Even German anthropologists themselves traced the roots of their own discipline to Herder's humanism. See, for example, Rudolf Virchow, opening address to the general assembly of the German Anthropological Society in Schweren, 22 September 1871, *CBDAG* 2 (1871): 42–47; and Adolf Bastian, *Die Vorgeschichte der Ethnologie: Deutschland's Denkfreunden gewidmet fur eine Mussestunde* (Berlin: Ferdinand Dümmler, 1881), 55. For Herder's own use of ethnographic data, see Gerald Broce, "Herder and Ethnography," *Journal of the History of the Behavioral Sciences* 22 (1986): 150–70. So tempting has it been to see in German historicism and humanism the origins of anthropological thinking that Teutonic ancestors have been found even for British anthropology. The most thorough version of this argument is Joan Leopold's *Culture in Comparative and Evolutionary Perspective: E. B. Tylor and the Making of "Primitive Culture"* (Berlin: Dietrich Reimer, 1980). See also George W. Stocking Jr., *Victorian Anthropology* (New York: Free Press, 1987), 20–25, 303–14; and A. L. Kroeber and Clyde Kluckhohn, *Culture: A Critical Review of Concepts and Definitions,* Papers of the Peabody Museum of American Archaeology and Ethnology 47 (Cambridge, Mass., 1952), 9–29.

5. Johann Gottfried von Herder, *Ideen zur Philosophie der Geschichte der Menschheit* (1784), 2 vols. (Berlin: Aufbau, 1965), 1:201–45.

6. Ibid., 230.

7. Herder, *Auch eine Philosophie der Geschichte zur Bildung der Menschheit* (1774; Stuttgart: Reclam, 1990).

8. Isaiah Berlin, *Vico and Herder: Two Studies in the History of Ideas* (New York: Viking, 1976). For a recent reappraisal of Herder that takes his ethnocentrism into account, see Paul Lawrence Rose, *Revolutionary Antisemitism in Germany from Kant to Wagner* (Princeton, N.J.: Princeton University Press, 1990), 97–109.

9. Immanuel Kant, *Anthropologie in pragmatischer Hinsicht* (Königsberg: Friedrich Nicolovius, 1800), 296–310.

10. Immanuel Kant, "Idea for a Universal History with a Cosmopolitan Intent" (1784), in *Perpetual Peace and Other Essays,* ed. and trans. Ted Humphrey (Indianapolis: Hackett, 1983), 29–40.

11. For a selection of excerpts relating to ethnocentrism and racism in the Enlightenment, including pieces by Kant and Herder, see Emmanuel Chukwudi Eze, ed., *Race and the Enlightenment: A Reader* (Cambridge: Blackwell, 1997). For a good survey of German and European ideas about race and ethnicity since the Middle Ages, see Léon Poliakov, *The Aryan Myth: A History of Racist and Nationalist Ideas in Europe,* trans. Edmund Howard (London: Sussex University Press, 1974). Poliakov discusses early German ideas on race and ethnicity in chap. 5 and the development of anthropology in chap. 11, "The Aryan Epoch."

12. Georg Wilhelm Friedrich Hegel, *Vorlesungen über die Philosophie der Geschichte* (Stuttgart: Reclam, 1961), 137, 163.

13. Leopold von Ranke, *Weltgeschichte* (1881), 5th ed. (Leipzig: Duncker & Humboldt, 1896), 1:vii–viii.

14. Leopold von Ranke, "Idee der Universalhistorie," in *Vorlesungseinleitungen,* ed. Volker Dotterweich and Walther Peter Fuchs, vol. 4 of *Leopold von Ranke: Aus Werk und Nachlass,* ed. Walther Peter Fuchs and Theodor Schieder (Munich: R. Oldenbourg, 1975), 72–89, 85–86.

15. Ranke, *Weltgeschichte,* 1:v.

16. Ranke, "Idee der Universalhistorie," 85.

17. Ranke relates the opposition of nature and culture to historical development in his 1855 lecture "Der Begriff des Fortschritts in der Geschichte," in Dotterweich and Fuchs, eds., *Vorlesungseinleitungen,* 255–61. He makes the same point in *Weltgeschichte,* 1:v.

18. See A. H. L. Heeren, *Ideen über die Politik, den Verkehr und den Handel der vornehmsten Völker der alten Welt,* 2 vols. (Göttingen: Vandenhoek & Ruprecht, 1793–96). Ryding also discusses Gervinus's attacks on Heeren. See Ryding, "Alternatives in Nineteenth-Century German Ethnology."

19. Georg Gottfried Gervinus, "Historische Briefe: Veranlaßt durch Heeren und das Archiv von Schlosser und Bercht," in *Gesammelte Kleine Historische Schriften* (Karlsruhe: Friedrich Wilhelm Hasper, 1838), 1–134.

20. Johann Gustav Droysen, *Rekonstruktion der ersten vollständigen Fassung der Vorlesungen* (1857), in *Historik,* ed. Peter Leyh (Stuttgart: Frommann-Holzboog, 1977), 1:1–412, 380, 312, 309, 312. Droysen's manuscript was continually updated and contains material that is clearly from later than 1857, such as references to the anthropologist Adolf Bastian, who was an unknown ship's doctor in 1857.

21. Ottokar Lorenz, "Die 'bürgerliche' und die naturwissenschaftliche Geschichte," *Historische Zeitschrift* 3 (1878): 458–85, 461–62, 483. Lorenz's essay is a response to an 1877 lecture by Emil Du Bois-Reymond, "Kulturgeschichte und Naturwissenschaft," reprinted in Emil Du Bois-Reymond *Vorträge über Philosophie und Gesellschaft,* ed. Siegried Wollgast (Hamburg: Felix Meiner, 1974), 105–58.

22. Ottokar Lorenz, *Die Geschichtswissenschaft in Hauptrichtungen und Aufgaben* (Berlin: Wilhelm Hertz, 1886), 1:226.

23. On Eduard Meyer's use of anthropology and his opposition to ethnography, see Wilfred Nippel, "Prolegomena zu Eduard Meyers Anthropologie," in *Eduard Meyer: Leben und Leistung eines Universalhistorikers,* ed. William M. Calder III and Alexander Demandt (Leiden: E. J. Brill, 1990), 311–28.

24. Eduard Meyer, introduction to *Elemente der Anthropologie,* vol. 1, pt. 1 of *Geschichte des Altertums,* 3d ed. (Stuttgart: Cotta, 1910), 84, 187–93.

25. Eduard Meyer, *Geschichte des Orients bis zur Begründung des Perserreichs,* vol. 1 of *Geschichte des Alterthums,* 1st ed. (Stuttgart: Cotta, 1884), 12. In that passage, however, he did allow that the people of India were "an eminently historical people." See also Meyer's *Zur Theorie und Methodik der Geschichte* (Halle: Max Niemeyer, 1902), 47. Roger Chickering relates Meyer's view of historical significance to the aftermath of the *Methodenstreit.* See Roger Chickering, "Universal History," in *Karl Lamprecht: A German Academic Life (1856–1915)* (Atlantic Highlands, N.J.: Humanities, 1993), 334–36.

26. On cultural scientists, see Smith, *Politics and the Sciences of Culture.* While the present account differs from Smith's interpretation of German anthropology, it also relies on his study of the other cultural sciences.

27. Karl Lamprecht, "Was ist Kulturgeschichte? Beitrag zu einer empirischen Historik," *Deutsche Zeitschrift für Geschichtswissenschaft,* n.s., 1 (1896–97): 75–150.

28. Wilhelm Wundt, "Ziele und Wege der Völkerpsychologie (1886)," in *Probleme der Völkerpsychologie* (Leipzig: Ernst Wiegandt, 1911), 1–35.

29. Teachers of "Anthropologie" in this philosophical sense included G. W. F. Hegel, Karl Friedrich Werder, Johann Friedrich Leopold George, Carl Ludwig Michelet, and Karl Heinrich Schultz-Schultzstein. For an indication of what was taught in these courses, see, for example, Carl Ludwig Michelet, *Anthropologie und Psychologie oder die Philosophie des subjectiven Geistes* (Berlin, 1840). Unless otherwise noted, all information on university course offerings comes from the *Vorlesungsverzeichnis der Friedrich-Wilhelm Universität zu Berlin.*

30. Komissionssitzung on Promotionsprüfung in Anthropologie und Völkerkunde, 25 February 1915, HU, Phil. Fak., 196, Promotionen, 345–46; dean of the Philosophy Faculty to Diedrich Westermann, 17 July 1922, HU, Phil. Fak., 197, Promotionen, 525. See dissertation exams for Heinrich Friedlaender, 3 March 1904, HU,

Phil. Fak., Promotionsvorgänge, 395, 521, and for Paul Hambruch, 25 July 1907, HU, Phil. Fak., Promotionsvorgänge, 433, 11. In 1886, the University of Munich did establish a professorship of physical anthropology, which was occupied first by Johannes Ranke. However, before the First World War, no other German university had a regular professorship of ethnology. See Hans Fischer, *Völkerkunde im National-Sozialismus: Aspekte der Anpassung, Affinität und Behauptung einer wissenschaftichen Disziplin* (Berlin: Dietrich Reimer, 1990). See also Ernst Grosse, "Ueber den Ethnologischen Unterricht," in *Festschrift für Adolf Bastian zu seinem 70. Geburtstag 26. Juni 1896* (Berlin: Dietrich Reimer, 1896), 595–604. In 1900, Zurich began offering a Ph.D. in physical anthropology. See "Eine neue anthropologische Professur," *CBDAG* 31 (1900): 24. Paris, by contrast, had an École d'Anthropologie since 1876, with five faculty members. See "Die École d'Anthropologie in Paris," *AA* 9 (1876): 272. See also Joy Harvey, "Evolutionism Transformed: Positivists and Materialists in the Sociéte d'Anthropologie de Paris from Second Empire to Third Republic," in *The Wider Domain of Evolutionary Thought,* ed. David Oldroyd and Ian Langham (Dordrecht: D. Reidel, 1983), 289–310; and Elizabeth A. Williams, *The Physical and the Moral: Anthropology, Physiology, and Philosophical Medicine in France, 1750–1850* (Cambridge: Cambridge University Press, 1994).

31. Although the academy of sciences did, in the end, recommend that the Ministry of Culture support the Berlin Anthropological Society's efforts to found a museum for its unique collections. Academy of Sciences (signed by Emil du Bois-Reymond) to Adalbert Falk (minister of culture), 14 August 1873, GStA PK, I. HA, Rep. 76Ve, Cultusministerium, Sekt. 15, Abt. XI, Nr. 2, Bd. 1, Bl. 49–51 (M).

32. The seminar was, in any case, considered a center for practical training rather than an academic institution. See Eduard Sachau, *Bericht über die Eröffnung des Seminars für Orientalische Sprachen an der Königlichen Friedrich-Wilhelms-Univerität und einige auf das Seminar bezügliche Schriftstücke* (Berlin: A. Asher, 1888). See also Jake W. Spidle, "Colonial Studies in Imperial Germany," *History of Education Quarterly* 13 (1973): 231–47.

33. Wilhelm von Bezold, evaluation of Franz Boas's habilitation, 15 March 1886, HU, Phil. Fak., Habilitationsvorgänge, 1213, Bl. 100; Heinrich Kiepert, evaluation of Boas's habilitation, 25 March 1886, HU, Phil. Fak., Habilitationsvorgänge, 1213, Bl. 101. Franz Boas, application for habilitation, HU, Phil. Fak., Habilitationsvorgänge, 1213, Bl. 96. Boas offered courses in oceanography, the geography of North America, and two semesters of practical exercises in traveling cartography (*Übungen in Itineraraufnahmen mit Excursionen*). He also offered a course in the history of polar expeditions and another in the ethnography of the northwest coast of America.

34. Adolf Bastian, *Der Mensch in der Geschichte; zur Begründung einer psychologischen Weltanschauung,* 3 vols. (1860; Osnabruck: Biblioverlag, 1968).

35. Minutes of the meeting of the Philosophy Faculty, 1 August 1866, HU, Phil. Fak., Promotionen "honoris causa" und Diplom-Erneuerungen, 1380, Bl. 56.

36. See E. Roth, "Nachruf für Adolf Bastian," *Globus* 87 (1905): 209.

37. Seler explained that the study of ancient America included "general anthropology" but was more similar to Egyptology, Assyriology, and Sinology, which

focused on linguistics and history. See Eduard Seler to the Philosophical Faculty, 7 November 1911, HU, Phil. Fak., 196, Promotionen, Bl. 299.

38. Bastian continued: "In contrast, the natural scientists of course cordially agreed" to participate in the anthropological society. Adolf Bastian to Rudolf Virchow, [October 1869?], NL Virchow, 117, pt. II, Bl. 20–21.

39. Bastian, *Die Vorgeschichte der Ethnologie,* 55.

40. Adolf Bastian to General Administration of the Royal Museums, December 1894, MfV, XIIa, 1178/95.

41. Bastian, *Die Vorgeschichte der Ethnologie,* 56–62.

42. Adolf Bastian, *Ethnologie und Geschichte in ihren Berührungspunkten unter Bezugnahme auf Indien,* vol. 2, *Ideale Welten in Wort und Bild* (Berlin: Emil Felber, 1892), 21, 27.

43. This venerable opposition of words to things and of reading to looking was given one of its classic formulations in Francis Bacon, *Novum Organum* (1620), trans. Peter Urbach and John Gibson (Chicago: Open Court, 1994), bk. 1, aphorisms 38–44, 59–60, pp. 53–56, 64–66. For a recent account of the role of this opposition in the Scientific Revolution, see Steven Shapin, *The Scientific Revolution* (Chicago: University of Chicago Press, 1996), esp. 74–78.

44. Robert Hartmann, "Untersuchungen über die Völkerschaften Nord-Ost-Afrikas," *ZfE* 1 (1869): 23–45, 135–58, 31–32.

45. Adolf Bastian, "Das natürliche System in der Ethnologie," 1 *ZfE* (1869): 1–23, 2.

46. Rudolf Virchow, "Eröffnungsrede," *CBDAG* 17 (1886): 67–80, 69.

47. The classic statement of these evolutionist arguments is in E. B. Tylor, *Primitive Culture* (1871; New York: Harper & Bros., 1958).

48. See, for example, Alexander Ecker, "Die Zwecke der Deutschen Gesellschaft für Anthropologie, Ethologie und Urgeschichte," presentation to the German Anthropological Society, 14 May 1870, *CBDAG* 1 (1870): 41–44, 49–53; and Moriz Hoernes, "Grundlinien einer Systematik der prähistorischen Archäologie," *ZfE* 25 (1893): 49–70.

49. In a review discussing evolutionist anthropology, Dilthey did not mention a single German anthropologist, despite the fact that Virchow wrote the preface to one of the books he considered and that Bastian was already a colleague at the University of Berlin. Dilthey's assumption that anthropology was not evolutionist is particularly interesting because he knew Bastian's work and thought highly of it. See Wilhelm Dilthey, "Literaturbrief," review of *Entstehung der Zivilisation,* by John Lubbock, and *Anfänge der Kultur,* by Lenormant, *Westermanns Monatsheften* 40 (1876): 102–6, and his review of *Reisen im östlichen Asien* (1867), by Adolf Bastian, *Westermanns Monatsheften* 22 (1867): 315–17, both reprinted in Dilthey, *Gesammelte Schriften* (Göttingen: Vandenhoeck & Ruprecht, 1974), 17:8–13, 286. Virchow wrote that British anthropologists were more theoretically inclined and advanced than the Germans but pointed out that they had "created certain general ideas about culture and civilization without securing themselves on the basics." See Virchow, opening address to the general assembly of the German Anthropological Society in Schweren, 1871.

50. Rudolf Virchow, preface to *Die vorgeschichtliche Zeit,* by John Lubbock (Jena: Hermann Castenoble, 1874), v. Despite the different reception of British evolutionism in Berlin, Lubbock approved of Virchow's preface to *Prehistoric Times.* See John Lubbock to Rudolf Virchow, 22 December 1873, NL Virchow, 1331. Elsewhere, Virchow cautioned that, although anthropologists would always "remain conscious" that they were dealing with a "piece of the history of humanity" when studying natural peoples, they should, for the time being, restrict themselves to gathering exact knowledge about particular groups. Rudolf Virchow, "Die Ziele und Mittel der modernen Anthropologie," *CBDAG* (1877): 1–7, 3.

51. Adolf Bastian, review of *Primitive Culture,* by Edward B. Tylor, *ZfE* 3 (1871): 361–62.

52. Felix Liebrecht, "Zur Culturgeschichte," review of *Researches into the Early History of Mankind,* by E. B. Tylor, *ZfE* 5 (1873): 77–105.

53. The Austrian anthropologist Wilhelm Schmidt noted that Tylor and Lubbock never drew the sharp distinction, made by many German anthropologists, between natural peoples (those without history) and historical peoples. See Wilhelm Schmidt, "Die Moderne Ethnologie," *Anthropos* 1 (1906): 134–63, 318–88, 592–644, 950–97, 602.

54. Adolf Bastian, *Zur Kenntniss Hawaii's* (Berlin: Ferdinand Dümmler, 1883), 125.

55. For Steinthal and Lazarus, see Ingrid Belke, *Moritz Lazarus und Heymann Steinthal: Die Begründer der Völkerpsychologie in ihren Briefen* (Tübingen: J. C. B. Mohr, 1971), 1:xiii—cxlii. On Steinthal, see Waltraud Bumann, *Die Sprachtheorie Heymann Steinthals: Dargestellt im Zusammenhang mit seiner Theorie der Geisteswissenschaft* (Meisenheim am Glan: Anton Hain, 1965).

56. Moritz Lazarus and Heymann Steinthal, "Einleitende Gedanken über Völkerpsychologie, als Einladung zu einer Zeitschrift für Völkerpsychologie und Sprachwissenschaft," *Zeitschrift für Völkerpsychologie und Sprachwissenschaft* 1 (1860): 1–73, 12. Steinthal and Lazarus wrote this argument almost a decade before the founding of the German Anthropological Society and initially had in mind versions of the discipline more medical and materialist than that practiced in Berlin.

57. Thus, for example, vol. 10 (1878) of the *Zeitschrift für Völkerpsychologie und Sprachwissenschaft* contains general articles on aesthetics, imagination, poetry (by Wilhelm Dilthey), ethics, and private property as well as several more specialized linguistic studies. These kinds of articles would never appear in the pages of the *Zeitschrift für Ethnologie.* Wilhelm Wundt, the Leipzig psychologist who, more than Steinthal and Lazarus, is today associated with *Völkerpsychologie,* similarly differentiated the discipline from anthropology.

58. Heymann Steinthal, *Die Mande-Neger-Sprachen* (Berlin: Ferdinand Dümmler, 1867), vi–vii, xiv–xv.

59. Heymann Steinthal, "Die sprachwissenschaftliche Richtung der Ethnologie," *VBGAEU* 4 (1872): 92–100, 94–95.

60. Adolf Bastian et al., comment on "Die sprachwissenschaftliche Richtung der Ethnologie," by Heymann Steinthal, *VBGAEU* 4 (1872): 99–100.

61. Robert Hartmann, in ibid., 100.

62. "Herr Hitzig spricht über Localisation psychischer Centren in der Hirn-
rinde," *VBGAEU* 6 (1874): 42–47. On Hitzig and Fritsch's experiments, see Philip J.
Pauly, "The Political Structure of the Brain: Cerebral Localization in Bismarckian
Germany," *International Journal of Neuroscience* 21 (1983): 145–50; and Robert M.
Young, *Mind, Brain, and Adaptation in the Nineteenth Century: Cerebral Localization
and Its Biological Context from Gall to Ferrier* (1970; New York: Oxford University
Press, 1990), 224–32.

63. Rudolf Virchow et al., comment on "Herr Hitzig spricht über Localisation
psychischer Centren in der Hirnrinde," *VBGAEU* 6 (1874): 47–51.

64. "Discussion über Aphasie," *VBGAEU* 6 (1874): 130–40, 132.

65. See also the similar debate about language vs. physical anthropology between
the Leipzig anthropologist Emil Schmidt and the Viennese linguist Friedrich Müller.
Emil Schmidt, "Physische Anthropologie und Sprachforschung," *Globus* 63 (1893):
109–10, 246; Friedrich Müller, "Anthropologie und Ethnologie oder Köpermessung
und Sprachforschung," *Globus* 63 (1893): 196–97; Emil Schmidt and Friedrich
Müller, "Physische Anthropologie und Sprachforschung," *Globus* 63 (1893): 311–13.
This discomfort with language explains the ambiguity that anthropologists displayed
toward the study of Asian cultures with written traditions, especially India and
China, as well as toward the archaeology of ancient America, which also included the
study of written inscriptions. While these areas were represented in the Berlin museum of ethnology because they were traditionally ignored by academic humanists,
anthropologists believed their study would someday be recognized as disciplines separate from anthropology. See Wilhelm Grübe (directoral assistant in the East Asian
Section of the Berlin Museum), memo, 24 March 1888, MfV, VII, vol. 1, 129/88; Eduard Seler (directorial assistant in the Ancient American Section of the Berlin Museum and professor) to the Philosophical Faculty, 7 November 1911, HU, Phil. Fak.,
196, Promotionen, Bl. 299.

66. The British Association for the Advancement of Science produced some of
the earliest anthropological questionnaires, which, like the German variety, sought
to prevent speculation on the part of the traveler. See George W. Stocking Jr., "The
Ethnographer's Magic: Fieldwork in British Anthropology from Tylor to Mali-
nowski," in *Observers Observed: Essays on Ethnograpic Fieldwork,* ed. George W.
Stocking Jr. (Madison: University of Wisconsin Press, 1983), 70–120, 71–73. ("The
Ethnographer's Magic" is reprinted in Stocking's *The Ethnographer's Magic and Other
Essays in the History of Anthropology* [Madison: University of Wisconsin Press, 1992],
12–59.) The earliest German questionnaire is the one produced in 1872 by the Berlin
Anthropological Society for the German navy. See Rudolf Virchow, Adolf Bastian, et
al., "Ratschläge für anthropologische Untersuchung auf Expeditionen der Marine,"
ZfE 4 (1872): 325–56.

67. Virchow, "Die Ziele und Mittel der modernen Anthropologie," 4.

68. [Felix von Luschan,] Königliches Museum für Völkerkunde in Berlin, *Anleitung für ethnographische Beobachtungen und Sammlungen in Afrika und Oceanien,* 3d
ed. (Berlin: Gebr. Unger, 1904), 3.

69. Ibid., 30, sec. T.

70. James Clifford has noted the similarity between anthropological notions of culture and anthropological collections. See James Clifford, "On Collecting Art and Culture," in *The Predicament of Culture: Twentieth-Century Ethnography, Literature, and Art* (Cambridge, Mass.: Harvard University Press, 1988).

71. Robert Hartmann to Rudolf Virchow, 4 December 1874, NL Virchow, 827.

72. See Adolf Bastian, review of *Culturgeschichte in ihrer natürlichen Entwicklung bis zur Gegenwart,* by Friedrich von Hellwald (Augsburg, 1875), *ZfE* 6 (1874): 412–17, 413 n. 1. Bastian used this review to discuss his own perspective on anthropology.

73. Adolf Bastian to Herman Costenable, 2 January 1860, Personal Papers of Adolf Bastian, Staats- und Universitätsbibliothek Bremen.

74. Adolf Bastian, "Ueber die priesterlichen Functionen unter Naturstämmen," *ZfE* 21 (1889): 109–54, 109.

75. "In der Zeichensprache (der Indianer) redet der Pantomime (im 'mimischen Tanz') als Dolmetschen (zu Nero's Zeit), und wie der König von Dahomey seine Gäste tanzend empfängt, stand in Thessalien die Tanzkunst in so hohem Ansehen, dass man sogar die ersten Männer im Staate und die Vorkämpfer in den Schlachten Vortänzer nannte (s. Lucian), = Meoh in Indonesian." Ibid., 126.

76. Karl von den Steinen, "Adolf Bastian: Gedächtnisfeier am 11. März 1905," *ZfE* 37 (1905): 233–56, 239. Steinen refers explicitly to Bastian's later writing, but the portion of the description cited here applies equally well to all Bastian's work. According to Steinen, his later writings also contained stock phrases that he mechanically inserted into the text in a way that indicated that he no longer had original thoughts.

77. Carl Vogt to Rudolf Virchow, 21 February 1870, Andree, 496–98.

78. J. D. E. Schmeltz, review of *Zur Lehre des Menschen in ethnischer Anthropologie,* by Adolf Bastian, *Internationale Archiv für Ethnographie* 9 (1896): 222–23, 223. Schmeltz refers in the quoted passage to all Bastian's works, not just the work under consideration in that review.

79. One anonymous American reviewer referred to one of Bastian's works as a well-indexed "flood of facts, names, and dates" and suggested that it be used as an encyclopedia rather than read as a narrative. See review of *Die Welt in ihren Spiegelungen unter dem Wandel des Völkergedankens,* by Adolf Bastian, *American Anthropologist* 1 (1888): 179. A German reviewer indicated a similar incomprehension of Bastian's works as narratives, in a review beginning, "Insofar as I have succeeded in understanding it, I will present a few details of the work to the readers of this journal." The reviewer proceeded to give several pages of quotations from the text without giving any commentary or conclusion. See K. Bruchmann, review of *Zur naturwissenschaftlichen Behandlungsweise der Psychologie durch und für die Völkerkunde,* by Adolf Bastian (Berlin, 1883), *Zeitschrift für Völkerpsychologie und Sprachwissenschaft* 16 (1886): 321–27.

80. *Berliner Tageblatt,* 10 November 1887, in GStA PK, I. HA, Rep. 76Ve, Cultusministerium, Sekt. 15, Abt. XI, Nr. 2, Bd. 7, unnumbered sheets (M).

81. For the conventional understanding of the German idea of *Kultur,* see Norbert Elias, "Sociogenisis of the Difference between *Kultur* and *Zivilisation* in German

Usage," in *The History of Manners* (1939), trans. Edmund Jephcott (New York: Pantheon, 1978), 3–50. Georg Bollenbeck's *Bildung und Kultur: Glanz und Elend eines deutschen Deutungsmusters* (Frankfurt a.M.: Insel, 1994) is an excellent account that corrects Elias's thesis by looking at the history of the concepts (*Begriffsgeschichte*) of *Bildung* and *Kultur* in the nineteenth and twentieth centuries. Alfred G. Meyer notes that German radicals had used the word *Kultur* to describe the progress that they hoped Napoleon would bring about in Europe. Meyer associates this definition of *Kultur* with Kant and the relativist notion with Herder. See Alfred G. Meyer, "Historical Notes on Ideological Aspects of the Concept of Culture in Germany and Russia," app. A in *Culture,* by Kroeber and Kluckhohn, 207–12.

82. David Blackbourn, "Progress and Piety: Liberalism, Catholicism, and the State in Imperial Germany," *History Workshop Journal* 26 (1988): 57–78. See also Michael B. Gross, "Kulturkampf and Unification: German Liberalism and the War against the Jesuits," *Central European History* 30 (1998): 545–66; and Helmut Walser Smith, *German Nationalism and Religious Conflict: Culture, Ideology, Politics, 1870–1914* (Princeton, N.J.: Princeton University Press, 1995).

83. Rudolf Virchow, 8 May 1875, *Stenographische Berichte über die Verhandlungen des Abgeordneten Haus,* 64. Sitzung, Bd. 3, pp. 1797–1801.

84. For an overview of the *Kulturkampf* laws, see Douglas W. Hatfield, "Kulturkampf: The Relationship of Church and State and the Failure of German Political Reform," *Church and State* 23 (1981): 465–84.

85. See Rudolf Virchow, 8 May 1875, *Stenographische Berichte über die Verhandlungen des Abgeordneten Haus,* 54. Sitzung, Bd. 2, pp. 1322–24, 1327.

86. Rudolf Virchow, 8 May 1875, *Stenographische Berichte über die Verhandlungen des Abgeordneten Haus,* 64. Sitzung, Bd. 3, pp. 1797–1801. The ban on Aristotle's writings on nature, Virchow was apparently unaware, in fact occurred only in Paris and was not accepted by the church as a whole. I am grateful to John A. Marino and Luce Giard for drawing my attention to Virchow's oversight.

87. Rudolf Virchow, 15 December 1868, *Stenographische Berichte über die Verhandlungen des Abgeordneten Haus,* 24. Sitzung, Bd. 1, p. 791.

88. Johannes Fabian has drawn attention to the centrality of notions of time to the construction of the other in anthropological discourse. He notes that anthropologists figure themselves as more modern than the supposedly primitive societies they study. This ideological time difference he calls *allochronism.* Fabian's study of "time and the other" has been very suggestive for the present argument, although I believe that German anthropology cannot be assimilated to British evolutionism as Fabian does, precisely because German notions of time differ in important and interesting ways from those of their British counterparts. See Johannes Fabian, *Time and the Other: How Anthropology Makes Its Object* (New York: Columbia University Press, 1983). See also the essays collected in Johannes Fabian, *Time and the Work of Anthropology: Critical Essays, 1971–1991* (Philadelphia: Harwood Academic, 1991), esp. "Culture, Time, and the Object of Anthropology," 191–206.

89. On humanism and humanities, see Anthony Grafton, *Defenders of the Text: The Traditions of Scholarship in an Age of Science, 1450–1800* (Cambridge, Mass.: Harvard University Press, 1991).

90. On the *Bildungsbürgertum,* see the essays collected in Werner Conze and Jürgen Kocka, eds., *Bildungsbürgertum im neunzehnten Jahrhundert,* 4 vols. (Stuttgart: Klett-Cotta, 1985–92).

91. Jean-Jacques Rousseau, "Discourse on the Origin and Foundations of Inequality among Men" (1755), in *Basic Political Writings,* trans. Donald A. Cress (Indianapolis: Hackett, 1987), 25–109, 33.

92. According to Bollenbeck, this optimistic reading of Rousseau was widespread in nineteenth-century Germany. See Bollenbeck, *Bildung und Kultur,* 112–19.

93. Reported in the *Kolnische Zeitung,* 9 August 1888, GStA PK, I. HA, Rep. 76Ve, Cultusministerium, Sekt. 1, tit. XI, Nr. 4, Bd. 2, Bl. 338–39 (M).

94. Adolf Bastian, *Zur Mythologie und Psychologie der Nigritier in Guinea mit Bezugnahme auf socialistische Elementargedanken* (Berlin: Dietrich Reimer, 1894), 110–11, 111n.

CHAPTER 3

1. A third German tradition of understanding of nature, scientific materialism, relied on and criticized both Kantian science and *Naturphilosophie* but was less relevant to anthropology's conception of nature. On German scientific materialism, see Frederick Gregory, *Scientific Materialism in Nineteenth Century Germany* (Dordrecht: D. Reidel, 1977). On German conceptions of nature, see Heinrich Schipperes, "Natur," in *Geschichtliche Grundbegriffe,* ed. Otto Brunner, Werner Konze, and Reinhardt Kosellek (Stuttgart: Klett, 1978), 4:215–44.

2. See Frederick Gregory, "Kant's Influence on Natural Scientists in the German Romantic Period," in *New Trends in the History of Science,* ed. R. P. W. Visser et al. (Amsterdam: Rodopi, 1989), 53–66. See also Frederick Gregory, *Nature Lost? Natural Science and the German Theological Traditions of the Nineteenth Century* (Cambridge, Mass.: Harvard University Press, 1992); and Ueli Hasler, *Beherrschte Natur: Die Anpassung der Theologie an die bürgerliche Naturauffassung im 19. Jahrhundert (Schleiermacher, Ritschl, Hermann)* (Bern: Peter Lang, 1982).

3. In his important study of a Kantian tradition of "teleomechanism" in nineteenth-century German biology, Timothy Lenoir minimizes the role of *Naturphilosophie.* Virchow, whom Lenoir places in the teleomechanist tradition, as well as German anthropologists generally, in fact synthesized *Naturphilosophie* with Kantianism. See Timothy Lenoir, *The Strategy of Life: Teleology and Mechanics in Nineteenth-Century German Biology* (Dordrecht: D. Reidel, 1982). Nicholas Jardine maintains, correctly I believe, that the generation of Virchow and Emil du Bois-Reymond exaggerated the extent to which they rejected *Naturphilosophie.* See Nicholas Jardine, "*Naturphilosophie* and the Kingdoms of Nature," in Jardine, Secord, and Spary, eds., *Cultures of Natural History,* 230–45.

4. This was, at least, the predominant reading of Kant in the second half of the nineteenth century. Ulrich Sieg argues that the return to Kantian philosophy in this period resulted from the discrediting of Left Hegelianism in the reactionary period after 1850 as well as from what he identifies as the implicit anti-Catholicism of neo-Kantian philosophy. See Ulrich Sieg, *Aufstieg und Niedergang des Marburger Neukani-*

anismus: Die Geschichte einer philosophischen Schulgemeinschaft (Würzburg: Königshausen & Neumann, 1994).

5. Immanuel Kant, *Metaphysische Anfangsgründe der Naturwissenschaft* (1786), in *Kant's gesammelte Schriften,* vol. 4 (Berlin: Georg Reimer, 1911), 465–565, 468.

6. See Immanuel Kant, *Die Religion innerhalb der Grenzen der blossen Vernunft* (1793), in *Kant's gesammelte Schriften,* vol. 6 (Berlin: Georg Reimer, 1914).

7. Friedrich Wilhelm Joseph von Schelling, *Ideas for a Philosophy of Nature* (1797), trans. Errol E. Harris and Peter Heath (Cambridge: Cambridge University Press, 1988), 30. On Schelling, see Andrew Bowie, *Schelling and Modern European Philosophy* (London: Routledge, 1993).

8. Anthropologists likely thought of idealist theories of embryology, such as those of Lorenz Oken and J. F. Meckel. As Stephen Jay Gould has pointed out, Oken's and Meckel's embryological theories did not necessarily imply the development of one species from another, although this seems to be how anthropologists read them. See Stephen Jay Gould, *Ontogeny and Phylogeny* (Cambridge, Mass.: Harvard University Press, 1977), 39–47. According to Robert J. Richards, Darwin himself read Ocken, Meckel, and others as evolutionists. See Robert J. Richards, *The Meaning of Evolution: The Morphological Construction and Ideological Reconstruction of Darwin's Theory* (Chicago: University of Chicago Press, 1992).

9. Rudolf Virchow, *Menschen- und Affenschädel,* Sammlung gemeinverständlicher Vorträge, vol. 96 (Berlin: C. G. Lüderitz, 1870), 36. See also Virchow's discussion of Darwin at the German Anthropological Society meeting in 1882, *CBDAG* 13 (1882): 80–84; and Adolf Bastian, review of *Die Anthropogenie,* by Ernst Haeckel (Leipzig, 1875), *ZfE* 7 (1875): 203–8.

10. The secondary literature on nineteenth-century German botany focuses on the acceptance of Darwinism rather than on the continuing importance of *Naturphilosophie.* Thus, Alexander Braun appears mostly as an outdated exception to Darwinian botany in Eugene Cittadino's *Nature as the Laboratory: Darwinian Plant Ecology in the German Empire, 1880–1900* (Cambridge: Cambridge University Press, 1990). For accounts of German botany more attentive to *Naturphilosophie,* see William Montgomery, "Evolution and Darwinism in German Biology, 1800–1883" (Ph.D. diss., University of Texas at Austin, 1974); and Thomas Junker, *Darwinismus und Botanik: Rezeption, Kritik und theoretische Alternativen im Deutschland des 19. Jahrhunderts* (Stuttgart: Deutscher Apotheker, 1989).

11. Alexander Braun, *Ueber die Bedeutung der Pflanzenkunde für die allgemeine Bildung* (Berlin: August Hirschwald, 1877).

12. See Adolf Bastian, review of *Völkerkunde,* by Oscar Peschel (Leipzig, 1874), *ZfE* 6 (1874): 148–49, 149; Adolf Bastian to General Administration of the Royal Museums, January 1894, MfV, VII, vol. 2, 53/94, and "Betrachtungen über zeitgemäße Förderung der Ethnologie und die darauf bezüglichen Sammlungen der Museen," printed pamphlet, 12 pp., in GStA PKB, I. HA, Rep. 76Ve, Cultusministerium, Sekt. 15, Abt. XI, Nr. 2, Bd. 8, unnumbered sheets (M). Bastian develops these botanical analogies most explicitly in his "Das natürliche System in der Ethnologie." The title of that article echoes the title of Alexander Braun's courses at the University of Berlin on the "Natürliche System in der Botanik" (see *Vorlesungsverzeichnis der Friedrich-*

Wilhelm Universität zu Berlin, 1867–77). For Braun's own idealist position on evolution and typology, see Alexander Braun, *Ueber die Bedeutung der Entwickelung in der Naturgeschichte* (Berlin: August Hirschwald, 1872).

13. Bastian, "Das natürliche System in der Ethnologie," 2.

14. Rudolf Virchow, *Göthe als Naturforscher und in besonderer Beziehung auf Schiller* (Berlin: August Hirschwald, 1861). See also Matthew Bell, *Goethe's Naturalistic Anthropology: Man and Other Plants* (Oxford: Clarendon, 1994).

15. For example, Georges Buffon views both nature and Scripture as similarly historical revelations about the earth's past: "All reason, all truth coming equally from God, there is no difference between the truths that have been revealed to us [in Scripture] and those that we have been allowed to discover by our [natural philosophical (scientific)] observations and researches." Georges Buffon, *Époques de la nature* (Paris, 1778), 6. For a British work exemplifying the complex relation of Scripture, history, and nature, see William Buckland, *Reliquiae Diluvianae; or, Observations on . . . Geological Phenomena, Attesting to the Action of a Universal Deluge* (London, 1823). Otto Zöcker, who attempted to rectify what he regarded as a lack of natural theology in Germany, is an exceptional example of German natural theology. He was especially important in the religious criticism of Darwinism and scientific materialism. See Gregory, *Nature Lost?* 112–59.

16. On the history of geology in the eighteenth and nineteenth centuries, especially in relation to the question of theology and history, see Charles Gillespie, *Genesis and Geology* (Cambridge, Mass.: Harvard University Press, 1951); Gabriel Gohau, *Les Sciences de la terre aux XVIIe et XVIIIe siècles: Naissance de la géologie* (Paris: Albin Michel, 1990); Stephen Jay Gould, *Time's Arrow, Time's Cycle: Myth and Metaphor in the Discovery of Geological Time* (Cambridge, Mass.: Harvard University Press, 1987); David R. Oldroyd, "Historicism and the Rise of Historical Geology," *History of Science* 17 (1979): 191–213, 227–57, and *Thinking about the Earth: A History of Ideas in Geology* (Cambridge, Mass.: Harvard University Press, 1996); and Martin J. S. Rudwick, *The Great Devonian Controversy: The Shaping of Scientific Knowledge among Gentlemanly Specialists* (Chicago: University of Chicago Press, 1985).

17. Martin Guntau presents German studies of the earth primarily as a theoretical discussion of neptunism and vulcanism. His account focuses on *Geologie* and pays, I believe, insufficient attention to *Geognosie*. See Martin Guntau, "The Natural History of the Earth," in Jardine, Secord, and Spary, eds., *Cultures of Natural History,* 211–29. Even in the late nineteenth century, German geologists tended to follow A. G. Werner's eighteenth-century project of *Geognosie,* especially as it was transmitted to them by the great mid-nineteenth-century geologist Bernard Cotta. See Bernard Cotta, *Leitfaden und Vademecum der Geognosie* (Dresden: Arnold, 1849). On the reception of Cotta, see, for example, Gustav Leonard, *Grundzüge der Geognosie und Geologie,* 3d ed. (Leipzig: C. F. Winter, 1874); and Friedrich Pfaff, *Allgemeine Geologie als Exacte Wissenschaft* (Leipzig: Wilhelm Engelmann, 1873). Oldroyd also finds Werner more interested in classification than in chronology. See Oldroyd, *Thinking about the Earth,* 97–105. Ernst P. Hamm studies K. E. A. von Hoff's *Geschichte der durch Überlieferung nachgewiesenen natürlichen Veränderungen der Erdobfläche* (1822–41) and finds even this unusually historical German study of the earth informed more by

statistical than by historical methods. See Ernst P. Hamm, "Bureaucratic *Statistik* or Actualism? K. E. A. von Hoff's *History* and the History of Geology," *History of Science* 31 (1993): 151–76. Martin Rudwick discusses an exception to this general lack of interest among Germans in historical studies of the earth. Oskar Friedrich von Fraas's popular *Vor der Sündfluth!* (1866) relied heavily on Figuier's *Earth before the Deluge,* a history of life on earth that included an account of human origins. Interestingly, while Fraas borrowed the illustrations from Figuier's work, he did not include the illustration of the emergence of humans, perhaps because of the tendency in Germany to separate human history from studies of nature. See Martin Rudwick, *Scenes from Deep Time* (Chicago: University of Chicago Press, 1992), 212–14.

18. Johann Gottfried Eichhorn, *Einleitung in das Alte Testament* (Leipzig: Weidmann, 1803), 1:iii.

19. See Hans W. Frei, *The Eclipse of Biblical Narrative: A Study in Eighteenth and Nineteenth Century Hermeneutics* (New Haven, Conn.: Yale University Press, 1974).

20. Rudolf Virchow, 12 March 1875, *Stenographische Berichte über die Verhandlungen des Abgeordneten Haus,* 28. Sitzung, Bd. 1, p. 704.

21. See Frei, *The Eclipse of Biblical Narrative,* esp. 53–59, 113–14, 142.

22. As Frederick Gregory argues, Darwinism in Germany was viewed primarily as part of a scientific assault on the dignity of man rather than on the biblical account of Creation. As Gregory writes, "Once Germans had been told that man's mind could be compared to urine, it came as no shock that man was now supposedly related to apes." In Germany, those who took offense at Darwin's "monkey doctrine" (*Affenlehre*) did so, not because it overturned (scriptural) narrative traditions of the development of humans, but rather because it continued the materialist assault on the peculiar dignity of humans. See Gregory, *Scientific Materialism in Nineteenth Century Germany,* 175. Alfred Kelly also supports the assertion that the "monkey doctrine" was one of the most important aspects of Darwinism as it was received in Germany. See Alfred Kelly, *The Descent of Darwin: The Popularization of Darwinism in Germany, 1860–1914* (Chapel Hill: University of North Carolina Press, 1981).

23. Fritsch, *Die Eingeborenen Süd-Afrika's ethnographisch und anatomisch Beschrieben,* xvii—xx. Fritsch's book was regularly referred to as an exemplar, especially for the photographic work. See, for example, Hermann von Jhering to Rudolf Virchow, 20 April 1880, NL Virchow, 996; and Alexander von Frantzius, "Am 1. Januar 1873," *CBDAG* 4 (1873): 1–2.

24. For explanations by German anthropologists of climate as an origin of racial variation, see Adolf Bastian, "Allgemeine Begriffe der Ethnologie," in *Anleitung zu Wissenschaftlichen Beobachtungen auf Reisen,* ed. Georg von Neumayer, 1st ed. (Berlin: Robert Oppenheimer, 1875), 516–33, 518; and Hermann Schaaffhausen, "Die Lehre Darwin's und die Anthropologie," *AA* 3 (1868): 259–66.

25. Rudolf Virchow, "Ueber den Transformismus," *AA* 18 (1889): 1–14.

26. Adolf Bastian, review of *Die Abstammung des Menschen und die geschlechtliche Zuchtwahl,* by Charles Darwin, *ZfE* 3 (1871): 349–59, 359.

27. See Adolf Bastian, "Die Grundlage der Ethnologie in den geographischen Provinzen," *ZfE* 5 (1873): 317–29.

28. German anthropologists did not, it should be noted, categorically reject all Darwin's work. The most important exceptions were the Darwinist anthropologists Hermann Schaaffhausen and Carl Vogt. Both Huxley and Darwin were named corresponding members of the Berlin Anthropological Society (in 1871 and 1877, respectively). Bastian, one of the more strident anti-Darwinists in the Berlin Anthropological Society, admired the "long series of sharp observations" that he recognized in all Darwin's writings, although he rejected evolution. See Adolf Bastian, review of *Expressions of the Emotions in Man and Animals,* by Charles Darwin, *ZfE* 4 (1872): 387–90, 387. Darwin's work on the expression of emotions interested the leaders of the Berlin Anthropological Society so much that they requested that naval officers collect information on this topic, among others, in foreign ports. See Virchow et al., "Ratschläge für anthropologische Untersuchung auf Expeditionen der Marine," 341–42. Robert Hartmann, who was especially interested in the use of animals by prehistoric and non-European peoples, cited Darwin's studies on domesticated animals quite favorably. See Robert Hartmann, "Studien zur Geschichte der Hausthiere (Das Kameel)," *ZfE* 1 (1869): 66–79, 232–51, 353–63, 68.

29. Adolf Bastian, review of *The Descent of Man,* by Charles Darwin (London, 1871), *ZfE* 3 (1871): 133–43, 136–37, review of *Expressions of the Emotions in Man and Animals,* and review of *Die Neuere Schöpfungsgeschichte,* by Arnold Dodel (Leipzig, 1875), *ZfE* 7 (1875): 273–79.

30. Virchow, *Menschen- und Affenschädel,* 27–31, 36.

31. Virchow, for example, stood up for his Munich colleague Johannes Ranke, who had been challenged for excluding evolution from an 1887 address on the state of the discipline (see Johannes Ranke, "Wissenschaftliche Jahresbericht des Generalsekretärs," *CBDAG* 18 [1887]: 87–100). Virchow proclaimed that it was appropriate to skip a discussion of evolution because evolution was not true. Rudolf Virchow, interpellation on Darwinism, *CBDAG* 18 (1887): 150–51.

32. Hermann Schaaffhausen, "Ueber die anthropologischen Fragen der Gegenwart," *AA* 2 (1867): 327–41, 328–30.

33. Schaaffhausen, "Die Lehre Darwin's und die Anthropologie."

34. More famous, although less significant for anthropology, is the controversy between Rudolf Virchow and Ernst Haeckel. While Ernst Haeckel was indeed one of the more prominent Darwinists, he was so far removed from the community of German anthropology that criticizing him did not represent a very important issue. For an excellent account of that controversy, see Richard Weikart, "The Role of Biologists in the Darwinism-Socialism Controversy in German," in *Socialist Darwinism: Evolution in German Socialist Thought from Marx to Bernstein* (San Francisco: International Scholars, 1998), 103–30.

35. Richard Neuhauss, "Zu Virchows siebzigstem Geburtstag," *Globus* 60 (1891): 225–27.

36. For an interpretation of the Neanderthal skull as a missing link between man and monkey, see Carl Vogt, "Ein Blick auf die Urzeiten des Menschengeschlechts," *AA* 1 (1866): 7–42.

37. Rudolf Virchow, "Untersuchung des Neanderthalschädels," *VBGAEU* 4 (1872): 157–65.

38. Rudolf Virchow, "Ueber den prähistorischen Menschen und über die Grenzen zwischen Species und Varietät," *CBDAG* 32 (1901): 81–91.

39. W. Krause, review of *Pithecanthropus erectus, eine menschenähnliche Uebergangsform aus Java,* by Eugen Dubois (Batavia, 1894), *VBGAEU* 27 (1895): 78–88

40. Rudolf Virchow, "Pithecanthropus erectus Dub.," *VBGAEU* 27 (1895): 723–49.

41. Robert Bogdan argues that, around the turn of the century in the United States, with the development of eugenics and the associated increasing scope of the medical profession, freaks came to be considered sick rather than simply different. These individuals thus became the province of medical knowledge and public pity rather than of legitimate popular interest. While Virchow certainly took freaks to be pathological and thus of scientific interest, he did not view this scientific mode of perception as exclusive of more general popular appreciation. See Robert Bogdan, *Freak Show: Presenting Human Oddities for Amusement and Profit* (Chicago: University of Chicago Press, 1988). See also the essays collected in Rosmarie Garland Thomson, ed., *Freakery: Cultural Spectacles of the Extraordinary Body* (New York: New York University Press, 1996).

42. Rudolf Virchow, *Die Eröffnung des pathologischen Museums der Königl. Friedrich-Wilhelms-Universität zu Berlin am 27. Juni 1899* (Berlin: August Hirschwald, 1899), 20.

43. Nigel Rothfels discusses the importance of Darwinism in "freaking" individuals in nineteenth-century Germany. See Nigel Rothfels, "Aztecs, Aborigines, and Ape-People: Science and Freaks in Germany, 1850–1900," in Thomson, ed., *Freakery,* 158–72.

44. Wilhelm Joest, "Haarmenschen Ram-a-Samy," *VBGAEU* 26 (1894): 433–35.

45. On the Stork Boy, see K. Maass, "Der Storch-Mensch," *VBAGEU* 30 (1898): 554–55; and K. Maass (Berlin) to the Berlin Anthropological Society, 20 November 1898, ABGAEU. On the Bear Lady, see K. Maass, "Zwei menschliche Missbildungen," *VBGAEU* 27 (1895): 412–13; and Rudolf Virchow and Max Bartels (Gutachten for the Bärenweib), 19 January 1898, ABGAEU.

46. See, for example, Rudolf Virchow, comment on "Affenmensch und Bärenmensch," by Max Bartels, *VBGAEU* 16 (1884): 106–13, 111.

47. Carl Vogt, *Mémoires sur les microcéphales ou hommes-singes* (Geneva: Mémoires de l'Institute Genevois, 1867), and "Ueber die Mikrocephalen oder Affen-Menschen," *AA* 2 (1867): 129–284.

48. Charles Darwin, *The Descent of Man and Selection in Relation to Sex* (1871), 2d ed. (London: John Murry, 1882), 35–36.

49. Virchow, *Menschen- und Affenschädel,* 27–31.

50. Johannes von Mierjeiewsky, "Ein Fall von Mikrocephalie," *VBGAEU* 4 (1872): 100–123.

51. "Microcephale (Familie Becker)," *CBDAG* 8 (1877): 131–35; Hermann Schaaffhausen, "Mikrocephale Becker," *CBDAG* 16 (1885): 137–38.

52. Rudolf Virchow, "Ueber Microcephalie," *VBGAEU* 9 (1877): 280–95, and

"Mikrocephalen," *VBGAEU* 10 (1878): 25–30. The Darwinist Schaaffhausen also acknowledged that microcephalics could not be considered a link between humans and animals, as Vogt had believed. See Schaaffhausen, "Mikrocephale Becker."

53. Johannes Ranke, "Zum Neujahr 1879," *CBDAG* (1879): 1–2.

54. Bernard Ornstein, "Ungewöhnliche Haarbildung in der Sacralgegend eines Griechen," *VBGAEU* 7 (1875): 91–92, and "Sacrale Trichose," *VBGAEU* 7 (1875): 279–81.

55. Interestingly, he did not recommend Darwin. See Bernhard Ornstein, "Schwanzbildung beim Menschen," *VBGAEU* 11 (1879): 303–5.

56. Rudolf Virchow, comment on "Geschwänzter Mensch," by Bernhard Ornstein, *VBGAEU* 17 (1885): 119–26.

57. Rudolf Virchow, lecture to the Berlin Medical Society, reported in "Miscellen und Bücherschau," *ZfE* 5 (1873): 243–44, and comment on "Affenmensch und Bärenmensch," by Max Bartels. See also P. Michelson, "Zum Capitel der Hypertrichoses," *Archiv für pathologische Anatomie und Physiologie und für klinische Medicin* (also known as *Virchows Archiv*) 100 (1885): 66–80.

58. Max Bartels, "Ueber abnorme Behaarung beim Menschen," *ZfE* 8 (1876): 110–29, 11 (1879): 145–94, and 13 (1881): 213–33.

59. In a report on observations of tailed humans in Borneo, Bartels claimed that tails were pathological, not atavistic. See Max Bartels, "Schwanzmenschen von Borneo," *VBGAEU* 18 (1886): 138–40.

60. Max Bartels, "Ueber abnorme Behaarung beim Menschen," 110.

61. There is an enormous literature on monsters. Two pieces that particularly helped me in formulating my thoughts on this topic are Donna Haraway, "The Promises of Monsters: A Regenerative Politics for Inappropriate/d Others," in *Cultural Studies,* ed. Lawrence Grossberg et al. (New York: Routledge, 1992), 295–337; and Evelleen Richards, "A Political Anatomy of Monsters, Hopeful and Otherwise: Teratogeny, Transcendentalism, and Evolutionary Theorizing," *Isis* 85 (1994): 377–411. Haraway notes the etymological relation of monsters and demonstrations and the importance of monsters as signifiers. Richards studies monsters as they actually functioned in nineteenth-century evolutionary theorizing.

62. Bartels, "Ueber abnorme Behaarung beim Menschen," 193.

CHAPTER 4

1. This chapter has been inspired by Stephen Jay Gould's analysis of the use of craniometry to construct racial hierarchies in U.S. anthropology. See Stephen Jay Gould, *The Mismeasure of Man* (New York: Norton, 1981).

2. Hartmann, "Untersuchungen über die Völkerschaften Nord-Ost-Afrikas," 33.

3. Felix von Luschan comments on the simplicity of the statistical methods of early anthropology in his *Völker, Rassen, Sprachen,* 1st ed. (Berlin: Weltverlag, 1922), 11. Only after the turn of the century did an anthropologist advocate testing the statistical significance of craniometric data with methods of standard deviation. See Paul

Bartels, "Über die Vergleichbarkeit kraniometrischer Reihen," *ZfE* 34 (1903): 935–51. (Whether Paul Bartels is related to Max Bartels is unknown.)

4. Hermann Welcker, "Kraniologische Mittheilungen," *AA* 1 (1866): 89–160, 93–94.

5. J. W. Spengel, "Zur Craniometrie," *ZfE* 9 (1877): 129–42. On the Göttingen craniometric agreement, see Benno Ottow, "K. E. von Baer als Kraniologe und die Anthropologen-Versammlung 1861 in Göttingen," *Sudhoffs Archiv* 50 (1966): 43–68.

6. Hermann von Jhering, "Zur Reform der Craniometrie," *ZfE* 5 (1873): 121–69.

7. Virchow explained craniometry to noncraniologists in the Berlin Anthropological Society in a lecture reprinted as "Über die Schädel der älteren Bevölkerung der Philippinen, insbesondere über künstlich verunstaltete Schädel derselben," *ZfE* 2 (1870): 151–58. The ratio of the length of a skull to its breadth was first proposed as a key craniological measurement by the Swedish anthropologist Magnus Gustav Retzius. A. Sasse remarks on the prevalence in German anthropology of the "simple Retzian formula of dolichocephaly and brachycephaly." See A. Sasse, "Zur wissenschaftlichen Kraniometrie," *AA* 2 (1867): 101–7.

8. Hermann von Jhering, "Zur Frage der Schädelmessung," *CBDAG* (1875): 62–63. Jhering also points out that anthropologists did not want to have to purchase the new craniometric instruments that a different method might require.

9. J. W. Spengel, "Zur Frage nach der Methode der Schädelmessung," *CBDAG* 6 (1875): 1–4, 2. Spengel was one of the most vocal proponents of Jhering's anthropometric methods.

10. Jhering agreed with Schaaffhausen's view of prognathism. See Hermann von Jhering, "Ueber das Wesen der Prognathie und ihr Verhältnis zur Schädelbasis," *AA* 5 (1872): 359–407, 406. Virchow also believed that a high degree of prognathy made a person look like an ape, although he did not believe that this resemblance implied a genetic relation between humans and apes. See Rudolf Virchow, "Ueber Negrito- und Igorroten-Schädel von den Philippinen," *VBGAEU* 4 (1872): 204–9.

11. Hermann Schaaffhausen, "Zur Messung und Horizontalstellung des Schädels," *AA* 11 (1879): 178–79. See also Schaaffhausen's comments on the Jhering-Spengel method, *CBDAG* 6 (1875): 116.

12. No anthropologist seems to have brought this charge against Schaaffhausen. However, almost a decade after the Frankfurt Agreement, Johannes Ranke pointed out that the degree of prognathy depended on the angle at which one places a skull. See Johannes Ranke, "Zur Frankfurter Verständigung und über Beziehungen des Gehirns zum Schädelbau," *CBDAG* 22 (1891): 115–18. Ranke was not criticizing Schaaffhausen's project but rather arguing that the development of the brain rather than the shape of the skull best differentiates humans and animals.

13. Hermann Schaaffhausen, "Ueber die heutige Schädellehre," *CBDAG* 20 (1889): 165–70.

14. J. W. Spengel pointed out explicitly that the differences between most German anthropologists and Schaaffhausen rested on Schaaffhausen's belief that he could learn about "psychic [*geistige*] function" by studying the skull. See Spengel, "Zur Frage nach der Methode der Schädelmessung."

15. Apparently, Schaaffhausen did not announce his heterodox craniometric views until 1875, after he had already begun issuing catalogs of skull collections. See Hermann Schaaffhausen, "Bericht über die Arbeiten zu Herstellung eines Gesamtcataloges der deutschen Schädelsammlungen," Sechste Allgemeine Versammlung der Deutschen Anthropologischen Gesellschaft in München 9–11 August 1875, attached to *CBDAG* 6 (1875): 56–59; and Spengel, "Zur Frage nach der Methode der Schädelmessung."

16. The proposal was made by the Munich anthropologists Johannes Ranke and Julius Kollmann. See Johannes Ranke to Rudolf Virchow, 30 November 1880, NL Virchow, 1729.

17. "1. Sitzung der Kraniometrischen Conferenz (9. August 1880)," and "2. Sitzung der Kraniometrischen Conferenz (10. August 1880)," Verhandlungen der XI. allgemeinen Versammlung der Deutsche Anthropologischen Gesellschaft in Berlin, 104–6, bound with *CBDAG* 11 (1880).

18. Johannes Ranke to Rudolf Virchow, 17 January 1882, NL Virchow, 1729.

19. For the text of the Frankfurt Agreement, see Julius Kollmann, Johannes Ranke, and Rudolf Virchow, "Verständigung über ein gemeinsames craniometrisches Verfahren," *AA* 15 (1884): 1–8. Also in *CBDAG* 14 (1883): 1–8. Outside Germany, these methods came to be known as "the method of Jhering," although, inside Germany, they were known as the "Frankfurt Agreement." See Otto Ammon, "Über die Wechselbeziehung des Kopfindex nach deutscher und französischer Messung," *Centralblatt für Anthropologie, Ethnologie und Urgeschichte* 2 (1897): 1–6. Nobody in Germany seems to have given Jhering credit for formulating the methods that would become standard there. Jhering complained that he had been attacked for his system when he first proposed it and that, when it was finally accepted, no one bothered to acknowledge him. Several years before the Frankfurt Agreement, Jhering had sired a child out of wedlock and, thinking the disgrace too great to allow him to pursue an academic career, had moved to Brazil to practice medicine. See Hermann von Jhering to Rudolf Virchow, 20 April 1880, 7 December 1885, NL Virchow, 996.

20. Rudolf Virchow, "Zur Frankfurter Verständigung," XXII Versammlung der Deutschen Anthropologischen Gesellschaft, Danzig, *CBDAG* 22 (1891): 121–24, 124.

21. This controversy was the most fundamental controversy in German craniometry but certainly not the only one. Indeed, the history of craniometry at this time consists largely of a series of very esoteric squabbles about technique. Jhering himself, commenting on the apparent triviality of these debates, remarked: "One could hardly think of a more comfortless task than to have to write a complete history of this science!" Jhering, "Zur Reform der Craniometrie," 121.

22. W. Krause, "Ueber die Aufgaben der wissenschaftlichen Kraniometrie," *AA* 1 (1866): 251–59, 251.

23. Important for this account of anthropological representation has been Lorraine Daston and Peter Galison, "The Image of Objectivity," *Representations* 40 (1992): 81–128. Daston and Galison characterize natural scientific aesthetics in the late nineteenth and the early twentieth centuries as "'noninterventionist' or 'mechanical' objectivity." They argue that objectivity in this period was understood as the

result of the restraint of scientists "from imposing their hopes, expectations, generalizations, aesthetics, even ordinary language on the image of nature" (p. 81).

24. As Joel Snyder has argued, representations that are held to be realistic presuppose a theory of vision that can account for this realism. Joel Snyder, "Picturing Vision," *Critical Inquiry* 6 (1980): 499–526. See also Joel Snyder and Neil Walsh Allen, "Photography, Vision, and Representation," *Critical Inquiry* 2 (1975): 143–69. Both these articles have been helpful in working out the argument of this section.

25. On the history of linear perspective, see Sam E. Edgerton Jr., *The Renaissance Rediscovery of Linear Perspective* (New York: Basic, 1975). For an account arguing that the realism of linear perspective based on the camera obscura was rejected in the mid-nineteenth century, see Jonathan Crary, *Techniques of the Observer: On Vision and Modernity in the Nineteenth Century* (Cambridge, Mass.: MIT Press, 1990).

26. Norman Bryson has cautioned against naturalizing linear perspective and qualifies it as a signifier of realism, as a socially specific convention indicating (to initiated observers) that the image they view is realistic. See Norman Bryson, *Vision and Painting: The Logic of the Gaze* (New Haven, Conn.: Yale University Press, 1983). On painting as recorded vision, see E. H. Gombrich, *Art and Illusion: A Study in the Psychology of Pictorial Representation* (Princeton, N.J.: Princeton University Press, 1960). For a good discussion of realistic art, including its relation to natural scientific knowledge, see Svetlana Alpers, *The Art of Describing: Dutch Art in the Seventeenth Century* (Chicago: University of Chicago Press, 1983).

27. See Snyder, "Picturing Vision"; and Snyder and Allen, "Photography, Vision, and Representation."

28. [Illegible] to the Faculty of Medicine of the University of Berlin, 1872, HU, Med. Fak., Habilitationsvorgänge, 1341/1, Bl. 140–41.

29. Gustav Fritsch, lecture on methods of representation in anthropology, *ZfE* 2 (1870): 172–74, 172.

30. The criticism of Haeckel as an inaccurate drawer was a common one among anthropologists, even those favorably disposed to his Darwinism. See, for example, the Darwinist Hermann Schaaffhausen's review of *Die Anthropogenie,* by Ernst Haeckel (Leipzig, 1875), *AA* 9 (1876): 109–10.

31. See Virchow et al., "Ratschläge für anthropologische Untersuchung auf Expeditionen der Marine," 352–53.

32. On anthropological photography in Berlin and Germany, see Thomas Theye, "'Wir wollen nicht glauben, sondern schauen': Zur Geschichte der ethnographischen Fotografie im deutschsprachigen Raum im 19. Jahrhundert," in *Der Geraubte Schatten: Photographie als ethnographsiches Dokument,* ed. Thomas Theye (Munich: Münchner Stadtmuseum, 1989), 60–119. The other essays in that catalog also deal with the topic of anthropological photography. The catalog itself presents an excellent selection of anthropological photographs, including previously unpublished material from the archive of the Berlin Anthropological Society. For nineteenth-century anthropological photographs, see also Elizabeth Edwards, ed., *Anthropology and Photography, 1860–1920* (New Haven, Conn.: Yale University Press, 1992).

33. Fritsch, lecture on methods of representation in anthropology, 173–74. See

also Virchow et al., "Ratschläge für anthropologische Untersuchung auf Expeditionen der Marine," 352–53.

34. For an excellent study of the conventions of viewing and making photographs in England at this time, see Jennifer Tucker, "Science Illustrated: Photographic Evidence and Social Practice in England, 1870–1920" (Ph.D. diss., Johns Hopkins University, 1996). Tucker finds that, although Victorian scientists hoped that photography could become an "objective" means of representation, they did not espouse naive notions of photographic realism. Rather, they sought conventions that would make photography objective and realistic.

35. A sheet of proofs of images of skulls for vol. 30 (1898) of the *Zeitschrift für Ethnologie* survives in the Virchow Papers on which Virchow has marked a dark spot on an image and complains: "The border is too sharp. It is not a depression." Virchow Papers, 2997.

36. Fritsch, lecture on methods of representation in anthropology, 174. The need for an illustrator to mediate photographs to the public was also partly a necessity of contemporary print technology. At the time, photographs could be rendered in print only by having an illustrator copy them as copper engravings or lithographs.

37. Fritsch, *Die Eingeborenen Süd-Afrika's ethnographisch und anatomisch Beschrieben,* 4–5.

38. Gustav Fritsch, "Die Bedeutung physiognomischer Darstellungen," *VBGAEU* 4 (1872): 11–14, 12.

39. For an early description of the Lucaesian apparatus, see Fritsch, lecture on methods of representation in anthropology, 172–74. See also Rudolf Virchow, "Coordinaten-Apparat von Lucae," *VBGAEU* 4 (1872): 282; and J. W. Spengel, "Ueber eine Modification des Lucaeschen Zeichen-Apparats," *ZfE* 6 (1874): 66–67.

40. Welcker, "Kraniologische Mittheilungen," 100–101.

41. See, for example, Theodor Landzert, "Welche Art bildlicher Darstellung braucht der Naturforscher? Beitrag zur Kenntnis der verschiedenen Darstellungsweisen vom Standpunkte des Naturforschers und Künstlers," *AA* 2 (1867): 1–16.

42. See J. Gildemeister, "Zur Schädelmessung," *CBDAG* 6 (1875): 27–29.

43. On Helmholtz's psychology of spatial perception, see Gary Hatfield, *The Natural and the Normative: Theories of Spatial Perception from Kant to Helmholtz* (Cambridge, Mass.: MIT Press, 1990); R. Steven Turner, *In the Eye's Mind: Vision and the Helmholtz-Hering Controversy* (Princeton, N.J.: Princeton University Press, 1994). Adolf Bastian extended this argument about the learned nature of fundamental categories of perception. See Adolf Bastian, "Raum und Zeit," *ZfE* 5 (1873): 43–49.

44. My analysis of geometric and perspectival projection has been aided by the analysis of Velázquez's *Las Meninas* in Michel Foucault, *The Order of Things: An Archaeology of the Human Sciences* (New York: Random House, 1970), 3–16. Geometric projection allowed anthropologists to solve the problem posed by the mirror represented in the center of that painting, which should reflect the position outside the image where both painter and viewer stand. Instead, the mirror reflects the subjects—King Philip IV and his wife, Mariana—whom Velázquez's self-representation paints. The painting forces the viewer to confront as impossible the seeming realism of

perspectival representation. By eschewing perspective altogether, anthropologists avoided this problem.

45. Friedrich Nietzsche, *On the Genealogy of Morality* (1887), ed. K. Ansell-Pearson, trans. C. Diethe (Cambridge: Cambridge University Press, 1994), essay 3, p. 12.

46. Wilhelm von Humboldt, "Über die Aufgabe des Geschichtsschreibers" (1821), in *Wilhelm von Humboldts Werke,* ed. A. Leitzmann (Berlin: B. Behr, 1905), 4:35–56.

47. Wilhelm Dilthey, *Einleitung in die Geisteswissenschaften,* 89–93.

48. Foucault, *The Order of Things,* 387.

CHAPTER 5

1. The title of this chapter is borrowed from Ralf Dahrendorf, "The German Idea of Truth," in *Society and Democracy in Germany* (1965; New York: Norton, 1979), 142–55. Dahrendorf's questions and approaches have been an important source and inspiration for the present chapter.

The epigraph is taken from E[rnst] Fr[iedel], "Urfideles Buddellied," in "Tisch-Lieder zum Fest Mahl deutscher Anthropologen im Zoologischen Garten in Berlin am 5. August 1880," printed pamphlet in LAB, Rep. 60, Nr. 5 (BGAEU), XI. Generalversammlung der Deutschen Anthropologischen Gesellschaft, 1880. These lyrics were to be sung to the tune of "Studio auf einer Reis', Juchheidi, Juchheida!"

Woodruff Smith and Paul Weindling both present nineteenth-century German anthropology as a liberal science because its theories implied liberal ideological positions. I argue in this chapter that the liberalism of German anthropology lay, not in its content, but rather in its social and epistemological form. See Smith, *Politics and the Sciences of Culture;* and Weindling, *Health, Race, and German Politics.*

2. Recent analyses of intellectual communities have illustrated the ways in which sociable practices form a ground for truth. Steven Shapin has shown how feudal, civic humanist, and Christian codes of gentlemanly conduct informed the production of knowledge about nature and the concept of truth in seventeenth-century England. See Steven Shapin, *A Social History of Truth: Civility and Science in Seventeenth-Century England* (Chicago: University of Chicago Press, 1994). Martin J. S. Rudwick demonstrates the importance of gentlemanly conventions to geological controversy in Victorian England. See Rudwick, *The Great Devonian Controversy.* Dena Goodman has shown the constitutive role played by salon sociability in the French Enlightenment. See Dena Goodman, *The Republic of Letters: A Cultural History of the French Enlightenment* (Ithaca, N.Y.: Cornell University Press, 1994). Jack Morrell and Arnold Thackray demonstrate how important specific rituals of social solidarity such as banquets and festivals were to the scientific practice of, and the idea of science formed by, the British Association for the Advancement of Science. See esp. Jack Morrell and Arnold Thackray, "Creating a Cultural Resource," in *Gentlemen of Science: Early Years of the British Association for the Advancement of Science* (Oxford: Clarendon, 1981), 95–163.

3. The most detailed account of the events leading up to German unification is Lothar Gall's biography of Bismarck. See Lothar Gall, *Bismarck: The White Revolutionary* (London: Allen & Unwin, 1986), vol. 1.

4. Otto von Bismarck, speech to the Budget Commission of the Prussian Parliament, 30 September 1862. quoted in ibid., 1:204.

5. For an excellent account of German dueling customs, see Kevin McAleer, *Dueling: The Cult of Honor in Fin-de-Siècle Germany* (Princeton, N.J.: Princeton University Press, 1994). On the tension between notions of truth in natural science and dueling, see Shapin, *A Social History of Truth*.

6. Virchow to an unknown Prussian battalion doctor, 3 April 1867, Andree, 482–83.

7. In 1881, the Progressives united with a group of secessionists from the National Liberals to form the German Free Thought Party (Deutsche Freisinnige Partei).

8. Alexander von Frantzius wrote to Virchow that the interests of Vienna were at odds with the rest of the society. See Alexander von Frantzius to Rudolf Virchow, 12 September 1874, Andree, 191–92. Vogt wrote to Virchow that Bismarck's division of Germany would have to hold true for the German Anthropological Society as well. See Carl Vogt to Virchow, 21 February 1870, Andree, 496–98. Similarly, Vogt believed that anti-German sentiments would make it impossible to start a branch of the German Anthropological Society in Prague. See Vogt to Virchow, 21 February 1870, Andree, 496–98. Virchow also seems to have considered Austrians poor anthropologists. While preparing to go to a conference in Austria, Virchow wrote to a colleague: "Tomorrow we go to Salzburg as men with the lowest expectations, for the Austrians have also shown themselves to be weak helpers." Virchow to Julius Kollmann, 10 August 1881, Andree, 263–64.

9. See Thomas Sprat, *History of the Royal Society* (1667), ed. Jackson I. Cope and Harold Whitmore Jones, facsimile ed. (St. Louis: Washington University Press, 1958), 25–34. See also J. R. Jacob, "Restoration, Reformation, and the Origins of the Royal Society," *History of Science* 13 (1975): 155–76.

10. Steven Shapin and Simon Schaffer, *Leviathan and the Air-Pump: Hobbes, Boyle, and the Experimental Life* (Princeton, N.J.: Princeton University Press, 1985), 332.

11. The term *Baconian* should not imply that this method sprang fully formed from the head of Francis Bacon. Indeed, Susan Cannon rightly suggests that, in the nineteenth century, the model for "Baconian" science was in fact the work of Alexander von Humboldt and that this "Humboldtian" science was not the blockheaded empiricism that it is often made out to be. I will return to Cannon's distinction below. See Susan F. Cannon, "Humboldtian Science," in *Science in Culture: The Early Victorian Period* (New York: Dawson, 1978), 73–110.

12. Joseph Ben-David, *The Scientist's Role in Society: A Comparative Study* (Englewood Cliffs, N.J.: Prentice-Hall, 1971), 73–74.

13. Jack Morrell and Arnold Thackray have shown how Baconian science allowed the members of the British Association for the Advancement of Science to contribute to a common project despite their varying interests and levels of expertise. See Morrell and Thackray, *Gentlemen of Science,* 267–75.

14. As Merton argued, because science both demanded and encouraged free

inquiry and communication based on commonly accessible data, its very practice fostered democracy. Robert K. Merton, "Science and the Social Order" (1938) and "The Normative Structure of Science" (1942), in his *The Sociology of Science: Theoretical and Empirical Investigations,* ed. Norman W. Storer (Chicago: University of Chicago Press, 1973), 254–66, 267–78. Shils called scientific communities "the prototype of the free society" and further emphasized that, because a scientific community could function only by applying its own standards to itself, it both fostered and required independence from external, especially state, authority. Edward A. Shils, "The Autonomy of Science," in *The Sociology of Science,* ed. Bernard Barber and Walter Hirsch (New York: Free Press, 1962), 610–22. Reprinted from Edward A. Shils, *The Torment of Secrecy: The Background and Consequences of American Security Policies* (New York: Free Press, 1956), 176–91. Joseph Needham concluded that, because scientific communities produce authorities through the assent of their members, "democracy might . . . almost in a sense be termed that practice of which science is the theory." For Needham, these "hidden connections between science and democracy" also explain why, in his view, science and democracy emerged together in the West and why science has been less successful in nondemocratic societies, such as feudal China or Nazi Germany. Joseph Needham, "On Science and Social Change" (1946), in *The Grand Titration: Science and Society in East and West* (Toronto: University of Toronto Press, 1969), 123–53, 145.

15. For critiques of the idea of an inherent connection between science and democracy, see Barry Barnes's classic "Making Out in Industrial Research," *Science Studies* 1 (1971): 157–75; and Herbert Mehrtens's more recent "The Social System of Mathematics and National Socialism: A Survey," in *Science, Technology, and National Socialism,* ed. Monika Renneberg and Mark Walker (Cambridge: Cambridge University Press, 1994), 291–311.

16. Keith M. Anderton has argued that Emil du Bois-Reymond, Hermann von Helmholtz, and Rudolf Virchow developed a "scientific agnosticism" that allowed them to retreat behind what du Bois-Reymond called the "absolute limits of science" in times of political crisis. In times more favorable to political participation, these scientists did take political stands, especially around issues of education. Anderton shows that their apparent apoliticism was in fact deeply political. See Keith M. Anderton, "The Limits of Science: A Social, Political, and Moral Agenda for Epistemology in Nineteenth-Century Germany" (Ph.D. diss., Harvard University, 1993).

17. [Adolf Bastian?], discussion of lecture by Rudolf Virchow at the Assembly of German Scientists and Doctors, *ZfE* 1 (1869): 393–95, 393.

18. Adolf Bastian, review of *Kant's Psychologie,* by J. B. Meyer (Berlin, 1870), *ZfE* 3 (1871): 68–71, 69.

19. Rudolf Virchow, opening address to the yearly meeting of the German Anthropological Society, *CBDAG* 6 (1875): 2–3.

20. Rudolf Virchow, "Festrede des Ehren-Präsidenten," *VBGAEU* 26 (1894): 497–541, 510.

21. Bastian, review of *The Descent of Man.*

22. Ludwig Wilser, "Die Rassen der Steinzeit," *CBDAG* 34 (1903): 185–87, 187.

23. Wilhelm von Gossler, opening address to the German Anthropological Society, *CBDAG* 12 (1881): 1–3, 1. Gossler would replace Robert von Puttkamer as minister of culture the following year.

24. Virchow, preface to *Die vorgeschichtliche Zeit,* vii. The broad interdisciplinarity of anthropology was stated programmatically in Rudolf Virchow et al., "Die Deutsche Gesellschaft für Anthropologie, Ethnologie und Urgeschichte," *CBDAG* 1 (1870): 1–4. As late as 1912, Felix von Luschan noted that, although anthropology, ethnology, and prehistory had become more specialized, the three disciplines were still basically united. See Felix von Luschan, "Anthropologie: Rückblicke und Ausblicke, Eröffnungsrede der 43. allgemeinen Versammlung der Deutschen Anthropologischen Gesellschaft in Weimar, 1912," *CBDAG* 43 (1912): 6–14.

25. This view of philosophy is surely partial since, in the nineteenth century, as today, philosophers have a lively associational life and their knowledge is certainly as social as any.

26. F. A. von Hartsen, review of *Grundlinien eines Systems der Aesthetik,* by Adolf Horwica (Leipzig, 1869), *ZfE* 1 (1869): 318–20, 319.

27. The prehistoric map project was initiated in 1871. See "Protocoll über die 1. Sitzung der 2. allgemeinen Versammlung der Deutschen Anthropologischen Gesellschaft zu Schweren, am 22. September 1871, im Saale des Schauspielhauses," *CBDAG* 2 (1871): 41–80.

28. Woldt informed Virchow: "I recently wrote many short articles about the anthropological society that . . . have the purpose of increasing the society's membership." August Woldt to Rudolf Virchow, 12 December 1877, NL Virchow, 2369. Virchow also wrote directly to the editor of the *Vossische Zeitung,* urging him to continue reporting the Berlin Anthropological Society's meetings and even offering assistance in writing the articles. Virchow explained that such articles would increase public interest in, and thus support for, the society. See Virchow to unknown correspondent [from the context of the letter clearly an editor of the *Vossische Zeitung*], 5 November 1876, Andree, 487.

29. Articles on anthropology society meetings from the *Vossische Zeitung* and other newspapers can be found in Virchow's newspaper clipping collection, NL Virchow, 3002–18.

30. See, for example, the *Berliner Börsen Courier,* 1 December 1889, NL Virchow, 3002; and *Die Post,* 17 August 1894, GStA PK, I. HA, Rep. 76Ve, Cultusministerium, Sekt. 1, Tit. XI, Nr. 4, Bd. 3, Bl. 14 (M).

31. Julius Stinde, "Kleine Chronik," *Berliner Tageblatt,* 10 August 1880, in LAB, Rep. 60, Nr. 4 (BGAEU), Zeitungsausschnitte, 1879–85.

32. "Geschwänzte Menschen," *Kölnische Zeitung,* 31 March 1877, ABGAEU.

33. Schaaffhausen, "Ueber die anthropologischen Fragen der Gegenwart," 329.

34. [Adolf Bastian (attribution made on stylistic grounds)], discussion of the *Philosophencongress* in Frankfurt, *ZfE* 1 (1869): 389–93, 393. I am grateful to C. N. Dugan for assistance with the Greek.

35. When Friedrich Wilhelm IV became king of Prussia in 1840, he declared

that he would stamp out "the dragon seed of Hegelianism." Under his reign, historians such as Leopold von Ranke took over the privileged position formerly occupied by philosophers in Prussia. On Hegelians, historians, and Prussian politics, see Herbert Schnädelbach, *Philosophy in Germany, 1831–1933* (Cambridge: Cambridge University Press, 1984).

36. Bastian, "Raum und Zeit," 47.

37. Bastian, "Das natürliche System in der Ethnologie."

38. Bastian, "Die Grundlage der Ethnologie in den geographischen Provinzen."

39. Such distinctions between knowledge and the things known, as well as between the internal text of knowledge and its external context, are always misleading. For externalism and internalism, see Steven Shapin, "Discipline and Bounding: The History and Sociology of Science as Seen through the Externalism-Internalism Debate," *History of Science* 30 (1992): 333–69. Two paradigmatic works dealing with the relation of internal and external factors are Robert Merton, *Science, Technology, and Society in Seventeenth-Century England* (1938; New York: Howard Fertig, 1970); and Thomas S. Kuhn, *The Structure of Scientific Revolutions* (Chicago: University of Chicago Press, 1970). For a study of these two works and their bearing on internalist and externalist accounts of science, see Michael D. King, "Reason, Tradition, and the Progressiveness of Science," *History and Theory* 10 (1971): 3–32.

40. Foucault, *The Order of Things,* 378. While Foucault seems to be thinking especially of the structural anthropology of Claude Lévi-Strauss in his discussion of ethnology, it applies, I believe, to earlier German anthropology as well. Foucault holds that psychoanalysis and structuralist linguistics also address the fundamental concept of the modern *episteme*. See ibid., 373–86.

41. Bastian, "Das natürliche System in der Ethnologie," 6.

42. Bastian himself seems to have believed that religions could give an anthropologist a kind of shortcut to a people's ethnic thoughts. However, in statements that he wrote for the Berlin Anthropological Society and for the Royal Museum of Ethnology, Bastian presented the more common view that one had to study all aspects of a given people before one could infer their ethnic thoughts. On Adolf Bastian's notion of the unity of humans, see Klaus-Peter Koepping, *Adolf Bastian and the Psychic Unity of Mankind: The Foundations of Anthropology in Nineteenth Century Germany* (St. Lucia: University of Queensland Press, 1983). See also Annemarie Fiedermutz-Laun, *Der kulturhistorische Gedanke bei Adolf Bastian* (Wiesbaden: Franz Steiner, 1970). Bastian's *Der Mensch in der Geschichte* is the standard primary source on his philosophical views. For much briefer accounts of Bastian's thought, see his "Das natürliche System in der Ethnologie," and his review of *Völkerkunde*. Even more understandable is Thomas Achelis's popularization of Bastian's thought, *Moderne Völkerkunde, deren Entwicklung und Aufgabe* (Stuttgart: Ferdinand Enke, 1896).

43. Rudolf Virchow et al., "Ueber Gräberfelder und Burgwälle der Nieder-Lausitz und des überoderischen Gebietes," *VBGAEU* 4 (1872): 226–38.

44. See Cannon, "Humboldtian Science."

45. Thomas Nipperdey, "Verein als soziale Struktur in Deutschland im späten

18. und frühen 19. Jahrhundert: Eine Fallstudie zur Modernisierung I," in *Gesellschaft, Kultur, Theorie* (Göttingen: Vandenhoeck & Ruprecht, 1976), 174-205.

46. For a good general model of German associations, see Herbert Freudenthal, *Vereine in Hamburg: Ein Beitrag zur Geschichte und Volkskunde der Geselligkeit* (Hamburg: Museum für Hamburgische Geschichte, 1968). See also Michael John, "Associational Life and the Development of Liberalism in Hannover, 1848-66," in *In Search of a Liberal Germany: Studies in the History of German Liberalism from 1789 to the Present*, ed. Konrad H. Jarausch and Larry Eugene Jones (New York: Berg, 1990), 161-86.

47. See Roger Chickering, *We Men Who Feel Most German: A Cultural Study of the Pan-German League, 1886-1914* (Boston: Allen & Unwin, 1984), esp. 152-82. For a study of another pressure group, see Marilyn Shevin Coetzee, *The German Army League: Popular Nationalism in Wilhelmine Germany* (New York: Oxford University Press, 1990). For a study placing nationalist pressure groups in the larger context of the Wilhelmine political-economic conjuncture, see Geoff Eley, *Reshaping the German Right: Radical Nationalism and Political Change after Bismarck* (New Haven, Conn.: Yale University Press, 1980).

48. On extra-academic scientific societies in nineteenth-century Germany, see Andreas W. Daum, *Wissenschaftspopularisierun im 19. Jahrhundert: Bürgerliche Kultur, naturwissenschaftliche Bildung und die deutsche Öffentlichkeit, 1848-1914* (München: R. Oldenbourg, 1998), 85-191. Christoph Meinl interprets the festive meetings and presentations of the Chemischen Gesellschaft in Imperial Germany as attempts to compensate for the lack of prestige of natural scientists in a society that valued the aristocracy and the military more than intellectual and scientific achievement. See Christopher Meinl, "August Wilhelm Hofmann—'Regierender Oberchemiker,'" in *Die Allianz von Wissenschaft und Industrie: August Wilhelm Hofmann (1818-1892)*, ed. Christoph Meinl and Hartmut Scholz (Weinheim: VCH, 1992), 27-64.

49. The classic works on German republicanism and liberalism are James Sheehan, *German Liberalism in the Nineteenth Century* (Chicago: University of Chicago Press, 1978); and Krieger, *The German Idea of Freedom*. The assertion of peculiar traditions of German liberalism has fallen out of favor since the pathbreaking work of David Blackbourn and Geoff Eley. Blackbourn and Eley have rightly taken to task histories of the German *Sonderweg,* or special path to modernity, for their implicit, ideological celebrations of England and the United States. However, this does not constitute an argument against the existence of peculiarly German political traditions. See David Blackbourn and Geoff Eley, *The Peculiarities of German History: Bourgeois Society and Politics in Nineteenth-Century Germany* (Oxford: Oxford University Press, 1985). See also Geoff Eley, "Introduction 1: Is There a History of the *Kaiserreich?"* in *Society, Culture, and the State in Germany, 1870-1930,* ed. Geoff Eley (Ann Arbor: University of Michigan Press, 1996). For more recent assessments (which, it should be noted, contradict the normative but not the major historical theses of Sheehan and Krieger), see the essays collected in Jarausch and Jones, eds., *In Search of a Liberal Germany.*

50. In the "Fest-Lieder zur 29. allgemeinen Versammlung der Deutschen

Anthropologischen Gesellschaft in Braunschweig 4. bis 6. August 1898," ABGAEU, it is noted explicitly that conference participants and their wives are to bring the society's songbook to meals, excursions, and other "festivities."

51. Information about the festivities of the German Anthropological Society generally and the Mainz meeting in particular comes from J. Howard Gore, "The German Anthropological Congress," *American Anthropologist* 2 (1889): 313–19. Accounts of the annual German Anthropological Society meetings printed each year in their *Correspondenz-Blatt* are restricted almost exclusively to stenographic reports of the academic proceedings of the conference. The highbrow *Vossische Zeitung* printed summaries of the presentations given at monthly Berlin society meetings but did not include any material on the sociability surrounding the presentations. Menus, songbooks, and other meeting programs can be found in the ABGAEU, the GStA PK, and the LAB.

52. In a letter to Rudolf Virchow, the newspaper reporter August Woldt mentioned complaints from members about the quality of the restaurant that the Berlin Anthropological Society patronized after its meetings. Woldt stressed the importance of postmeeting refreshments to most members of the society. See August Woldt to Rudolf Virchow, 12 December 1877, NL Virchow, 2369. Excursions were usually recorded in the *Verhandlungen der Berliner Gesellschaft für Anthropologie, Ethnologie und Urgeschichte*.

53. "Hallstattlied," in a book of festive songs written for the German Anthropological Society (1892), ABGAEU.

54. See "Miscellen und Bücherschau," *VBGAEU* 3 (1871): 134–44; Johanna Mestorf to Wilhelm von Gossler (minister of culture), 24 August 1884, GStA PK, I. HA, Rep. 76Ve, Cultusministerium, Sekt. 15, Abt. XI, Nr. 2, Bd. 5, unnumbered sheets (M); German Anthropological Society 1880 Prehistory Exhibition Commission to Robert von Puttkamer (minister of culture), 21 June 1880, GStA PK, I. HA, Rep. 76Ve, Cultusministerium, Sekt. 1, Tit. XI, Nr. 4, Bd. 1, Bl. 328–29 (M). On Mestorf, see also Richard Andree, "Johanna Mestorf zum 80. Geburtstag," *Globus* 95 (1909): 212–15.

55. While conducting archaeological fieldwork in Syria, Luschan was assisted by Hochstetter in taking anthropological photographs. See Felix von Luschan to Rudolf Virchow, 29 August 1890, NL Virchow, 1345; and Luschan to Friedrich Ratzel, 22 May 1894, NL Luschan, K. 21, Copie-Buch VI, 254. In 1905, Hochstetter also assisted her spouse in taking anthropometric measurements in South Africa. See Luschan to Royal Museum of Ethnology, 14 September 1905, MfV, IB58, 1832/1905. Luschan relied on her, as well as his students, to assist in photographing the Africans performing at the 1896 colonial exhibition in Berlin. See Luschan, *Beiträge*, 4. Both Luschan and Hochstetter were accomplished photographers and together won a gold medal at an 1896 international amateur photography exhibition. See NL Luschan, box 23.

56. On homosociality, learned societies, and republicanism, see Dena Goodman, "Masculine Self-Governance and the End of Salon Culture," in *The Republic of Letters*, 233–80. On gender and French revolutionary republicanism, see Lynn Hunt, *Politics, Culture, and Class in the French Revolution* (Berkeley and Los Angeles: University of California Press, 1984); and Dorinda Outram, *The Body and the French Rev-*

olution: Sex, Class, and Political Culture (New Haven, Conn.: Yale University Press, 1989).

57. Rudolf Virchow, opening address to the 1880 German Anthropological Society meeting in Berlin, *CBDAG* 12 (1881): 4–5, 4.

58. See n. 49 above.

59. Wilhelm von Gossler (minister of culture) to Kaiser Wilhelm and Robert von Puttkamer (minister of the interior), 4 August 1884, GStA PK, I. HA, Rep. 76Ve, Cultusministerium, Sekt. 1, Tit. XI, Nr. 4, Bd. 2, Bl. 257–58 (M).

60. Adolf Bastian to General Administration of the Royal Museums, 5 April 1884, in MfV, IV, 144a/85.

61. President of the police to Wilhelm von Gossler (minister of culture), 18 June 1883, and Ministry of the Interior, Ministry of Justice, and Ministry of Culture to the police president, 28 January 1884, GStA PK, I. HA, Rep. 76Ve, Cultusministerium, Sekt. 1, Tit. XI, Nr. 4, Bd. 2, Bl. 209–12, 214–15 (M).

62. Virchow et al., "Die Deutsche Gesellschaft für Anthropologie, Ethnologie und Urgeschichte," 5. The prohibition against voting to decide the truth generally forms the limit of democracy in science and therefore constitutes an important exception to accounts such as Merton's that present science as inherently democratic. For an exception to this prohibition on voting, see Ronald Bayer, "Politics, Science, and the Problem of Psychiatric Nomenclature: A Case Study of the American Psychiatric Association Referendum on Homosexuality," in *Scientific Controversies: Case Studies in the Resolution and Closure of Disputes in Science and Technology,* ed. H. Tristam Engelhardt Jr. and Arthur L. Caplan (Cambridge: Cambridge University Press, 1987), 381–400.

63. See Byron A. Boyd, *Rudolf Virchow: The Scientist as Citizen* (New York: Garland, 1991), 136.

64. Rudolf Virchow, *Die Freiheit der Wissenschaft im modernen Staat* (Berlin: Wiegandt, Hempel & Parey, 1877), 7, 12.

65. Rudolf Virchow and [?] Dücker, "Westfällische Funde," *VBGAEU* 2 (1870): 170–71, 240–41.

66. Alexander von Frantzius to Rudolf Virchow, 30 July 1876, Andree, 208–10.

67. That many regarded anthropology as a dilettantish pursuit was often noted in speeches given at German Anthropological Society meetings. See, for example, [?] Zittel, "Eröffnung der Generalversammlung," *CBDAG* 6 (1875): 67–72.

68. In addition to their contribution of empirical information, the lay members of the society were also valued for their contribution of yearly dues. See Alexander von Frantzius to Rudolf Virchow, 30 July 1876, Andree, 208–10.

69. Adolf Bastian to Rudolf Virchow, June 1870, NL Virchow, 117, pt. II, Bl. 18–19.

70. Adolf Bastian to Rudolf Virchow, 1880, NL Virchow, 117, pt. I, Bl. 37–38.

71. That the discussions were themselves published threatened to undermine the distinction between published and oral anthropology. Bastian, for example, regarded the publication of discussions as problematic, admitting that "many points could be

found in the *Transactions of the Berlin Society* that do not taste excessively of strict scholarship." Adolf Bastian, defense of the Berlin Anthropological Society, *ZfE* 4 (1872): 249–50, 249. The *Transactions* (*VBGAEU*), at least by the 1890s, were edited from stenographic reports. See Rudolf Virchow to Johannes Ranke, 4 July 1880, Andree, 396; and Alexander von Frantzius to Virchow, 9 October 1873, NL Virchow, 646. Instead of having stenographic reports taken of their meetings, as they did earlier in the century, by 1895 members were asked to write down and report their own comments to the editor of the journal. This meant that the oral form of discussion would have been cleaned up and recast as a written text. See the program for Berlin Anthropological Society meeting, 14 December 1895, NL Virchow, 2661. Even the reports of German Anthropological Society meetings, for which there was a stenographer, were edited before being published.

CHAPTER 6

1. Virchow, "Die Ziele und Mittel der modernen Anthropologie."

2. Historians have been virtually unanimous in presenting this study—incorrectly, in my view—as a blow against anti-Semitism, as a demonstration that there was neither a Jewish nor a German race. The only historian to recognize that Virchow believed that the study proved Germany to be racially "Aryan" is Léon Poliakov. See Poliakov, *The Aryan Myth,* 264–66. George L. Mosse recognized the equivocal nature of this study, although he did not discuss Virchow's own conclusions about the German and Jewish races. See George L. Mosse, *Toward the Final Solution: A History of European Racism* (New York: Howard Fertig, 1978), 90–93. Otherwise, historians have generally coordinated their presentation of the school survey with Virchow's well-known liberalism and opposition to anti-Semitism and assumed that Virchow's study disproved the existence of German and Jewish races. The earliest presentation of the study as a blow against racial notions of Germany is in Carl Posner, *Rudolf Virchow* (Vienna: Rikola, 1921), 67. See also Erwin Heinz Ackerknecht, *Rudolf Virchow: Doctor, Statesman, Anthropologist* (Madison: University of Wisconsin Press, 1953), 212–16; Smith, *Politics and the Sciences of Culture,* 103; Weindling, *Health, Race, and German Politics,* 48–49. The conventional account of Virchow's study is also presented in John M. Efron, *Defenders of the Race: Jewish Doctors and Race Science in Fin-de-Siècle Europe* (New Haven, Conn.: Yale University Press, 1994). Efron does an excellent job, however, of situating the study in a wider context of German discussions of Jewish racial separateness. Sander Gilman notes with Mosse that Virchow categorized Jews and Germans separately, although both Gilman and Mosse maintained the view that the study undermined the notion of a physically distinct Jewish race. See Sander Gilman, "The Jewish Nose: Are Jews White? or, The History of the Nose Job," in *The Jew's Body* (New York: Routledge, 1991), 169–93, 177. While the present chapter contradicts Gilman's brief account of the school survey, it has, more generally, been aided and inspired by Gilman's work.

3. The members of the commission in charge of the study were Alexander Ecker, Wilhelm His, Wilhelm Krause, Hermann Schaaffhausen, Albert Kölliker, Gustav Lucae, and Hermann Welcker as well as Virchow. See "Protocoll über die 1. Sitzung der 2. allgemeinen Versammlung der Deutschen Anthropologischen Gesellschaft zu

Schweren, am 22. September 1871, im Saale des Schauspielhauses," 59. See also Rudolf Virchow, report on the statistical study of the skull form, in *Die vierte Allgemeine Versammlung der Deutschen Anthropologischen Gesellschaft zu Wiesbaden,* 28–30, attached to *CBDAG* 4 (1873).

4. Rudolf Virchow, "Berichterstattung über die statistischen Erhebungen bezüglich der Farbe der Augen, der Haare und der Haut," *CBDAG* 7 (1876): 91–102.

5. Virchow used the term *Rasse* throughout his reports of the study. *Rassen* were each associated with a physical *Typus,* although it was believed that several races could have the same *Typus,* for example, Jews and Walloons.

6. Virchow, "Die Ziele und Mittel der modernen Anthropologie."

7. Most historians have seen the German Anthropological Society study as a response to the assertion of the French anthropologist Armand de Quatrefages in *La Race prussienne* (Paris, 1871) that German troops behaved barbarously in the Franco-Prussian War because Prussians, who led the attack, were not German at all but rather Finns. Quatrefages asserted that a Prussian-dominated unified Germany was therefore "une erreur anthropologique" (p. 104) that "menaced all of Europe with a second Thirty Years' War" (p. 1). Although opposition to Quatrefages's theory may indeed have added zeal to the work of pro-Prussian and anti-French anthropologists, the physical anthropology of the Germans was a project central to German anthropologists even before Quatrefages's attack, as the articles in the *Archiv für Anthropologie,* from its founding in 1866, indicate. Furthermore, Virchow had, to his own satisfaction at least, already demolished Quatrefages's account on methodological grounds before he began his own study. See Rudolf Virchow, "Über die Methode der wissenschaftlichen Anthropologie: Eine Antwort an Hrn. de Quatrefages," *ZfE* 4 (1872): 300–320. When the German Anthropological Society study was finally completed, Virchow's reports mention only in passing that it disproved Quatrefages's hypothesis.

8. Rudolf Virchow, report on the school statistics, *Sechste Allgemeine Versammlung der Deutschen Anthropologischen Gesellschaft in München, 9–11 August 1875,* 47–50, attached to *CBDAG* 6 (1875).

9. Virchow, report on the statistical study of skull form. This was not the first time that Jews had been excluded from statistical surveys. Hermann Hölder excluded Jewish and French subjects from his "Beiträge zur Ethnographie von Württemberg," *AA* 2 (1867): 51–99. Ian Hacking notes that, in 1769, Prussia separated Jews from non-Jews in its statistical surveys, resulting in the *General-Judentabellen* and *Provinzial-Judenfamilien-Listen.* See Ian Hacking, *The Taming of Chance* (Cambridge: Cambridge University Press, 1990), 23. Of course, the eighteenth-century Prussian statistics did not include surveys of racial characteristics. In the nineteenth century, Prussia ceased to count Jews separately in its censuses. The anti-Semitic petition presented to Bismarck in 1882 demanded a restoration of the special census for Jews as well as the exclusion of Jews from public positions and the end of Jewish immigration. See Peter Pulzer, *The Rise of Political Anti-Semitism in Germany and Austria* (1964; London: Peter Halban, 1988), 91.

10. The question of a separate Jewish race had interested physical anthropologists since the late eighteenth century, although this question had never before been pursued on the grand scale of Virchow's study. On the question of a Jewish race in

German anthropology, see Annegret Kiefer, *Das Problem einer "Jüdischen Rasse": Eine Diskussion zwischen Wissenschaft und Ideologie (1870–1930)* (Frankfurt: Peter Lang, 1991). Kiefer's discussion of Virchow's study of schoolchildren (pp. 26–31) gives a conventional account of it as a challenge to anti-Semitism.

11. Virchow, report on the school statistics, 32–36. Michael B. Gross shows how liberal adversaries of the *Kulturkampf* feared that anti-Catholicism would lead to anti-Semitism. See Gross, "Kulturkampf and Unification."

12. As heroic and important as it was, Virchow's opposition to anti-Semitism should not be exaggerated. Werner Kümmel is, as far as I know, the only historian to deal with the subtleties of Virchow's relation to Jews. As Kümmel shows, Virchow's attitude was fairly typical for liberals: Jews were in Germany to stay and were capable of being assimilated into mainstream German society. Virchow's declaration in the Prussian House of Deputies on 21 March 1890 confirms Kümmel's interpretation: "The Jews are simply here. You cannot strike them dead" ("Die Juden sind einmal da. Sie können sie nicht totschlagen"). This position did not tolerate cultural and religious difference between Jews and non-Jews, advocating instead eliminating this difference. It was only after Adolf Stoecker began attacking him in the 1880s that Virchow came to be regarded as an unequivocal enemy of anti-Semitism. See Werner Kümmel, "Rudolf Virchow und der Antisemitismus," *Medizinhistorisches Journal* 3 (1968): 165–79.

13. Virchow, report on the school statistics, 32–36.

14. The ability of states to order teachers to participate in this study was made possible by the 1872 School Supervision Law, part of the *Kulturkampf* legislation, which decreased church control of schooling and increased the state's influence in education. See Marjorie Lamberti, *State, Society, and the Elementary School in Imperial Germany* (New York: Oxford University Press, 1989).

15. See, for example, Alexander Ecker to Rudolf Virchow, 8 February 1876, Andree, 83–84; and Adalbert Falk (minister of culture) to the Berlin Anthropological Society, 10 August 1874, 12 October 1874, printed in *CBDAG* 6 (1875): 32–36.

16. Rudolf Virchow, address to the German Anthropological Society, *CBDAG* 6 (1875): 2–3, 3.

17. See Oscar Fraas, report on the school statistics, 36–37, attached to *CBDAG* 6 (1875).

18. "Anthropologische Erhebungen in den Schulen," *VBGAEU* 7 (1875): 90. See Georg von Mayr, report on the school statistic in Munich, in *Sechste Allgemeine Versammlung der Deutschen Anthropologischen Gesellschaft in München. 9–11 August 1875*, 50–55.

19. This story was first reported by E. B. Tylor in his "Address to the Department of Anthropology of the British Association," reprinted in the *Journal of the Anthropological Institute of Great Britain and Ireland* 9 (1879): 235–46, 245–46. It was then cited in Alfred C. Haddon, *History of Anthropology* (London: Watts, 1910). Finally, it was cited in Ackerknecht, *Rudolf Virchow*, 213.

20. A copy of this pamphlet, "Der Vorstand der deutschen anthropologischen

Gesellschaft an die Lehrer der höheren Unterrichtsanstalten und der Volksschulen," exists in NL Virchow, 2642.

21. I draw this conclusion from the fact that eye color was the only color that anthropologists recommended be measured comparatively and was the first category given in each of the eleven combinations.

22. Mosse is surely correct in observing that "the survey must have made Jewish children conscious of their minority status and their supposedly different origins." Mosse, *Toward the Final Solution,* 91.

23. Jack Goody shows how lists organize thought, action, and objects and are thus a kind of cosmological representation. The *Schulstatistik* tables functioned similarly. See Jack Goody, "What's in a List," in *The Domestication of the Savage Mind* (Cambridge: Cambridge University Press, 1977), 74–111.

24. See "Cassenbericht," in *Sechste Allgemeine Versammlung der Deutschen Anthropologischen Gesellschaft in München. 9–11 August 1875,* 21–22. Hamburg never conducted the survey. As Mosse notes, the Hamburg government explained that the survey conflicted with ideas of personal liberty. Mosse, *Toward the Final Solution.* (One Jewish school from Hamburg did complete the survey and sent it separately to Virchow.) See Rudolf Virchow, "Gesammtbericht über die von der deutschen anthropologischen Gesellschaft veranlassten Erhebungen über die Farbe der Haut, der Haare und der Augen der Schulkinder in Deutschland," *AA* 16 (1886): 275–475, 283–84.

25. See the tabulation for Altenburg, Saxony, in Virchow Papers, 2644.

26. These maps were by the cartographer Daniel Gottlob Reymann. Some copies survive in the Virchow Papers, 2644, as well as in the ABGAEU.

27. Virchow gives some information on his map coloring in his "Berichterstattung über die statistischen Erhebungen bezüglich der Farbe der Augen, der Haare und der Haut," 101. More finished versions of these maps appear in Virchow, "Gesammtbericht."

28. ". . . ein recht respectabler Gegensatz gegen die wirklichen Germanen." Virchow, "Berichterstattung über die statistischen Erhebungen bezüglich der Farbe der Augen, der Haare und der Haut," 102.

29. Rudolf Virchow, "Gesammtbericht über die Statistik der Farbe der Augen, der Haare und der Haut der Schulkinder in Deutschland," *CBDAG* 16 (1885): 89–100, 91.

30. The last explanation had recently been put forward in the Berlin Anthropology Society's journal and seems to have been the most commonly held among German anthropologists at the time the survey results were evaluated. See Richard Andree, "Rothe Haare," *ZfE* 10 (1878): 335–45. Virchow cites James Cowles Prichard's *Researches into the Physical History of Mankind* (London, 1844), 4:597, as the source for the view that Jews took on the physical characteristics of the population into which they became assimilated.

31. Virchow, "Gesammtbericht" (*CBDAG*), 91.

32. Virchow, "Gesammtbericht" (*AA*), 368.

33. Virchow, "Gesammtbericht" (*CBDAG*), 92.

34. Virchow, "Gesammtbericht" (*AA*), 299–300.

35. Such newspaper reports survive in the Virchow Papers. See, for example, *Nichtpolitische Zeitung* (Munich), 13 August [1874?]; and Victor Böhmert, "Die sächsische Erhebungen über die Farbe der Haut, der Haare und der Augen der schulpflichtigen Jugend (Aus dem statistischen Bureau des Köngl. Ministeriums des Innern)," *Wissenschaftliche Beilage der Leipziger Zeitung,* 23 November 1876, 581–85, Virchow Papers, 2644.

36. While I have found no direct evidence of popular memories of this study in Germany, there is such evidence in Austria, where a similar survey was conducted several years later. An 1890 article in the *Wiener Familien Journal* begins: "Our younger readers will certainly still remember that one day in school they were examined to find out what kind of hair and eyes they had and if their skin was whitish or brownish: in short if they were blond or brunet." C. Falkenhorst, "Von Blonden und Brünetten," *Wiener Familien Journal,* vol. 8 (1890), Virchow Papers, 3003.

37. I estimate that 81 percent of all children in Germany between the ages of six and fourteen participated in the survey. I arrived at this figure using German census data from 1871 and 1880. Since the age group measured by anthropologists was six to fourteen, while the census included groups from from five to nine and from ten to fourteen, I subtracted one-fifth from the total of the age group five to nine to reflect the absence of five-year-old children, on the assumption that there were an equal number of children of each age. I thus calculated as follows (figures are in thousands). For census year 1871,

$$4,626 \text{ (age 5--9)} \times \tfrac{4}{5} = 3,701 \text{ (age 6--9)} + 4,270 \text{ (age 10--14)}$$
$$= 7,971 \text{ (total 6--14)}.$$

For census year 1880,

$$5,171 \text{ (age 5--9)} \times \tfrac{4}{5} = 4,137 \text{ (age 6--9)} + 4,676 \text{ (age 10--14)}$$
$$= 8,813 \text{ (total 6--14)}.$$

I then averaged the total population of six- to fourteen-year-old children for 1871 and 1880 to estimate the number of children in this age group in Germany at the time of the study (the mid-1870s): 8,392. The number measured was 6,759, or 81 percent of the relevant age group. This figure does not reflect the teachers also directly involved in the study and the parents indirectly involved. For the statistics, see B. R. Mitchell, *European Historical Statistics, 1750–1970* (London: Macmillan, 1975).

38. I do not mean to assert that the survey of German races itself caused German anti-Semitism. Indeed, studies of hair, eye, and skin color were conducted in Belgium, Switzerland, and German-speaking Austria before 1885, although there is no indication of whether these studies also excluded Jews or of how they were conducted. Virchow used the results of these other studies to bolster his assertion of the peculiar blondness (and therefore whiteness) of the population of Germany. See Rudolf Virchow, "Die Verbreitung des blonden und des brünetten Typus in Mitteleuropa," *Sitzungsberichte der Königlich Preussischen Akademie der Wissenschaften zu Berlin* 5 (1885): 39–47, 39–40.

39. Johannes Ranke, "Somatisch-anthropologische Beobachtungen," in *An-*

leitung zur deutschen Landes- und Volksforschung, ed. Alfred Kirchhoff (Stuttgart: J. Engelhorn, 1889), 329–80, 332–39.

40. Julius Kollmann, "Die Verbreitung des blonden und des brünetten Typus in Mitteleuropa," *CBDAG* 16 (1885): 33–35.

41. See Virchow, "Gesammtbericht" (*CBDAG*).

42. While Nietzsche does not specify that "the more careful ethnographical maps of Germany" to which he refers are Virchow's, he does name Virchow elsewhere in that passage. The contemporary anthropologist Otto Ammon also identified the maps to which Nietzsche referred as Virchow's (see n. 43 below). Friedrich Nietzsche, *On the Genealogy of Morals,* trans. Walter Kaufmann and R. J. Hollingdale (New York: Random House, 1967), essay 1, p. 5. Kaufmann and Hollingdale translate "unge-heuern Nachschlag" as "tremendous *counterattack.*" However, Nietzsche's association in this paragraph of primitive races and socialism suggests that "monstrous *atavism*" renders his meaning more accurately. Nietzsche actually claims to use Virchow's map against the view, which he attributes to Virchow, that the brown people were of Celtic origin. Virchow, however, never presented a definite view on the origin of the non-Jewish brown type. At one point, he did argue against the view (held by Quatrefages) that the non-Jewish brown type was Slavic in origin and suspected instead a mixture of Celts, Romans, Illyrians, and Rhaetians. See Rudolf Virchow, "Die Verbreitung des blonden und des brünetten Typus in Mitteleuropa."

43. Otto Ammon, *Die Gesellschaftsordnung und ihre natürliche Grundlagen: Ent-wurf einer Sozial-Anthropologie zum Gebrauch für alle Gebildeten, die sich mit sozialen Fragen befassen* (Jena: Gustav Fischer, 1895), 173–74.

44. I discuss this study in terms of skills and tacit knowledge in my "Anti-Semi-tism as Skill: Rudolf Virchow's Schulstatistik and the Racial Composition of Ger-many," *Central European History* 32 (1999): 409–29.

45. Virchow, "Über die Methode der wissenschaftlichen Anthropologie."

46. The phrase comes from Michael Burleigh and Wolfgang Wippermann, *The Racial State: Germany, 1933–1945* (Cambridge: Cambridge University Press, 1991).

CHAPTER 7

1. The title of this chapter, "The Secret of Primitive Accumulation," is taken from the title of chap. 6, vol. 1, of Karl Marx, *Capital,* trans. Samuel Moore and Ed-ward Aveling (New York: International, 1967). I try to make an argument similar to one made by Marx, albeit in reference to a different historical moment, when he writes, "As a matter of fact, the methods of primitive accumulation are anything but idyllic. . . . And the history of this, their expropriation, is written in the annals of mankind in letters of blood and fire" (pp. 668–69).

2. There is an enormous literature on consumer culture and commodities in this period. The three most useful analyses for the present argument are Georg Lukács, "Reification and the Consciousness of the Proletariat," in *History and Class Conscious-ness,* trans. Rodney Livingstone (Cambridge, Mass.: MIT Press, 1971), 83–222; Walter Benjamin, *Charles Baudelaire: A Lyric Poet in the Era of High Capitalism,* trans. Harry Zohn (London: Verso, 1983); and the essays collected in Victoria de Grazia and Ellen

Furlough, eds., *The Sex of Things: Gender and Consumption in Historical Perspective* (Berkeley and Los Angeles: University of California Press, 1996).

3. This chapter is an essay in economic anthropology in the tradition of Marx's analysis of commodities in *Capital* and Marcel Mauss's analysis of gifts in *The Gift: Forms and Functions of Exchange in Archaic Societies* (1950), trans. Ian Cunnison (London: Cohen & West, 1969). Recently, anthropologists have developed analyses of exchange that seek to overcome the gift/commodity distinction, which Mauss himself found problematic. See Marshall Sahlins, *Stone Age Economics* (New York: Aldine, 1972); Pierre Bourdieu, *Outline of a Theory of Practice,* trans. Richard Nice (Cambridge: Cambridge University Press, 1972); Maurice Godelier, "The Rationality of Economic System," in *Rationality and Irrationality in Economics,* trans. Brian Pearce (London: New Left, 1972), 243–319; and C. A. Gregory, *Gifts and Commodities* (London: Academic, 1982). Marilyn Strathern demonstrates the importance of not only analyzing exchange as a way in which goods are distributed but also considering the specific meanings of exchanges and goods in various societies. See Marilyn Strathern, *The Gender of the Gift: Problems with Women and Problems with Society in Melanesia* (Berkeley and Los Angeles: University of California Press, 1988). The transformation of objects into anthropological evidence has recently been the subject of much excellent work. Most important for the present account has been Nicholas Thomas, *Entangled Objects: Exchange, Material Culture, and Colonialism in the Pacific* (Cambridge, Mass.: Harvard University Press, 1991). Thomas observes that, long before anthropologists distinguished gift and commodity economies, the two systems were inextricably linked in a global system. Thomas studies both the consumption of European goods by the indigenous populations of colonies in the Pacific and the collection of indigenous goods by Europeans. These goods, Thomas argues, are not merely blank spaces within systems of exchange but rather "entangled" in, that is, given meaning by, those systems. Furthermore, Thomas shows, both European and colonized indigenous societies conceive of themselves in terms of theories of exchange. Differences in systems of exchange not only provide "modern" societies with a means of differentiating themselves from "primitive" societies but also allow Fijians, for example, to differentiate themselves from European societies. See also Arjun Appadurai, "Introduction: Commodities and the Politics of Value," in *The Social Life of Things: Commodities in Cultural Perspective,* ed. Arjun Appadurai (Cambridge: Cambridge University Press, 1986), 3–63, 5; Igor Kopytoff, "The Cultural Biography of Things: Commoditization as Process," in Appadurai, ed., *The Social Life of Things,* 64–91; Barbara Kirschenblatt-Gimblett, "Objects of Ethnography," in *Exhibiting Cultures: The Poetics and Politics of Museum Display,* ed. Ivan Karp and Steven D. Lavine (Washington, D.C.: Smithsonian Institution Press, 1990), 386–443; and James Clifford, "On Collecting Art and Culture." See also the essays collected in George W. Stocking Jr., ed., *Objects and Others: Essays on Museums and Material Culture* (Madison: University of Wisconsin Press, 1985), esp. James Clifford, "Objects and Selves—an Afterward," 236–46.

4. On the history of the Marshall Islands, see Francis X. Hezel, *The First Taint of Civilization: A History of the Caroline and Marshall Islands in the Pre-Colonial Days, 1521–1885* (Honolulu: University of Hawaii Press, 1983). For Kabua and German imperialism, see pp. 290–306. The first German merchants arrived in the Marshall Islands in 1859. The Marshalls became a German protectorate in 1885, administered

by a concession company. Germany formally established colonial rule in the Marshalls in 1899.

5. Kabua to Kaiser Wilhelm II, 2 February 1909, and Bernhard Dernburg (Imperial Colonial Office) to Geheimes Zivilkabinett, 9 July 1909, GStA PK, I. HA, Rep. 89, Geheimes Zivilkabinett, Nr. 20489, Bl. 32–35, 31 (M).

6. Geheimes Zivilkabinett to Bernhard Dernburg, 18 August 1909, Dernburg to Geheimes Zivilkabinett, 27 August 1909, and Geheimes Zivilkabinett to Dernburg, 28 September 1909, GStA PK, I. HA, Rep. 89, Geheimes Zivilkabinett, Nr. 20489, Bl. 36–38 (M).

7. See General Administration of the Royal Museums to Adalbert Falk (minister of culture), 19 May 1870, and Falk's reply, 15 July 1870, MfV, IB 50, 523/70, 726/70. The context of the statement was an attempt by Leipzig anthropologists to have German embassy personnel collect for them. See also Otto von Bismarck to General Consul Gerlich (Calcutta), 14 September 1888, and Gerlich to Bismarck, 21 September 1888, BAP, Auswärtiges Amt, 37865, Bl. 87–88, 96–99; and Wilhelm von Gossler (minister of culture) to Bismarck, 29 November 1888, BAP, Auswärtiges Amt, 37866, Bl. 20–21.

8. The legislation was first suggested by the Royal Museums in Berlin to the minister of culture, who passed it on to Bismarck to propose to the Bundesrath. See General Administration of the Royal Museums to Ministry of Culture, March 1888, GStA PK, I. HA, Rep. 76Ve, Cultusministerium, Sekt. 15, Abt. XI, Nr. 2, Bd. 7, unnumbered sheets (M); Wilhelm von Gossler (minister of culture) to Bismarck, 11 February 1889, GStA PK, I. HA, Rep. 76Ve, Cultusministerium, Sekt. 15, Abt. XI, Nr. 2, Bd. 8, unnumbered sheets (M); Bundesrath, "Anweisung betreffend die Behandlung der aus den Deutschen Schutzgebieten eingehenden wissenschaftlichen Sendungen," 3 August 1889, MfV, IB 46, vol. 1, 763/90; and "Runderlass, betr. die ethnographischen und naturwissenschaftlichen Sammlungen der in den Schutzgebieten befindlichen Beamten und Militärpersonen," *Kolonialblatt* (1896), 669, in MfV, IB 46, vol. 1, 763/90. On the effects of this law on German anthropology museums outside Berlin, see Wolfgang Lustig, "'Außer ein paar zerbrochenen Pfeilen nichts zu verteilen . . .'— Ethnographische Sammlungen aus den detuschen Kolonien und ihre Verteilung an Museen 1889 bis 1914," *Mitteilungen aus dem Museum für Völkerkunde Hamburg* 18 (1988): 157–78.

9. These are the only years for which figures are available. The figures are taken from MfV, IB 46, vol. 2, 1360/96, 1111/98, 888/00, 1169/1901; vol. 3, 1457/02, 1549/04, 1870/06, 1858/07.

10. See George A. Dorsey, "Notes on the Anthropological Museums of Central Europe," *American Anthropologist,* n.s., 1 (1899): 462–74, 468–69.

11. Schlözer (German Embassy in Rio de Janeiro) to Otto von Bismarck, 3 September 1888, Foreign Office to Wilhelm von Gossler, 27 September 1888, Richard Schöne to Gossler, 16 October 1888, Wilhelm von Gossler to Bismarck, 7 November 1888, Foreign Office to Wilhelm von Gossler, 12 December 1888, and Wilhelm von Gossler to Bismarck, 3 January 1889, GStA PK, I. HA, Rep. 76Ve, Cultusministerium, Sekt. 15, Abt. XI, Nr. 2, Bd. 8, unnumbered sheets (M). German Embassy in Brazil to Imperial Chancellor Leo von Caprivi, 24 January 1892, GStA PK, I. HA,

Rep. 76Ve, Cultusministerium, Sekt. 15, Abt. XI, Nr. 2, Bd. 9, unnumbered sheets (M).

12. The documents relevant to the exchanges with Siam are the following: Richard Schöne (general director of the Royal Museums) to Wilhelm von Gossler (minister of culture), 2 January 1882, GStA PK, I. HA, Rep. 76Ve, Cultusministerium, Sekt. 15, Abt. XI, Nr. 2, Bd. 3, unnumbered sheets (M); Foreign Office to Geheimes Zivilkabinett, 14 August 1882, Professor Dr. Lessing (director of the Museum of Applied Arts) to Geheimes Zivilkabinett, 14 March 1883, Geheimes Zivilkabinett to royal house-minister, 19 May 1883, Ministry of Culture and Ministry of War to Kaiser Wilhelm I, 10 February 1883, Foreign Ministry to Ministry of State and Ministry of Culture, 12 May 1882, Ministry of Culture to Geheimes Zivilkabinett, 29 August 1882, 22 February 1883, Geheimes Zivilkabinett to Ministry of Culture, 19 May 1883, and Ministry of Culture to Geheimes Zivilkabinett, 5 February 1886, 5 February 1887, GStA PK, I. HA, Rep. 89, Geheimes Zivilkabinett, Nr. 20489, Bl. 79, 80, 85–87, 91–95, 98–99, 105–7, 133, 161–64 (M).

13. Luschan, *Völker, Rassen, Sprachen*. Volker Harms treats the use of colonial military violence to acquire artifacts in "Ethnographische Kunstobjekte als Beute des europäischen Kolonialismus," *Kritische Berichte* 23 (1995): 15–31.

14. Chief of the Admiralty to Board of Directors of the Berlin Anthropological Society, 8 August 1873, ABGAEU.

15. Virchow et al., "Ratschläge für anthropologische Untersuchung auf Expeditionen der Marine," 329.

16. Ibid., 341.

17. Ibid., 325.

18. Gustav Thaulow, "Rathschläge für anthropologische Untersuchungen auf Expedition der Marine," *ZfE* 6 (1874): 102–18.

19. General Administration of the Royal Museums to Ministry of Culture, 8 August 1873, GStA PK, I. HA, Rep. 76Ve, Cultusministerium, Sekt. 15, Abt. XI, Nr. 2, Bd. 1, Bl. 42–48 (M).

20. Adolf Bastian to General Administration of the Royal Museums, 22 April 1874, Admiralty to General Administration of the Royal Museums, 25 May 1874, and General Administration of the Royal Museums to Admiralty, 27 October 1874, MfV, IB 48, vol. 1, 670/74.

21. See Ulrich, memo, 5 February 1897, MfV, XIII, vol. 1, 143/97.

22. Admiralty to Dr. Friedländer (director of the Coin-Cabinet), 28 July 1882, MfV, IB 48, vol. 1, 1717/82.

23. Felix von Luschan to Commanding Admiral von Knorr, 7 August 1897, MfV, IB 48, vol. 1, 1009/97.

24. The museum did not trust the purchasing decisions of the untrained paymaster and sought a way to have the officer control purchases without insulting the paymaster. See, for example, Felix von Luschan to Lieutenant Kuthe, 9 January 1899, MfV, IB 48, vol. 1, 32/99.

25. Felix von Luschan to Rear Admiral Alfred von Tirpitz, 5 November 1898,

MfV, IB 48, vol. 1, 1223/98. Unfortunately, there is no specific information about the training that Kuthe received.

26. See, for example, Felix von Luschan to Lieutenant Kuthe, 4 April 1899, MfV, IB 48, vol. 1, 32/99.

27. Lieutenant Kuthe to Imperial Command, 25 April 1899, and Kuthe, "Ethnographischer Bericht über die Eigeborenen der Musa Halbinsel (Nordwestlicher Teil von Neu-Mecklenburg)" (51 pp.) (1899), MfV, IB 48, vol. 1, 822/99.

28. See the permanent secretary of the Imperial Navy Office to the director of the Royal Museum of Ethnology, 28 November 1902, MfV, IB 48, vol. 1, 1626/02.

29. Luschan to the commander of the *Seagull,* 10 December 1900, MfV, IB 48, vol. 1, 894/00.

30. See, for example, Luschan's worries about "pieces made for trade" in Felix von Luschan to Captain Schack, 5 October 1899, MfV, IB 48, vol. 1, 1047/99, and his complaints about tourist curios in Luschan to Edgar Walden, 29 May 1908, MfV, IB71, vol. 2, 1136/08.

31. Adolf Bastian to General Administration of the Royal Museum, 21 July 1900, forwarded to the imperial chancellor, 13 September 1900, BAP, Auswärtiges Amt, 37869, Bl. 75–76. See also the minister of culture to the imperial chancellor, 21 July 1900, BAP, Auswärtiges Amt, 37869, Bl. 75–76.

32. Captain von Frantzius to the chief of the Admiralty, 9 March 1887, MfV, IB 48, vol. 1, 645/87.

33. Luschan rather than Bastian, the museum's director, served as the main liaison between anthropologists and the military. This may have been in part because of Bastian's evident inability or unwillingness to write about anthropology in a clear, generally understandable language. As the Heidelberg anthropologist Alexander von Frantzius (no known relation to the lieutenant commander) explained, for communicating the museum's wishes to the navy, Bastian is "unfortunately the least useful because of his totally inappropriate style." Alexander von Frantzius to Rudolf Virchow, 5 November 1872, Andree, 161–63.

34. The *Schutztruppen* were nominally under the authority of the navy, although, in practice, imperial governors commanded them.

35. See, for example, Felix von Luschan to the governor of East Africa, 16 December 1896, and Luschan to the Imperial Landeshauptmannschaft of Togo, 20 April 1897, MfV, IB 46, vol. 2, 1503/96, 474/97.

36. For an excellent discussion of the historiography of the Maji Maji uprising, see Marcia Wright, "Maji Maji: Prophecy and Historiography," in *Revealing Prophets: Prophecy in East African History,* ed. David M. Anderson and Douglas H. Johnson (London: James Currey, 1995), 124–42. For an account of the Maji Maji rebellion based not only on German sources but also on African oral history sources, see G. C. K. Gwassa, "African Methods of Warfare during the Maji Maji War, 1905–1907," in *War and Society in Africa,* ed. Bethwell A. Ogot (London: Frank Cass, 1972), 123–48. For an article connecting the Maji Maji uprising to the history of African nationalism, see Terence Ranger, "The Connection between 'Primary Resistance' Movements and Modern Mass Nationalism in East and Central Africa," *Journal of African History* 9

(1968): 437–53, 631–41. See also Iliffe, *A Modern History of Tanganyika;* Wright, "East Africa"; Woodruff D. Smith, *The German Colonial Empire* (Chapel Hill: University of North Carolina Press, 1978), 91–107; and Horst Gründer, *Geschichte der deutschen Kolonien,* 2d ed. (Munich: Ferdinand Schöningh, 1991), 154–69.

37. Foreign Office, Colonial Division, to Felix von Luschan, 7 May 1906, MfV, IB 78, 1009/06. See also the report on the objects by Karl Weule on the *Admiral* in the Red Sea to [Luschan], 30 December 1906, MfV, IB 78, 38/07.

38. Poisoned arrows also represented a real threat to anthropologists working with them. Oswald Richter, a volunteer in the Berlin museum, jabbed himself with a poisoned arrow from Semang while he was a student in Dresden and died from the wound several years later. See O. Nöffer, preface to "Über die Idealen und Praktischen Aufgaben der Ethnographischen Museen," by Oswald Richter, *Museumskunde* 4 (1908): 92–93.

39. Felix von Luschan to Wilhelm Foy, director of the anthropology museum in Cologne, 13 July 1907, Luschan to the director of the Colonial Section of the Foreign Office, 15 March 1907, Luschan to the director of the Colonial Section of the Foreign Office, 12 April 1907, Luschan, memo, 30 July 1907, Luschan to the permanent secretary of the Imperial Colonial Office, 3 June 1907, Luschan, memo, 30 July 1907, and Colonial Section of the Foreign Office to Luschan, 18 April 1907, MfV, IB 78, 308/07. When it was learned that the museum planned to destroy some objects in its possession, other individuals and museums in Germany, whose access to anthropological objects had been limited by the 1889 colonial collection law, claimed them. See Lauchheim (in Württemburg) to Luschan, 1 October 1907, and Luschan's response, 10 December 1907, MfV, IB 78, 1831/07; Willy Sangmeister to Luschan, 15 July 1907, MfV, IB 78, 1413/07.

40. Rudolf Virchow, "Anthropologie und prähistorische Forschungen," in Neumayer, ed., *Anleitung zu Wissenschaftlichen Beobachtungen auf Reisen* (1st ed.), 571–90.

41. Luschan to Wilhelm Waldeyer, 10 May 1906, MfV, IB 39, vol. 1, 849/06.

42. Felix von Luschan to Imperial Government of East Africa in Dar es Salaam, 31 March 1906, MfV, IB 39, vol. 1, 589/06. It is not clear whether the governor sent the skulls that Luschan requested.

43. Felix von Luschan to Imperial Government of East Africa in Dar es Salaam, 11 July 1906, MfV, IB 39, vol. 2, 1240/06.

44. Imperial Government of East Africa in Dar es Salaam to Felix von Luschan, 3 October 1906, MfV, IB 39, vol. 2, 1240/06. Dr. Dempwolf, captain, Medical Corps, in Triga, German East Africa, to Luschan, 4 December 1906, MfV, IB 39, vol. 2, 1288/06.

45. As one of Luschan's contacts in East Africa wrote, "Only a rebellion or a battle can provide series of skulls; the Hehe are so opposed to 'desecration of the dead' that officials declined to burn the corpses of plague victims because that would lead to unrest and concealment of cases of the plague." Dr. Dempwolf to Felix von Luschan, 16 April 1907, MfV, IB 39, vol. 2, 1288/06. Once the Maji Maji uprising had been put down, the governor of East Africa wrote that there would be few opportunities to get freshly severed heads for Luschan. See the imperial governor of German East Africa to Royal Museum of Ethnology, 6 July 1906, MfV, IB 39, vol. 1, 589/06.

46. Reinhold Hensel, "Die Schädel der Corados," *ZfE* 2 (1870): 195–203.

47. Thus, when writing of the 150 skulls that he purchased in New Guinea, Meyer commented, "Here I did not have to steal them, as I did in the Philippines." A. B. Meyer to Rudolf Virchow, 22 October 1873, NL Virchow, 1429.

48. Felix von Luschan to Herr Biallowons, German East Africa, 3 January 1907, MfV, IB 39, vol. 2, 2330/06.

49. Felix von Luschan to Dr. E. Schulz, imperial judge, Apia, Samoa, 30 January 1911, Schulz to Luschan, 22 March 1911, 17 May 1911, and Luschan to Shulz, 22 July 1911, MfV, IB 39, vol. 4, 168/11.

50. Anneli Yaam to Felix von Luschan, 29 February 1904, MfV, IB 39, vol. 1, 461/01.

51. Anneli Yaam to Felix von Luschan, 7 April 1904, MfV, IB 39, vol. 1, 657/04; Luschan to Yaam, 11 May 1904, MfV, IB 39, vol. 1, 579/04; Luschan to Yaam, 14 November 1905, MfV, IB 39, vol. 1, 2170/05.

52. A number of Virchow's hair samples are in the Museum of Natural History in Berlin. While working with Virchow's literary remains in the archive of the Academy of Sciences in Berlin, I was also surprised by item 2693, "Head Hair Samples, 7 bundles (no date)."

53. The German Anthropological Society considered hair important enough to set up a "hair commission" in 1884 to standardize methods for taking hair samples. The commission was made up of the Berlin Anthropologists Virchow, Fritsch, and Wilhelm Waldeyer as well as the Munich anthropologist Johannes Ranke. See "Bericht der Haarkommission," *CBDAG* 16 (1885): 129–34. The Leipzig geography professor Oscar Peschel held the slightly idiosyncratic view that hair constituted the most important racial characteristic. See Oscar Peschel, *Völkerkunde,* 2d ed. (Leipzig: Duncker & Humboldt, 1875), 102. Although taking hair was relatively easy, people did sometimes resist giving anthropologists locks of hair. See Otto Finsch's description of his collection of 192 hair samples in "Die Schädelsammlung meiner Südsee-Reisen 1879/82, nach 25 jähriger Vergessenheit ihrer Bestimmung zugeführt," ABGAEU.

54. Virchow first introduced the *Negritofrage* in December 1870 with two skulls from the Philippines. A. B. Meyer, a contact of Virchow's traveling in the Philippines, presented evidence of the relation of Philippine and Papuan Negritos based on their hair form. Meyer soon managed to disinter seven skeletons, which he mailed to Virchow. On the basis of these skeletons, Virchow concluded that Negritos had no relation to Africans or to Australians. While hair could not decide the *Negritofrage,* it did arouse anthropologists' interest when no skeletal remains were available. See A. B. Meyer to Rudolf Virchow, 25 April 1872, NL Virchow, 1429; Virchow, "Ueber Negrito- und Igorroten-Schädel von den Philippinen"; and [?] Pincus, "Die Haare der Negritos auf den Philippinen," *VBGAEU* 5 (1873): 155–56.

55. Luschan, "Anthropologie, Ethnologie und Urgeschichte," 37–38.

56. Luschan, *Beiträge,* 9.

57. Luschan, "Anthropologie, Ethnologie und Urgeschichte," 38.

58. Ibid., 5.

59. This informant was working on German soldiers in Baden. See Otto Ammon to Rudolf Virchow, 14 May 1890, Andree, 19–20.

60. Luschan, "Anthropologie, Ethnologie und Urgeschichte," 31–32. One of Luschan's students noted about the dynamometer: "It is the only [instrument] that gives the subjects any joy and attracts them to measurement. They are driven by curiosity about their strength to submit willingly to the entire procedure of anthropological evaluation. That, more than its scientific value, is the significance of the dynamometer." Krum Drontschilow, *Beiträge zur Anthropologie der Bulgaren* (Braunschweig: Vieweg, 1914), 25. This dissertation is located in HU, Phil. Fak., Promotionsvorgänge, Nr. 553, Bl. 224–79.

61. Luschan, "Bericht über eine im Sommer 1905 ausgeführte Reise in Süd Afrika," in BAP, Auswärtiges Amt, 37582, Bl. 109.

62. In the period before Germany took colonies, Bastian discussed sending medical students to the Dutch colonial service. See Adolf Bastian to Rudolf Virchow, September 1879, November 1879, NL Virchow, 117, pt. I, Bl. 29–33. Virchow's colleague in the medical faculty of the University of Berlin, Wilhelm Waldeyer, writes of former students currently in the military in German East Africa who wish to collect for him. See Wilhelm Waldeyer to Foreign Office, 2 January 1892, BAP, Reichskolonialamt, 6109, Bl. 52.

63. See S. Weissenberg, "Ueber die Formen der Hand und des Fusses," *ZfE* 27 (1895): 82–111.

64. See Luschan, "Anthropologie, Ethnologie und Urgeschichte," 6–7.

65. See Franz Boas and Ales Hrdlicka, "Facial Casts," *American Anthropologist,* n.s., 7 (1905): 169; and Luschan, "Anthropologie, Ethnologie und Urgeschichte," 6.

66. Otto Finsch, *Gesichtsmasken von Völkertypen der Südsee und dem malayischen Archipel nach Leben abgegossen in den Jahren 1879–1882* (Bremen: Homeyer & Meyer, 1887), 2.

67. Hermann von Schlagintweit relates that copies of a series of casts that he made in Asia had been reproduced and sold to museums in London, St. Petersburg, Calcutta, Bombay, Madras, Paris, and Cambridge, Massachusetts. See Hermann von Schlagintweit to Rudolf Virchow, 13 May 1873, *Briefe an Rudolf Virchow* (Berlin: Litteraturarchiv-Gesellschaft, 1921), 47–48. Copies of Otto Finsch's plaster casts could be purchased in Castan's Panopticon in Berlin and the Berlin museum of ethnology. Museums in Paris, Florence, St. Petersburg, Sydney, Berlin, Dresden, Bremen, and Leiden all displayed Finsch's collection. See Finsch, *Gesichtsmasken.* Frederick Starr of the Anthropology Department at the University of Chicago exchanged sixteen plaster casts of Pueblo Indians for casts of an entire Dinka body and a series of plaster masks made by Franz Stuhlmann. See Frederick Starr to Felix von Luschan, 26 April 1901, MfV, IB 39, vol. 1, 503/01.

68. The Red Eagle Order was founded in the eighteenth century as a group of thirty noblemen who were supposed to be particularly honest and were required to donate money to charities. By the second half of the nineteenth century, the Red Eagle Order became significantly larger and no longer required particular duties from its

members. The Crown Order was founded by King Wilhelm in 1861 to commemo-
rate his own ascension to the throne. The two orders were nominally equal, although
the Red Eagle seems to have been slightly more esteemed, perhaps because it was an
older order. For an English translation of the statutes of the Red Eagle and the Crown
Orders, see William E. Hamelman, *Of Red Eagles and Royal Crowns* (Dallas: Taylor,
1978). For an excellent discussion of the role of orders in German society and their
commoditization in the later nineteenth century, see Alastair Thomson, "Honours
Uneven: Decorations, the State, and Bourgeois Society in Imperial Germany," *Past
and Present* 144 (1994): 171–204.

69. For an excellent account of the role of orders in the culture and politics of an-
thropological collecting in New Mecklenburg, see Rainer Buschmann, "Franz Bolu-
minski and the Wonderland of Carvings: Towards an Ethnography of Collection
Activity," *Baessler-Archiv* 44 (1996): 185–210. Cornelia Essner considers aspects of
Bastian's use of royal orders to get artifacts in "Berlins Völkerkunde-Museum in der
Kolonialära: Anmerkungen zum Verhältnis von Ethnologie und Kolonialismus in
Deutschland," in *Berlin in Geschichte und Gegenwart: Jahrbuch des Landesarchivs
Berlin,* ed. Hans J. Reichhardt (Berlin: Siedler, 1986), 65–94. For the similar use of
orders by the Munich museum, see Smolka, *Völkerkunde in München,* 146–49.

70. Georg Wislicenus explains the ubiquity of black tie in the colonies to justify
including formal evening wear in a list of necessary equipment for traveling scientists.
See Wislicenus, "Einige Winke für die Ausrüstung und die Ausführung von
Forschungsreisen," 744.

71. Adolf Bastian to Rudolf Virchow, November 1879, NL Virchow, 117, pt. I,
Bl. 31–33.

72. There is no indication in the records of the Ministry of Culture or the Prussian king's Privy Council that anyone not of European descent was ever even nominated for an order. Indeed, in the 1870s, it was considered problematic to give
Prussian orders to German Jews. It appears that one donor was given a thank-you letter from the kaiser rather than an order for his collection at least partly because he was
"of the Mosaic confession." See Adalbert Falk (minister of culture) to Kaiser Wilhelm
I, 5 July 1879, GStA PK, Rep. 89, Geheimes Zivilkabinett, Nr. 20489, Bl. 35–36 (M).

73. Richard Schöne (general director of the Royal Museums) reported this. See
Richard Schöne to the minister of culture, 6 January 1883, GStA PK, I. HA, Rep.
76Ve, Cultusministerium, Sekt. 15, Abt. XI, Nr. 2, Bd. 4, unnumbered sheets (M).

74. Max Braun to Adolf Bastian, 27 June 1898, MfV, IB 48, Bd. 1, 927/98.

75. Two of Bastian's younger colleagues reported Bastian's turn of phrase independently. See Felix von Luschan to Ministry of Culture, 23 December 1904, MfV, IB
46, Bd. 3, 1977/04; and Steinen, *Unter den Naturvölkern Zentral-Brasiliens,* vii–viii,
132.

76. Virchow made a similar argument about preserving the supposedly primitive
before modernity destroyed it in his opening address to the general assembly of the
German Anthropological Society in Schweren, 1871, 46. Bastian was also aware that
he was collecting from societies that were being "quickly changed by European culture" and others that were "in the process of dying out." Bastian's views were reported

by Adalbert Falk. See Adalbert Falk (minister of culture) to Kaiser Wilhelm I, May 1878, GStA PK, I. HA, Rep. 89, Geheimes Zivilkabinett, Nr. 20489, Bl. 25–26 (M). Anthropologists were often correct in believing that the people they studied were dying off. Especially in the South Pacific, colonized societies often suffered from increased deathrates and decreased birthrates as a result of various aspects of European rule, which occasionally led to the extinction of entire societies. In 1899, Luschan learned that the population of the Hermit and Anchor Islands would soon be totally extinct and asked his contact on the HMS *Seagull* to visit them and collect skulls and hair samples before they had all died. (Body parts could not be collected in the South Pacific from graveyards because the acidity of the soil causes corpses to decompose quickly.) See Felix von Luschan to Lieutenant Kuthe, 4 April 1899, MfV, IB 48, vol. 1, 32/99; and Max Moszkowski to Virchow Foundation, 4 December 1909, ABGAEU.

77. Reported in Richard Schöne to Wilhelm von Gossler, 23 May 1885, GStA PK, I. HA, Rep. 76Ve, Cultusministerium, Sekt. 15, Abt. XI, Nr. 2, Bd. 6, Bl. 32–33 (M).

78. This "salvage ethnology" was also an important motivation in British anthropology. See Stocking, *Victorian Anthropology*.

79. For the text of the speech, see Bernd Sösemann, "Die sog. Hunnenrede Wilhelms II: Textkritische und interpretatorische Bemerkungen zur Ansprache des Kaisers vom 27. Juli 1900 in Bremerhaven," *Historische Zeitschrift* 222 (1976): 342–58.

80. On the Boxer uprising, see Joseph W. Esherick, *The Origins of the Boxer Uprising* (Berkeley and Los Angeles: University of California Press, 1987). On Germany's role in this uprising, see especially chaps. 5 and 7.

81. Bastian to General Administration of the Royal Museums, 23 January 1901, BAP, Auswärtiges Amt, 37869, Bl. 100–102. See also Bastian to Lucanus (chief of the Geheimes Zivilkabinett), 27 November 1900, GStA PK, Rep. 89, Geheimes Zivilkabinett, Nr. 20490, Bl. 230–32 (M); Imperial Foreign Office to Imperial Ambassador Mumm von Schwarzenstein in Beijing, 9 January 1901, and Ministry of Culture to the imperial chancellor, 7 March 1901, BAP, Auswärtiges Amt, 37869, Bl. 79, 99; and Mumm to Imperial Chancellor Bernhard von Bülow, 24 July 1901, BAP, Auswärtiges Amt, 37870, Bl. 15–16.

82. Nietzsche, *On the Genealogy of Morality* (Ansell-Pearson/Diethe), essay 2, p. 12.

CHAPTER 8

1. My understanding of the museum as a contested space has been shaped by Susan Leigh Star and James R. Griesemer, "Institutional Ecology, 'Translations,' and Boundary Objects: Amateurs and Professionals in Berkeley's Museum of Vertebrate Zoology, 1907–39," *Social Studies of Science* 19 (1989): 387–420. For an exemplary interpretation of a museum that accounts for its multiple creators, see Donna Haraway, "Teddy Bear Patriarchy," in *Primate Visions: Gender, Race, and Nature in the World of Modern Science* (New York: Routledge, 1989), 26–58. For museums as places to establish ideological hegemonies, see Tony Bennet, *The Birth of the Museum: History, Theory, Politics* (London: Routledge, 1995). For the role of museums in creating national identities in new nations, see Flora E. S. Kaplan, ed., *Museums and the Making of "Our-*

NOTES TO PAGES 173-174

selves": The Role of Objects in National Identity (London: Leicester University Press, 1994). For accounts more directly concerned with nineteenth-century anthropology museums, see Annie E. Coombes, *Reinventing Africa: Museums, Material Culture, and Popular Imagination in Late Victorian and Edwardian England* (New Haven, Conn.: Yale University Press, 1994); David K. van Keuren, "Museums and Ideology: Augustus Pitt-Rivers, Anthropological Museums, and Social Change in Later Victorian England," *Victorian Studies* 28 (1984): 171–89; and Michael Hog, *Ethnologie und Öffentlichkeit: Ein entwicklungsgeschichtlicher Überblick* (Frankfurt: Peter Lang, 1990). William Ryan Chapman argues that anthropologists thought about the broad questions of their discipline by arranging artifacts in museums. See William Ryan Chapman, "Arranging Ethnology: A. H. L. F. Pitt Rivers and the Typological Tradition," in Stocking, ed., *Objects and Others*, 15–48. For accounts of museums as symbolizing European mastery over the world, see Paula Findlen, *Possessing Nature: Museums, Collecting, and Scientific Culture in Early Modern Italy* (Berkeley and Los Angeles: University of California Press, 1993); and Anthony Pagden, *The Fall of Natural Man: The American Indian and the Origins of Comparative Ethnology* (Cambridge: Cambridge University Press, 1982), 12. For a more theoretical account of the museum as a form of knowledge, see John V. Pickstone, "Museological Science? The Place of the Analytical/Comparative in Nineteenth-Century Science, Technology, and Medicine," *History of Science* 32 (1994): 111–38.

2. As Raymond Williams has shown, anxieties about a modern urban economy replacing a traditional pastoral economy emerged even in classical antiquity. See Raymond Williams, *The Country and the City* (London: Chatto & Windus, 1973).

3. See, for example, Adolf Bastian to General Administration of the Royal Museums, December 1894, MfV, XIIa, vol. 1, 1178/95.

4. See, for example, Adolf Bastian to General Administration of the Royal Museums, 31 October 1899, MfV, I/1, vol. 1, 1134/99.

5. The anthropologist Oswald Richter, for example, worried about artifacts becoming "objects of speculation for the world market." See Oswald Richter, "Über die Idealen und Praktischen Aufgaben der Ethnographischen Museen," *Museumskunde* 2 (1906): 189–218; 3 (1907): 14–25, 99–120; 4 (1908): 92–106, 156–68, 224–35; 5 (1909): 102–13, 166–74, 231–36; 6 (1910): 40–60, 131–37. The quotation is from 4 (1908): 95.

6. Felix von Luschan to Edgar Walden, 29 May 1908, MfV, IB71, vol. 2, 1136/08.

7. For example, Luschan found the Berlin Museum's Oceanic and African collections superior to those of the British Museum "because here [in Berlin] we have systematic series, while the Brit. Museum possesses only individual 'curiosities.'" Felix von Luschan to Adolf Bastian, 25 October 1899, MfV, Ic, vol. 4, 639/99.

8. Adolf Bastian, memo, 1885, MfV, IB Litt C., vol. 1, 216a/85.

9. Bastian, *Die Vorgeschichte der Ethnologie;* Adolf Bastian to General Administration of the Royal Museums, 28 January 1899, MfV, Ic, Bd. 4, 467/99; Felix von Luschan to Rear-Admiral Franz Strauch, 29 November 1897, MfV, IB 46, Bd. 2, 1427/97.

10. [?] Castan and Rudolf Virchow, "Australier von Queensland," *VBGAEU* 16 (1884): 407–18, 417; Felix von Luschan to Direction of the Royal Museum of Ethnology, 7 November 1900, MfV, I/1, Bd. 1, 985/00.

11. Steinen, *Unter den Naturvölkern Zentral-Brasiliens,* viii.

12. "Aktstudien von Rasse Typen meist aufgenommen durch Prof. Gustav Fritsch," box in the Archive of the Berliner Gesellschaft für Anthropologie, Ethnologie und Urgeschichte, Schloß Charlottenburg, Berlin.

13. On nineteenth-century erotic photographs of males, see F. Valentine Hooven, "The Birth of Beefcake," in *Beefcake: The Muscle Magazine of America, 1950–1970* (Cologne: Benedikt Taschen, 1995), 16–51. On pornography and representations of prostitution, see Walter Kendrick, *The Secret Museum: Pornography in Modern Culture* (New York: Viking, 1987), 1–32. The essays collected in Lynn Hunt, ed., *The Invention of Pornography: Obscenity and the Origins of Modernity, 1500–1800* (New York: Zone, 1993), also present pornography as an important aspect of modern sensibilities and view it as directed against traditional religious and political authorities. Anthropologists thus may have figured themselves as modern men by consuming pornography.

14. See Adolf Bastian to Adalbert Falk (minister of culture), 3 January 1878, GStA PK, I. HA, Rep. 76Ve, Cultusministerium, Sekt. 15, Abt. III, Nr. 2, Bd. I, unnumbered sheets (M).

15. Adolf Bastian to General Administration of the Royal Museums, 23 August 1876, GStA PK, I. HA, Rep. 76Ve, Cultusministerium, Sekt. 15, Abt. III, Nr. 2, Bd. I, unnumbered sheets (M).

16. Adolf Bastian to Rudolf Virchow, 29 August 1878, NL Virchow, 117, pt. I, Bl. 25–26.

17. Adolf Bastian to Adalbert Falk (minister of culture), 3 January 1878, GStA PK, I. HA, Rep. 76Ve, Cultusministerium, Sekt. 15, Abt. III, Nr. 2, Bd. I, unnumbered sheets (M).

18. Walter Benjamin has provided the classic account of these arcades in his studies of Paris. See Walter Benjamin, *Das Passagen-Werk,* ed. Rolf Tiedemann, 2 vols. (Frankfurt a.M.: Suhrkamp, 1982), and *Charles Baudelaire.* Especially relevant to the present discussion are the sections of the *Passagen-Werk* entitled "Eisenkonstruktion" (pp. 211–31), "Traumhaus, Museum, Brunnenhalle" (pp. 511–23), and "Panorama" (pp. 655–65). Benjamin mentions Castan's panopticon on p. 517. See also Susan Buck-Morss, *The Dialectics of Seeing: Walter Benjamin and the Arcades Project* (Cambridge, Mass.: MIT Press, 1989).

19. Bastian's proposal and the state's reaction are reported by D. C. in the *Vossische Zeitung,* 24 January 1901, MfV, I/1, vol. 1, 94/01. There are unfortunately no other sources documenting this plan. If it were true that Bastian had proposed this iron and glass construction, it would lend further support to the thesis that anthropological display was based on a type of vision related to the covered galleries.

20. See Dorsey, "Notes on the Anthropological Museums of Central Europe," 471.

21. On the Berlin museum of ethnology's cases, see [?] Klutmann, *Das Königliche Museum für Völkerkunde in Berlin,* offprint from the *Zeitschrift für Bauwesen* (Berlin: Ernst & Korn, 1887); Richter, "Über die Idealen und Praktischen Aufgaben der Ethnographischen Museen," 4 (1908): 226; and Panzer, Inc., Berlin, to Royal Museum of Ethnology, 10 October 1904, MfV, Ic, vol. 6, 1575/04.

22. Bastian to General Administration of the Royal Museums, 30 April 1889, MfV, Ic, vol. 2, 426/89.

23. As the museum's architect explained, this design assisted in creating the kind of all-encompassing vision that anthropologists desired: "This kind of display . . . allows for a grouping of the objects that makes easier an overview [*Übersicht*] according to individual ethnic groups, which is especially important in ethnological collections." Klutmann, "Das Königliche Museum für Völkerkunde in Berlin," 8.

24. Alfred Grünwedel to General Administration of the Royal Museums, 11 April 1905, MfV, VIC, vol. 2, 733/05.

25. See *Führer durch das Museum für Völkerkunde*, 7th ed. (Berlin: W. Spemann, 1898).

26. See Dorsey, "Notes on the Anthropological Museums of Central Europe," 468–69.

27. See Alfred Grünwedel, memo, 3 March 1898, MfV, VI, vol. 1, 232/98.

28. Richter, "Über die Idealen und Praktischen Aufgaben der Ethnographischen Museen," 5 (1909): 169.

29. "Die Klemm'sche ethnologische Sammlung," *CBDAG* 1 (1870): 47–48.

30. Lee Rust Brown explains the aesthetics of non-Darwinian natural history museums in his study of the Royal Museum of Natural History in Paris. See Lee Rust Brown, "The Emerson Museum," *Representations* 40 (1992): 57–80. According to Brown, the Paris museum presented specimens not as part of a developmental narrative but rather as illustrations of the classification of species of plants and animals. The museum gave meaning to nature, Brown argues, neither by relating it to a divine creation, nor by placing it in a narrative of gradual development, but rather by presenting it to the classifying consciousness of the visitor. Classification was an activity in which an observer in the present gave meaning to nature. The display cases in the Paris museum, arranged by Georges Cuvier, did not simply exhibit individual specimens to the public; rather, they were "like transparent windows through which the visitor could 'see' families, orders, and classes" (p. 64). The Paris museum, as Brown shows, consisted of multiple layers of transparency. The visitor peered through the glass panes of the cases to the specimens contained within and, through those specimens, to the classifications that they represented.

31. See Adolf Bastian, *Die Seele indischer und hellenischer Philosophie in den Gespenstern moderner Geisterseherei* (Berlin: Weidmann, 1886), and *Der Buddhismus als religions-philosophisches System* (Berlin: Weidmann, 1893).

32. This description and interpretation of the ceiling mosaic comes from "Eröffnung des Museums für Völkerkunde," *Deutscher Reichs- und königlicher Preußischer Staatsanzeiger*, 18 December 1886, in MfV, I, vol. 1, 397a/86.

33. Otto von Bismarck and Robert von Puttkamer to Kaiser Wilhelm I, 21 January 1881, GStA PK, I. HA, Rep. 89, Geheimes Zivilkabinett, 20489, Bl. 52–60 (M).

34. It was Rudolf Virchow who legitimized Schliemann's discoveries in Germany—not as contributions to classical philology but as contributions to natural science. See Rudolf Virchow to Heinrich Schliemann, 4 June 1880, *Die Korrespondenz zwischen Heinrich Schliemann und Rudolf Virchow, 1876–1890*, ed. Joachim Herrmann

et al. (Berlin: Akademie, 1990), 195. Schliemann's finds remained classified as natural scientific and anthropological throughout the lifetime of their discoverer. See Virchow to Schliemann, 8 November 1889, ibid., 523–24. For Virchow's friendship with Schliemann, see David A. Trail, *Schliemann of Troy: Treasure and Deceit* (New York: St. Martin's, 1995), 186–95. Trail provides a good biography of Schliemann, with much detail about his excavations.

35. For Voss on the patriotic significance of the prehistory collection, see Albert Voss to General Administration of the Royal Museums, 29 July 1901, MfV, I/1, vol. 2, 775/01.

36. Wilhelm von Gossler, who served as minister of culture during the crucial years of the founding of the Berlin museum, supported German anthropology largely because he believed that it was a patriotic science primarily about German prehistory. Even in his address at the opening ceremonies of the museum, when he could not have helped but notice that German prehistory represented only one part of anthropology, Gossler held fast to his view of the museum of ethnology as a patriotic display. He maintained that, because the non-Europeans displayed at the museum were, like prehistoric Germans, dependent on the "soil of their home" (*heimatlichen Boden*), viewing their artifacts also increased German patriotism. See Wilhelm von Gossler, address at the opening ceremonies of the Royal Museum of Ethnology, 18 December 1886, MfV, I, vol. 1, 397a/86.

37. Königliche Museen zu Berlin, *Das Koenigliche Museum für Völkerkunde am 18. Dezember 1886* (Berlin: Gebr. Unger, 1886).

38. The fourth floor also contained office space for the Berlin Anthropological Society and the museum's library. The Berlin Anthropological Society was allowed to meet in the museum and use the fourth floor in exchange for giving their collection of artifacts and their library to the museum. The anthropology society was also required to present objects from its physical anthropological collection to the public. See the contract between the Berlin Anthropological Society and the Royal Museum of Ethnology, MfV, IV, 133/88.

39. It is not clear why physical anthropology, which was so central to German anthropology, was marginalized in the museum. I speculate that it had to do with Bastian's equivocal interest in physical anthropology. On the original plans for the physical anthropology display, see Board of Directors of the Berlin Anthropological Society to Adalbert Falk (minister of culture), 24 May 1878, ABGAEU. On the contents of the physical anthropology display, see Wilhelm Waldeyer and Max Bartels to Konrad von Studt (minister of culture), 23 July 1900, ABGAEU. Bastian was never enthusiastic about displaying physical anthropological objects in the museum of ethnology, and, although Luschan favored such exhibits, the collection never flourished. See Otto Finsch to Felix von Luschan, 13 February 1900, "Finsch, Otto," NL Luschan, Bl. 40; and Luschan to General Administration of the Royal Museums, 9 December 1891, MfV, Ic, vol. 2, 1490/91.

40. Dorsey, "Notes on the Anthropological Museums of Central Europe," 468–69.

41. Adolf Bastian to Rudolf Virchow, 18 January 1876, NL Virchow, 117, pt. I, Bl. 19–22.

42. Bastian to General Administration of the Royal Museums, 2 March 1886, MfV, Ic, vol. 1, 48/85. Overcrowding was a problem in most nineteenth-century museums because curators usually displayed everything that they possessed. See Kenneth Hudson, *A Social History of Museums: What the Visitors Thought* (London: Macmillan, 1975), 77–78.

43. Memo to General Administration of the Royal Museums, 25 July 1889, MfV, III, vol. 1. 715/89.

44. Ozeanische Sammlung, "Protokoll über die Revision," 3 February 1905, MfV, IIIa, vol. 1, 216/1905.

45. See Luschan to Zoological Museum, 4 April 1905, MfV, IB 39, vol. 1, 1776/04. The curator Alfred Grünwedel had to admit to the General Administration of the Royal Museums that he could not produce a complete list even of the Indian collection for which he was responsible. See Alfred Grünwedel to General Administration of the Royal Museums, 16 March 1891, MfV, IIIa, vol. 1, 319/21.

46. Leo Frobenius, *Der Ursprung der afrikanischen Kulturen* (Berlin: Gebrüder Borntraeger, 1898), 301–2.

47. Adolf Bastian to General Administration of the Royal Museums, 12 July 1899, MfV, I/1, vol. 1, 712/99.

48. Dorsey, "Notes on the Anthropological Museums of Central Europe," 468–69.

49. See Ulrich, memo, 1 March 1898, MfV, VI, vol. 1, 232/98. The poor guidebooks must have seemed particularly burdensome because visitors were not allowed to bring even their own reference books into the museum but had instead to leave them in the coat check. See Willy Pastor to Management of the Museum für Völkerkunde, 28 March 1905, and the response of the Museum, 29 March 1905, MfV, XII, vol. 2, 635/1905.

50. Felix von Luschan to General Administration of the Royal Museums, 12 October 1903, MfV, I/1, vol. 2, 1286/03.

51. Wilhelm Waldeyer, as reported in "XXI Kongreß der Anthropologen," *Rheinisch Westfälischen Zeitung,* 13 August 1890, clipping, NL Virchow, 3003.

52. Felix von Luschan to John Frazer, 25 March 1897, MfV, VIa, vol. 3, 321/97. The original is in English.

53. Expert Commission of the Prehistory Section of the Royal Museum of Ethnology to General Administration of the Royal Museums, 18 February 1893, MfV, vol. 1, 203/93.

54. Richter, "Über die Idealen und Praktischen Aufgaben der Ethnographischen Museen," 6 (1910): 47.

55. "Ausstellung am Kurfürstendamm" (printed leaflet), NL Virchow, 1587.

56. Felix von Luschan to General Administration of the Royal Museums, 19 October 1896, MfV, IB 46, vol. 2, 1209/96.

57. Felix von Luschan to Captain (Medical Corps) Dr. Steinbach, 27 November 1897, MfV, IB 46, vol. 2, 1427/97.

58. The other anthropologists cited in the museum's promotional pamphlet were

the Berliner Karl Weule and the Hamburger Georg Thilenius. Weule would soon move to the Leipzig museum. "Urteile: Deutsches Kolonial-Museum" (1906), MfV, IB46a, 665/06; and "Urteile: Deutsches Kolonial-Museum" (n.d.), BAP, Reichskolonialamt, 6361, Bl. 5–11.

59. See Albert Voss to General Administration of the Royal Museums, 3 November 1899, MfV, I/1, vol. 1, 1178/99.

60. See Oswald Richter to Direction of the Indian Section, 21 October 1906, MfV, XII, vol. 3, 1876/06.

61. Felix von Luschan to General Administration of the Royal Museums, 7 December 1907, MfV, XII, vol. 3, 2324/07.

62. Steinen, "Adolf Bastian"; Bernhard Ankermann, "Die Entwicklung der Ethnologie seit Adolf Bastian," *ZfE* 58 (1926): 221–30, 227.

63. Fritz Graebner, "Adolf Bastian's 100. Geburtstag," *Ethnologica* 3 (1927): ix–xii.

64. See also Felix von Luschan to "Herr Hofrath," 8 January 1891, NL Luschan, K. 21, Copie-Buch IV, Bl. 275–78.

65. See Felix von Luschan to General Administration of the Royal Museums, 31 March 1905, MfV, VII, vol. 3, 660/05.

66. Leo Frobenius, *Ausfahrt: Von der Völkerkunde zum Kulturproblem* (Frankfurt a.M.: Frankfurter Societäts-Druckerei, 1925), 58.

67. General Administration of the Royal Museums to Wilhelm von Gossler, 10 September 1889, GStA PK, I. HA, Rep. 76Ve, Cultusministerium, Sekt. 15, Abt. III, Nr. 2, Bd. IV, unnumbered sheets (M).

68. Susan Sheets-Pyenson discusses this system of display in natural history museums in her *Cathedrals of Science: The Development of Colonial Natural History Museums during the Late Nineteenth Century* (Kingston: McGill-Queen's University Press, 1988), 6–8.

69. Adolf Bastian to General Administration of the Royal Museums, 28 January 1899, MfV, Ic, Bd. 4, 467/99.

70. See *Vossische Zeitung,* 26 June 1900, 1 July 1900, and 7 July 1900.

71. See the minutes of a discussion on remodeling the museum, 7 November 1900, MfV, I/1, vol. 1, 985/00. As these minutes show, curators did not seriously consider separating out the prehistory collection from the ethnological collection of the museum, although the general museum direction suggested doing so. By 1924, the prehistory collection had, however, been moved out of the museum of ethnology.

72. For the directors' responses, see Felix von Luschan to Direction of the Royal Museum of Ethnology, 7 November 1900, Alfred Grünwedel to Direction of the Royal Museum of Ethnology, 15 November 1900, F. W. K. Müller, memo, 15 November 1900, Adolf Bastian to General Administration of the Royal Museums, 17 November 1900, Albert Voss to General Administration of the Royal Museums, 24 November 1900, and Karl von den Steinen to Direction of the Royal Museum of Ethnology, 26 November 1900, MfV, I/1, vol. 1, 985/00.

73. F. W. K. Müller, memo, 15 November 1900, MfV, I/1, vol. 1, 985/00.

74. Felix von Luschan, "Ziele und Wege eines modernen Museums für Völkerkunde," *Globus* 88 (1905): 238–40, 238.

75. In the United States, Franz Boas similarly viewed specialists as the primary audience of the museum and eventually withdrew from the museum to the university department as a way to avoid the exigencies of conducting anthropology in a setting that also had to communicate with the public. See Ira Jacknis, "Franz Boas and the Exhibits: On the Limitations of the Museum Method of Anthropology," in Stocking, ed., *Objects and Others,* 75–111.

76. See Felix von Luschan to General Administration of the Royal Museums, 12 October 1903, MfV, I/1, vol. 2, 1286/03; and Luschan, "Ziele und Wege eines modernen Museums für Völkerkunde."

77. It was only after the Second World War that the entire museum of ethnology moved to its present location in Dahlem. However, the museum did build a storage space in Dahlem in 1906 and moved significant numbers of artifacts there in the 1920s. See Sigrid Westphal-Hellbusch, "Zur Geschichte des Museums," *Baessler-Archiv: Beiträge zur Völkerkunde* 21 (1973): 1–99.

CHAPTER 9

1. H. H. Frese makes a related argument about the connection of the culture-historical method to museum arrangement in the ethnology museum in Cologne, where Graebner worked after he left Berlin. Frese regards the culture-historical method as a way for curators to connect the various geographic areas displayed in the museum, which earlier anthropology had presented simply as parallels. See H. H. Frese, *Anthropology and the Public: The Role of Museums* (Leiden: E. J. Brill, 1960), 57–62. Woodruff Smith regards the culture-historical method as a rejection of the liberal anthropology of Bastian and Virchow in favor of an aggressive imperialist discourse, ominously foreshadowing First World War annexationism and National Socialist doctrines of *Lebensraum* and *Geopolitik.* See Woodruff D. Smith, "The Diffusionist Revolt," in *Politics and the Sciences of Culture,* 140–61, "Friedrich Ratzel and the Origins of *Lebensraum,*" *German Studies Review* 3 (1980): 61–68, and *The Ideological Origins of Nazi Imperialism* (New York: Oxford University Press, 1986). Smith especially focuses on Friedrich Ratzel, an important influence on the Swedish political scientist Rudolf Kjellén, whose conceptions of *Geopolitik* helped shape Nazi imperialist thinking. Smith makes a persuasive argument about one of the terrible offspring of diffusionist anthropology and about the homologous morphology of diffusionism with one strand of colonialist ideology. While I disagree with Smith's presentation of Ratzel's thought and his explanation of the origin of culture-historical anthropology, I do not dispute his account of Nazi geopolitics as one of the many offspring of this new direction in anthropology.

2. See Alfred Götze, memo, 23 December 1896, MfV, XIIa, vol. 1, 1544/96. These tours were organized and encouraged by two private organizations promoting education, the Central Office for Workers' Welfare Facilities and the Association for Popular Courses by Berlin College and University Teachers. Public lectures and tours in the museum of ethnology are listed in MfV, XIIa, vols. 1–2. In 1896, Viennese archaeologist Moritz Hoernes presented as novel the idea that anthropology and prehistory

museums should have labels and guides addressing, not just specialists, but also laypersons. See Hoernes to [Rudolf Virchow?], 3 February 1896, ABGAEU.

3. Kaiser Wilhelm II, speech to a conference on education reform at the Prussian Ministry of Culture, 4 December 1890, in *Reden Kaiser Wilhelms II.,* ed. Axel Matthes (Munich: Rogner & Bernhard, 1976), 30–40, 34. On the kaiser's education reforms, see James C. Albisetti, *Secondary School Reform in Imperial Germany* (Princeton, N.J.: Princeton University Press, 1983).

4. Woodruff D. Smith argues that, after the turn of the century, this Leipzig group began to gain preeminence over Berlin cultural scientists. See his *Politics and the Sciences of Culture,* 204ff. Roger Chickering has suggested that scholars at Leipzig were peculiarly dedicated to reconciling the sciences of culture and the sciences of nature, much as scholars in Berlin were dedicated to preserving the distinction. See Chickering, *Karl Lamprecht,* 294.

5. See "Gesellschaftsnachrichten," *CBDAG* (1876): 9. Indeed, the interests of the Leipzig museum were regarded as contrary to the interests of the German Anthropological Society, so much so that the museum's director, Hermann Obst, was passed over for a leadership position in the German Anthropological Society. See Alexander Frantzius to Rudolf Virchow, 12 September 1874, Andree, 191–92.

6. On the *Methodenstreit,* see Chickering, *Karl Lamprecht,* esp. chaps. 6 and 7.

7. Karl Lamprecht, *Deutsche Geschichte,* 3d ed. (Berlin: R. Gaertner, 1902), 1:xv–xvii.

8. For Ratzel, see, in addition to the works by Woodruff Smith cited in n. 1 above, Johannes Steinmetzler, *Die Anthropogeographie Friedrich Ratzels und ihre ideengeschichtliche Wurzeln* (Bonn: Selbstverlag des geographischen Instituts der Universität Bonn, 1956); Harriet Wanklyn, *Friedrich Ratzel: A Biographical Memoir and Bibliography* (Cambridge: Cambridge University Press, 1961); Günther Buttmann, *Friedrich Ratzel: Leben und Werk eines deutschen Geographen, 1844–1904* (Stuttgart: Wissenschaftlich Verlagsgesellschaft, 1977); and James M. Hunter, *Perspective on Ratzel's Political Geography* (Lanham, Md.: University Press of America, 1983). Hunter deals extensively with questions about Ratzel's relation to imperialism and geopolitics and notions of *Lebensraum.* Both Hunter and Wanklyn argue against the view that Ratzel's use of the term *Lebensraum* indicates support for imperialism.

9. For Ratzel's initial enthusiasm about German anthropology, see his "Die deutsche Gesellschaft für Anthropologie, Ethnologie und Urgeschichte," *Globus* 17 (1870): 204.

10. As early as 1870 German anthropologists suggested the possibility of a historical link between certain Pacific Islanders and Africans, which was to become one of the most common diffusionist hypotheses in the twentieth century, as an answer to the so-called *Negritofrage.* The American anthropologist Clyde Kluckhohn noted this similarity between the methods of diffusionism and those of physical anthropology in his discussion of the *Kulturkreislehre,* the Austrian variant of diffusionism. See Clyde Kluckhohn, "Some Reflections on the Method and Theory of the 'Kulturkreislehre,'" *American Anthropologist,* n.s., 38 (1936): 157–96, 167.

11. Rudolf Virchow, "Gesichtsurnen," *VBGAEU* 2 (1870): 174.

12. Virchow, "Anthropologie und prähistorische Forschungen," 584.

13. Bastian, "Die Grundlage der Ethnologie in den geographischen Provinzen." For a contemporary explication of the importance of geography in Bastian's ethnology, see Thomas Achelis, "Bastians Lehre von den geographischen Provinzen," *Ausland* 63 (1890): 361–64.

14. Johannes Fabian discusses Ratzel's arguments against the "allochronism" of other anthropologists. See Fabian, *Time and the Other,* 18–21.

15. Friedrich Ratzel, *Anthropogeographie,* vol. 2, *Die Geographische Verbreitung des Menschen* (1891; Stuttgart: J. Engelshorns, 1912), 460. See also Friedrich Ratzel, "Die geographische Methode in der Ethnographie," *Geographische Zeitschrift* 3 (1897): 268–78.

16. Analytic statements explicate a thing by drawing logical conclusions from its definition because the predicate is contained in the subject (for example, "Circles are round"). Synthetic statements, on the other hand, bring together properties not necessarily related to each other (for example, "That circle is blue"). Ethnology was analytic, Virchow suggested, because it dealt with things in terms of their essential nature rather than their accidental connections. As a "synthetic" discipline, culture history did not treat human societies themselves, only the histories of their mutual interactions. Rudolf Virchow, review of *Völkerkunde,* vol. 3, *Kulturvölker der Alten und Neuen Welt,* by Friedrich Ratzel (Leipzig, 1888), *ZfE* 20 (1888): 248–49, 248.

17. In the 1890s, Thomas Achelis, a Bremen anthropologist and *Gymnasium* director, published less esoteric defenses of the discipline against attempts either to merge it with or to subordinate it to history. Thomas Achelis, "Ethnologie und Geschichte," *Ausland* 63 (1890): 548–52, 566–70, and "Ethnologie, Geographie und Geschichtsschreibung," *Globus* 69 (1896): 62–66.

18. Friedrich Ratzel, "Geschichte, Völkerkunde und historische Perspektive," in *Kleine Schriften von Friedrich Ratzel,* ed. Hans Helmolt (Munich: R. Oldenbourg, 1906), 2:488–525, 501–2. Originally published in *Historische Zeitschrift* 93 (1904): 1–46.

19. Ibid., 498.

20. Ibid., 498–501.

21. Ibid., 525.

22. Ibid., 506–9.

23. Frobenius was never employed by the museum but did conduct research there as an independent scholar. On Frobenius, see Jahnheinz Jahn, *Leo Frobenius: The Demonic Child,* trans. Reinhard Sander (Austin, Tex.: African and Afro-American Studies and Research Center, 1974); Suzanne Marchand, "Leo Frobenius and the Revolt against the West," *Journal of Contemporary History* 32 (1997): 153–70; and Renée Sylvain, "Leo Frobenius: From *Kulturkreis* to *Kulturmorphologie,*" *Anthropos* 91 (1996): 483–94.

24. Frobenius, *Der Ursprung der afrikanischen Kulturen,* ix.

25. Ibid., 7; Leo Frobenius, *Die Weltanschauung der Naturvölker* (Weimar: Emil Felber, 1898), and *Die naturwissenschaftliche Culturlehre* (Berlin: Ferdinand Dümmler, 1899).

26. For Frobenius's rejection of history as a ground for interpretation in anthropology, see *Der Ursprung der afrikanischen Kulturen,* 5. Frobenius cited Ratzel as an opponent of history in anthropology, despite the latter's strong advocacy of precisely the opposite. While Ratzel's most explicit call for undermining the distinction between history and anthropology came five years after Frobenius's book, Ratzel had insisted on historicizing anthropological topics from the beginning.

27. Frobenius, *Der Ursprung der afrikanischen Kulturen,* 298.

28. Ibid., 299; Frobenius, *Die Weltanschauung der Naturvölker,* vii. Bernard Ankermann, a Berlin convert to the culture-historical method, similarly argued that Asian culture "brought new impulses to a stagnating Negro culture, for Africa has, as far as we know, never given, only received." Bernard Ankermann, "Kulturkreise und Kulturschichten in Afrika," *ZfE* 37 (1905): 54–84, 55.

29. On Graebner, see the obituary by Julius E. Lips, "Fritz Graebner: March 4, 1877 to July 13, 1934," *American Anthropologist,* n.s., 37 (1935): 320–26. On his employment at the Royal Museum of Ethnology, see MfV, Ic, vol. 7, 803/06.

30. For information on Ankermann, see the biographical dictionary at the end of Theye, ed., *Der Geraubte Schatten.*

31. Graebner, "Adolf Bastian's 100. Geburtstag." See chap. 8 above.

32. Fritz Graebner, "Kulturkreise und Kulturschichten in Ozeanien," *ZfE* 37 (1905): 28–53, 28.

33. " . . . ob nicht auch die sogenannten geschichtslosen Völker historischer Darstellung zugänglich sind." Ibid., 29.

34. Ibid., 30.

35. See ibid., 29 n. 3.

36. Bernard Ankermann, "Die Lehre von den Kulturkreisen," *CBDAG* 42 (1911): 156–62, 160.

37. Kluckhohn also noted that Graebner's source criticism was informed by the methods of historians. See Kluckhohn, "Some Reflections on the Method and Theory of the 'Kulturkreislehre,'" 161.

38. Fritz Graebner, "Quellenkritik," in *Methode der Ethnologie* (1911; Oosterhout: Anthropological Publications, 1966), 7–54. *Methode der Ethnologie* would become a fundamental text of the discipline for the next quarter century. See Wilhelm Mühlmann, *Methodik der Völkerkunde* (Stuttgart: Ferdinand Enke, 1938).

39. Ankermann, "Kulturkreise und Kulturschichten in Afrika," 71. See also p. 56 n. 1.

40. Graebner, "Kulturkreise und Kulturschichten in Ozeanien," 44, 53.

41. See Ankermann, "Kulturkreise und Kulturschichten in Afrika," 71ff. Virchow, it will be remembered, had concluded a link between the Near East and East Africa from his physical anthropological examination of the Nubian show at the Berlin zoo.

42. Fritz Graebner, comments on "Die Entstehung des Gottesgedankens insonderheit bei den amerikanische Urzeitvölkern," by Kurt Breysig, *ZfE* 37 (1905): 216–21, 218.

43. Ankermann, "Die Lehre von den Kulturkreisen," 156, 162.

44. Graebner, *Methode der Ethnologie,* 92. Kluckhohn refers to this as an "indispensable book" on *Kulturkreislehre.* Kluckhohn also cites works by Ratzel, Frobenius, Ankermann, and Wilhelm Schmidt. See Kluckhohn, "Some Reflections on the Method and Theory of the 'Kulturkreislehre,'" 159 n. 2.

45. Wilhelm Schmidt, "Kulturkreise und Kulturschichten in Südamerika," *ZfE* 45 (1913): 1014–1130, 1116. Schmidt made a similar argument against Bastian's understanding of natural peoples as peoples without history and against his understanding of anthropology as a study of universal human nature. See Schmidt, "Die Moderne Ethnologie." Schmidt may have overstated the success of the culture-historical method, for anthropologists such as Paul Ehrenreich and Karl von den Steinen continued to defend some form of idealistic universalism against the historical method. Neither Ehrenreich nor Steinen, however, defended the notion of pure natural peoples representing a universal human nature. They merely advocated considering the development of various societies as independent parallel phenomena. Even before the development of the culture-historical method in Berlin, Steinen had criticized attempts to see in various natural peoples the "stone age" or the earliest form of all history. Still, he did not become a proponent of the culture-historical method in the twentieth century. See Karl von den Steinen, *Unter den Naturvölkern Zentral-Brasiliens,* 1st ed. (Berlin: Dietrich Reimer, 1894), 203, 205. Ehrenreich explained cultural parallels as convergences of separate histories rather than as cultural borrowings or as the necessary working out of a universal human nature. See Paul Ehrenreich, "Zur Frage der Beurtheilung und Bewerthung ethnographischer Analogien," *CBDAG* 34 (1903): 176–80. Ehrenreich doubted both Bastian's explanation and the culture-historical explanations for "ethnographic analogies" and was more concerned with studying material in the present than with speculating about its origin. See Paul Ehrenreich, *Die Mythen und Legenden der Südamerikanischen Urvölker und ihre Beziehungen zu denen Nordamerikas und der alten Welt,* supplement to *ZfE* 37 (1905). Although Luschan was more sympathetic than Ehrenreich to culture-historical questions, he also supported Ehrenreich's methods. See his comments included in Ehrenreich, "Zur Frage der Beurtheilung und Bewerthung ethnographischer Analogien," 180. Luschan indicated at least a partial acceptance of diffusionism and the culture-historical method. See Felix von Luschan, "Prähistorische Zusammenhänge zwischen Europa und dem tropischen Afrika," *CBDAG* 42 (1911): 65–67. As early as 1907, he expressed cautious interest in the question of the relations of Melanesians and Africans. See Felix von Luschan to Dr. Dempwolf, Captain (Medical Corps), Triga, German East Africa, 8 August 1907, MfV, IB 39, vol. 2, 1288/06.

46. On Wilhelm Schmidt, see Ernest Brandewie, *When Giants Walked the Earth: The Life and Times of Wilhelm Schmidt SVD* (Fribourg: Fribourg University Press, 1990).

47. As Wilhelm Schmidt noted, the move away from ahistorical accounts of natural peoples to culture history did not find any parallel developments in England, France, or the United States, although he did regard W. H. R. Rivers, Franz Boas, and A. van Gennep as partial exceptions to this rule. See Wilhelm Schmidt, "Die kulturhistorische Methode in der Ethnologie," *Anthropos* 3 (1911): 1010–36, 1016–17. On

Rivers's diffusionism, see George W. Stocking Jr., *After Tylor: British Social Anthropology, 1888–1951* (Madison: University of Wisconsin Press, 1995), 179–232.

48. See Kluckhohn, "Some Reflections on the Method and Theory of the 'Kulturkreislehre,'" 159 n. 1.

49. See, for example, Richard Thurnwald, "Anleitung zur völkerkundlichen Feldarbeit," in *Lehrbuch der Völkerkunde,* ed. Richard Thurnwald and Konrad Theodor Preuss, 2d ed. (Stuttgart: Ferdinand Enke, 1939), 405–22; and Mühlmann, *Methodik der Völkerkunde.*

50. Walter Krickeberg, review of *Lehrbuch der Völkerkunde,* by Konrad Theodor Preuss (1937), *ZfE* 69 (1937): 464–66, 465.

51. Karl Weule, "Die Praktischen Aufgaben der Völkermuseen auf Grund Leipziger Erfahrungen," *CBDAG* 41 (1910): 74–78. Weule was responding to a reassertion of the Berlin museum methods in Oswald Richter's 1906–10 series in *Museumskunde,* "Über die Idealen und Praktischen Aufgaben der Ethnographischen Museen."

52. Konrad Theodor Preuss to General Administration of the Royal Museums, 12 August 1910, MfV, IIc, vol. 1, 1431/10.

53. See, for example, Konrad Theodor Preuss to General Administration of the Royal Museums, 12 August 1910, MfV, IIc, vol. 1, 1431/10.

54. See Lips, "Fritz Graebner."

55. Sometime before 1924, the prehistoric collections and the East Asian collections moved to the neighboring Applied Arts Museum (known today as the Martin-Gropius Bau). See [?] Egeka, "Die Neuordnung des Museums für Völkerkunde," *Berliner Tageblatt,* 26 October 1924, MfV, I, vol. 2, 758/24. In 1926, the Berlin Anthropological Society (and with it, presumably, its physical anthropology collections) also moved to the Kunstgewerbe Museum to make more room for instructive displays in the museum of ethnology. See memo from 1926 (no day or month given), MfV, IV, 1314/26.

56. The most notable descendant of these debates was the so-called Berlin museum war of the early 1920s, which involved the distinction between anthropological objects and art and the appropriate methods of displaying the objects of non-Europeans. Related to this question was the development in Germany of expressionist art that followed "primitive" art found in anthropology museums. On the Berlin museum war, see Karl Scheffler, *Berliner Museumskrieg* (Berlin: Bruno Cassierer, 1921). On anthropology and expressionist and cubist art, see James Clifford, "On Ethnographic Surrealism," *Comparative Studies in Society and History* 23 (1981): 539–64; Arthur C. Danto, "Artifact and Art," in *Art/Artifact: African Art in Anthropology Collections* (New York: Center for African Art, 1988), 18–32; and Jill Lloyd, *German Expressionism: Primitivism and Modernity* (New Haven, Conn.: Yale University Press, 1991).

57. Ankermann emphasizes the empirical nature of culture history in his "Die Lehre von den Kulturkreisen." Later, he even held that culture history and Bastian's anthropology could be translated into each other theoretically and that their difference was merely in the focus of the former on the historical development of contem-

porary mixed cultures and of the latter on the search for original pure cultures. See Ankermann, "Die Entwicklung der Ethnologie seit Adolf Bastian."

58. Ankermann also later attributed the development of the culture-historical method to the fact that German anthropology was a museum science. He held that the curators could discern patterns of relations among cultures because the museum presented them with so many artifacts from around the world. See Ankermann, "Die Entwicklung der Ethnologie seit Adolf Bastian," 228.

59. This transition follows a pattern that John V. Pickstone outlines for the development of sciences from an amateur stage of cataloging and classification to a professional stage of analytic depth in which scientists seek to understand specific realities beyond the surface of the objects collected. This phenomenon is illustrated well by Graebner's call to go beyond appearances to cultures. Pickstone maintains that this epistemological transformation generally occurs with the institutional transition of the discipline from a private society to a public museum, a hypothesis supported by the case of German anthropology. While Pickstone follows Michel Foucault's scheme of *epistemes* from *The Order or Things,* he differs from Foucault in regarding the newer, analytic stage as preserving within it the older stage of cataloging and classification. He thus has a more dialectical understanding of historical change than Foucault and one that better describes the conservative process of change that occurred in anthropology after the turn of the century. The museum of ethnology did not simply negate the empiricism of German anthropology; rather, the two interacted dialectically, as did the two modes of knowledge, the cataloging and the analytic. Pickstone has developed this argument in a number of articles. See esp. John V. Pickstone, "Ways of Knowing: Towards a Historical Sociology of Science, Technology, and Medicine," *British Journal of the History of Science* 26 (1993): 433–58, and "Museological Science?"

60. Ankermann, "Kulturkreise und Kulturschichten in Afrika," 83.

61. Albrecht Penck, "Das Alter des Menschengeschlechtes," *ZfE* 40 (1908): 390–407.

62. In 1911, R. R. Schmidt presented the combination of human history, paleontology, and earth history as a methodology that had only recently been accepted. See R. R. Schmidt, "Die Grundlagen für die Diluvialchronologie und Paläethnologie Westeuropas," *ZfE* 43 (1911): 945–74.

63. See, for example, Josef Bayer, "Über das Alter des Menschengeschlechts," *ZfE* 44 (1912): 180–87; and E. Werth, "Die geologische Datierung der Paläolithfundstätte von Markkleeberg," *ZfE* 47 (1915): 234–41.

64. Oskar Montelius, "Vorgeschichtliche Chronologie," *ZfE* 42 (1910): 955–62, 960–61.

65. See chap. 3 above. The quotation is from Gustav Fritsch, *Die Eingeborenen Süd-Afrika's ethnographisch und anatomisch Beschrieben,* xx.

66. Gustav Fritsch, "Verwertung von Rassenmerkmalen für allgemeine Vergleichungen," *ZfE* 43 (1911): 272–80, 272.

67. Gustav Fritsch, "Die Entwicklung und Verbreitung der Menschenrassen," *ZfE* 42 (1910): 580–86; discussion of Fritsch's lecture, *ZfE* 42 (1910): 924–29. Paul

Ehrenreich opposed Fritsch's understanding of human races as developing over time. Ehrenreich was more concerned than most anthropologists to keep biological and cultural questions separate from each other and thus would not have been predisposed to accept any kind of Darwinism. He also, as we saw above, opposed the culture-historical method. See, for example, Paul Ehrenreich, review of *Natur und Urgeschichte des Menschen,* by Moritz Hoernes (Vienna, 1909), *ZfE* 42 (1910): 363–64.

68. For Hans Friedenthal's Darwinism, see his "Die Stellung des Menschen im zoologischen System," *ZfE* 42 (1910): 989–94, and "Über die Behaarung der Menschenrassen und Menschenaffen," *ZfE* 43 (1911): 974–79.

69. See *Vorlesungsverzeichnis der Friedrich-Wilhelm Universität zu Berlin* (1878–).

70. Julius Kollmann, "Neue Gedanken über das alte Problem von der Abstammung des Menschen," *CBDAG* 36 (1905): 9–20.

71. Felix von Luschan, obituary for Gustav Schwalbe, *CBDAG* 42 (1916): 15–18, 15.

72. Hans Virchow, "Eine Tätowierte," *ZfE* 43 (1911): 270–71, and "Ein Kraftmensch," *ZfE* 45 (1914): 639.

CHAPTER 10

1. An important inspiration for German fieldwork was likely the 1898 Torres Straits expedition, in which a number of Cambridge anthropologists collected firsthand observations of indigenous populations in the South Pacific. However, the conventions of fieldwork were by no means fully elaborated by Cambridge anthropologists at this time, and German anthropologists had, in any case, to adapt this new approach to their own cultural and political context. On the Torres Straits expedition, see Anita Herle and Sandra Rouse, eds., *Cambridge and the Torres Strait: Centenary Essays on the 1898 Anthropological Expedition* (Cambridge: Cambridge University Press, 1998); Kuklick, "The Politics of Perception"; and Stocking, "The Ethnographer's Magic." For excellent discussion of fieldwork in a broad range of disciplines, including anthropology, see the essays collected in Henrika Kuklick and Robert E. Kohler, eds., *Science in the Field, Osiris* 11 (1997).

2. Clifford Geertz has written that "'Being There' authorially, palpably on the page, is . . . as difficult a trick to bring off as 'being there' personally." Geertz considers anthropological fieldwork at a relatively developed stage, after conventions and practices of the field had already been established. However, prior to the construction of the field, anthropologists could not have simply selected a region for study and gone there. To echo Gertrude Stein's famous quip about Oakland: There was no there there. German fieldwork was successful insofar as it was able to construct a "there" there by cooperating with colonists and borrowing techniques from colonial administration. See Clifford Geertz, "Being There: Anthropology and the Scene of Writing," in *Works and Lives: The Anthropologist as Author* (Stanford, Calif.: Stanford University Press, 1988), 1–24, 23.

3. Mary Louise Pratt discusses the differentiation of professional and amateur field reports in "Fieldwork in Common Places," in *Writing Culture: The Politics and*

Poetics of Ethnography, ed. James Clifford and George E. Marcus (Berkeley and Los Angeles: University of California Press, 1986), 27–50.

4. Felix von Luschan (no title, n.d.), NL Luschan, box 8.

5. Richard Thurnwald, "Über Völkerkundemuseen, ihre wissenschaftliche Bedingungen und Ziele," *Museumskunde* 8 (1912): 197–215, 200.

6. Fritsch, *Die Eingeborenen Süd-Afrika's ethnographisch und anatomisch Beschrieben,* xx—xxi.

7. Schmidt, "Die Moderne Ethnologie," 594.

8. See Fritsch, *Die Eingeborenen Süd-Afrika's ethnographisch und anatomisch Beschrieben.*

9. Reinhold Hensel, "Die Coroados der brasilianischen Provinz Rio Grande del Sul," *ZfE* 1 (1869): 124–35.

10. Adolf Bastian to Adalbert Falk (minister of culture), 16 May 1878, GStA PK, I. HA, Rep. 76Ve, Cultusministerium, Sekt. 15, Abt. XI, Nr. 2, Bd. 1, Bl. 126–28 (M). It is not clear why Bastian uses the term *authentic Bora* to refer to original sources.

11. As the minister of culture explained to the kaiser about one of Bastian's trips, "the purpose of this journey will be primarily to establish appropriate contacts and introduce useful correspondents to the requirements of systematic collecting." Adalbert Falk (minister of culture) to Kaiser Wilhelm I, May 1878, GStA PK, I. HA, Rep. 89, Geheimes Zivilkabinett, Nr. 20489, Bl. 25–26 (M). Bastian's own correspondence confirms the primary importance of making contacts with local colonists during his travels. See Adolf Bastian (in Lima) to Rudolf Virchow, 16 July 1875, and Bastian (in Batavia) to Virchow, November 1879, NL Virchow, 117, pt. I, Bl. 31–33.

12. Steinen, "Adolf Bastian," 243.

13. In 1908, the anthropologist Oswald Richter called sending out museum employees to collect, rather than relying on amateur suppliers already working in the colonies, a new trend, first pioneered by the Berlin museum. See Richter, "Über die Idealen und Praktischen Aufgaben der Ethnographischen Museen," 4 (1908): 96–97. Richard Thurnwald, a German anthropologist who developed fieldwork methodologies, commented on the distinctions between traveling to collect and extended fieldwork. See Thurnwald, "Anleitung zur völkerkundlichen Feldarbeit," 406.

14. Felix von Luschan to the Imperial Navy Office, 22 December 1892, MfV, IB 48, vol. 1, 891/93.

15. The Colonial Section of the Foreign Office acknowledged the insufficiency of colonial collecting in a letter to Richard Schöne (general director of the Royal Museums), 20 May 1893, MfV, IB 46, vol. 1, 671/93.

16. Felix von Luschan to General Administration of the Royal Museums, 7 March 1907, MfV, IB71, vol. 1, 435/07.

17. On Thurnwald's expeditions, see Marion Melk-Koch, *Auf der Such nach der menschlichen Gesellschaft: Richard Thurnwald* (Berlin: Dietrich Reimer, 1989). Luschan requested twenty-five thousand marks for Thurnwald's expedition and fifty thousand marks for Stephan's expedition. The Baessler Foundation gave Thurnwald

an additional twenty thousand marks, which still did not bring Thurnwald's funding up even to the level of the museum's portion of the support for Stephan's expedition. Stephan's expedition received additional funding from the navy. See Felix von Luschan to General Administration of the Royal Museum, 22 February 1907, MfV, IB71, vol. 1, 435/07; and Richard Thurnwald, "Im Bismarckarchipel und auf den Salomoinseln, 1906–1909," *ZfE* 42 (1910): 98–147.

18. Felix von Luschan to the commander of the *Möwe,* 10 December 1900, MfV, IB 48, vol. 1, 894/00.

19. Dernburg announced this new policy in a January 1907 lecture reprinted in Bernhard Dernburg, *Zielpunkte des Deutschen Kolonialwesens* (Berlin: Ernst Siegfried Mittler & Sohn, 1907). On Dernburg's reforms, see Smith, *The German Colonial Empire,* 183–209; and W. O. Henderson, *The German Colonial Empire, 1884–1919* (London: Frank Cass, 1993), 100–105. On Dernburg himself, see Werner Schiefel, *Bernhard Dernburg, 1865–1937: Kolonialpolitiker und Bankier im wilhelminischen Deutschland* (Zürich: Atlantis, 1974).

20. Admiral Alfred von Tirpitz to Foreign Office, Colonial Section, 29 April 1907; Tirpitz to Bernhard Dernburg, 9 June 1907, MfV, IB71, vol. 1, 1176/07. Tirpitz refers in the letter of 9 June 1907 to the similar argument by the expedition's leader, Emil Stephan, in Stephan's *Südseekunst: Beiträge zur Kunst des Bismarck-Archipels und zur Urgeschichte der Kunst überhaupt* (Berlin: Dietrich Reimer, 1907), 30–31. See also Emil Stephan and [?] Furstenan, "Die deutsche Marine Expedition 1907/08," *Marine-Rundschau,* August/September 1907, 10067–69. Proofs in MfV, IB71, vol. 1, 1349/07.

21. Stephan and Furstenan, "Die deutsche Marine Expedition 1907/08."

22. Bernhard Dernburg to Tirpitz, 22 May 1907, MfV, IB71, vol. 1, 1176/07. See also Acting Governor Krauss, memo, 13 May 1907, MfV, IB71, vol. 1, 1176/07.

23. See Smith, *The German Colonial Empire,* 163–64.

24. Felix von Luschan to Emil Stephan, 28 January 1908, MfV, IB71, vol. 1, 98/08.

25. Felix von Luschan to Emil Stephan, 6 June 1907, MfV, IB71, vol. 1, 1093/07.

26. For a brief account of Stephan's life, see Fritz Graebner, obituary for Emil Stephan, *Globus* 95 (1909): 81.

27. Emil Stephan to Felix von Luschan, 14 October 1904, MfV, IB 48, vol. 2, 17/05.

28. Ibid.

29. See Felix von Luschan to Admiral Alfred von Tirpitz, 5 January 1907, and Tirpitz's adjutant to Luschan, 1 February 1907, MfV, IB48, vol. 3, 25/07.

30. Emil Stephan, "Beiträge zur Psychologie der Bewohner von Neupommern: Nebst ethnographische Mitteilungen über die Barriai und über die Insel Hunt (Duror)," *Globus* 88 (1905): 205–10, 216–21, 205–6.

31. Stephan, *Südseekunst,* 3.

32. Emil Stephan to Felix von Luschan, 14 September 1904, Luschan to the Baessler Foundation, 4 November 1904, Luschan to Eduard Sachau (director of the Seminar for Oriental Languages), 4 November 1904, Luschan to Carl Meinhof, 9

November 1904, and Luschan to the director of the Colonial Section of the Foreign Office, 14 November 1904, MfV, IB 48, vol. 2, 1751/04. 311/05; Luschan to General Administration of the Royal Museums, 16 February 1905, MfV, IB 48, vol. 2, 311/05.

33. Stephan, *Südseekunst.*

34. Nolde never completed this book, but he did outline it in his autobiographical *Jahre der Kämpfe, 1902-1914* (1934; Cologne: Dumont, 1967), 194-98. On Picasso and the issue of "primitivism" generally, see Danto, "Artifact and Art." On Nolde and "primitivism" in German expressionism, see Lloyd, *German Expressionism.*

35. See Alfred Grünwedel to Wilhelm von Bode, 2 January 1905, Grünwedel to Bode, 24 January 1905, Bode to Grünwedel, 15 March 1905, and Grünwedel to Bode, 3 May 1905, MfV, IB 50, 107/05, 2058/04. See also W. v. Seidlitz, "Ein Deutsches Museum für Asiatische Kunst," *Museumskunde* 1 (1905): 181-97.

36. See, for example, August Köhler (Imperial Landeshauptmann of Togo) to the Colonial Office of the Foreign Office, 4 August 1899, BAP, Reichskolonialamt, 6360, Bd. 1, Bl. 53; German Colonial Society to Ministry of Culture, 1904, MfV, IB 50, 1978/04.

37. *Deutsche Kolonialzeitung,* no. 16, 10 April 1907, in MfV, IB71, Die Expedition des Marine-Stabsarztes Dr. Stephan nach der Südsee, vol. 1, 772/07.

38. Emil Stephan, "First Report of the German Navy Expedition," 20 November 1907, MfV, IB71, Die Expedition des Marine-Stabsarztes Dr. Stephan nach der Südsee, vol. 1, 154/08.

39. Felix von Luschan to Augustin Krämer, 14 November 1905, MfV, IB 48, vol. 2, 2171/05. Luschan did, however, persuade the Imperial Navy Office to give Stephan a medal and support the publication of his book. Luschan to Imperial Navy Office, 14 April 1905, and Admiral Alfred von Tirpitz (head of the Imperial Navy Office) to Luschan, 29 May 1905, MfV, IB 48, vol. 2, 771/1905, 1329/05.

40. Fritz Graebner, preface to *Neu-Mecklenburg (Bismarck-Archipel): Die Küste von Umuddu bis Kap St. Georg. Forschungsergebnisse bei den Vermessungsfahrten von S.M.S. Möwe im Jahre 1904,* by Emil Stephan and Fritz Graebner (Berlin: Dietrich Reimer, 1907), n.p.

41. "Psychologische Beobachtungen," in Stephan and Graebner, *Neu-Mecklenburg,* 23-30.

42. Stephan, "Beiträge zur Psychologie der Bewohner von Neupommern," 205.

43. Ibid., 216-21.

44. Kurt Lampert (Royal Natural History Cabinett in Stuttgart) to Felix von Luschan, 15 July 1907, MfV, IB71, vol. 1, 1036/07.

45. Felix von Luschan to Otto Schlaginhaufen, 25 June 1907, and Luschan to Jacobi (Dresden museum of ethnology), 29 June 1907, MfV, IB71, vol. 1, 1234/07.

46. Felix von Luschan to Edgar Walden, 8 April 1907, MfV, IB71, vol. 1, 511/07. Wilhelm Müller to Luschan, 28 May 1907, MfV, IB71, vol. 1, 571/07.

47. See Stephan, "First Report of the German Navy Expedition." See also Otto Schlaginhaufen, *Muliama: Zwei Jahren unter Südsee-Insulaner* (Zürich: Orell Füssli, 1959), 10-33.

48. See Edgar Walden's report written en route to the Pacific, "Die deutsche Südsee-Expedition," *Berliner Tageblatt,* 23 October 1907, in MfV, IB71, vol. 1, 2031/07.

49. See Felix von Luschan to Edgar Walden, 29 May 1908, MfV, IB71, vol. 2, 1136/08.

50. Emil Stephan, journal, 20 December 1907, MfV, IB71, vol. 2, 702/08.

51. Ibid.

52. On the setup of the camp, see Augustin Krämer-Bannow, "Der Verlauf der Deutschen Marine Expedition, 1907–1909," *Zeitschrift der Gesellschaft für Erdkunde zu Berlin* 46 (1911): 14–23, 16; Elisabeth Krämer-Bannow, *Bei kunstsinnigen Kannibalen der Südsee: Wanderungen auf Neu-Mecklenburg, 1908–1909* (Berlin: Dietrich Reimer, 1916), 7–17; Schlaginhaufen, *Muliama,* 39–49; Otto Schlaginhaufen, journal, 11, 12 December 1907, and Emil Stephan, journal, 9 December 1907, MfV, IB71, vol. 2, 702/08.

53. Emil Stephan, journal, 24 February 1908, MfV, IB71, vol. 2, 128/1908.

54. Emil Stephan, journal, 12, 15, 22 December 1907, 6 January 1908, MfV, IB71, vol. 2, 702/08.

55. Schlaginhaufen, *Muliama,* 43–62.

56. Claude Lévi-Strauss suggests that such scenes of writing signify authority, for they involve one of the gestures through which power is wielded. See Claude Lévi-Strauss, "The Writing Lesson," in *Tristes Tropiques* (1955), trans. John Weightman and Doreen Weightman (New York: Pocket, 1973), 331–43. Jacques Derrida remarks that the difference between writing and not-writing (but speaking) that Lévi-Strauss's analysis presupposes is itself an artifact of European imperialism. See Derrida, *Of Grammatology,* 101–40.

57. Emil Stephan, journal, 12 December 1907, and Otto Schlaginhaufen, journal, 13 December 1907, 14 December 1907, MfV, IB71, vol. 2, 702/08.

58. Emil Stephan, journal, 16 December 1907, MfV, IB71, vol. 2, 702/08.

59. Schlaginhaufen, *Muliama,* 49–62.

60. Stephan noted that Chinese merchants were an important source of artifacts but that they often could not give sufficient information about the objects that they sold. Emil Stephan, journal, 18 December 1907, MfV, IB71, vol. 2, 702/08.

61. Although Stephan considered the prices "shameless," he still bought a number of items. Emil Stephan, journal, 18 February 1908, and Otto Schlaginhaufen, journal, 18 February 1908, MfV, IB71, vol. 2, 888/08.

62. Emil Stephan, journal, 26 December 1907, MfV, IB71, vol. 2, 702/08.

63. Otto Schlaginhaufen, journal, 17 December 1907, MfV, IB71, vol. 2, 702/08.

64. Emil Stephan, journal, 14 December 1907, MfV, IB71, vol. 2, 702/08.

65. Emil Stephan, journal, 27 December 1907, MfV, IB71, vol. 2, 702/08.

66. Otto Schlaginhaufen, journal, 12, 13 January 1908, MfV, IB71, vol. 2, 702/08. Within his own camp, Stephan also acted as a judicial authority, having his own police soldiers beaten publicly on two occasions. The first charge was leaving a campfire un-

attended and burning down a house; the second charge was raping the wife of a Chinese merchant. See Emil Stephan, journal, 31 January, 8 February 1908, MfV, IB71, vol. 2, 888/08.

67. Emil Stephan, journal, 22 December 1907, MfV, IB71, vol. 2, 702/08.

68. Emil Stephan, journal, 12, 15 December 1907, MfV, IB71, vol. 2, 702/08.

69. Emil Stephan, journal, 6 January 1908, MfV, IB71, vol. 2, 702/08.

70. Emil Stephan, report to the Imperial Navy Office, mid-February 1908, MfV, IB71, vol. 2, 976/08.

71. Otto Schlaginhaufen to the Imperial Navy Office, 9 July 1908, MfV, IB71, vol. 3, 1680/08. Stephan's only surviving report was written at the request of the local government of New Mecklenburg on the reasons for population decline in the region, a question related to labor recruitment policy. Although the Colonial Office in Berlin had specifically forbidden him to comment on this question, the local colonial government requested this report. Stephan and Schlaginhaufen had made a census of every village and may also have worked out family trees. On the basis of this work, Stephan reported to the colonial government that the population around Muliama would be extinct within three generations. This was not, however, because of colonial labor recruitment, or the alcohol and venereal diseases introduced by Europeans, or the military expeditions led against indigenous inhabitants by the Germans. The reason for the population decline, Stephan argued, could only be centuries of inbreeding in the small island communities. Although European imperialism was not the cause of this depopulation, colonial efforts would certainly suffer from the disappearance of local sources of labor and taxation. Stephan suggested that, if possible, Melanesians from other parts of the Pacific be brought to the area to breed with the inhabitants around his station or, failing that, that women from Germany's African colonies be brought to New Mecklenburg in order to "freshen up the blood." Emil Stephan, "Ursachen des Volksrückganges und Vorschläge zu seiner Erhaltung auf Grund von Untersuchungen über die Bevölkerung von Muliama," report presented to the Colonial Government in New Mecklenburg in 1908. Handwritten copy in MfV, IB71, vol. 2, 995/08. See also Emil Stephan to Admiral Alfred von Tirpitz, January 1908, MfV, IB71, vol. 2, 740/08; and Stephan, journal, 24 December 1907, MfV, IB71, vol. 2, 702/08.

72. Krämer-Bannow, *Bei kunstsinnigen Kannibalen der Südsee,* 3–4.

73. Felix von Luschan to Otto Schlaginhaufen, 26 August 1908, MfV, IB71, vol. 3, 1729/08.

74. Thiel hosted the members of the expedition regularly and was decorated for his services. See Schlaginhaufen, *Muliama;* Emil Stephan to Felix von Luschan, 19 November 1907, and Bernhard Dernburg to Wilhelm von Bode, 17 February 1908, MfV, IB71, vol. 1, 31/08.

75. Krämer, "Der Verlauf der Deutschen Marine Expedition, 1907–1909," 17.

76. Otto Schlaginhaufen, report to the Imperial Navy Office, 5 September 1908, IB 71, vol. 4, 2404/08.

77. On Krämer, see Dietrich Schleip, "Ozeanische Ethnographie und koloniale Praxis: Das Beispiel Augustin Krämer," *Tribus* 38 (1989): 121–48.

78. See Augustin Krämer, "Gouvernmentale Übergriffe in ethnographische

Arbeitsgebiete und Mittel zur Abhilfe," *Globus* 96 (1909): 264-66, 266. Schlaginhaufen saw the appointment of a second collector as a "vote of no confidence" in his own collecting abilities (Otto Schlaginhaufen to Felix von Luschan, 10 August 1908, IB 71, vol. 4, 2266/08). While Luschan had a high opinion of Krämer as a collector, he did not seem to trust him to carry out the slow, methodical work that he hoped to initiate with the expedition. He turned to the elusive Walden, who soon rejoined the expedition, to make sure that his instructions were carried out. Luschan to Edgar Walden, 27 October 1908, IB 71, vol. 4, 2268/08.

79. Krämer, "Der Verlauf der Deutschen Marine Expedition, 1907–1909," 17.

80. On this expedition, see Fischer, *Die Hamburger Südsee-Expedition*. For an analysis of the goals and methods of the expedition as well as its contradictory interactions with other colonial goals, see Rainer F. Buschmann, "Tobi Captured: Converging Ethnographic and Colonial Visions on a Caroline Island," *ISLA: A Journal of Micronesian Studies* 4 (1996): 317–40.

81. Krämer, "Gouvernmentale Übergriffe in ethnographische Arbeitsgebiete und Mittel zur Abhilfe."

82. This was true not only for Krämer but also, it seems, for the other members of the Hamburg expedition. See the series published from the Hamburg expedition, esp. Georg Thilenius, "Plan der Expedition," in *Allgemeines, in Ergebnisse der Südsee-Expedition, 1908–1910* (Hamburg: L. Friedrichsen, 1927), 1:1–40; and Augustin Krämer, *Palau,* in ibid.

83. Augustin Krämer, comment at meeting of the German Anthropological Society, *CBDAG* 42 (1911): 171–72.

84. Augustin Krämer, "Über Museums- und Feldmonographen," *CBDAG* 43 (1912): 22–24.

CONCLUSION

1. Carl Meinhof, "Aus dem Seelenleben der Eingeborenen," *Jahrbuch über die deutschen Kolonien* 3 (1910): 84–100, 84.

2. On Thurnwald's attempts to make anthropology useful to colonialism, see Gothsch, *Die deutsche Völkerkunde und ihr Verhältnis zum Kolonialismus*. For an example of Thilenius's similar endeavors, see Georg Thilenius, "Arbeitsweise der Naturvölker," in *Deutsches Kolonial-Lexikon* (Leipzig: Quelle & Meyer, 1920), 1:79–81.

3. Of course, there was no simple path from anthropology to racial hygiene to Nazism. Darwinist anthropology did become increasingly racist and eventually provided a major source of ideological support for National Socialism. On developments in German racial anthropology into the twentieth century, see Massin, "From Virchow to Fischer"; Proctor, "From *Anthropologie* to *Rassenkunde* in the German Anthropological Tradition"; and Weindling, *Health, Race, and German Politics*.

4. Felix von Luschan to Rittergutsbesitzer Wilhelm von Arnim, 15 December 1908, MfV, IB 39, vol. 3, 2661/08.

5. Felix von Luschan, lecture notes from after the First World War, NL Luschan, K. 15.

6. See, for example, Felix von Luschan, lecture notes, NL Luschan, K. 12, 14, 15.

7. The *Politisch-Anthropologische Revue* began in 1902, the *Archiv für Rassen- und Gesellschaftsbiologie* in 1904.

8. W. Schallmayer, "Zum Einbruch der Naturwissenschaften in das Gebiet der Geisteswissenschaften," *Archiv für Rassen- und Gesellschafts-Biologie* 1 (1904): 586–97, 589, 596.

9. On the recent revelations about Conze and Schieder, see Hans-Ulrich Wehler, "In den Fusstapfen der kaempfenden Wissenschaft," *Frankfurter Allgemeine Zeitung,* 4 January 1999, 48; and Götz Aly, "Stakkato der Vertreibung, Pizzikato der Entlastung," *Frankfurter Allgemeine Zeitung,* 3 February 1999, 46.

10. See Michael Burleigh, *Germany Turns Eastwards: A Study of Ostforschung in the Third Reich* (Cambridge: Cambridge University Press, 1988). On Nazi population policy in Eastern Europe, see Götz Aly, *"Final Solution": Nazi Population Policy and the Murder of the European Jews* (New York: Oxford University Press, 1999).

11. Mühlmann, *Methodik der Völkerkunde,* 247.

12. Wilhelm Mühlmann, *Rassen- und Völkerkunde: Lebensprobleme der Rassen, Gesellschaften und Völker* (Braunschweig: Friedrich Vieweg & Sohn, 1936), iii, 534–37. See also the positive review of that work and its opposition to racial mixing in the *Zeitschrift für Ethnologie,* the official organ of the Berlin Anthropological Society. Arthur Hintze, review of Wilhelm Mühlmann, *Rassen- und Völkerkunde* (1936), *ZfE* 69 (1937): 452–53.

13. Wilhelm Mühlmann, *Geschichte der Anthropologie* (Bonn: Universitäts-Verlag Bonn, 1948).

14. In 1997, Felicitas Heimann-Jelinek of the Vienna Jewish Museum curated an exhibition entitled "Masken: Versuch über die Schoa," which documented the collection for the Vienna anthropology museum of plaster masks and skulls from Jews, Szinti, and Roma in concentration camps. This exhibition was reviewed by Amos Elon, "Death for Sale," *New York Review of Books,* 20 November 1997, 41. The exhibition further pursued discoveries by Götz Aly about the procurement of plaster casts and body parts from interred Jews by the German anatomist Hermann Voss, at the Reich University of Posen. See Götz Aly, "Das Posener Tagebuch des Anatomen Hermann Voss," in *Biedermann und Schreibtischtäter: Materialien zur detuschen Täter-Biographie* (Berlin: Rotbuch, 1987), 14–66, esp. 55.

15. Miklos Nyiszli, an inmate of Auschwitz who performed dissections for Mengele, remembered: "I had to keep any organs of possible scientific interest, so that Dr. Mengele could examine them. Those which might interest the Anthropological Institute at Berlin-Dahlem were preserved in alcohol. These parts were specially packed to be sent through the mails. Stamped 'War Material—Urgent,' they were given top priority in transit. In the course of my work at the crematorium I dispatched an impressive number of such packages. I received, in reply, either precise scientific observations or instructions. In order to classify this correspondence I had to set up special files. The directors of the Berlin-Dahlem Institute always warmly thanked Dr. Mengele for this rare and precious material." Miklos Nyiszli, *Auschwitz: A Doctor's Eye Witness Account* (1960), trans. Tibère Kremer and Richard Seaver (New York:

Arcade, 1993), 63. On doctors in Nazi death camps, see Robert Jay Lifton, *The Nazi Doctors: Medical Killing and the Psychology of Genocide* (New York: Basic, 1986). On Mengele's anthropological research, see pp. 284–87, 337–83. See also Weindling, *Health, Race, and German Politics,* 552–64; and Benno Müller-Hill, *Murderous Science: Elimination by Scientific Selection of Jews, Gypsies, and Others in Germany, 1933–1945,* trans. George R. Fraser (Plainview, N.Y.: Cold Springs Harbor Laboratory Press, 1998), 71–94.

16. The most recent and the most extensively researched account of the period of German colonization in Namibia is Jan-Bart Gewald, *Herero Heroes: A Socio-Political History of the Herero of Namibia, 1890–1923* (Oxford: James Currey, 1999). See also Helmut Bley, *South-West Africa under German Rule, 1894–1914* (1968), trans. Hugh Ridley (Evanston, Ill.: Northwestern University Press, 1971); Jon M. Bridgman, *The Revolt of the Hereros* (Berkeley and Los Angeles: University of California Press, 1981); and Horst Drechsler, *"Let Us Die Fighting": The Struggle of the Herero and Nama against German Imperialism (1884–1915)* (1966), trans. Bernd Zöllner (London: Zed, 1980).

17. The standard account of the war has been that it began with Herero attacks on German settlers. However, Gewald has marshaled significant evidence suggesting that German troops, fearful of a Herero attack, fired the first shots in panic. See Gewald, *Herero Heroes,* 141–91.

18. For arguments—which I do not find persuasive—against the genocidal interpretation of the war with the Herero, see Brigitte Lau, "Uncertain Certainties— the Herero-German War of 1904," in *History and Historiography* (Windhoek: Discourse/MSORP, 1995), 39–52; and esp. Gunter Spraul, "Der 'Volkermord' an den Herero: Untersuchungen zu einer neuen *Kontinuitätsthese," Geschichte in Wissenschaft und Unterricht* 39 (1988): 713–39.

19. See Roger Boyes, "Germany Apologises for 1904 Slaughter of Africans," *The Times* (London), 9 June 1998, 16.

20. See Gewald, *Herero Heroes,* 141–91.

21. Felix von Luschan to Oberleutnant Ralf Zürn, 15 April, 21 June 1905, MfV, IB 39, vol. 1, 775/05.

22. See Felix von Luschan to Ernst A. Böttcher, 8 October 1906, and Böttcher to Luschan, 18 October 1906, MfV, IB 39, vol. 2, 1675/06. Luschan declared the rumor to be a "mystification."

23. Felix von Luschan to Oberleutnant Ralf Zürn, 21 June 1905, MfV, IB 39, vol. 1, 775/05.

24. Felix von Luschan to Oberleutnant Ralf Zürn, 21 June 1905, and Zürn to Luschan, 25 June 1905, MfV, IB 39, vol. 1, 775/05.

25. See Gewald, *Herero Heroes,* 189–90 n. 256. Gewald's information comes from a letter of 31 July 1908 from the German colonial secretary to the governor of Southwest Africa, Namibian National Archives, Windhoek, Zentralbureau 2027, SAWW.II.d.8. He also cites a photograph in *Meine Kreigs-Erlebnisse in Deutsch-Südwest-Afrika, Von Einem Offizier Der Schutztruppe* (Minden: Wiköhler, 1907), 114, with the following caption: "A chest of Herero skulls was recently sent by troops from

German Southwest Africa to the pathological institute in Berlin, where they will be subjected to scientific measurements. The skulls, from which Herero women have removed the flesh with the aid of glass shards to make suitable for shipment, come from Hereros who have been hanged or who have fallen." This caption is also cited in Gesine Krüger, *Kriegsbewältigung und Geschichtsbewußtsein: Realität, Deutung und Verarbeitung des deutschen Kolonialkrieges in Namibia 1904 bis 1907* (Göttingen: Vandenhoeck & Ruprecht, 1999), 98.

26. Leonard Schultze, introduction to *Zoologische und anthropologische Ergebnisse einer Forschungsreise im westlichen und zentralen Südafrika ausgeführt in den Jahren 1903–1905,* ed. Leonard Schultze (Jena: Gustav Fischer, 1908), viii. Schultze is cited in Gewald, *Herero Heroes,* 189 n. 256. See also H. von Eggeling, "Anatomische Untersuchungen an den Köpfen von vier Hereros, einem Herero- und einem Hottentottenkind," in Schultze, ed., *Zoologische und anthropologische Ergebnisse einer Forschungsreise im westlichen und zentralen Südafrika,* 322–48.

27. See Wilhelm Waldeyer, forward to "Cerebra Hererica" and "Cerebra Hererica," by Sergio Sergi, in Schultze, ed., *Zoologische und anthropologische Ergebnisse einer Forschungsreise im westlichen und zentralen Südafrika,* 1–321.

28. There is obviously no space here to discuss in any more than a suggestive way the enormous topic of continuities between German imperialism and Nazi expansionism or even between anthropology in the two periods. Woodruff Smith has done interesting work on ideological continuities. See Smith, *The Ideological Origins of Nazi Imperialism.*

29. See Léopold Sédar Senghor, forward to *Leo Frobenius, 1873–1973: An Anthology,* ed. Eike Haberland (Wiesbaden: Franz Steiner, 1973). See also Janet G. Vaillant, *Black, French, and African: A Life of Léopold Sédar Senghor* (Cambridge, Mass.: Harvard University Press, 1990); and Jahn, *Leo Frobenius.* Suzanne Marchand discusses Leo Frobenius and the inspiration that he provided to those, including Eric Wolff and Léopold Sédar Senghor, who wished to move away from Eurocentric definitions of culture and history in "Leo Frobenius and the Revolt against the West."

30. Yambo Ouologuem, *Bound to Violence* (1968), trans. Ralf Mannheim (New York: Harcourt Brace Jovanovich, 1971). J. M. Ita discusses this book as a response to Senghor's reading of Frobenius in "Frobenius, Senghor, and the Image of Africa," in *Modes of Thought: Essays on Thinking in Western and Non-Western Societies,* ed. Robin Horton and Ruth Finnegan (London: Faber & Faber, 1973), 306–36.

31. Aimé Césaire, *Discourse on Colonialism* (1955; New York: Monthly Review Press, 1972), 14, 56.

BIBLIOGRAPHY

ARCHIVES

Archiv der Berliner Gesellschaft für Anthropologie, Ethnologie und Urgeschichte, Schloß Charlottenberg, Berlin.

Archiv der Humboldt-Universität, Berlin.

Archiv des Museums für Völkerkunde, Berlin.

Archiv der Staatlichen Museen, Berlin.

Brandenburgisches Landeshauptarchiv, Potsdam.

Bundesarchiv Potsdam. Records of the Imperial German Government.

Geheimes Staatsarchiv Preußischer Kulturbesitz, Berlin. Records of the Prussian Government.

Landesarchiv Berlin (Stadtarchiv).

Nachlaß Adolf Bastians, Staatsbibliothek, Bremen.

Nachlaß Felix von Luschans, Handschriftenabteilung, Staatsbibliothek Berlin (Haus II).

Nachlaß Rudolf Virchows, Akademie der Wissenschaften, Berlin.

PERIODICALS

American Anthropologist

Anthropos

Archiv für Anthropologie

Archiv für pathologische Anatomie und Physiologie und für klinische Medicin (also known as *Virchows Archiv*)

Archiv für Rassen- und Gesellschafts-Biologie

Ausland

Baessler-Archiv: Beiträge zur Völkerkunde

Centralblatt für Anthropologie, Ethnologie und Urgeschichte

Correspondenz-Blatt der Deutschen Anthropologischen Gesellschaft

Deutsche Zeitschrift für Geschichtswissenschaft

Ethnologica

Globus

Historische Zeitschrift

Internationale Archiv für Ethnographie

Jahrbuch über die deutschen Kolonien

Journal of the Royal Anthropological Institute of Great Britain and Ireland

Koloniale Rundschau

Mittheilungen der anthropologischen Gesellschaft in Wien

Museumskunde

Politisch-Anthropologische Revue

Sitzungsberichte der Königlich Preussischen Akademie der Wissenschaften zu Berlin

Stenographische Berichte über die Verhandlungen des Abgeordneten Haus

Stenographische Berichte über die Verhandlungen des Reichstags

Verhandlungen der Berliner Gesellschaft für Anthropologie, Ethnologie und Urgeschichte

Vorlesungsverzeichnis der Friedrich-Wilhelm Universität zu Berlin

Zeitschrift für Ethnologie

Zeitschrift der Gesellschaft für Erdkunde zu Berlin

Zeitschrift für Völkerpsychologie und Sprachwissenschaft

PUBLISHED PRIMARY SOURCES

Achelis, Thomas. *Moderne Völkerkunde, deren Entwicklung und Aufgabe.* Stuttgart: Ferdinand Enke, 1896.

Ammon, Otto. *Die Gesellschaftsordnung und ihre natürliche Grundlagen: Entwurf einer Sozial-Anthropologie zum Gebrauch für alle Gebildeten, die sich mit sozialen Fragen befassen.* Jena: Gustav Fischer, 1895.

Bacon, Francis. *Novum Organum.* 1620. Translated by Peter Urbach and John Gibson. Chicago: Open Court, 1994.

Bastian, Adolf. *Das Beständige in den Menschenrassen und die Spielweite ihrer Veränderlichkeit: Prolegomena zu einer Ethnologie der Culturvölker.* Berlin: Dietrich Reimer, 1868.

———. *Der Buddhismus als religions-philosophisches System.* Berlin: Weidmann, 1893.

———. *Ethnologie und Geschichte in ihren Berührungspunkten unter Bezugnahme auf Indien.* Vol. 2, *Ideale Welten in Wort und Bild.* Berlin: Emil Felber, 1892.

———. *Zur Kenntniss Hawaii's.* Berlin: Ferdinand Dümmler, 1883.

————. *Der Mensch in der Geschichte: Zur Begründung einer psychologischen Weltanschauung.* 1860. 3 vols. Osnabruck: Biblioverlag, 1968.

————. *Zur Mythologie und Psychologie der Nigritier in Guinea mit Bezugnahme auf socialistische Elementargedanken.* Berlin: Dietrich Reimer, 1894.

————. *Offner Brief an Herrn Professor Dr. E. Häckel, Verfasser der "Natürlichen Schöpfungsgeschichte."* Berlin: Wiegandt, Hempel & Parey, 1874.

————. *Die Seele indischer und hellenischer Philosophie in den Gespenstern moderner Geisterseherei.* Berlin: Weidmann, 1886.

————. *Die Vorgeschichte der Ethnologie: Deutschland's Denkfreunden gewidmet fur eine Mussestunde.* Berlin: Ferdinand Dümmler, 1881.

Bauausführungen der Berliner Terrain und Bau Aktiengesellschaft: Passage-Kaufhaus (Friedrichstraßen-Passage). n.p., n.d.

Blumenbach, Johann Friedrich. *The Anthropological Treatises of Johann Friedrich Blumenbach.* 1865. Edited and translated by Thomas Bendyshe. Boston: Milford, 1973.

Braun, Alexander. *Ueber die Bedeutung der Entwickelung in der Naturgeschichte.* Berlin: August Hirschwald, 1872.

————. *Ueber die Bedeutung der Pflanzenkunde für die allgemeine Bildung.* Berlin: August Hirschwald, 1877.

Briefe an Rudolf Virchow. Berlin: Litteraturarchiv-Gesellschaft, 1921.

Buckland, William. *Reliquiae Diluvianae; or, Observations on . . . Geological Phenomena, Attesting to the Action of a Universal Deluge.* London, 1823.

Buffon, Georges. *Époques de la nature.* Paris, 1778.

Cotta, Bernard. *Leitfaden und Vademecum der Geognosie.* Dresden: Arnold, 1849.

Darwin, Charles. *The Descent of Man and Selection in Relation to Sex.* 2d ed. London: John Murry, 1882.

Dernburg, Bernhard. *Zielpunkte des Deutschen Kolonialwesens.* Berlin: Ernst Siegfried Mittler & Sohn, 1907.

Deutsches Kolonial-Lexikon. Leipzig: Quelle & Meyer, 1920.

Dilthey, Wilhelm. *Einleitung in die Geisteswissenschaften.* 1883. Stuttgart: B. G. Teubner, 1914.

————. *Gesammelte Schriften.* Vol. 17. Göttingen: Vandenhoeck & Ruprecht, 1974.

Droysen, Johann Gustav. *Rekonstruktion der ersten vollständigen Fassung der Vorlesungen.* 1857. In *Historik* (vol. 1), ed. Peter Leyh. Stuttgart-Bad Cannstatt: Frommann-Holzboog, 1977.

Du Bois-Reymond, Emil. "Kulturgeschichte und Naturwissenschaft." In *Vorträge über Philosophie und Gesellschaft,* ed. Siegried Wollgast, 105–58. Hamburg: Felix Meiner, 1974.

Eichhorn, Johann Gottfried. *Einleitung in das Alte Testament.* Leipzig: Weidmann, 1803.

Festschrift für Adolf Bastian zu seinem 70. Geburtstag 26. Juni 1896. Berlin: Dietrich Reimer, 1896.

Finsch, Otto. *Gesichtsmasken von Völkertypen der Südsee und dem malayischen Archipel nach Leben abgegossen in den Jahren 1879–1882.* Bremen: Homeyer & Meyer, 1887.

Fritsch, Gustav. *Die Eingeborenen Süd-Afrika's: Atlas enthaltend dreissig Tafeln Racentypen.* Breslau: Ferdinand Hirt, 1872.

———. *Die Eingeborenen Süd-Afrika's ethnographisch und anatomisch Beschrieben.* Breslau: Ferdinand Hirt, 1872.

Frobenius, Leo. *Ausfahrt: Von der Völkerkunde zum Kulturproblem.* Frankfurt a.M.: Frankfurter Societäts-Druckerei, 1925.

———. *Die naturwissenschaftliche Culturlehre.* Berlin: Ferdinand Dümmler, 1899.

———. *Der Ursprung der afrikanischen Kulturen.* Berlin: Gebrüder Borntraeger, 1898.

———. *Die Weltanschauung der Naturvölker.* Weimar: Emil Felber, 1898.

Führer durch das Museum für Völkerkunde. 1st–8th eds. Berlin: W. Spemann, 1886–1900.

Gervinus, Georg Gottfried. *Gesammelte Kleine Historische Schriften.* Karlsruhe: Friedrich Wilhelm Hasper, 1838.

Goldschmidt, Albert. *Berlin, Potsdam und Umgebungen: Praktischer Wegweiser.* Berlin: Albert Goldschmidt, 1892.

Graebner, Fritz. "Adolf Bastian's 100. Geburtstag." *Ethnologica* 3 (1927): ix–xii.

———. *Methode der Ethnologie.* 1911. Oosterhout: Anthropological Publications, 1966.

Haddon, Alfred C. *History of Anthropology.* London: Watts & Co., 1910.

Hagenbeck, Carl. *Von Tieren und Menschen: Erlebnisse und Erfahrungen.* Berlin: Vita Deutsches, 1909.

Heeren, A. H. L. *Ideen über die Politik, den Verkehr und den Handel der vornehmsten Völker der alten Welt.* 2 vols. Göttingen: Vandenhoek & Ruprecht, 1793–96.

Hegel, Georg Wilhelm Friedrich. *Vorlesungen über die Philosophie der Geschichte.* Stuttgart: Reclam, 1961.

Helmholtz, Hermann von. *Ueber das Verhältniss der Naturwisenschaften zur Gesammtheit der Wissenschaften.* Heidelberg: Georg Mohr, 1862.

Herder, Johann Gottfried von. *Auch eine Philosophie der Geschichte zur Bildung der Menschheit.* 1774. Stuttgart: Reclam, 1990.

———. *Ideen zur Philosophie der Geschichte der Menschheit.* 1784. 2 vols. Berlin: Aufbau, 1965.

Herrmann, Joachim, Evelin Maas, Christian Andree, and Lousie Hallof, eds. *Die Korrespondenz zwischen Heinrich Schliemann und Rudolf Virchow, 1876–1890.* Berlin: Akademie, 1990.

Humboldt, Wilhelm von. "Über die Aufgabe des Geschichtschreibers." 1821. In *Wil-*

helm von Humboldts Werke, ed. Albert Leitzmann, 4:35–56. Berlin: B. Behr, 1905.

Kant, Immanuel. *Anthropologie in pragmatischer Hinsicht.* 1798. Königsberg: Friedrich Nicolovius, 1800.

———. "Idea for a Universal History with a Cosmopolitan Intent." In *Perpetual Peace and Other Essays,* trans. and ed. Ted Humphrey, 29–40. Indianapolis: Hackett, 1983.

———. *Metaphysische Anfangsgründe der Naturwissenschaft.* 1786. In *Kant's gesammelte Schriften,* 4:465–565. Berlin: Georg Reimer, 1911.

———. *Die Religion innerhalb der Grenzen der blossen Vernunft.* 1793. In *Kant's gesammelte Schriften,* vol. 6. Berlin: Georg Reimer, 1914.

Klemm, Gustav. *Allgemeine Cultur-Geschichte der Menschheit.* Vol. 1, *Die Einleitung und die Urzustände der Menschheit.* Leipzig: B. G. Teubner, 1843.

Klutmann, [?]. *Das Königliche Museum für Völkerkunde in Berlin.* Berlin: Ernst & Korn, 1887.

Königliche Museen zu Berlin. *Das Koenigliche Museum für Völkerkunde am 18. Dezember 1886.* Berlin: Gebr. Unger, 1886.

Königliches Museum für Völkerkunde in Berlin. *Anleitung für ethnographische Beobachtungen und Sammlungen in Afrika und Oceanien.* 3d ed. Berlin: Gebr. Unger, 1904.

Kracauer, Siegfried. "Abschied von der Lindenpassage." 1930. In *Das Ornament der Masse,* 326–32. Frankfurt a.M.: Suhrkamp, 1963.

Krämer, Augustin. *Palau.* In *Ergebnisse der Südsee-Expedition, 1908–1910,* ed. Georg Thilenius. Hamburg: L. Friedrichsen, 1917.

Krämer-Bannow, Elisabeth. *Bei kunstsinnigen Kannibalen der Südsee: Wanderungen auf Neu-Mecklenburg, 1908–1909.* Berlin: Dietrich Reimer, 1916.

Ledebur, Leopold von. *Geschichte der Königlichen Kunstkammer in Berlin.* Berlin: E. G. Mittler, 1831. Reprinted from *Allgemeines Archiv für die Geschichtskunde des Preußischen Staates* 6 (1831): 3ff.

———. *Das Königliche Museum Vaterländischer Alterthümer im Schlosse Monbijou zu Berlin.* Berlin: Königliche Akademie der Wissenschaften, 1838.

———. *Leitfaden für die Königliche Kunstkammer und das ethnographische Cabinet zu Berlin.* Berlin, 1844.

Leonard, Gustav. *Grundzüge der Geognosie und Geologie.* 3d ed. Leipzig: C. F. Winter, 1874.

Lorenz, Ottokar. *Die Geschichtswissenschaft in Hauptrichtungen und Aufgaben.* Berlin: Wilhelm Hertz, 1886.

Lubbock, John. *Die Entstehung der Civilization und der Urzustand des Menschengeschlechtes.* Jena: Hermann Castenoble, 1875.

———. *Die vorgeschichtliche Zeit.* Jena: Hermann Castenoble, 1874.

Luschan, Felix von. *Beiträge zur Völkerkunde der Deutschen Schutzgebiete: Erweiterte*

Sonderausgabe aus dem "Amtlichen Bericht über die Erste Deutsche Kolonial-Ausstellung" in Treptow 1896. Berlin: Dietrich Reimer, 1897.

———. *Völker, Rassen, Sprachen.* Berlin: Weltverlag, 1922.

Matthes, Axel, ed. *Reden Kaiser Wilhelms II.* Munich: Rogner & Bernhard, 1976.

Meinecke, Gustav Hermann, and Rudolf Hellgrewe, eds. *Deutschland und seine Kolonien im Jahre 1896: Amtlicher Bericht über die erste Deutsche Kolonial-Ausstellung.* Berlin: Dietrich Reimer, 1897.

Meyer, Eduard. *Geschichte des Alterthums.* 1st—3d eds. Stuttgart: Cotta, 1884–1910.

———. *Zur Theorie und Methodik der Geschichte.* Halle: Max Niemeyer, 1902.

Michelet, Carl Ludwig. *Anthropologie und Psychologie oder die Philosophie des subjectiven Geistes.* Berlin, 1840.

Michelson, P. "Zum Capitel der Hypertrichoses." *Archiv für pathologische Anatomie und Physiologie und für klinische Medicin* 100 (1885): 66–80.

Mühlmann, Wilhelm. *Geschichte der Anthropologie.* Bonn: Universitäts-Verlag Bonn, 1948.

———. *Methodik der Völkerkunde.* Stuttgart: Ferdinand Enke, 1938.

———. *Rassen- und Völkerkunde: Lebensprobleme der Rassen, Gesellschaften und Völker.* Braunschweig: Friedrich Vieweg & Sohn, 1936.

Neumayer, Georg von, ed. *Anleitung zu Wissenschaftlichen Beobachtungen auf Reisen in Einzel-Abhandlungen.* 1st ed. Berlin: Robert Oppenheimer, 1875. 3d ed. Hannover: Dr. Max Jänecke, 1906.

Nolde, Emil. *Jahre der Kämpfe, 1902–1914.* 1934. Cologne: Dumont, 1967.

Nyiszli, Miklos. *Auschwitz: A Doctor's Eye Witness Account.* 1960. Translated by Tibère Kremer and Richard Seaver. New York: Arcade, 1993.

Ouologuem, Yambo. *Bound to Violence.* 1968. Translated by Ralf Mannheim. New York: Harcourt, Brace, Jovanovich, 1971.

Peschel, Oscar. *Völkerkunde.* 2d ed. Leipzig: Duncker & Humboldt, 1875.

Pfaff, Friedrich. *Allgemeine Geologie als Exacte Wissenschaft.* Leipzig: Wilhelm Engelmann, 1873.

Quatrefages, Armand de. *La Race prussienne.* Paris: Hachette, 1871.

Ranke, Johannes. *Der Mensch.* Leipzig: Bibliographisches Institut, 1894.

———. "Somatisch-anthropologische Beobachtungen." In *Anleitung zur deutschen Landes- und Volksforschung,* ed. Alfred Kirchhoff. Stuttgart: J. Engelhorn, 1889.

Ranke, Leopold von. *Leopold von Ranke: Aus Werk und Nachlass.* Edited by Walther Peter Fuchs and Theodor Schieder. Munich: R. Oldenbourg, 1975.

———. *Weltgeschichte.* 1881. 5th ed. Leipzig: Duncker & Humboldt, 1896.

Ratzel, Friedrich. *Anthropogeographie.* 3 vols. Stuttgart: J. Engelshorns, 1912.

———. "Die geographische Methode in der Ethnographie." *Geographische Zeitschrift* 3 (1897): 268–78.

————. *Kleine Schriften von Friedrich Ratzel,* ed. Hans Helmolt. 2 vols. Munich: R. Oldenbourg, 1906.

Rousseau, Jean-Jacques. "Discourse on the Origin and Foundations of Inequality among Men (1755)." In *Basic Political Writings,* trans. Donald A. Cress. Indianapolis: Hackett, 1987.

Sachau, Eduard. *Bericht über die Eröffnung des Seminars für Orientalische Sprachen an der Königlichen Friedrich-Wilhelms-Univerität und einige auf das Seminar bezügliche Schriftstücke.* Berlin: A. Asher, 1888.

Scheffler, Karl. *Berliner Museumskrieg.* Berlin: Bruno Cassierer, 1921.

Schelling, Friedrich Wilhelm Joseph von. *Ideas for a Philosophy of Nature.* 1979. Translated by Errol E. Harris and Peter Heath. Cambridge: Cambridge University Press, 1988.

Schlaginhaufen, Otto. *Muliama: Zwei Jahren unter Südsee-Insulaner.* Zürich: Orell Füssli, 1959.

Schultze, Leonard ed. *Zoologische und anthropologische Ergebnisse einer Forschungsreise im westlichen und zentralen Südafrika ausgeführt in den Jahren 1903–1905.* Jena: Gustav Fischer, 1908.

Sprat, Thomas. *History of the Royal Society.* 1667. Edited by Jackson I. Cope and Harold Whitmore Jones. Facsimile ed. St. Louis: Washington University Press, 1958.

Steinen, Karl von den. *Unter den Naturvölkern Zentral-Brasiliens: Reiseschilderung und Ergebnisse der Zweiten Schingú-Expedition, 1887–1888.* 1st ed. Berlin: Dietrich Reimer, 1894. 2d ed. Berlin: Dietrich Reimer, 1897.

Steinthal, Heymann. *Die Mande-Neger-Sprachen.* Berlin: Ferdinand Dümmler, 1867.

Stephan, Emil. *Südseekunst: Beiträge zur Kunst des Bismarck-Archipels und zur Urgeschichte der Kunst überhaupt.* Berlin: Dietrich Reimer, 1907.

Stephan, Emil, and Fritz Graebner. *Neu-Mecklenburg (Bismarck-Archipel): Die Küste von Umuddu bis Kap St. Georg. Forschungsergebnisse bei den Vermessungsfahrten von S. M. S. Möwe im Jahre 1904.* Berlin: Dietrich Reimer, 1907.

Thilenius, Georg. *Allgemeines.* In *Ergebnisse der Südsee-Expedition, 1908–1910.* Hamburg: L. Friedrichsen & Co., 1927.

Thurnwald, Richard, and Konrad Theodor Preuss, eds. *Lehrbuch der Völkerkunde.* 2d ed. Stuttgart: Ferdinand Enke, 1939.

Tylor, E. B. *Primitive Culture.* 1871. New York: Harper & Bros., 1958.

Virchow, Rudolf. *Die Eröffnung des pathologischen Museums der Königl. Friedrich-Wilhelms-Universität zu Berlin am 27. Juni 1899.* Berlin: August Hirschwald, 1899.

————. *Die Freiheit der Wissenschaft im modernen Staat.* Berlin: Wiegandt, Hempel & Parey, 1877.

————. *Göthe als Naturforscher und in besonderer Beziehung auf Schiller.* Berlin: August Hirschwald, 1861.

————. *Menschen- und Affenschädel.* Sammlung gemeinverständlicher Vorträge 96. Berlin: C. G. Lüderitz, 1870.

Waitz, Theodor. *Anthropologie der Naturvölker.* Leipzig: Friedrich Fleischer, 1859.

Wundt, Wilhelm. *Probleme der Völkerpsychologie.* Leipzig: Ernst Wiegandt, 1911.

SECONDARY SOURCES

Ackerknecht, Erwin. *Rudolf Virchow: Doctor, Statesman, Anthropologist.* Madison: University of Wisconsin Press, 1953.

Albisetti, James C. *Secondary School Reform in Imperial Germany.* Princeton, N.J.: Princeton University Press, 1983.

Alpers, Svetlana. *The Art of Describing: Dutch Art in the Seventeenth Century.* Chicago: University of Chicago Press, 1983.

Altick, Richard D. *The Shows of London.* Cambridge, Mass.: Harvard University Press, 1978.

Aly, Götz. *"Final Solution": Nazi Population Policy and the Murder of the European Jews.* New York: Oxford University Press, 1999.

————. "Das Posener Tagebuch des Anatomen Hermann Voss." In *Biedermann und Schreibtischtäter: Materialien zur detuschen Täter-Biographie,* 14–66. Berlin: Rotbuch, 1987.

————. "Stakkato der Vertreibung, Pizzikato der Entlastung." *Frankfurter Allgemeine Zeitung,* 3 February 1999, 46.

Anderton, Keith M. "The Limits of Science: A Social, Political, and Moral Agenda for Epistemology in Nineteenth-Century Germany." Ph.D. diss., Harvard University, 1993.

Andree, Christian. *Rudolf Virchow als Prähistoriker.* 2 vols. Cologne: Bohlau, 1976.

Appadurai, Arjun, ed. *The Social Life of Things: Commodities in Cultural Perspective.* Cambridge: Cambridge University Press, 1986.

Asad, Talal, ed. *Anthropology and the Colonial Encounter.* New York: Humanities, 1973.

Bakhtin, Mikhail. *The Dialolgic Imagination.* Edited by Michael Holquist. Translated by Caryl Emerson and Michael Holquist. Austin: University of Texas Press, 1981.

Barnes, Barry. "Making Out in Industrial Research." *Science Studies* 1 (1971): 157–75.

Batra, Roger. *The Artificial Savage: Modern Myths of the Wild Man.* Translated by Christopher Follett. Ann Arbor: University of Michigan Press, 1997.

Bayer, Ronald. "Politics, Science, and the Problem of Psychiatric Nomenclature: A Case Study of the American Psychiatric Association Referendum on Homosexuality." In *Scientific Controversies: Case Studies in the Resolution and Closure of Dis-*

putes in Science and Technology, ed. H. Tristam Engelhardt Jr. and Arthur L.
Caplan, 381–400. Cambridge: Cambridge University Press, 1987.

Belke, Ingrid. *Moritz Lazarus und Heymann Steinthal: Die Begründer der Völkerpsychologie in ihren Briefen.* Tübingen: J. C. B. Mohr, 1971.

Bell, Matthew. *Goethe's Naturalistic Anthropology: Man and Other Plants.* Oxford: Clarendon, 1994.

Ben-David, Joseph. *Scientific Growth: Essays on the Social Organization and Ethos of Science.* Edited by Gad Freudenthal. Berkeley and Los Angeles: University of California Press, 1991.

———. *The Scientist's Role in Society: A Comparative Study.* Englewood Cliffs, N.J.: Prentice-Hall, 1971.

Benjamin, Walter. *Charles Baudelaire: A Lyric Poet in the Era of High Capitalism.* Translated by Harry Zohn. London: Verso, 1983.

———. *Das Passagen-Werk.* Edited by Rolf Tiedemann. 2 vols. Frankfurt a.M.: Suhrkamp, 1982.

Bennet, Tony. *The Birth of the Museum: History, Theory, Politics.* London: Routledge, 1995.

Berlin, Isaiah. *Vico and Herder: Two Studies in the History of Ideas.* New York: Viking, 1976.

Bernal, Martin. *Black Athena.* Vol. 1. New Brunswick, N.J.: Rutgers University Press, 1987.

Bhabha, Homi. *The Location of Culture.* New York: Routledge, 1994.

Bitterli, Urs. *Die "Wilden" und die "Zivilisierten": Grundzüge einer Geistes- und Kulturgeschichte der europäisch-überseeischen Begegnung.* Munich: C. H. Beck, 1976.

Blackbourn, David. "Progress and Piety: Liberalism, Catholicism, and the State in Imperial Germany." *History Workshop Journal* 26 (1988): 57–78.

Blackbourn, David, and Geoff Eley. *The Peculiarities of German History: Bourgeois Society and Politics in Nineteenth-Century Germany.* Oxford: Oxford University Press, 1985.

Blackbourn, David, and Richard J. Evans, eds. *The German Bourgeoisie: Essays on the Social History of the German Middle Class from the Late Eighteenth to the Early Twentieth Century.* London: Routledge, 1991.

Bley, Helmut. *South-West Africa under German Rule, 1894–1914.* 1968. Translated by Hugh Ridley. Evanston, Ill.: Northwestern University Press, 1971.

Bogdan, Robert. *Freak Show: Presenting Human Oddities for Amusement and Profit.* Chicago: University of Chicago Press, 1988.

Bollenbeck, Georg. *Bildung und Kultur: Glanz und Elend eines deutschen Deutungsmusters.* Frankfurt a.M.: Insel, 1994.

Bourdieu, Pierre. *Outline of a Theory of Practice.* Translated by Richard Nice. Cambridge: Cambridge University Press, 1972.

Bowie, Andrew. *Schelling and Modern European Philosophy.* London: Routledge, 1993.

Boyd, Byron A. *Rudolf Virchow: The Scientist as Citizen.* New York: Garland, 1991.

Boyes, Roger. "Germany Apologises for 1904 Slaughter of Africans" *The Times,* 9 June 1998, 16.

Brandewie, Ernest. *When Giants Walked the Earth: The Life and Times of Wilhelm Schmidt SVD.* Fribourg: Fribourg University Press, 1990.

Bravo, Michael T. "The Accuracy of Ethnoscience: A Study of Inuit Cartography and Cross-Cultural Commensurability." Manchester Papers in Social Anthropology, no. 2. Manchester: University of Manchester, Department of Social Anthropology, 1996.

Bridgman, Jon M. *The Revolt of the Hereros.* Berkeley and Los Angeles: University of California Press, 1981.

Broce, Gerald. "Herder and Ethnography." *Journal of the History of the Behavioral Sciences* 22 (1986): 150–70.

Brown, Lee Rust. "The Emerson Museum." *Representations* 40 (1992): 57–80.

Bruch, Rüdiger vom. *Wissenschaft, Politik und öffentliche Meinung: Gelehrtenpolitik im Wilhelminischen Deutschland (1890–1914).* Husum: Matthiesen, 1980.

Bruckner, Sierra Ann. "The Tingle-Tangle of Modernity: Popular Anthropology and the Cultural Politics of Identity in Imperial Germany." Ph.D. diss., University of Iowa, 1999.

Bryson, Norman. *Vision and Painting: The Logic of the Gaze.* New Haven, Conn.: Yale University Press, 1983.

Buck-Morss, Susan. *The Dialectics of Seeing: Walter Benjamin and the Arcades Project.* Cambridge, Mass.: MIT Press, 1989.

Buddensieg, Tilmann, Kurt Duwell, and Klaus-Jürgen Sembach, eds. *Wissenschaften in Berlin.* Berlin: Gebrüder Mann, 1987.

Bumann, Waltraud. *Die Sprachtheorie Heymann Steinthals. Dargestellt im Zusammenhang mit seiner Theorie der Geisteswissenschaft.* Meisenheim am Glan: Anton Hain, 1965.

Burleigh, Michael. *Germany Turns Eastwards: A Study of Ostforschung in the Third Reich.* Cambridge: Cambridge University Press, 1988.

Burleigh, Michael, and Wolfgang Wippermann. *The Racial State: Germany, 1933–1945.* Cambridge: Cambridge University Press, 1991.

Buschmann, Rainer F. "Franz Boluminski and the Wonderland of Carvings: Towards an Ethnography of Collection Activity." *Baessler-Archiv* 44 (1996): 185–210.

———. "Tobi Captured: Converging Ethnographic and Colonial Visions on a Caroline Island." *ISLA: A Journal of Micronesian Studies* 4 (1996): 317–40.

Buttmann, Günther. *Friedrich Ratzel: Leben und Werk eines deutschen Geographen, 1844–1904.* Stuttgart: Wissenschaftlich Verlagsgesellschaft, 1977.

Cahan, David. *An Institution for an Empire: The Physikalisch-Technische Reichsanstalt, 1871–1918.* Cambridge: Cambridge University Press, 1989.

Cannon, Susan F. *Science in Culture: The Early Victorian Period.* New York: Dawson, 1978.

Césaire, Aimé. *Discourse on Colonialism.* 1955. New York: Monthly Review Press, 1972.

Chickering, Roger. *Karl Lamprecht: A German Academic Life (1856–1915).* Atlantic Highlands, N.J.: Humanities, 1993.

———. *We Men Who Feel Most German: A Cultural Study of the Pan-German League, 1886–1914.* Boston: George Allen & Unwin, 1984.

Christ, Karl. *Römische Geschichte und deutsche Geschichtswissenschaft.* München: C. H. Beck, 1982.

Cittadino, Eugene. *Nature as the Laboratory: Darwinian Plant Ecology in the German Empire, 1880–1900.* Cambridge: Cambridge University Press, 1990.

Clifford, James. "On Ethnographic Surrealism." *Comparative Studies in Society and History* 23 (1981): 539–64.

———. *The Predicament of Culture: Twentieth-Century Ethnography, Literature, and Art.* Cambridge, Mass.: Harvard University Press, 1988.

Clifford, James, and George E. Marcus, eds. *Writing Culture: The Politics and Poetics of Ethnography.* Berkeley and Los Angeles: University of California Press, 1986.

Cocks, Geoffrey, and Konrad H. Jarausch. *German Professions, 1800–1950.* New York: Oxford University Press, 1990.

Coetzee, Marilyn Shevin. *The German Army League: Popular Nationalism in Wilhelmine Germany.* New York: Oxford University Press, 1990.

Cohn, Bernard S. *Colonialism and Its Forms of Knowledge: The British in India.* Princeton, N.J.: Princeton University Press, 1996.

Conn, Steven. *Museums and American Intellectual Life, 1876–1926.* Chicago: University of Chicago Press, 1998.

Conze, Werner, and Jürgen Kocka, eds. *Bildungsbürgertum im neunzehnten Jahrhundert.* 4 vols. Stuttgart: Klett-Cotta, 1985–92.

Coombes, Annie E. *Reinventing Africa: Museums, Material Culture, and Popular Imagination in Late Victorian and Edwardian England.* New Haven, Conn.: Yale University Press, 1994.

Cooper, Frederick, and Ann Laura Stoler, eds. *Tensions of Empire: Colonial Cultures in a Bourgeois World.* Berkeley and Los Angeles: University of California Press, 1997.

Crary, Jonathan. *Techniques of the Observer: On Vision and Modernity in the Nineteenth Century.* Cambridge, Mass.: MIT Press, 1990.

Dahrendorf, Ralf. *Society and Democracy in Germany.* Garden City, N.Y.: Doubleday, 1967.

Danto, Arthur C. "Artifact and Art." In *Art/Artifact: African Art in Anthropology Collections*, 18–32. New York: Center for African Art, 1988.

Danziger, Kurt. *Constructing the Subject: Historical Origins of Psychological Research.* Cambridge: Cambridge University Press, 1990.

Daston, Lorraine, and Peter Galison. "The Image of Objectivity." *Representations* 40 (1992): 81–128.

Daum, Andreas W. *Wissenschaftspopularisierun im 19. Jahrhundert: Bürgerliche Kultur, naturwissenschaftliche Bildung und die deutsche Öffentlichkeit, 1848–1914.* München: R. Oldenbourg, 1998.

Debrunner, Hans Werner. *Presence and Prestige: Africans in Europe.* Basel: Basler Afrika Bibliographien, 1979.

de Grazia, Victoria, and Ellen Furlough, eds. *The Sex of Things: Gender and Consumption in Historical Perspective.* Berkeley and Los Angeles: University of California Press, 1996.

Derrida, Jacques. *Of Grammatology.* Translated by Gayatri Chakravorty Spivak. Baltimore: Johns Hopkins University Press, 1976.

Desmond, Adrian. *The Politics of Evolution: Morphology, Medicine, and Reform in Radical London.* Chicago: University of Chicago Press, 1989.

Dirks, Nicholas B. "History as a Sign of the Modern." *Public Culture* 2 (1990): 25–32.

———, ed. *Colonialism and Culture.* Ann Arbor: University of Michigan Press, 1992.

Drechsler, Horst. *"Let Us Die Fighting": The Struggle of the Herero and Nama against German Imperialism (1884–1915).* 1966. Translated by Bernd Zöllner. London: Zed, 1980.

Edgerton, Sam E., Jr. *The Renaissance Rediscovery of Linear Perspective.* New York: Basic, 1975.

Edwards, Elizabeth, ed. *Anthropology and Photography, 1860–1920.* New Haven, Conn.: Yale University Press, 1992.

Efron, John M. *Defenders of the Race: Jewish Doctors and Race Science in Fin-de-Siècle Europe.* New Haven, Conn.: Yale University Press, 1994.

Eley, Geoff. *Reshaping the German Right: Radical Nationalism and Political Change after Bismarck.* New Haven, Conn.: Yale University Press, 1980.

———, ed. *Society, Culture, and the State in Germany, 1870–1930.* Ann Arbor: University of Michigan Press, 1996.

Elias, Norbert. *The History of Manners.* 1939. Translated by Edmund Jephcott. New York: Pantheon, 1978.

Elon, Amos. "Death for Sale." *New York Review of Books,* 20 November 1997, 41.

Engelhardt, Dietrich von. "Der Biludungsbegriff in der Naturwissenschaft des 19. Jahrhunderts." In *Bildungsbürgertum im 19. Jahrhundert* (vol. 2), ed. Reinhart Koselleck, 106–16. Stuttgart: Klett-Cotta, 1990.

Esherick, Joseph W. *The Origins of the Boxer Uprising.* Berkeley and Los Angeles: University of California Press, 1987.

Essner, Cornelia. "Berlins Völkerkunde-Museum in der Kolonialära: Anmerkungen zum Verhältnis von Ethnologie und Kolonialismus in Deutschland." In *Berlin in Geschichte und Gegenwart: Jahrbuch des Landesarchivs Berlin,* ed. Hans J. Reichhardt, 65–94. Berlin: Siedler, 1986.

———. *Deutsche Afrikareisende im neunzehnten Jahrhundert.* Stuttgart: Franz Steiner, 1985.

Eze, Emmanuel Chukwudi, ed. *Race and the Enlightenment: A Reader.* Cambridge: Blackwell, 1997.

Fabian, Johannes. *Time and the Other: How Anthropology Makes Its Object.* New York: Columbia University Press, 1983.

———. *Time and the Work of Anthropology: Critical Essays, 1971–1991.* Philadelphia: Harwood Academic, 1991.

Fiedermutz-Laun, Annemarie. *Der kulturhistorische Gedanke bei Adolf Bastian.* Wiesbaden: Franz Steiner, 1970.

Findlen, Paula. *Possessing Nature: Museums, Collecting, and Scientific Culture in Early Modern Italy.* Berkeley and Los Angeles: University of California Press, 1993.

Fischer, Hans. *Die Hamburger Südsee-Expedition: Über Ethnographie und Kolonialismus.* Frankfurt a.M: Syndikat, 1981.

———. *Völkerkunde im National-Sozialismus: Aspekte der Anpassung, Affinität und Behauptung einer wissenschaftichen Disziplin.* Berlin: Dietrich Reimer, 1990.

Foucault, Michel. *Discipline and Punish: The Birth of the Prison.* New York: Vintage, 1977.

———. *The Order of Things: An Archaeology of the Human Sciences.* New York: Random House, 1970.

Frei, Hans W. *The Eclipse of Biblical Narrative: A Study in Eighteenth and Nineteenth Century Hermeneutics.* New Haven, Conn.: Yale University Press, 1974.

Frese, Hermann Heinrich. *Anthropology and the Public: The Role of Museums.* Leiden: E. J. Brill, 1960.

Freudenthal, Herbert. *Vereine in Hamburg: Ein Beitrag zur Geschichte und Volkskunde der Geselligkeit.* Hamburg: Museum für Hamburgische Geschichte, 1968.

Friedrichsmeyer, Sara, Sara Lennox, and Susanne Zantop, eds. *The Imperialist Imagination: German Colonialism and Its Legacy.* Ann Arbor: University of Michigan Press, 1998.

Gadamer, Hans-Georg. *Truth and Method.* 1986. Translated by Joel Weinsheimer and Donald G. Marshall. New York: Crossroad, 1990.

Gall, Lothar. *Bismarck: The White Revolutionary.* London: Allen & Unwin, 1986.

Gareis, Sigrid. *Exotik in München: Museumsethnologische Konzeptionen im historischen Wandel am Beispiel des Staatlichen Museums für Völkerkunde München.* Munich: Anacon, 1990.

Gasman, Daniel. *The Scientific Origins of National Socialism: Social Darwinism in Ernst Haeckel and the German Monist League.* New York: American Elsevier, 1971.

Geary, Christraud M. "Political Dress: German-Style Military Attire and Colonial
    Politics in Bamum." In *African Crossroads: Intersections between History and An-
    thropology in Cameroon,* ed. Ian Fowler and David Zeitlyn, 165–92. Providence:
    Berghahn, 1996.

Geertz, Clifford. "Being There: Anthropology and the Scene of Writing." In *Works
    and Lives: The Anthropologist as Author,* 1–24. Stanford, Calif.: Stanford Univer-
    sity Press, 1988.

Gernsheim, Helmut, and Alison Gernsheim. *The History of Photography From the
    Camera Obscura to the beginning of the Modern Era.* New York: McGraw-Hill,
    1969.

Geus, Armin, and Hans Querner. *Deutsche Zoologische Gesellschaft, 1890–1990: Doku-
    mentation und Geschichte.* Stuttgart: Gustav Fischer, 1990.

Gewald, Jan-Bart. *Herero Heroes: A Socio-Poliical History of the Herero of Namibia,
    1890–1923.* Oxford: James Currey, 1999.

Gillespie, Charles. *Genesis and Geology.* Cambridge, Mass.: Harvard University Press,
    1951.

Gilman, Sander. *The Jew's Body.* New York: Routledge, 1991.

Giustiniani, Vito R. "Homo, Humanus, and the Meaning of 'Humanism.'" *Journal
    of the History of Ideas* 46 (1985): 167–95.

Godelier, Maurice. *Rationality and Irrationality in Economics.* Translated by Brian
    Pearce. London: New Left, 1972.

Gohau, Gabriel. *Les Sciences de la Terre aux XVIIe et XVIIIe Siècles: Naissance de la
    Géologie.* Paris: Albin Michel, 1990.

Goldgar, Anne. *Impolite Learning: Conduct and Community in the Republic of Letters,
    1680–1750.* New Haven, Conn.: Yale University Press, 1995.

Gombrich, E. H. *Art and Illusion: A Study in the Psychology of Pictorial Representation.*
    Princeton, N.J.: Princeton University Press, 1960.

Goodman, Dena. *The Republic of Letters: A Cultural History of the French Enlighten-
    ment.* Ithaca, N.Y.: Cornell University Press, 1994.

Goody, Jack. *The Domestication of the Savage Mind.* Cambridge: Cambridge Univer-
    sity Press, 1977.

Gordon, Robert J. *The Bushman Myth: The Making of a Namibian Underclass.* Boulder,
    Colo.: Westview, 1992.

Gothsch, Manfred. *Die deutsche Völkerkunde und ihr Verhältnis zum Kolonialismus: Ein
    Beitrag zur kolonialideologischen und kolonialpractischen Bedeutung der deutschen
    Völkerkunde in der Zeit von 1870 bis 1975.* Baden-Baden: Nomos, 1983.

Gould, Stephen Jay. *The Mismeasure of Man.* New York: Norton, 1981.

———. *Ontogeny and Phylogeny.* Cambridge, Mass.: Harvard University Press,
    1977.

———. *Time's Arrow, Time's Cycle: Myth and Metaphor in the Discovery of Geological
    Time.* Cambridge, Mass.: Harvard University Press, 1987.

Grafton, Anthony. *Defenders of the Text: The Traditions of Scholarship in an Age of Science, 1450–1800.* Cambridge, Mass.: Harvard University Press, 1991.

Gregory, C. A. *Gifts and Commodities.* London: Academic, 1982.

Gregory, Frederick. "Kant's Influence on Natural Scientists in the German Romantic Period." In *New Trends in the History of Science,* ed. R. P. W. Visser et al., 53–66. Amsterdam: Rodopi, 1989.

———. *Nature Lost? Natural Science and the German Theological Traditions of the Nineteenth Century.* Cambridge, Mass.: Harvard University Press, 1992.

———. *Scientific Materialism in Nineteenth Century Germany.* Dordrecht: D. Reidel, 1977.

Gross, Michael B. "Kulturkampf and Unification: German Liberalism and the War against the Jesuits." *Central European History* 30 (1998): 545–66.

Grosse, Pascal. "Eingeborene, Untertanen, oder Bürger?—Afrikaner aus den Kolonien in Deutschland, 1885–1914." Humboldt-Universität, Berlin, 1995. Typescript.

Grottanelli, Vinigi. "Ethnology and/or Cultural Anthropology in Italy: Traditions and Developments." *Current Anthropology* 18 (1977): 593–614.

Gründer, Horst. *Geschichte der deutschen Kolonien.* 2d ed. Munich: Ferdinand Schöningh, 1991.

Guha, Ranajit, and Gayatri Chakravorty Spivak, eds. *Selected Subaltern Studies.* New York: Oxford University Press, 1988.

Gupta, Akhil, and James Ferguson. "Beyond 'Culture': Space, Identity, and the Politics of Difference." *Cultural Anthropology* 7 (1992): 6–23.

Gwassa, G. C. K. "African Methods of Warfare during the Maji Maji War, 1905–1907." In *War and Society in Africa,* ed. Bethwell A. Ogot. London: Frank Cass, 1972.

Haberland, Eike, ed. *Leo Frobenius, 1873–1973: An Anthology.* Wiesbaden: Franz Steiner, 1973.

Hacking, Ian. *The Taming of Chance.* Cambridge: Cambridge University Press, 1990.

Hamelman, William E. *Of Red Eagles and Royal Crowns.* Dallas: Taylor, 1978.

Hamm, Ernst P. "Bureaucratic *Statistik* or Actualism? K. E. A. von Hoff's *History* and the History of Geology." *History of Science* 31 (1993): 151–76.

Haraway, Donna. *Primate Visions: Gender, Race, and Nature in the World of Modern Science.* New York: Routledge, 1989.

———. "The Promises of Monsters: A Regenerative Politics for Inappropriate/d Others." In *Cultural Studies,* ed. Lawrence Grossberg, Carly Nelson, and Paula A. Treichler, 295–337. New York: Routledge, 1992.

Harms, Volker. "Ethnographische Kunstobjekte als Beute des europäischen Kolonialismus." *Kritische Berichte* 23 (1995): 15–31.

———. "Das historische Verhältnis der deutschen Ethnologie zum Kolonialismus." *Zeitschrift für Kulturaustausch* 34 (1984): 401–16.

Harvey, Joy. "Evolutionism Transformed: Positivists and Materialists in the *Société d'Anthropologie de Paris* from Second Empire to Third Republic." In *The Wider Domain of Evolutionary Thought,* ed. David Oldroyd and Ian Langham, 289–310. Dordrecht: D. Reidel, 1983.

Harwood, Jonathan. "Mandarins and Outsiders in the German Professoriate, 1890–1933: A Study of the Genetics Community." *European History Quarterly* 23 (1993): 485–511.

———. *Styles of Scientific Thought: The German Genetics Community, 1900–1933.* Chicago: University of Chicago Press, 1993.

Hasler, Ueli. *Beherrschte Natur: Die Anpassung der Theologie an die bürgerliche Naturauffassung im 19. Jahrhundert (Schleiermacher, Ritschl, Hermann).* Bern: Peter Lang, 1982.

Hatfield, Douglas W. "Kulturkampf: The Relationship of Church and State and the Failure of German Political Reform." *Church and State* 23 (1981): 465–84.

Hatfield, Gary. *The Natural and the Normative: Theories of Spatial Perception from Kant to Helmholtz.* Cambridge, Mass.: MIT Press, 1990.

Hausen, Karin. *Deutsche Kolonialherrschaften in Afrika: Wirtschaftsinteressen und Kolonialverwaltung in Kamerun vor 1914.* Zurich: Atlantis, 1970.

Headrick, Daniel R. *The Tools of Empire: Technology and European Imperialism in the Nineteenth Century.* New York: Oxford University Press, 1981.

Henderson, W. O. *The German Colonial Empire, 1884–1919.* London: Frank Cass, 1993.

Herle, Anita, and Sandra Rouse, eds. *Cambridge and the Torres Strait: Centenary Essays on the 1898 Anthropological Expedition.* Cambridge: Cambridge University Press, 1998.

Hezel, Francis X. *The First Taint of Civilization: A History of the Caroline and Marshall Islands in the Pre-Colonial Days, 1521–1885.* Honolulu: University of Hawaii Press, 1983.

Hildebrand, Josephine, and Christian Theurerkauff, eds. *Die Brandenburgisch-Preussische Kunstkammer.* Berlin: Staatliche Museen Preußischer Kulturbesitz, 1981.

Hinsley, Curtis M. "The Museum Origins of Harvard Anthropology, 1866–1915." In *Science at Harvard University: Historical Perspectives,* ed. Clark A. Elliott and Margaret W. Rossiter, 121–45. Bethlehem, Pa.: Lehigh University Press, 1992.

———. *Savages and Scientists: The Smithsonian Institution and the Development of American Anthropology, 1846–1910.* Washington, D.C.: Smithsonian Institution Press, 1981.

Hobsbawm, Eric, and Terence Ranger, eds. *The Invention of Tradition.* Cambridge: Cambridge University Press, 1983.

Hog, Michael. *Ethnologie und Öffentlichkeit: Ein entwicklungsgeschichtlicher Überblick.* Frankfurt: Peter Lang, 1990.

Hooven, F. Valentine. "The Birth of Beefcake." In *Beefcake: The Muscle Magazine of America, 1950–1970.* Cologne: Benedikt Taschen, 1995.

Hücking, Renate, and Ekkehard Launer. *Aus Menschen Neger Machen: Wie sich das Handelshaus Woermann in Afrika Entwickelt hat.* Hamburg: Galgenberg, 1986.

Hudson, Kenneth. *A Social History of Museums: What the Visitors Thought.* London: Macmillan, 1975.

Hunt, Lynn. *Politics, Culture, and Class in the French Revolution.* Berkeley and Los Angeles: University of California Press, 1984.

———, ed. *The Invention of Pornography: Obscenity and the Origins of Modernity, 1500–1800.* New York: Zone, 1993.

Hunter, James M. *Perspective on Ratzel's Political Geography.* Lanham, Md.: University Press of America, 1983.

Iggers, Georg G. *The German Conception of History: The National Tradition of Historical Thought from Herder to the Present.* Middletown, Conn.: Wesleyan University Press, 1968.

Iliffe, John. *A Modern History of Tanganyika.* Cambridge: Cambridge University Press, 1979.

Ita, J. M. "Frobenius, Senghor, and the Image of Africa." In *Modes of Thought: Essays on Thinking in Western and Non-Western Societies,* ed. Robin Horton and Ruth Finnegan, 306–36. London: Faber & Faber, 1973.

Jacob, J. R. "Restoration, Reformation, and the Origins of the Royal Society." *History of Science* 13 (1975): 155–76.

Jaeger, Friedrich, and Jörn Rüsen. *Geschichte des Historismus.* Munich: C. H. Beck, 1992.

Jahn, Jahnheinz. *Leo Frobenius: The Demonic Child.* Translated by Reinhard Sander. Occasional Publication. Austin, Tex.: African and Afro-American Studies and Research Center, 1974.

Jarausch, Konrad H., and Larry Eugene Jones, eds. *In Search of a Liberal Germany: Studies in the History of German Liberalism from 1789 to the Present.* New York: Berg, 1990.

Jardine, Nick Jardine, J. A. Secord, and E. C. Spary, eds. *Cultures of Natural History.* Cambridge: Cambridge University Press, 1997.

Jay, Martin. *Downcast Eyes: The Denigration of Vision in Twentieth-Century French Thought.* Berkeley and Los Angeles: University of California Press, 1993.

Jelavich, Peter. *Berlin Cabaret.* Cambridge, Mass.: Harvard University Press, 1993.

Jonas, Hans. "The Nobility of Sight: A Study in the Phenomenology of the Senses." In *The Phenomenon of Life: Toward a Philosophical Biology.* Chicago: University of Chicago Press, 1982.

Junker, Thomas. *Darwinismus und Botanik: Rezeption, Kritik und theoretische Alternativen im Deutschland des 19. Jahrhunderts.* Stuttgart: Deutscher Apotheker, 1989.

Kaplan, Flora E. S., ed. *Museums and the Making of "Ourselves": The Role of Objects in National Identity.* London: Leicester University Press, 1994.

Karp, Ivan, and Steven D. Lavine. *Exhibiting Cultures: The Poetics and Politics of Museum Display.* Washington, D.C.: Smithsonian Institution Press, 1990.

Kelly, Alfred. *The Descent of Darwin: The Popularization of Darwinism in Germany, 1860–1914.* Chapel Hill: University of North Carolina Press, 1981.

Kendrick, Walter. *The Secret Museum: Pornography in Modern Culture.* New York: Viking, 1987.

Keuren, David K. van. "Museums and Ideology: Augustus Pitt-Rivers, Anthropological Museums, and Social Change in Later Victorian England." *Victorian Studies* 28 (1984): 171–89.

Kiefer, Annegret. *Das Problem einer "Jüdischen Rasse": Eine Diskussion zwischen Wissenschaft und Ideologie (1870–1930).* Frankfurt: Peter Lang, 1991.

King, Michael D. "Reason, Tradition, and the Progressiveness of Science." *History and Theory* 10 (1971): 3–32.

Knoll, Arthur J. *Togo under Imperial Germany, 1884–1914.* Stanford, Calif.: Hoover Institution Press, 1978.

Koepping, Klaus-Peter. *Adolf Bastian and the Psychic Unity of Mankind: The Foundations of Anthropology in Nineteenth Century Germany.* St. Lucia: University of Queensland Press, 1983.

Kramer, Fritz. "Empathy—Reflections on the History of Ethnology in Pre-Facist Germany: Herder, Creuzer, Bastian, Bachofen, and Frobenius." *Dialectical Anthropology* 9 (1985): 337–47.

———. *Verkehrte Welten: Zur imaginäre Ethnographie des neunzehten Jahrhunderts.* Frankfurt a.M.: Syndikat, 1977.

Krieger, Leonard. *The German Idea of Freedom.* Boston: Beacon, 1957.

———. *Ranke: The Meaning of History.* Chicago: University of Chicago Press, 1977.

Kroeber, A. L., and Clyde Kluckhohn. *Culture: A Critical Review of Concepts and Definitions.* Papers of the Peabody Museum of American Archaeology and Ethnology 47. Cambridge, Mass., 1952.

Krüger, Gesine. *Kriegsbewältigung und Geschichtsbewußtsein: Realität, Deutung und Verarbeitung des deutschen Kolonialkrieges in Namibia 1904 bis 1907.* Göttingen: Vandenhoeck & Ruprecht, 1999.

Kuhn, Thomas S. *The Structure of Scientific Revolutions.* Chicago: University of Chicago Press, 1970.

Kuklick, Henrika. *The Savage Within: The Social History of British Anthropology, 1885–1945.* Cambridge: Cambridge University Press, 1991.

Kuklick, Henrika, and Robert E. Kohler, eds. *Science in the Field. Osiris* 11 (1997).

Kümmel, Werner. "Rudolf Virchow und der Antisemitismus." *Medizinhistorisches Journal* 3 (1968): 165–79.

Kuper, Adam. *Anthropology and Anthropologists: The Modern British School.* London: Routledge & Kegan Paul, 1996.

Lamberti, Marjorie. *State, Society, and the Elementary School in Imperial Germany.* New York: Oxford University Press, 1989.

Lau, Brigitte. "Uncertain Certainties—the Herero-German War of 1904." In *History and Historiography,* 39–52. Windhoek: Discourse/MSORP, 1995.

Lebovics, Hermann. *True France: The Wars over Cultural Identity, 1900–1945.* Ithaca, N.Y.: Cornell University Press, 1992.

Lehmann, Alfred. "Zeitgenössische Bilder der ersten Völkerschauen." In *Von fremden Völkern und Kulturen: Beiträge zur Völkerkunde,* ed. W. Lang, 31–38. Düsseldorf: Droste, 1955.

Lenoir, Timothy. *The Strategy of Life: Teleology and Mechanics in Nineteenth Century German Biology.* Dordrecht: D. Reidel, 1982.

Leopold, Joan. *Culture in Comparative and Evolutionary Perspective: E. B. Tylor and the Making of "Primitive Culture."* Berlin: Dietrich Reimer, 1980.

Letkemann, Peter. "Das Berliner Panoptikum: Namen, Häuser und Schicksale." *Mitteilungen des Vereins für die Geschichte Berlins* 69 (1973): 317–26.

Lévi-Strauss, Claude. *Tristes tropiques.* 1955. Translated by John Weightman and Doreen Weightman. New York: Pocket, 1973.

Lifton, Robert Jay. *The Nazi Doctors: Medical Killing and the Psychology of Genocide.* New York: Basic, 1986.

Lloyd, Jill. *German Expressionism: Primitivism and Modernity.* New Haven, Conn.: Yale University Press, 1991.

Lukács, Georg. "Reification and the Consciousness of the Proletariat." In *History and Class Consciousness,* trans. Rodney Livingstone, 83–222. Cambridge, Mass.: MIT Press, 1971.

Lustig, Wolfgang. "'Außer ein paar zerbrochenen Pfeilen nichts zu verteilen . . .'— Ethnographische Sammlungen aus den detuschen Kolonien und ihre Verteilung an Museen 1889 bis 1914." *Mitteilungen aus dem Museum für Völkerkunde Hamburg* 18 (1988): 157–78.

MacKenzie, John M. *Orientalism: History, Theory, and the Arts.* Manchester: Manchester University Press, 1995.

———, ed. *Imperialism and Popular Culture.* Manchester: Manchester University Press, 1986.

Majluf, Natalia. "'Ce n'est pas le Pérou,' or the Failure of Authenticity: Marginal Cosmopolitans at the Paris Universal Exhibition of 1855." *Critical Inquiry* 23 (1997): 818–93.

Marchand, Suzanne L. *Down from Olympus: Archaeology and Philhellenism in Germany, 1750–1970.* Princeton, N.J.: Princeton University Press, 1996.

———. "Leo Frobenius and the Revolt against the West," *Journal of Contemporary History* 32 (1997): 153–70.

————. "The Rhetoric of Artifacts and the Decline of Classical Humanism: The Case of Josef Strzygowski." *History and Theory* 33 (1994): 106–30.

Marx, Christoph. *"Völker ohne Schrift und Geschichte": Zur historischen Erfassung des vorkolonialen Schwarzafrika in der deutschen Forschung des 19. und frühen 20. Jahrhunderts.* Stuttgart: Franz Steiner, 1988.

Marx, Karl. *Capital: A Critique of Political Economy.* 1867. Translated by Samuel Moore and Edward Aveling. Vol. 1. New York: International, 1967.

Mauss, Marcel. *The Gift: Forms and Functions of Exchange in Archaic Societies.* 1950. Translated by Ian Cunnison. London: Cohen & West, 1969.

McAleer, Kevin. *Dueling: The Cult of Honor in Fin-de-Siècle Germany.* Princeton, N.J.: Princeton University Press, 1994.

Meek, Ronald L. *Social Science and the Ignoble Savage.* Cambridge: Cambridge University Press, 1976.

Mehrtens, Herbert. "The Social System of Mathematics and National Socialism: A Survey." In *Science, Technology and National Socialism,* ed. Monika Renneberg and Mark Walker, 291–311. Cambridge: Cambridge University Press, 1994.

Meinl, Christoph. "August Wilhelm Hofmann—'Regierender Oberchemiker.'" In *Die Allianz von Wissenschaft und Industrie: August Wilhelm Hofmann (1818–1892),* ed. Christoph Meinl and Hartmut Scholz, 27–64. Weinheim: VCH, 1992.

Melk-Koch, Marion. *Auf der Such nach der menschlichen Gesellschaft: Richard Thurnwald.* Berlin: Dietrich Reimer, 1989.

Merton, Robert K. *Science, Technology, and Society in Seventeenth-Century England.* 1938. New York: Howard Fertig, 1970.

————. *The Sociology of Science: Theoretical and Empirical Investigations.* Edited by Norman W. Storer. Chicago: University of Chicago Press, 1973.

Mitchell, B. R. *European Historical Statistics, 1750–1970.* London: Macmillan, 1975.

Mitchell, Timothy. *Colonizing Egypt.* Cambridge: Cambridge University Press, 1988.

Montgomery, William. "Evolution and Darwinism in German Biology, 1800–1883." Ph.D. diss., University of Texas at Austin, 1974.

Morrell, Jack, and Arnold Thackray. *Gentlemen of Science: Early Years of the British Association for the Advancement of Science.* Oxford: Clarendon, 1981.

Mosse, George L. *Toward the Final Solution: A History of European Racism.* New York: Howard Fertig, 1978.

Muhlack, Ulrich. "Bildung zwischen Neuhumanismus und Historismus." In *Bildungsbürgertum im neunzehnten Jahrhundert* (vol. 20), ed. Reinhart Koselleck. Stuttgart: Klett-Cotta, 1990.

Müller-Hill, Benno. *Murderous Science: Elimination by Scientific Selection of Jews, Gypsies, and Others in Germany, 1933–1945.* Translated by George R. Fraser. Plainview, N.Y.: Cold Springs Harbor Laboratory Press, 1998.

Needham, Joseph. *The Grand Titration: Science and Society in East and West.* Toronto: University of Toronto Press, 1969.

Nietzsche, Friedrich. *On the Genealogy of Morality.* 1887. Edited by K. Ansell-Pearson. Translated by C. Diethe. Cambridge: Cambridge University Press, 1994.

Nippel, Wilfred. "Prolegomena zu Eduard Meyers Anthropologie." In *Eduard Meyer: Leben und Leistung eines Universalhistorikers,* ed. William M. Calder III and Alexander Demandt, 311–28. Leiden: E. J. Brill, 1990.

Nipperdey, Thomas. *Gesellschaft, Kultur, Theorie.* Göttingen: Vandenhoeck & Ruprecht, 1976.

Nyhart, Lynn K. *Biology Takes Form: Animal Morphology and the German Universities, 1800–1900.* Chicago: University of Chicago Press, 1995.

Oldroyd, David R. "Historicism and the Rise of Historical Geology." *History of Science* 17 (1979): 191–213, 227–57.

———. *Thinking about the Earth: A History of Ideas in Geology.* Cambridge, Mass.: Harvard University Press, 1996.

Oldroyd, David R., and Ian Langham, eds. *The Wider Domain of Evolutionary Thought.* Dordrecht: D. Reidel, 1983.

Olesko, Kathryn M. *Physics as a Calling: Discipline and Practice in the Königsberg Seminar for Physics.* Ithaca, N.Y.: Cornell University Press, 1991.

Oosterhuis, Harry, ed. *Homosexuality and Male Bonding in Pre-Nazi Germany: The Youth Movement, the Gay Movement, and Male Bonding before Hitler's Rise.* New York: Haworth, 1991.

Ophir, Adi, and Steven Shapin. "The Place of Knowledge: A Methodological Survey." *Science in Context* 4 (1991): 3–22.

Ottow, Benno. "K. E. von Baer als Kraniologe und die Anthropologen-Versammlung 1861 in Göttingen." *Sudhoffs Archiv* 50 (1966): 43–68.

Outram, Dorinda. *The Body and the French Revolution: Sex, Class, and Political Culture.* New Haven, Conn.: Yale University Press, 1989.

Pagden, Anthony. *The Fall of Natural Man: The American Indian and the Origins of Comparative Ethnology.* Cambridge: Cambridge University Press, 1982.

Pauly, Philip J. "The Political Structure of the Brain: Cerebral Localization in Bismarckian Germany." *International Journal of Neuroscience* 21 (1983): 145–50.

Penny, H. Glenn, III. "Cosmopolitan Visions and Municipal Displays: Museums, Markets, and the Ethnographic Project in Germany, 1868–1914." Ph.D. diss., University of Illinois at Urbana-Champaign, 1999.

Pickering, Andrew, ed. *Science as Practice and Culture.* Chicago: University of Chicago Press, 1992.

Pickstone, John V. "Museological Science? The Place of the Analytical/Comparative in Nineteenth-Century Science, Technology, and Medicine." *History of Science* 32 (1994): 111–38.

———. "Ways of Knowing: Towards a Historical Sociology of Science, Technology, and Medicine." *British Journal of the History of Science* 26 (1993): 433–58.

Pohle, Hermann, and Gustav Mahr, eds. *Festschrift zum hundertjährigen Bestehen der Berliner Gesellschaft für Anthropologie, Ethnologie und Urgeschichte, 1869–1969.* Vol. 1. Berlin: Berliner Gesellschaft für Anthropologie, Ethnologie und Urgeschichte, 1969.

Poliakov, Léon. *The Aryan Myth: A History of Racist and Nationalist Ideas in Europe.* Translated by Edmund Howard. London: Sussex University Press, 1974.

Posner, Carl. *Rudolf Virchow.* Vienna: Rikola, 1921.

Pratt, Mary Louise. *Imperial Eyes: Travel Writing and Transculturation.* London: Routledge, 1992.

Prein, Philip. "Guns and Top Hats: African Resistance in German South West Africa, 1907–1915." *Journal of Southern African Studies* 20 (1994): 99–121.

Proctor, Robert. *Racial Hygiene: Medicine under the Nazis.* Cambridge, Mass.: Harvard University Press, 1988.

Pulzer, Peter. *The Rise of Political Anti-Semitism in Germany and Austria.* 1964. London: Peter Halban, 1988.

Ranger, Terence. "The Connection between 'Primary Resistance' Movements and Modern Mass Nationalism in East and Central Africa." *Journal of African History* 9 (1968): 437–53, 631–41.

Richards, Evelleen. "A Political Anatomy of Monsters, Hopeful and Otherwise: Teratogeny, Transcendentalism, and Evolutionary Theorizing." *Isis* 85 (1994): 377–411.

Richards, Robert J. *The Meaning of Evolution: The Morphological Construction and Ideological Reconstruction of Darwin's Theory.* Chicago: University of Chicago Press, 1992.

Ricoeur, Paul. "Phenomenology and Hermeneutics." 1975. In *From Text to Action: Essays in Hermeneutics, II,* trans. Kathleen Blamey and John B. Thompson, 25–52. Evanston, Ill.: Northwestern University Press, 1991.

Ringer, Fritz K. *The Decline of the German Mandarins.* Cambridge, Mass.: Harvard University Press, 1969.

———. *Fields of Knowledge: French Academic Culture in Comparative Perspective, 1890–1920.* Cambridge: Cambridge University Press, 1992.

Rose, Paul Lawrence. *Revolutionary Antisemitism in Germany from Kant to Wagner.* Princeton, N.J.: Princeton University Press, 1990.

Rosenberry, William. *Anthropologies and Histories: Essays in Culture, History, and Political Economy.* New Brunswick, N.J.: Rutgers University Press, 1989.

Rothfels, Nigel T. "Bring 'Em Back Alive: Carl Hagenbeck and Exotic Animal and People Trades in Germany, 1848–1914." Ph.D. diss., Harvard University, 1994.

Rudwick, Martin J. S. *The Great Devonian Controversy: The Shaping of Scientific Knowledge among Gentlemanly Specialists.* Chicago: University of Chicago Press, 1985.

———. *Scenes from Deep Time.* Chicago: University of Chicago Press, 1992.

Ryding, James N. "Alternatives in Nineteenth-Century German Ethnology: A Case Study in the Sociology of Science." *Sociologicus* 25 (1975): 1–28.

Sahlins, Marshall. *Stone Age Economics*. New York: Aldine, 1972.

Said, Edward W. *Culture and Imperialism*. New York: Vintage, 1993.

———. *Orientalism*. New York: Pantheon, 1978.

———. "Representing the Colonized: Anthropology's Interlocutors." *Critical Inquiry* 15 (1989): 205–25.

Schaffer, Simon. "Natural Philosophy and Public Spectacle in the Eighteenth Century." *History of Science* 21 (1983): 1–43.

———. "From Physics to Anthropology—and Back Again." Prickly Pear Pamphlet no. 3. Cambridge: Prickly Pear, 1994.

Schiefel, Werner. *Bernhard Dernburg, 1865–1937: Kolonialpolitiker und Bankier im wilhelminischen Deutschland*. Zürich: Atlantis, 1974.

Schiller, Francis. *Paul Broca: Founder of French Anthropology, Explorer of the Brain*. Berkeley and Los Angeles: University of California Press, 1979.

Schipperes, Heinrich. "Natur." In *Geschichtliche Grundbegriffe* (vol. 4), ed. Otto Brunner, Werner Konze, and Reinhardt Kosellek, 215–44. Stuttgart: Klett, 1978.

Schleip, Dietrich. "Ozeanische Ethnographie und koloniale Praxis: Das Beispiel Augustin Krämer." *Tribus* 38 (1989): 121–48.

Schleunes, K. A. *Schooling and Society*. Oxford: Berg, 1989.

Schnädelbach, Herbert. *Philosophy in Germany, 1831–1933*. Cambridge: Cambridge University Press, 1984.

Schumaker, Lynette L. "The Lion in the Path: Fieldwork and Culture in the History of the Rhodes-Livingstone Institute, 1937–1964." Ph.D. diss., University of Pennsylvania, 1994.

Schwartz, Vanessa R. *Spectacular Realities: Early Mass Culture in Fin-de-Siècle Paris*. Berkeley and Los Angeles: University of California Press, 1998.

Shapin, Steven. "Discipline and Bounding: The History and Sociology of Science as Seen through the Externalism-Internalism Debate." *History of Science* 30 (1992): 333–69.

———. *The Scientific Revolution*. Chicago: University of Chicago Press, 1996.

———. *A Social History of Truth: Civility and Science in Seventeenth-Century England*. Chicago: University of Chicago Press, 1994.

Shapin, Steven, and Simon Schaffer, *Leviathan and the Air-Pump: Hobbes, Boyle, and the Experimental Life*. Princeton, N.J.: Princeton University Press, 1985.

Sheehan, James. *German Liberalism in the Nineteenth Century*. Chicago: University of Chicago Press, 1978.

Sheets-Pyenson, Susan. *Cathedrals of Science: The Development of Colonial Natural History Museums during the Late Nineteenth Century*. Kingston: McGill-Queen's University Press, 1988.

Shils, Edward A. "The Autonomy of Science." 1956. In *The Sociology of Science,* ed. Bernard Barber and Walter Hirsch, 610–22. New York: Free Press, 1962.

Sieg, Ulrich. *Aufstieg und Niedergang des Marburger Neukanianismus: Die Geschichte einer philosophischen Schulgemeinschaft.* Würzburg: Königshausen & Neumann, 1994.

Smith, Bernard. *European Vision and the South Pacific.* 1959. New Haven, Conn.: Yale University Press, 1985.

Smith, Helmut Walser. *German Nationalism and Religious Conflict: Culture, Ideology, Politics, 1870–1914.* Princeton, N.J.: Princeton University Press, 1995.

Smith, Woodruff D. "Friedrich Ratzel and the Origins of *Lebensraum.*" *German Studies Review* 3 (1980): 61–68.

———. *The German Colonial Empire.* Chapel Hill: University of North Carolina Press, 1978.

———. *The Ideological Origins of Nazi Imperialism.* New York: Oxford University Press, 1986.

———. *Politics and the Sciences of Culture in Germany, 1840–1920.* New York: Oxford University Press, 1991.

Smolka, Wolfgang J. *Völkerkunde in München: Voraussetzungen, Möglichkeiten und Entwicklungslinien ihrer Institutionalisierung, ca. 1850–1933.* Berlin: Duncker & Humboldt, 1994.

Snyder, Joel. "Picturing Vision." *Critical Inquiry* 6 (1980): 499–526.

Snyder, Joel, and Neil Walsh Allen. "Photography, Vision, and Representation." *Critical Inquiry* 2 (1975): 143–69.

Sösemann, Bernd. "Die sog. Hunnenrede Wilhelms II: Textkritische und interpretatorische Bemerkungen zur Ansprache des Kaisers vom 27. Juli 1900 in Bremerhaven." *Historische Zeitschrift* 222 (1976): 342–58.

Southard, Robert. *Droysen and the Prussian School of History.* Lexington: University Press of Kentucky, 1995.

Spidle, Jake W. "Colonial Studies in Imperial Germany." *History of Education Quarterly* 13 (1973): 231–47.

Spivak, Gayatri Chakravorty, "Can the Subaltern Speak?" In *Marxism and the Interpretation of Culture,* ed. Cary Nelson and Lawrence Grossberg, 271–313. Urbana: University of Illinois Press, 1988.

Spraul, Gunter. "Der 'Volkermord' an den Herero: Untersuchungen zu einer neuen Kontinuitätsthese." *Geschichte in Wissenschaft und Unterricht* 39 (1988): 713–39.

Stallybrass, Peter, and Allon White. *The Politics and Poetics of Transgression.* Ithaca, N.Y.: Cornell University Press, 1986.

Star, Susan Leigh, and James R. Griesemer. "Institutional Ecology, 'Translations,' and Boundary Objects: Amateurs and Professionals in Berkeley's Museum of Vertebrate Zoology, 1907–39." *Social Studies of Science* 19 (1989): 387–420.

Steinmetzler, Johannes. *Die Anthropogeographie Friedrich Ratzels und ihre ideengeschichtliche Wurzeln.* Bonn: Selbstverlag des geographischen Instituts der Universität Bonn, 1956.

Stocking, George W., Jr. *After Tylor: British Social Anthropology, 1888–1951.* Madison: University of Wisconsin Press, 1995.

———. *The Ethnographer's Magic and Other Essays in the History of Anthropology.* Madison: University of Wisconsin Press, 1992.

———. *Victorian Anthropology.* New York: Free Press, 1987.

———, ed. *Bones, Bodies, Behavior: Essays on Biological Anthropology.* Madison: University of Wisconsin Press, 1988.

———, ed. *Colonial Situations: Essays on the Contextualization of Ethnographic Knowledge.* Madison: University of Wisconsin Press, 1991.

———, ed. *Functionalism Historicized: Essays in British Social Anthropology.* Madison: University of Wisconsin Press, 1984.

———, ed. *Objects and Others: Essays on Museums and Material Culture.* Madison: University of Wisconsin Press, 1985.

———, ed. *Observers Observed: Essays on Ethnographic Fieldwork.* Madison: University of Wisconsin Press, 1983.

———, ed. *Volksgeist as Method and Ethic: Essays on Boasian Ethnography and the German Anthropological Tradition.* Madison: University of Wisconsin Press, 1996.

Stoler, Ann Laura. *Race and the Education of Desire: Foucault's History of Sexuality and the Colonial Order of Things.* Durham, N.C.: Duke University Press, 1995.

Strathern, Marilyn. *The Gender of the Gift: Problems with Women and Problems with Society in Melanesia.* Berkeley and Los Angeles: University of California Press, 1988.

Terry, Jennifer, and Jacqualine Urla, eds. *Deviant Bodies: Critical Perspective on Difference in Science and Popular Culture.* Bloomington: Indiana University Press, 1995.

Theye, Thomas, ed. *Der Geraubte Schatten: Photographie als ethnographsiches Dokument.* Munich: Münchner Stadtmuseum, 1989. Exhibition catalog, Münchener Stadtmuseum and the Haus der Kulturen der Welt, Berlin.

———, ed. *Wir und die Wilden: Einblick in eine kannibalische Beziehung.* Hamburg: Rowohlt, 1984.

Thiel, Paul. "Berlin präsentiert sich der Welt: Die Berliner Gewerbeausstellung 1896 in Treptow." In *Die Metropole: Industriekultur in Berlin im 20. Jahrhundert,* ed. Jochen Bobert, Tilman Fichter, and Eckhart Gillen, 16–27. Munich: C. H. Beck, 1986.

Thode-Arora, Hilke. "'Charakteristische Gestalten des Volkslebens': Die Hagenbeckschen Südasien-, Orient-, und Afrika Völkerschauen." In *Fremde Erfahr-*

ungen: Asiaten und Afrikaner in Deutschland, Österreich und der Schweiz bis 1945,
ed. Gerhard Höpp. Berlin: Das Arabische Buch, 1996.

————. "Das Eskimo-Tagebuch von 1880: Eine Völkerschau aus der Sicht eines
Teilnehmers." *Kea: Zeitschrift für Kulturwissenschaften* 2 (1991): 87–115.

————. *Für fünfzig Pfennig um die Welt: Die Hagenbeckschen Völkerschauen.* New
York: Campus, 1989.

Thomas, Nicholas. *Entangled Objects: Exchange, Material Culture, and Colonialism in
the Pacific.* Cambridge, Mass.: Harvard University Press, 1991.

Thomson, Alastair. "Honours Uneven: Decorations, the State, and Bourgeois Society
in Imperial Germany." *Past and Present* 144 (1994): 171–204.

Thomson, Rosmarie Garland, ed. *Freakery: Cultural Spectacles of the Extraordinary
Body.* New York: New York University Press, 1996.

Trail, David A. *Schliemann of Troy: Treasure and Deceit.* New York: St. Martin's Press,
1995.

Tucker, Jennifer. "Science Illustrated: Photographic Evidence and Social Practice in
England, 1870–1920." Ph.D. diss., Johns Hopkins University, 1996.

Turner, R. Steven. "German Science, German Universities: Historiographical Perspectives from the 1980s." In *"Einsamkeit und Freiheit" neu besichtigt,* ed. Gert
Schubring, 24–36. Stuttgart: Franz Steiner, 1991.

————. "The Growth of Professorial Research in Prussia, 1818–1948: Causes and
Context." *Historical Studies in the Physical Sciences* 3 (1971): 137–82.

————. *In the Eye's Mind: Vision and the Helmholtz-Hering Controversy.* Princeton,
N.J.: Princeton University Press, 1994.

————. "University Reformers and Professorial Scholarship in Germany, 1760–
1806." In *The University in Society: Studies in the History of Higher Education,* ed.
Lawrence Stone, 2:495–531. Princeton, N.J.: Princeton University Press, 1974.

Vaillant, Janet G. *Black, French, and African: A Life of Léopold Sédar Senghor.* Cambridge, Mass.: Harvard University Press, 1990.

Viswanathan, Gauri. *Masks of Conquest: Literary Study and British Rule in India.* New
York: Columbia University Press, 1989.

Wanklyn, Harriet. *Friedrich Ratzel: A Biographical Memoir and Bibliography.* Cambridge: Cambridge University Press, 1961.

Wehler, Hans-Ulrich. *Bismarck und der Imperialismus.* Berlin: Kiepenheuer & Witsch,
1969.

————. "In den Fusstapfen der kaempfenden Wissenschaft." *Frankfurter Allgemeine
Zeitung,* 4 January 1999, 48.

————. *The German Empire, 1871–1918.* 1973. Translated by Kim Traynor. Leam-
ington Spa: Berg, 1985.

Weikart, Richard. *Socialist Darwinism: Evolution in German Socialist Thought from
Marx to Bernstein.* San Francisco: International Scholars, 1998.

Weindling, Paul. *Health, Race, and German Politics between National Unification and Nazism, 1870–1945.* Cambridge: Cambridge University Press, 1989.

Westphal-Hellbusch, Sigrid. "Zur Geschichte des Museums." *Baessler-Archiv: Beiträge zur Völkerkunde* 21 (1973): 1–99.

White, Allon. "Pigs and Pierrots: Politics of Transgression in Modern Fiction." *Raritan* 2 (1982): 51–70.

White, Richard. *The Middle Ground: Indians, Empires, and Republics in the Great Lakes Region, 1650–1815.* Cambridge: Cambridge University Press, 1991.

Williams, Elizabeth A. "Anthropological Institutions in Nineteenth-Century France." *Isis* 76 (1985): 331–48.

———. *The Physical and the Moral: Anthropology, Physiology, and Philosophical Medicine in France, 1750–1850.* Cambridge: Cambridge University Press, 1994.

Williams, Raymond. *The Country and the City.* London: Chatto & Windus, 1973.

Winkelmann, Ingeburg. "Die bürgerliche Ethnographie im Dienste der Kolonialpolitik des Deutschen Reiches (1870–1918)." Ph.D. diss., Humboldt-Universität zu Berlin, 1966.

Winter, Kurt, *Rudolf Virchow.* Leipzig: Urania, 1956.

Wolf, Eric R. *Europe and the People without History.* Berkeley and Los Angeles: University of California Press, 1982.

Wright, Marcia. "East Africa." In *The Cambridge History of Africa,* ed. J. D. Fage and Roland Oliver, 6:539–91. Cambridge: Cambridge University Press, 1985.

———. "Maji Maji: Prophecy and Historiography." In *Revealing Prophets: Prophecy in East African History,* ed. David M. Anderson and Douglas H. Johnson, 124–42. London: James Currey, 1995.

Young, Robert. *Colonial Desire: Hybridity in Theory, Culture, and Race.* London: Routledge, 1995.

———. *White Mythologies: Writing History and the West.* London: Routledge, 1990.

Young, Robert M. *Darwin's Metaphor: Nature's Place in Victorian Culture.* Cambridge: Cambridge University Press, 1985.

———. *Mind, Brain, and Adaptation in the Nineteenth Century: Cerebral Localization and Its Biological Context from Gall to Ferrier.* 1970. New York: Oxford University Press, 1990.

Zantop, Susanne. *Colonial Fantasies: Conquest, Family, and Nation in Precolonial Germany, 1770–1870.* Durham, N.C.: Duke University Press, 1997.

Zimmerman, Andrew. "Anti-Semitism as Skill: Rudolf Virchow's Schulstatistik and the Racial Composition of Germany." *Central European History* 32 (1999): 409–29.

———. "German Anthropology and the 'Natural Peoples': The Global Context of Colonial Discourse." In *German Colonialism: Another Sonderweg?* Special issue of *European Studies Journal* 16 (1999): 95–112.

————. "Geschichtslose und Schriftlose Völker in Spreeathen: Anthropologie als Kritik der Geschichtswissenschaft im Kaiserreich." *Zeitschrift für Geschichtswissenschaften* 47 (1999): 197–210.

————. "Looking beyond History: The Optics of German Anthropology and the Critique of Humanism." *Studies in History and Philosophy of Biological and Biomedical Sciences* (in press).

————. "Science and *Schaulust* in the Berlin Museum of Ethnology." In *Wissenschaft und Öffentlichkeit in Berlin,* ed. Constantin Goschler, 66–88. Wiesbaden: Franz Steiner, 2000.

————. "Selin, Pore, and Emil Stephan in the Bismarck Archipelago: A 'Fresh and Joyful Tale' of the Origin of Fieldwork." *Journal of the Pacific Arts Association* (in press).

꧃

Note: Italicized page numbers indicate figures.